SOME PLANTS

GREG CURTIS   MATHEW TIMMONS

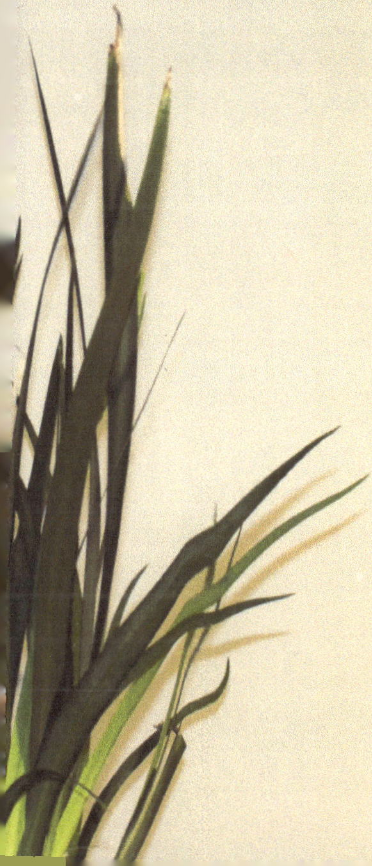

INSERT BLANC PRESS

Los Angeles

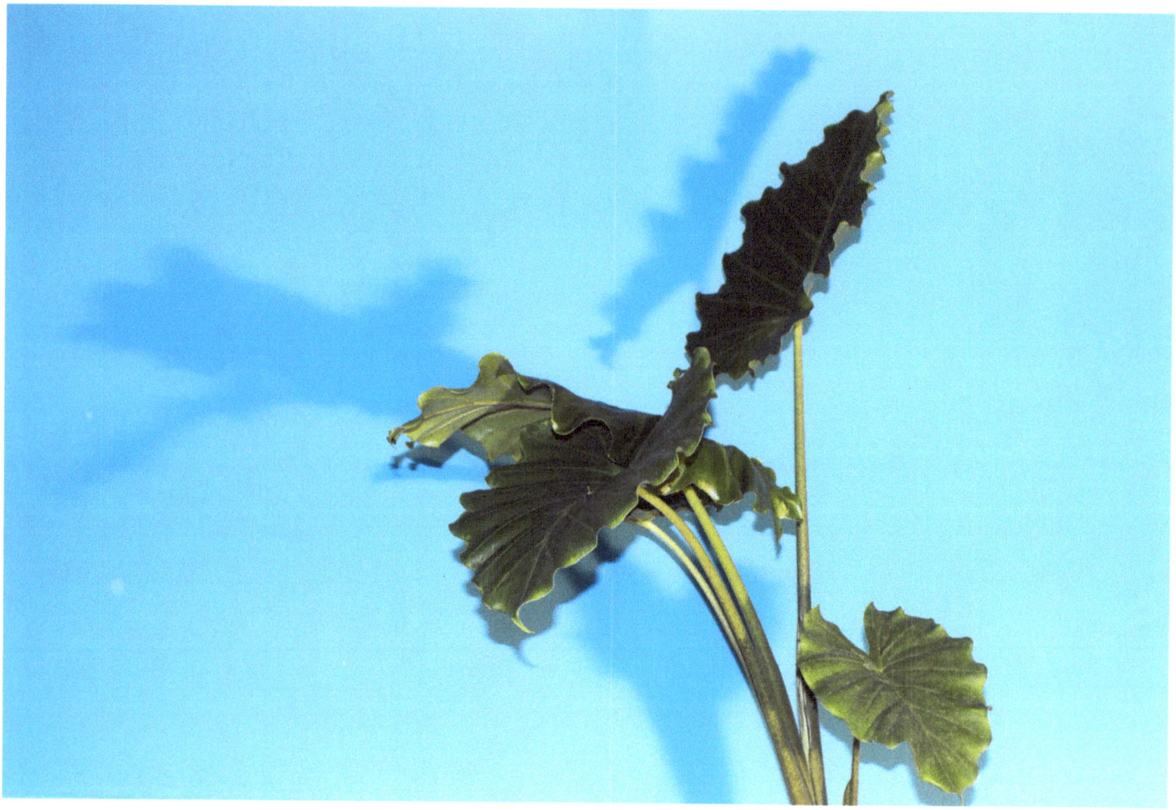

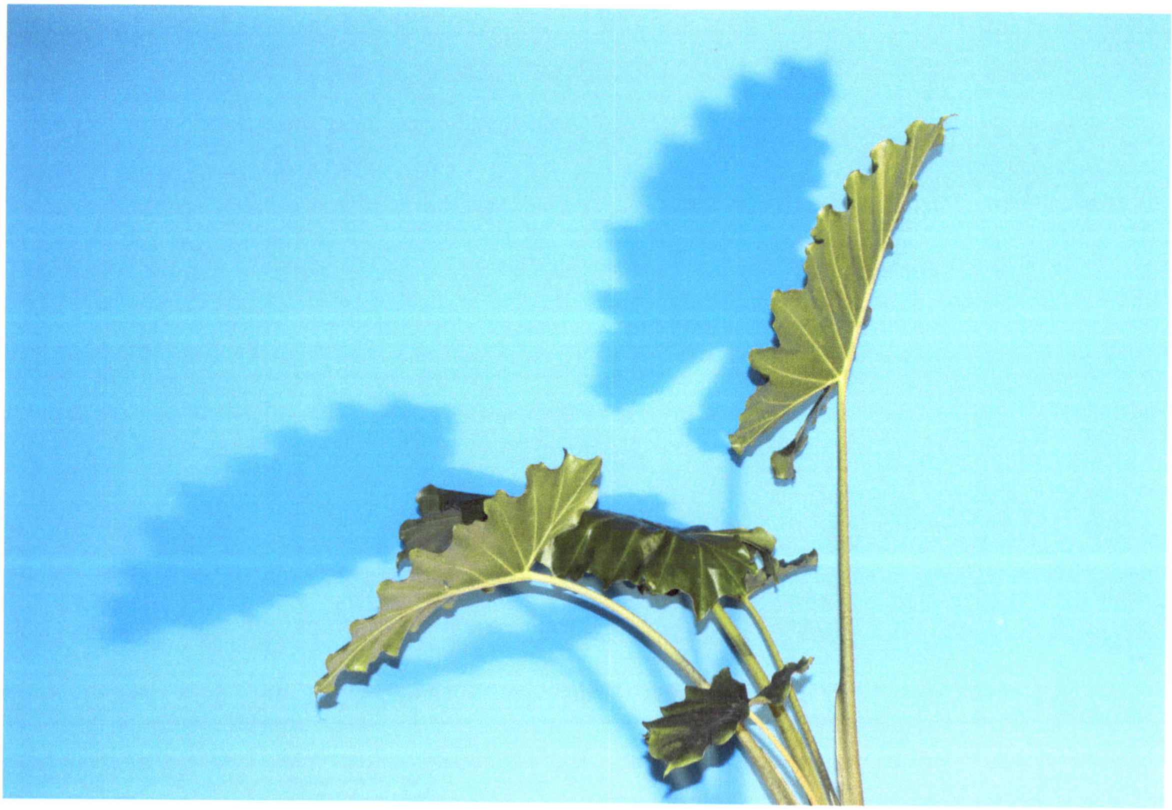

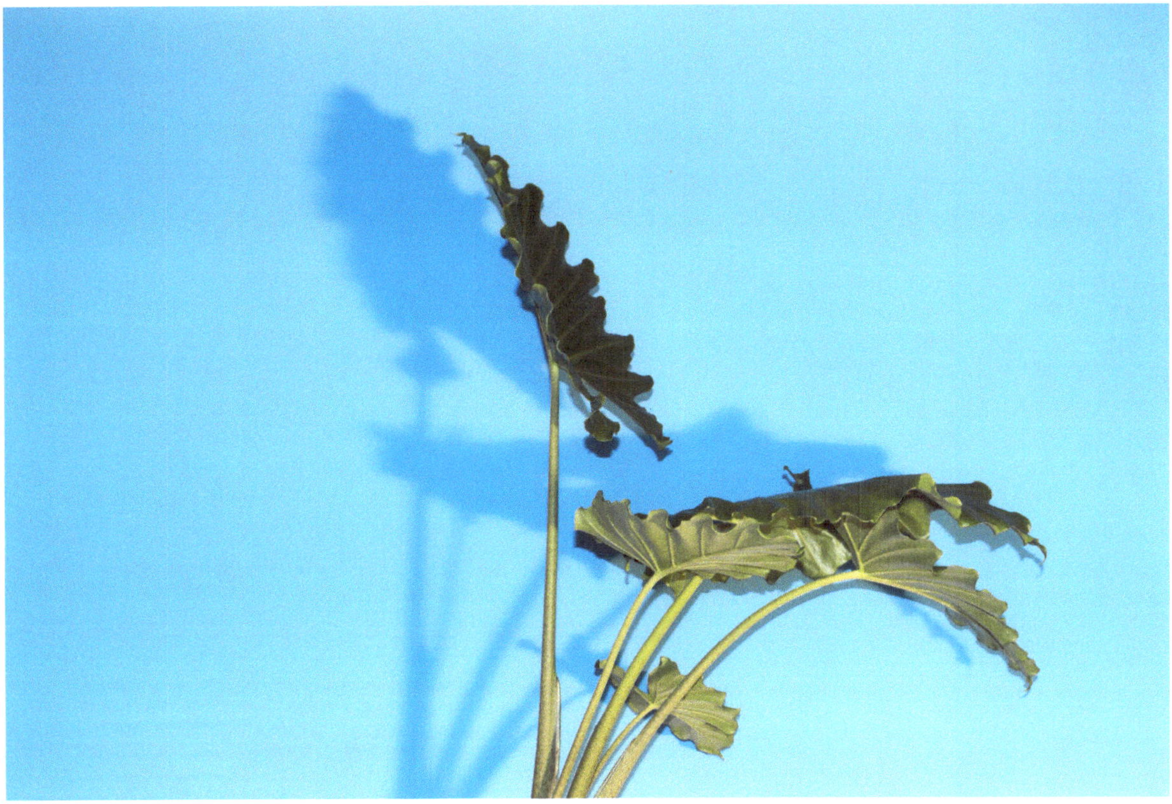

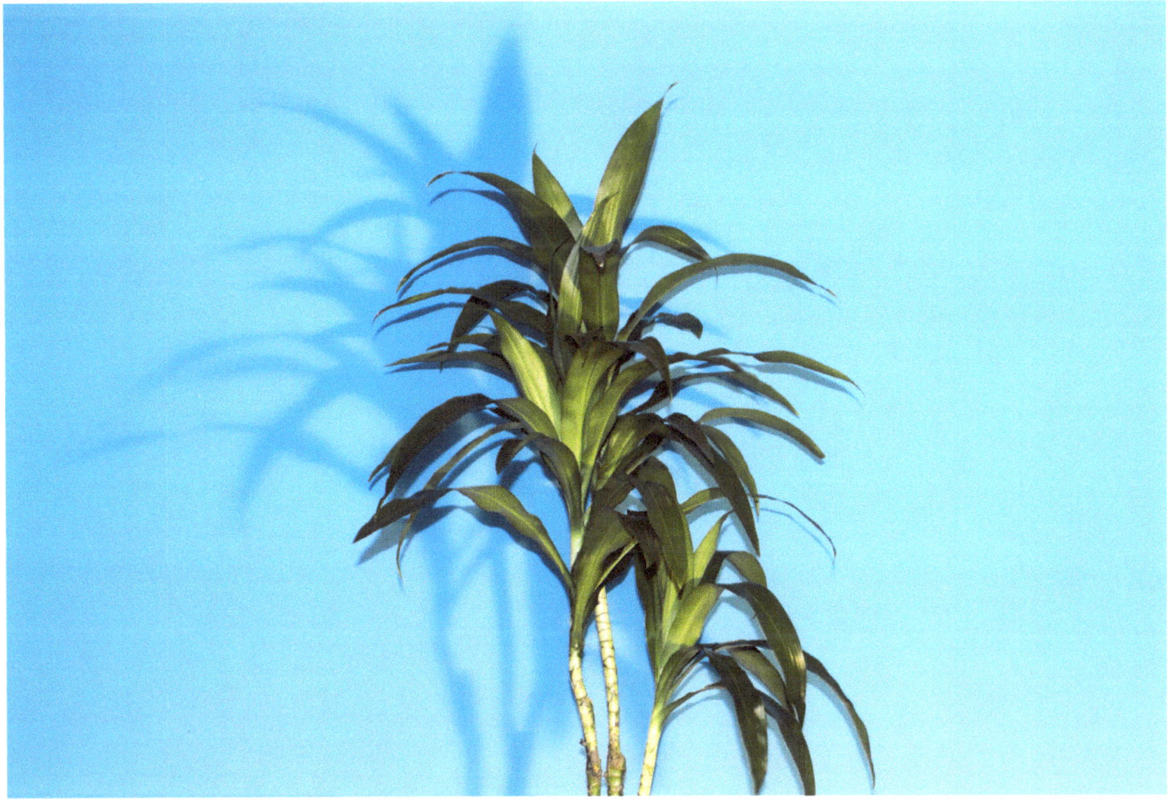

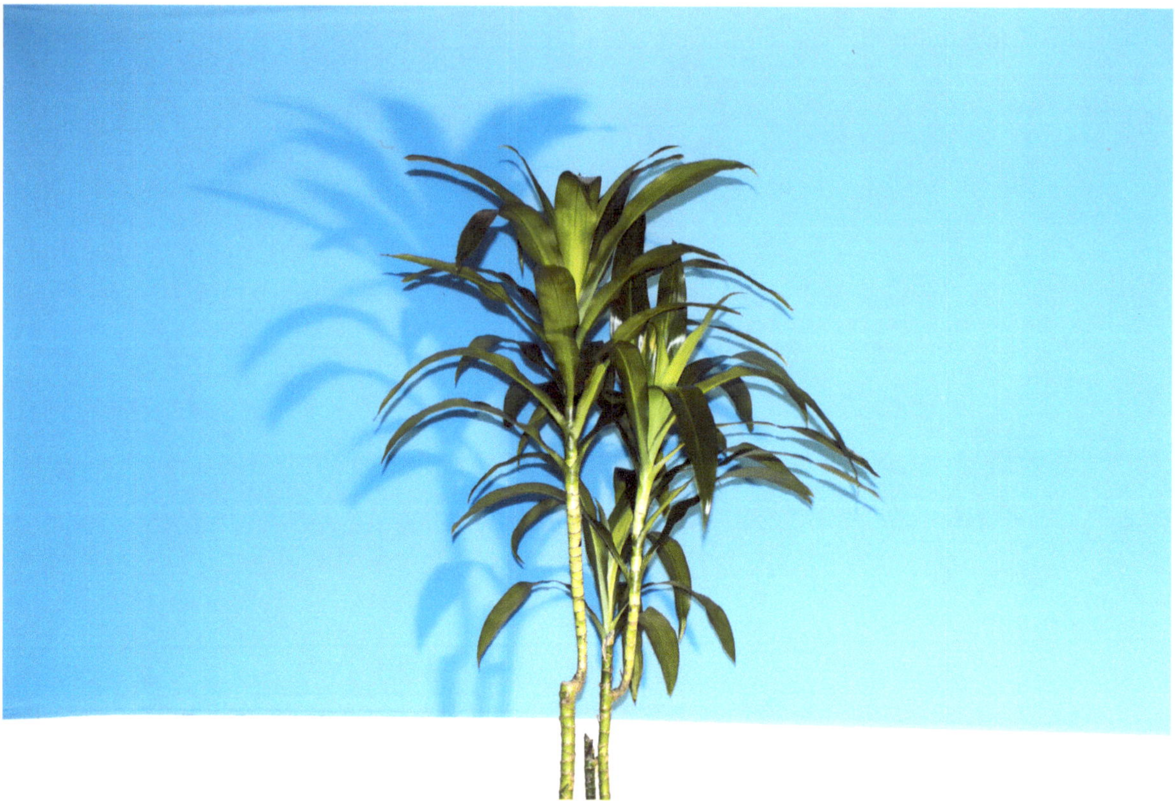

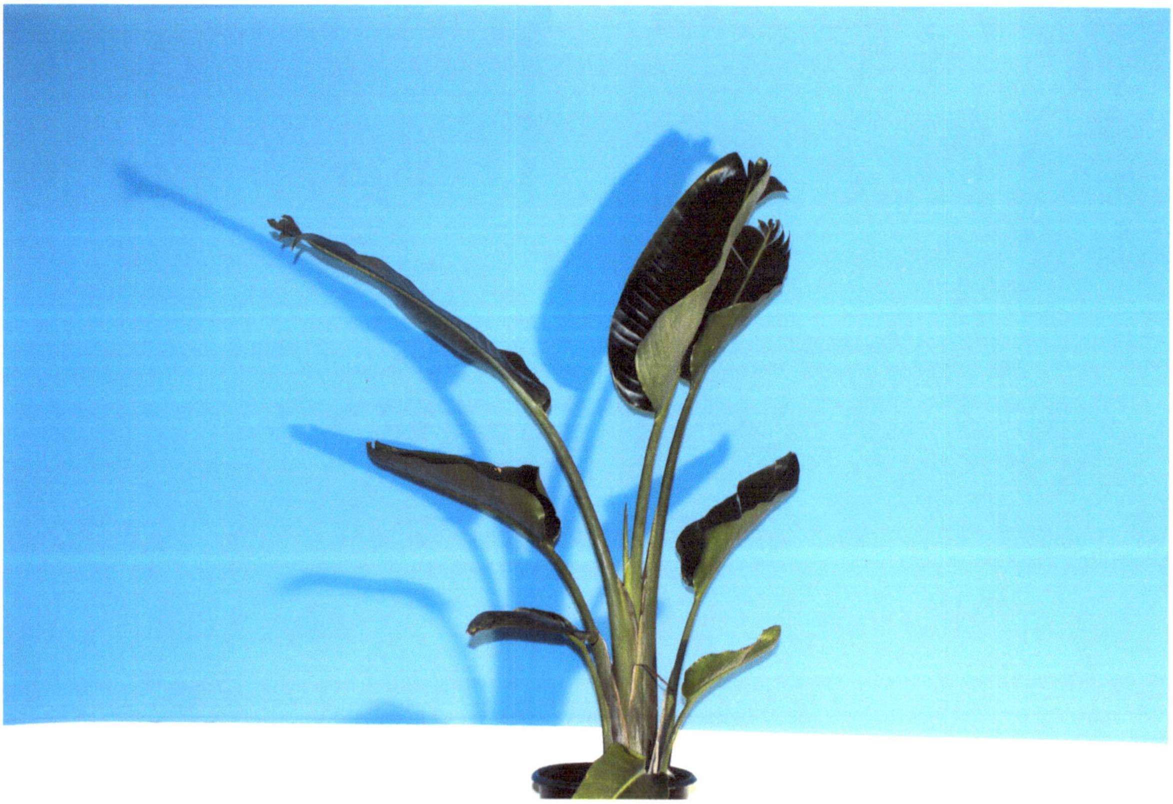

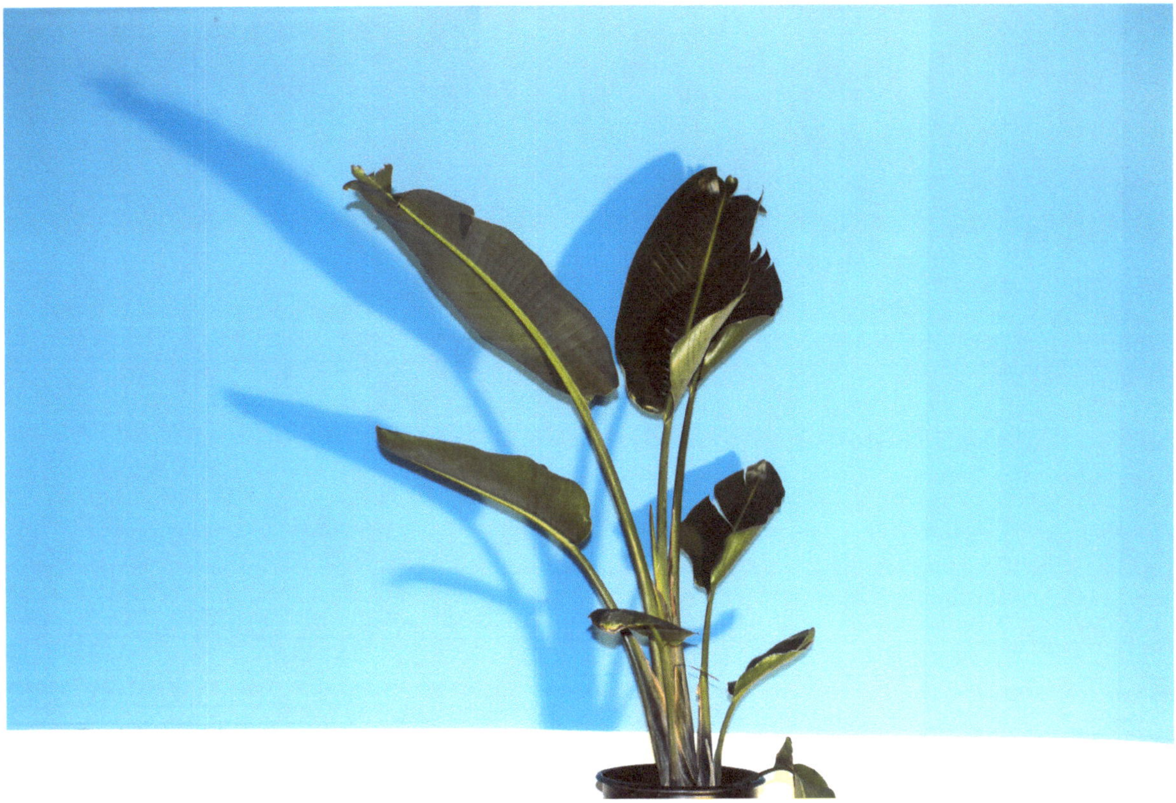

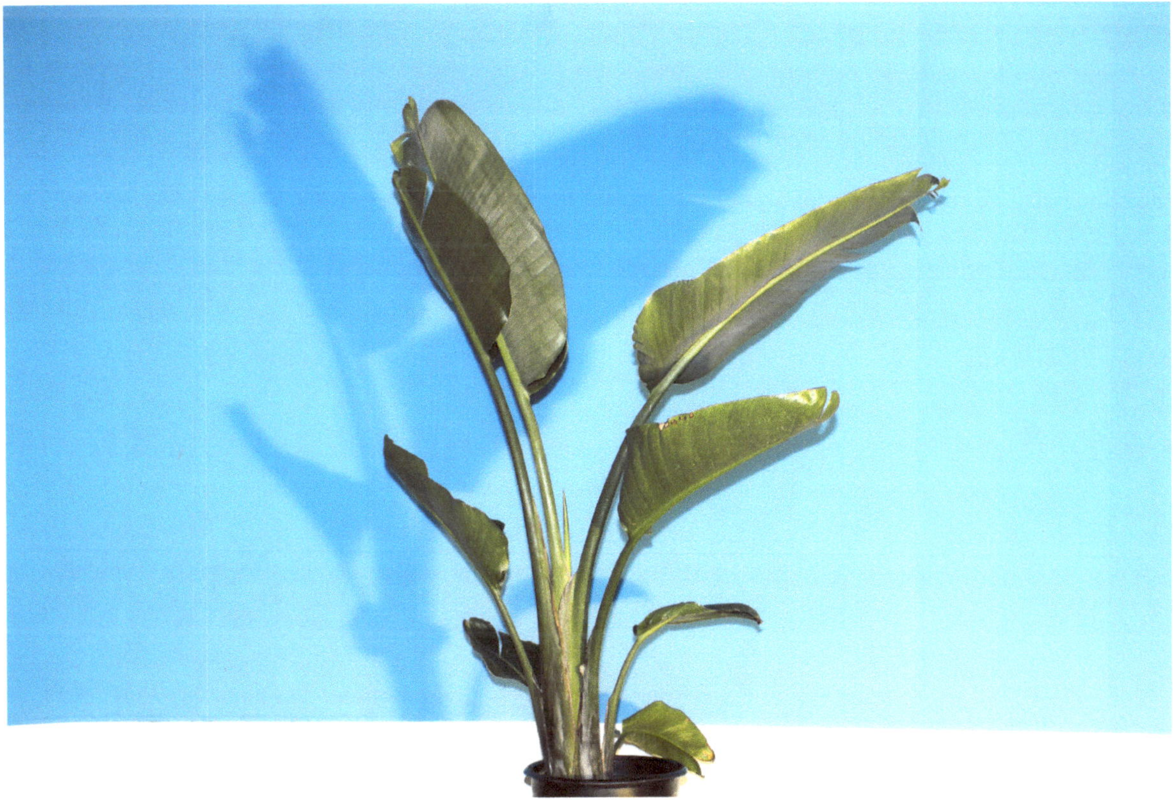

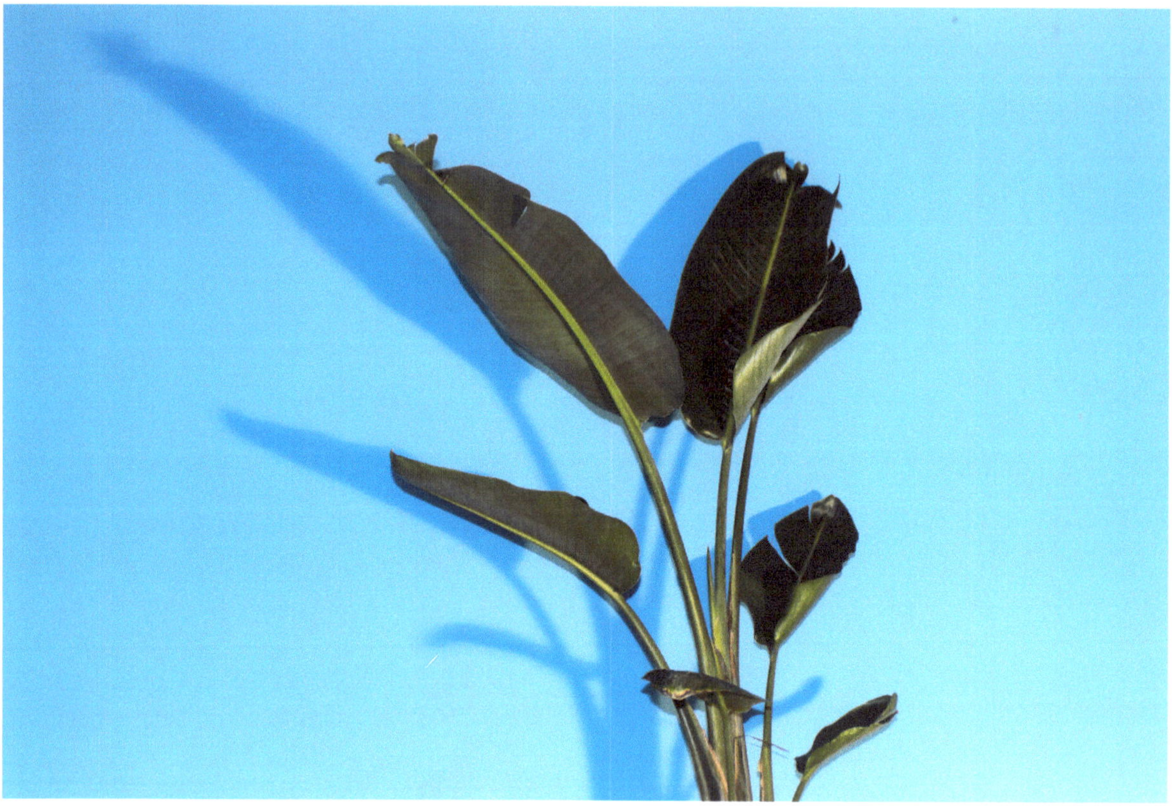
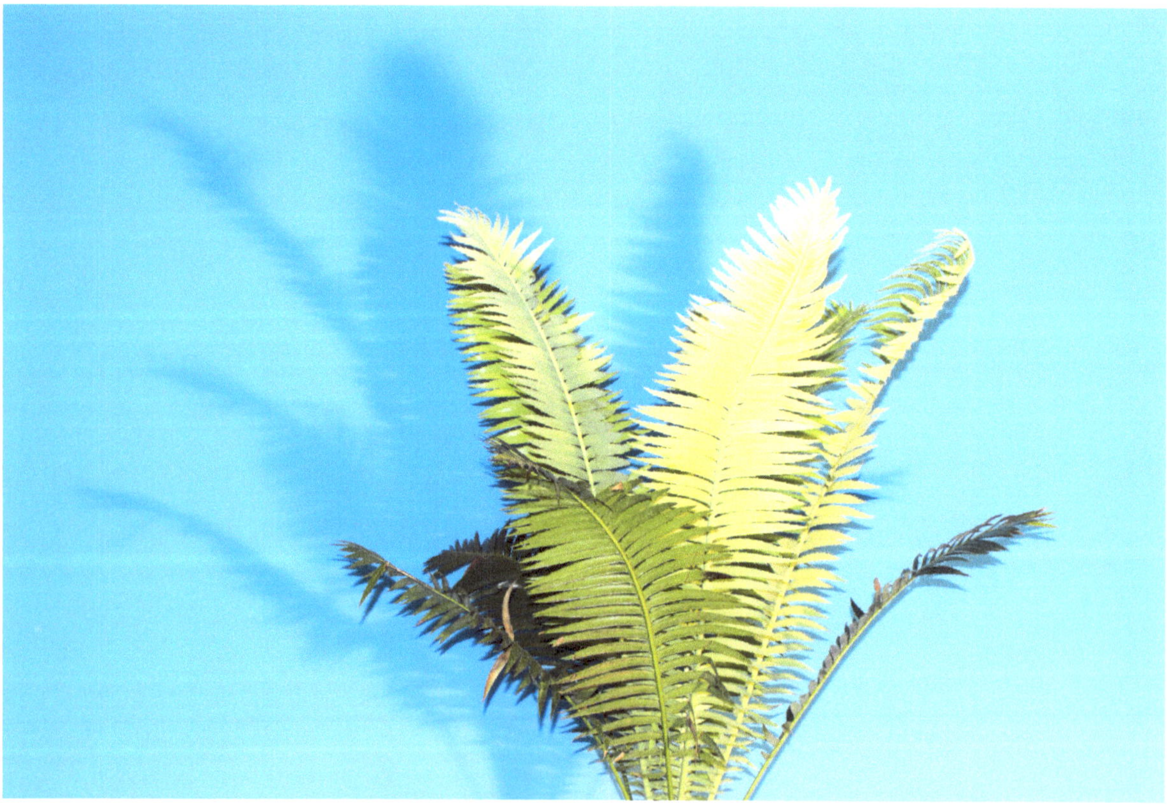

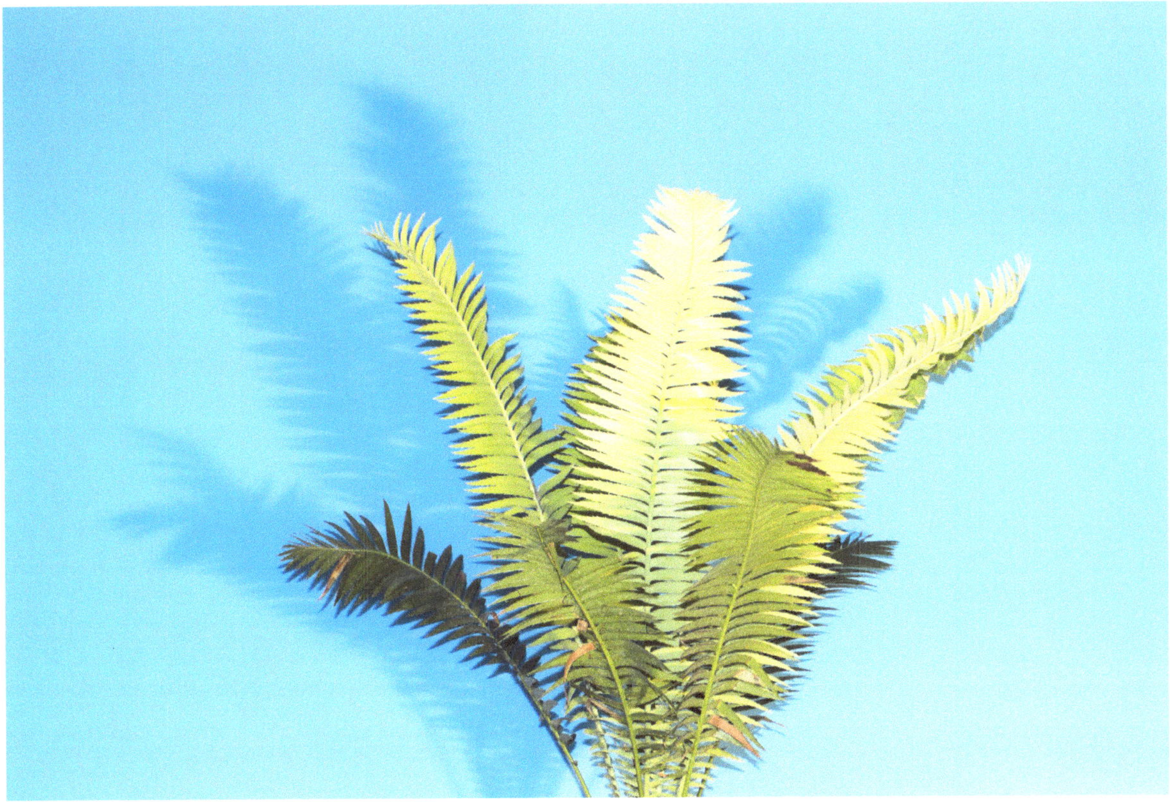

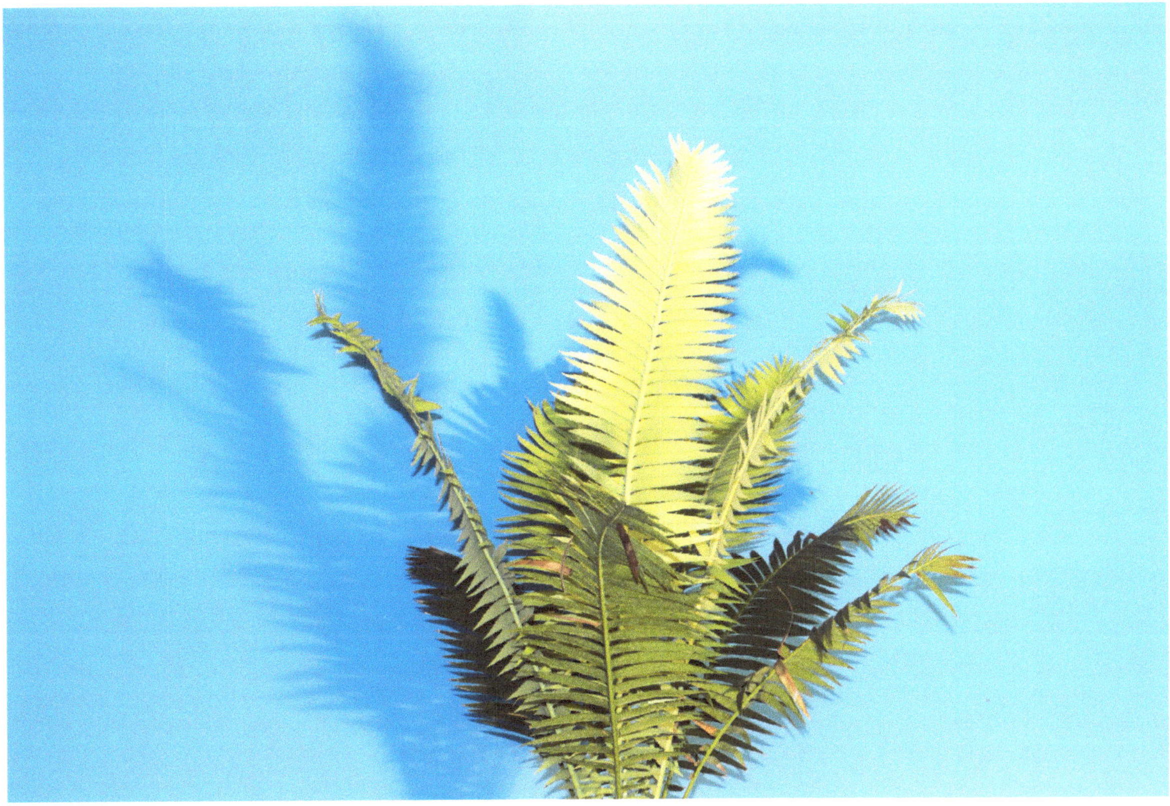

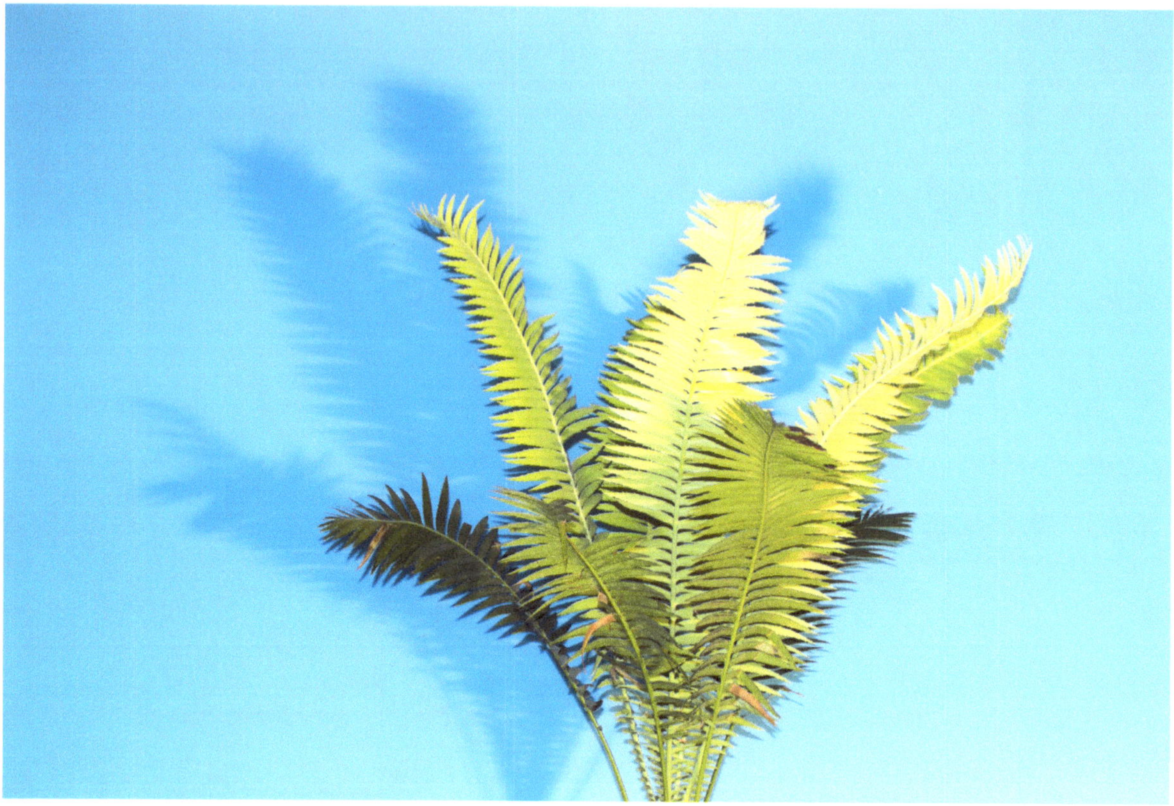

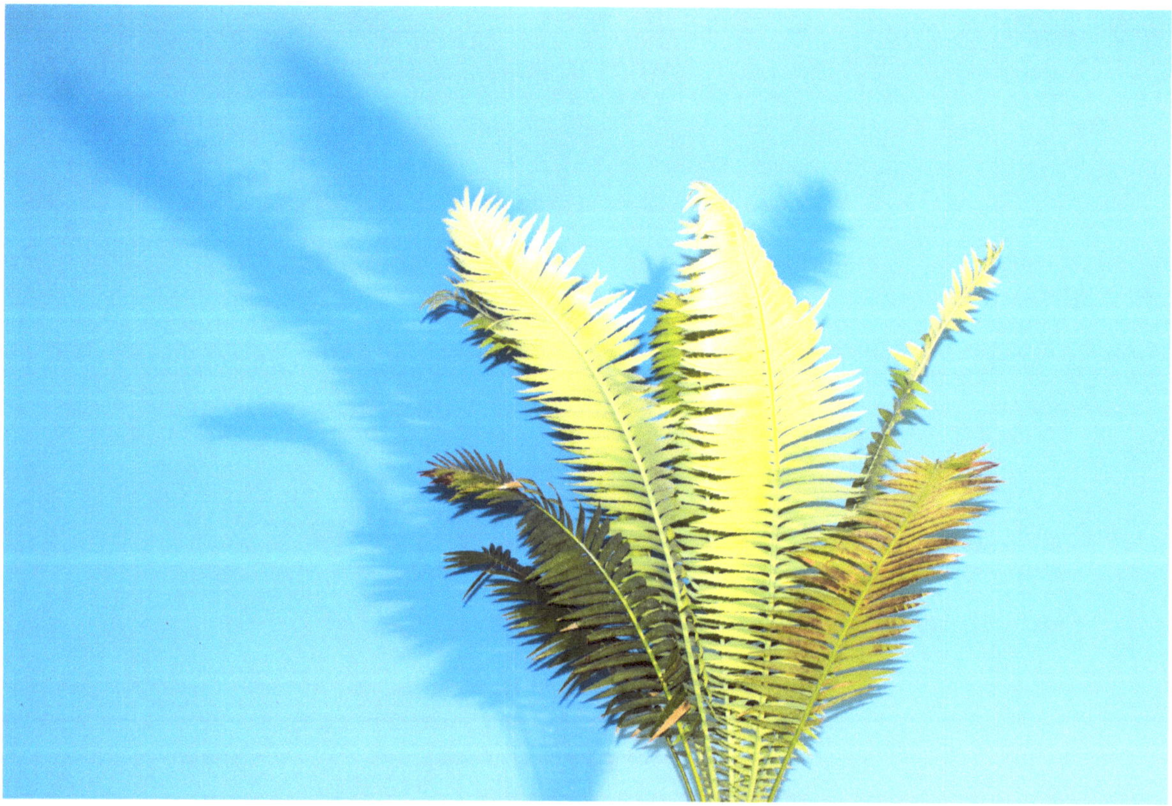

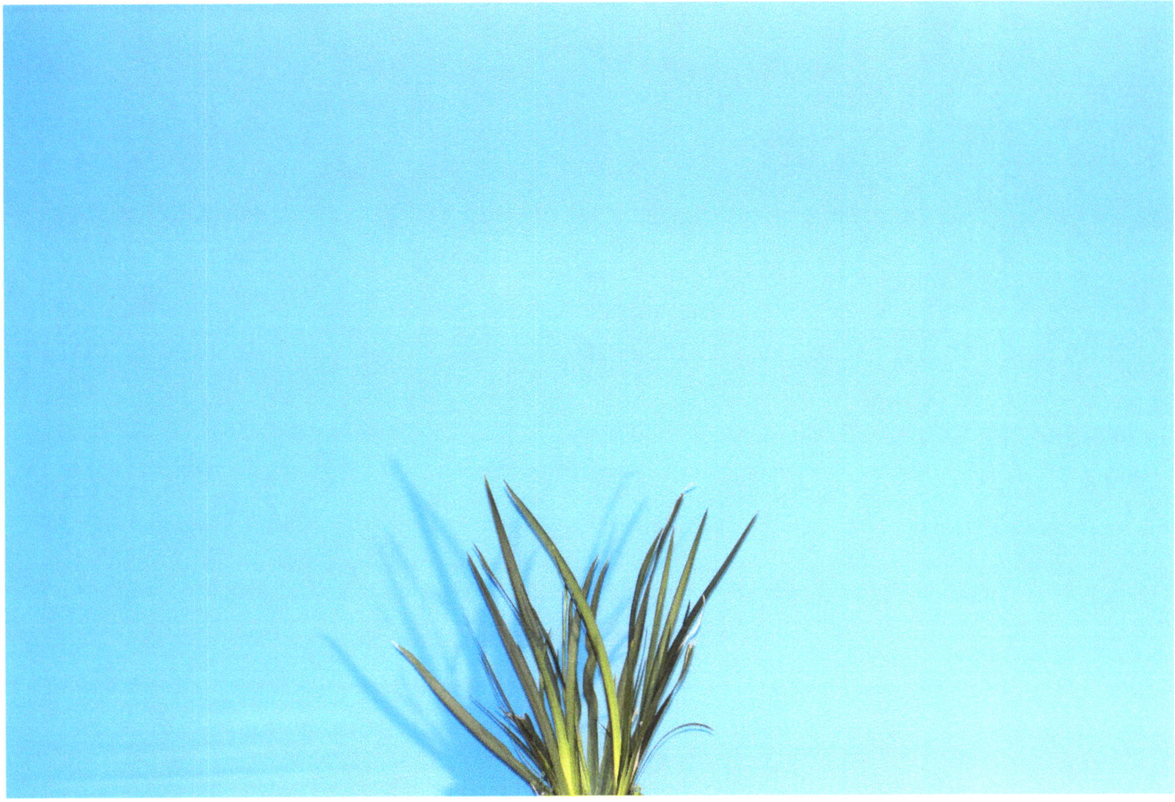

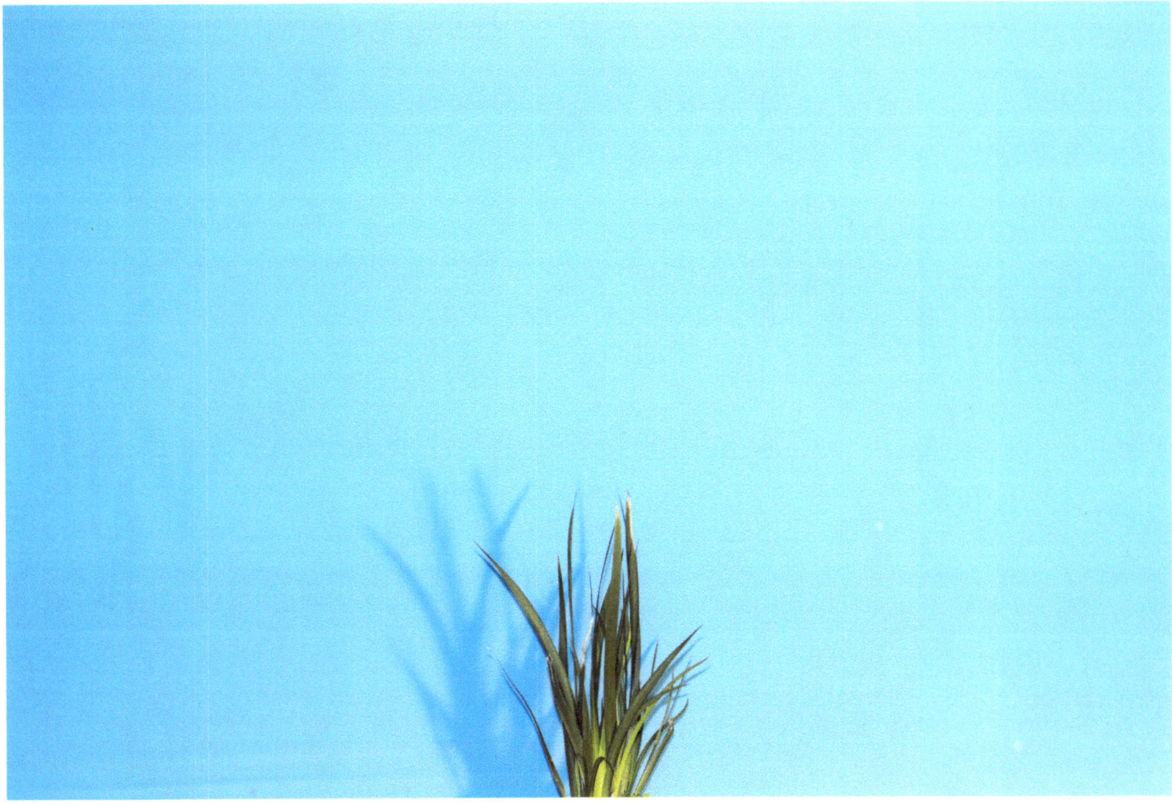

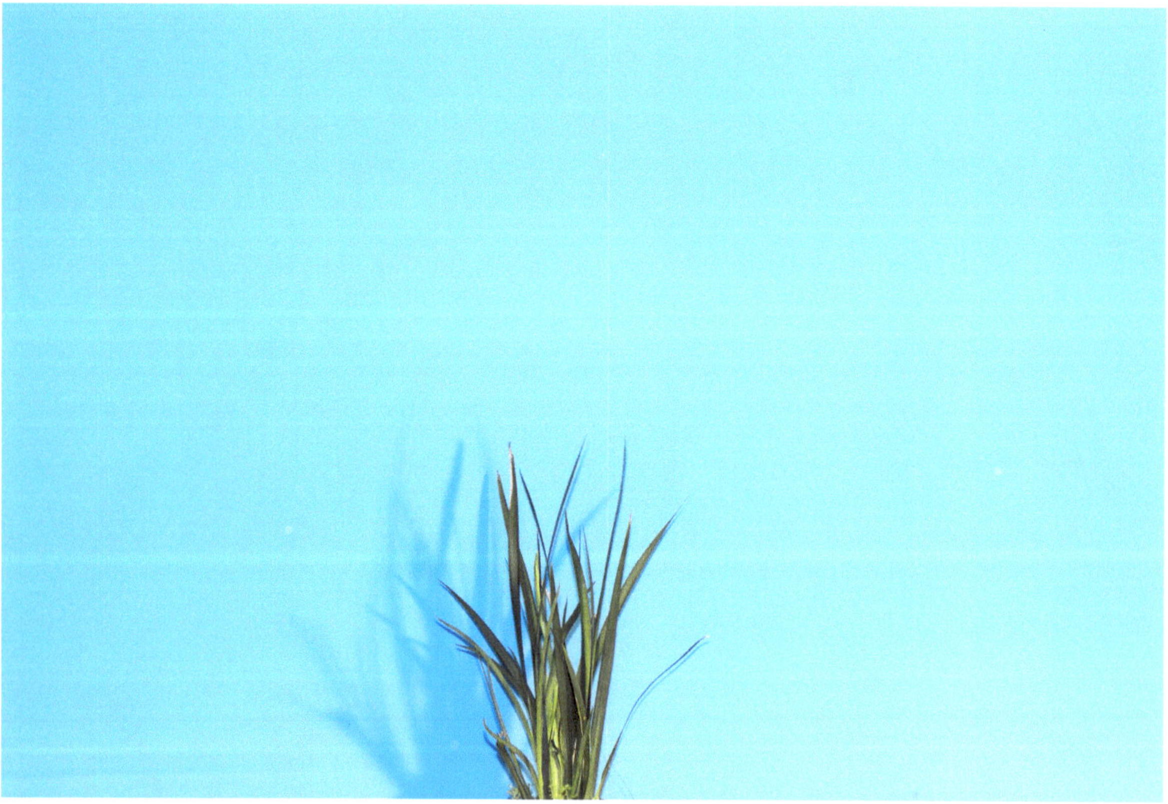

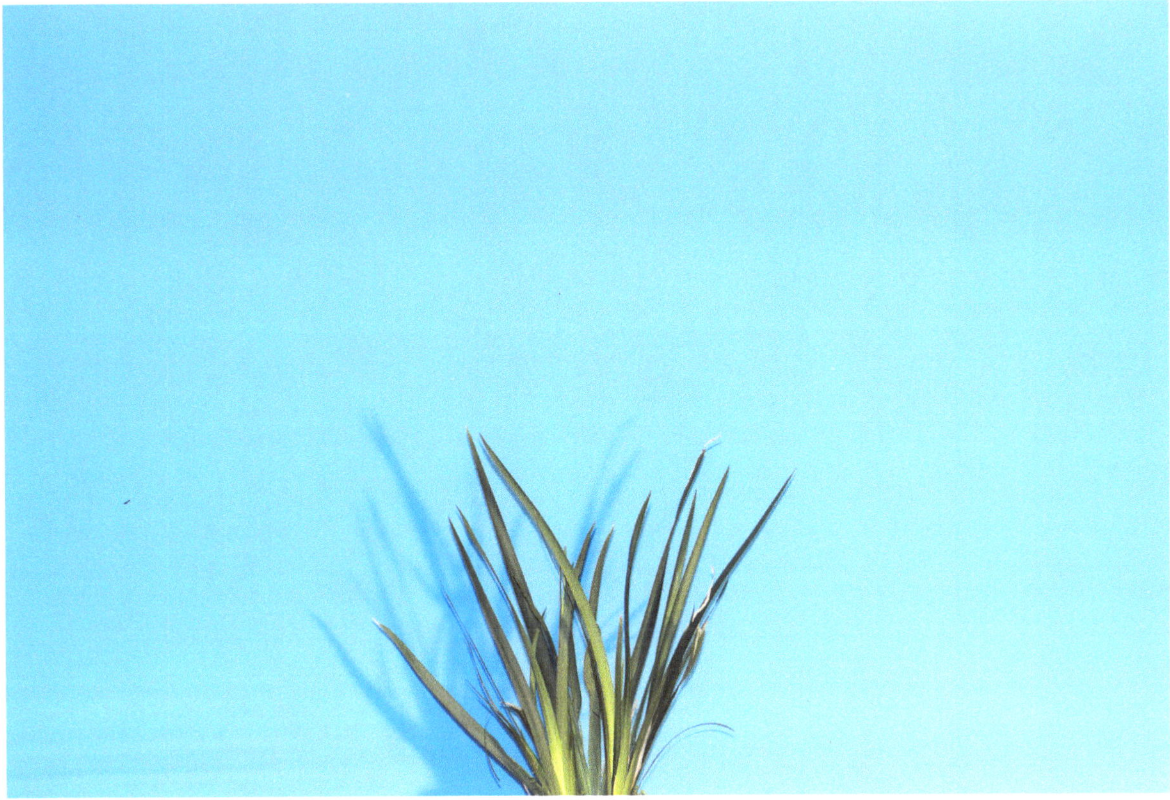

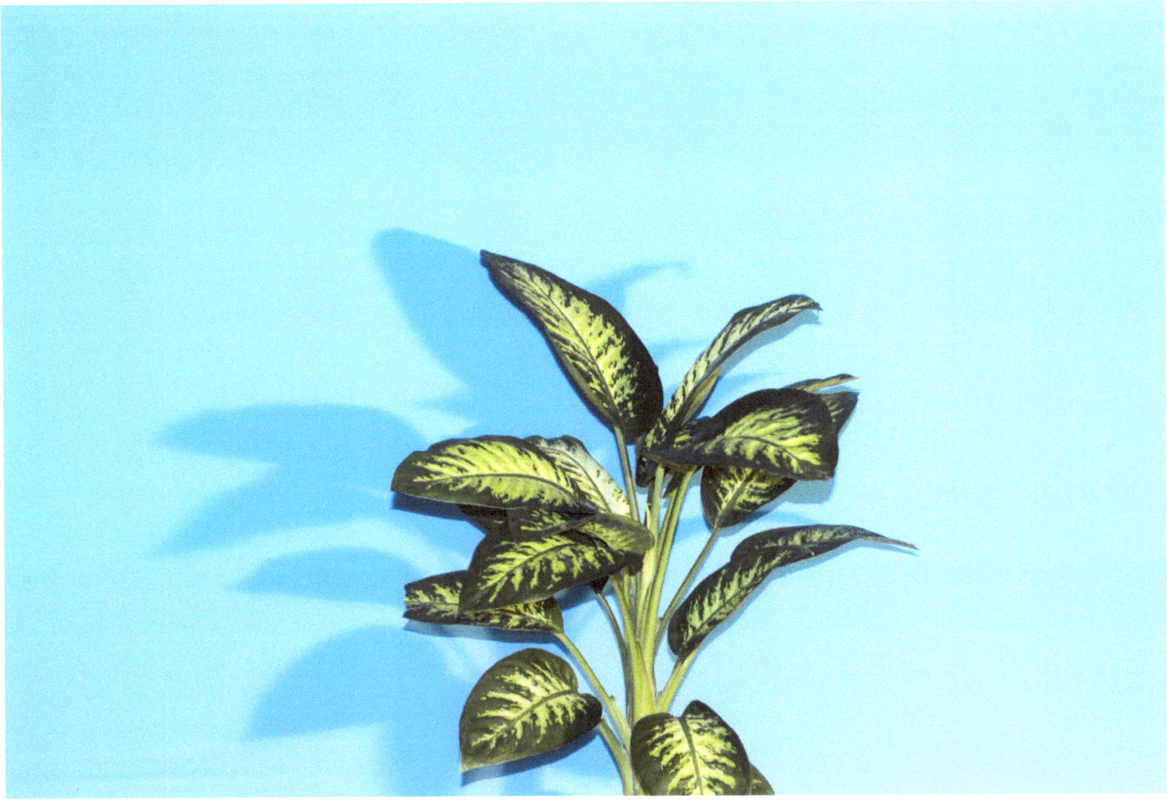

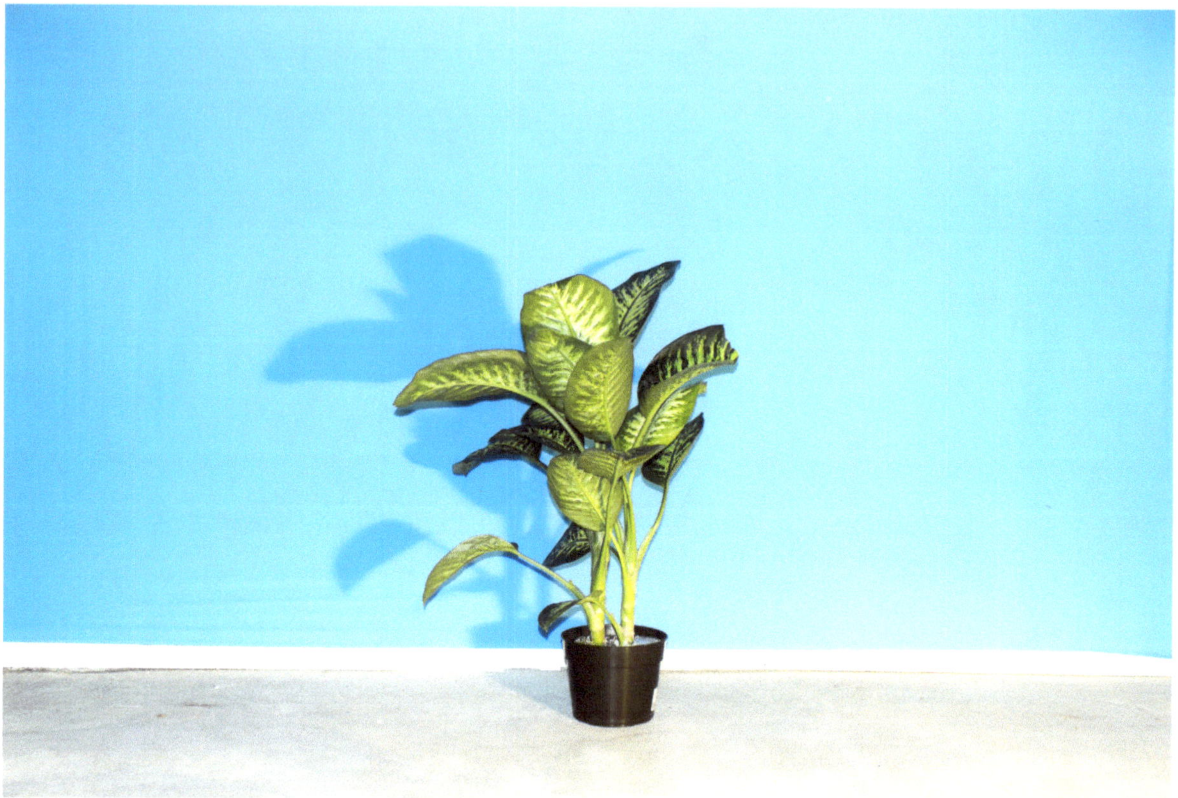

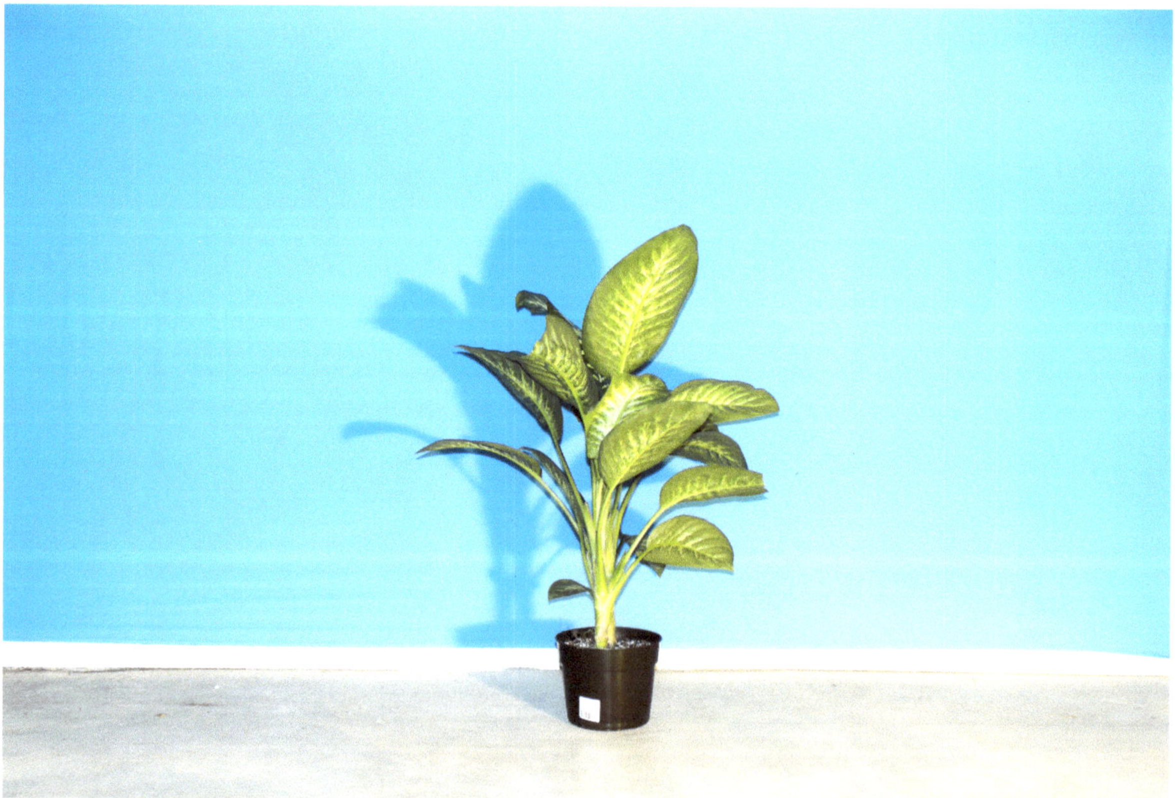

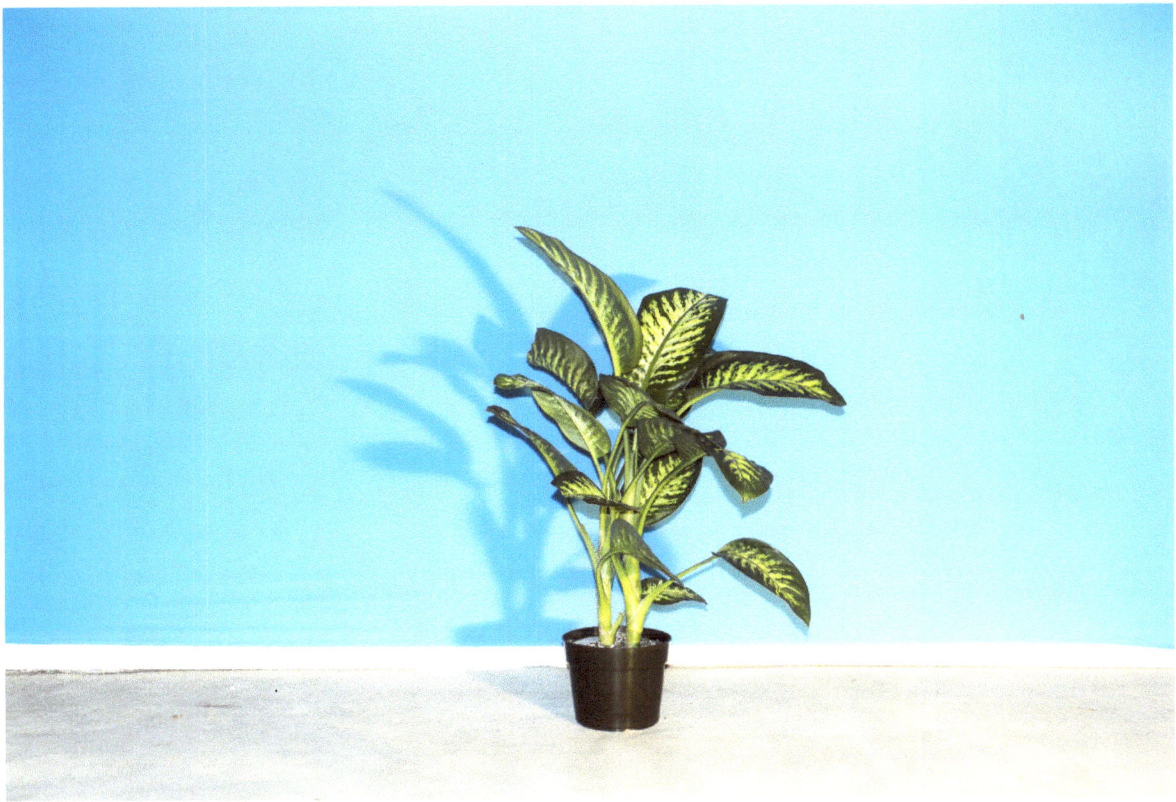

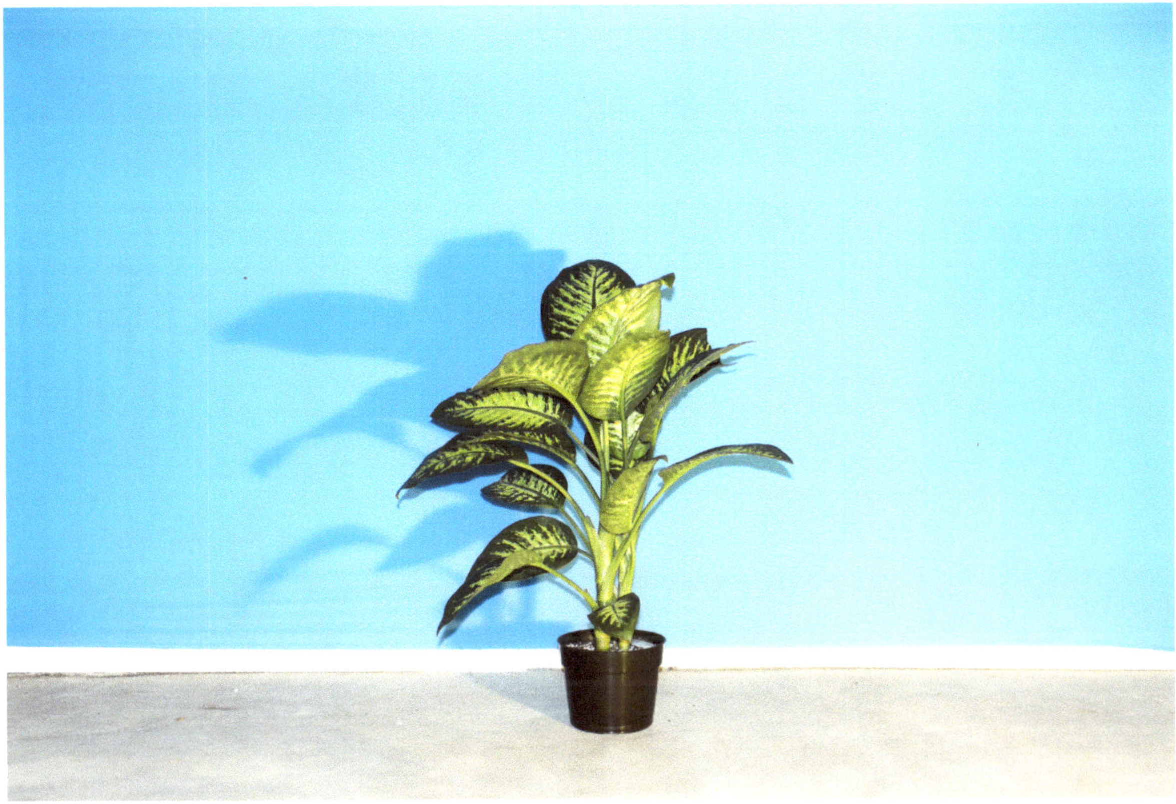

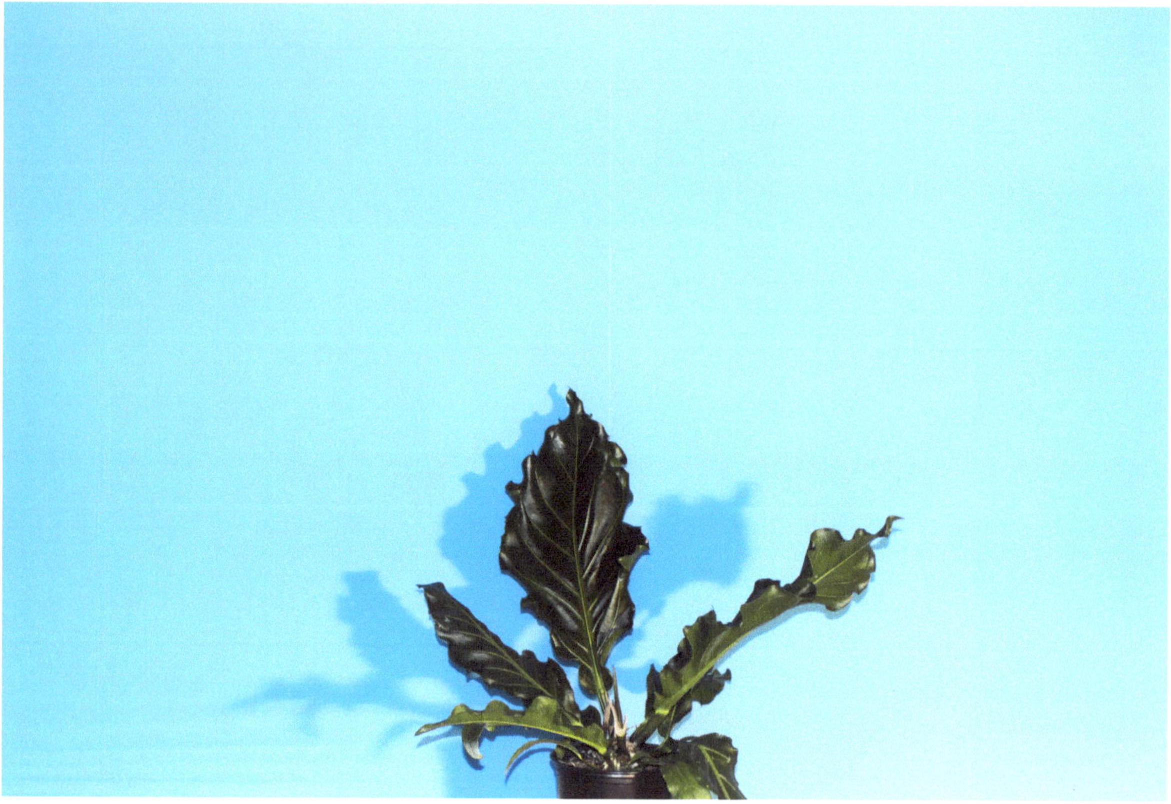

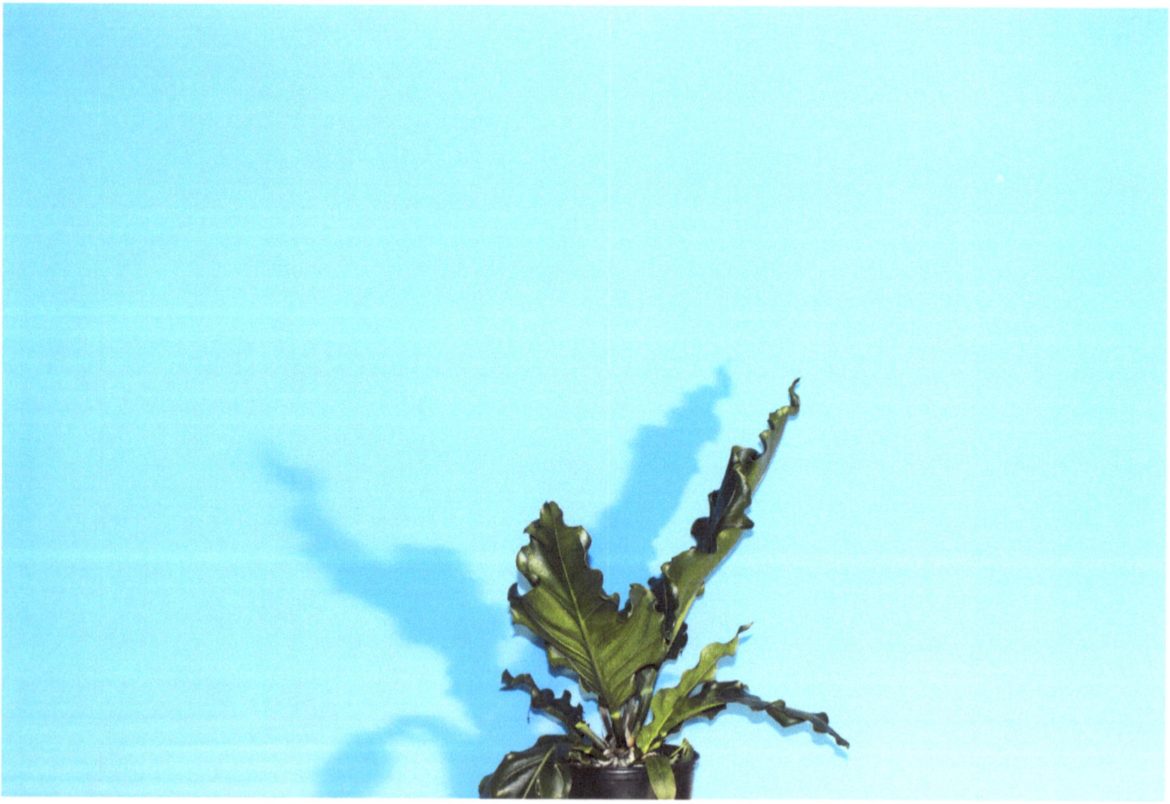

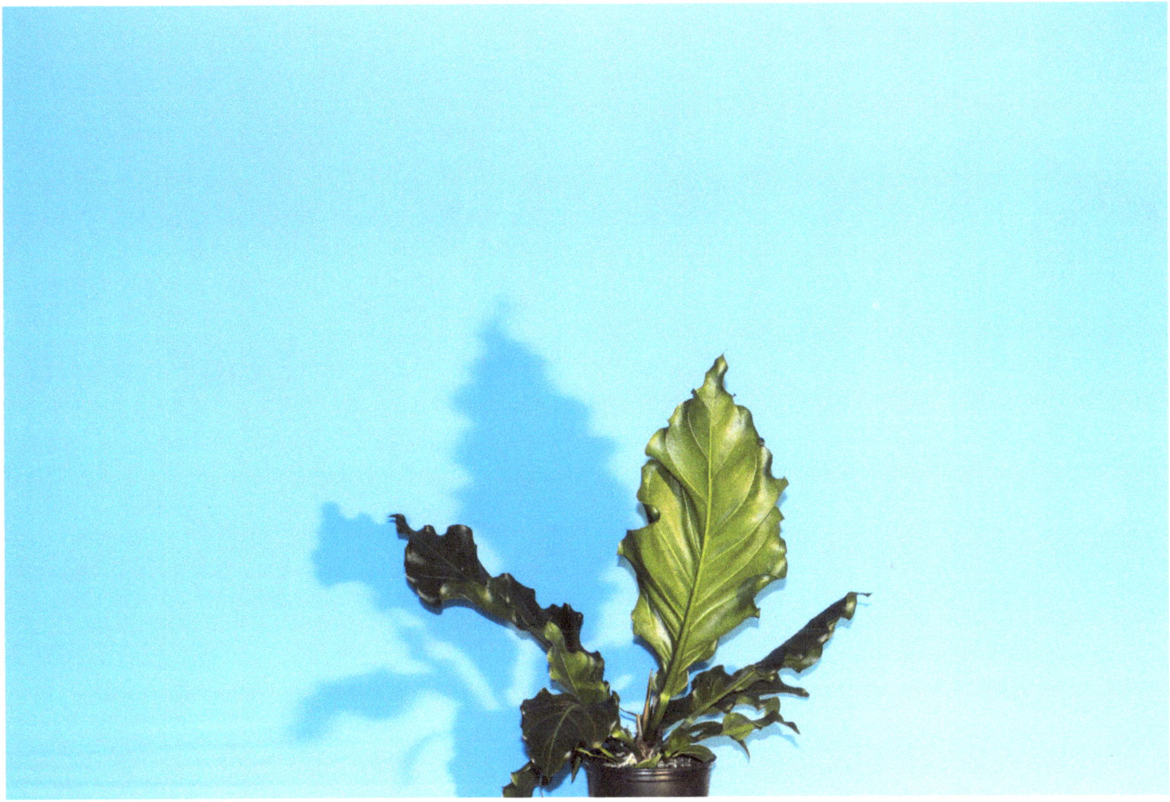

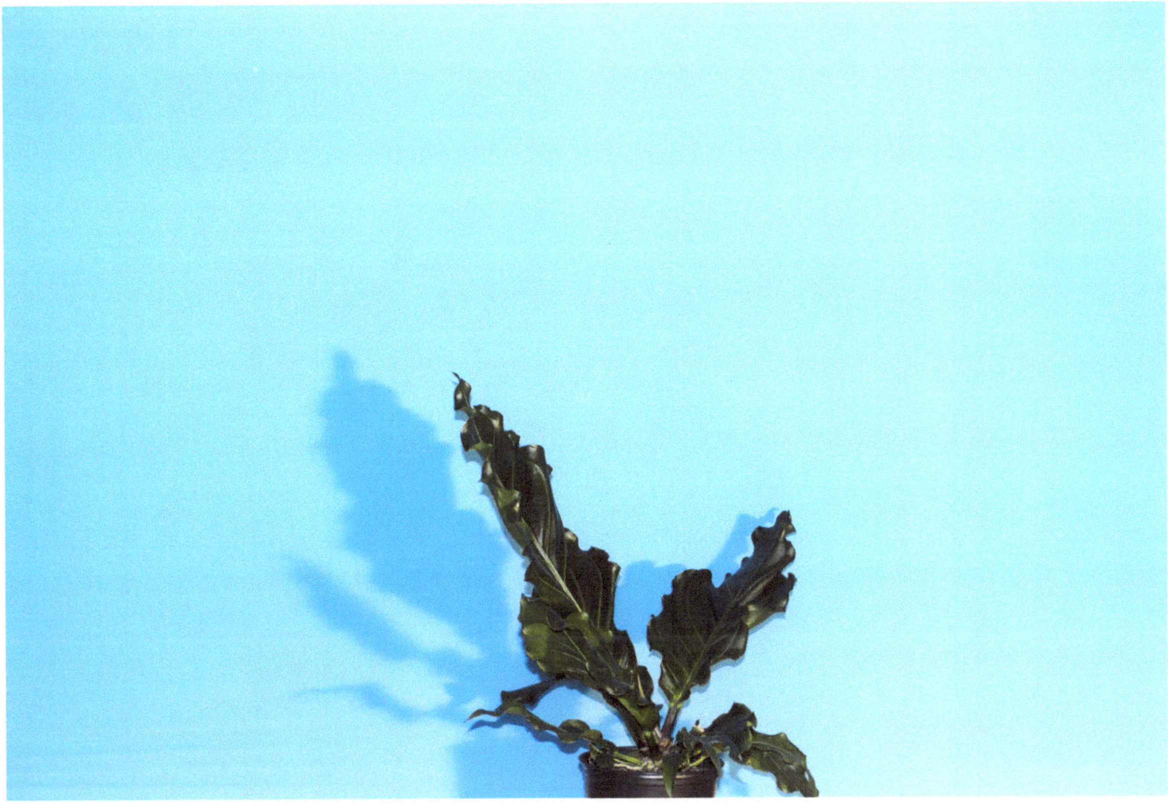

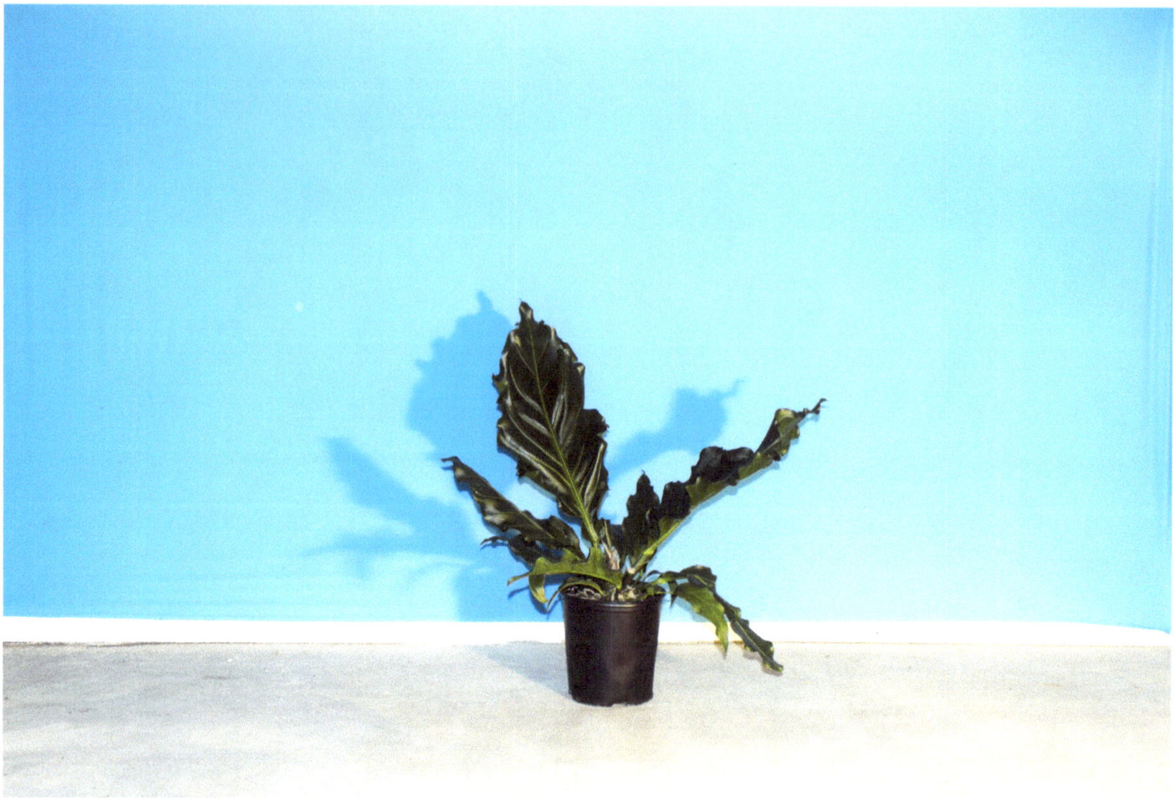

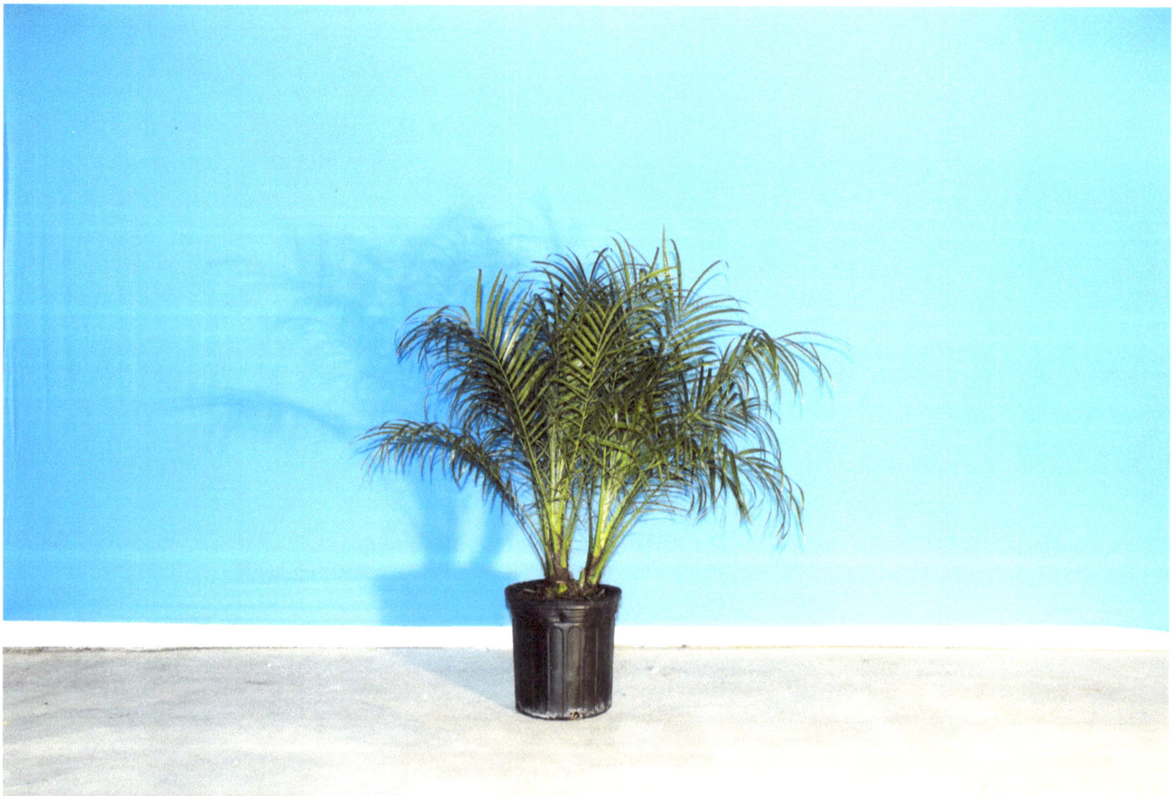

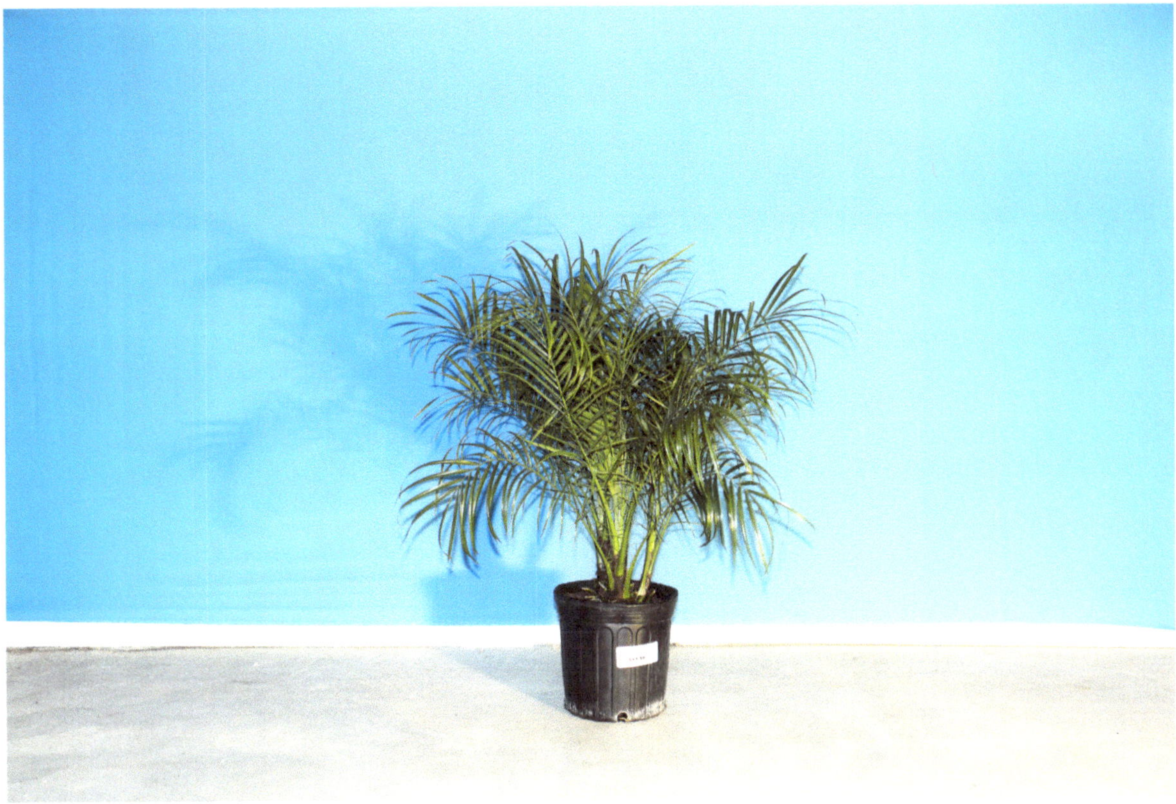

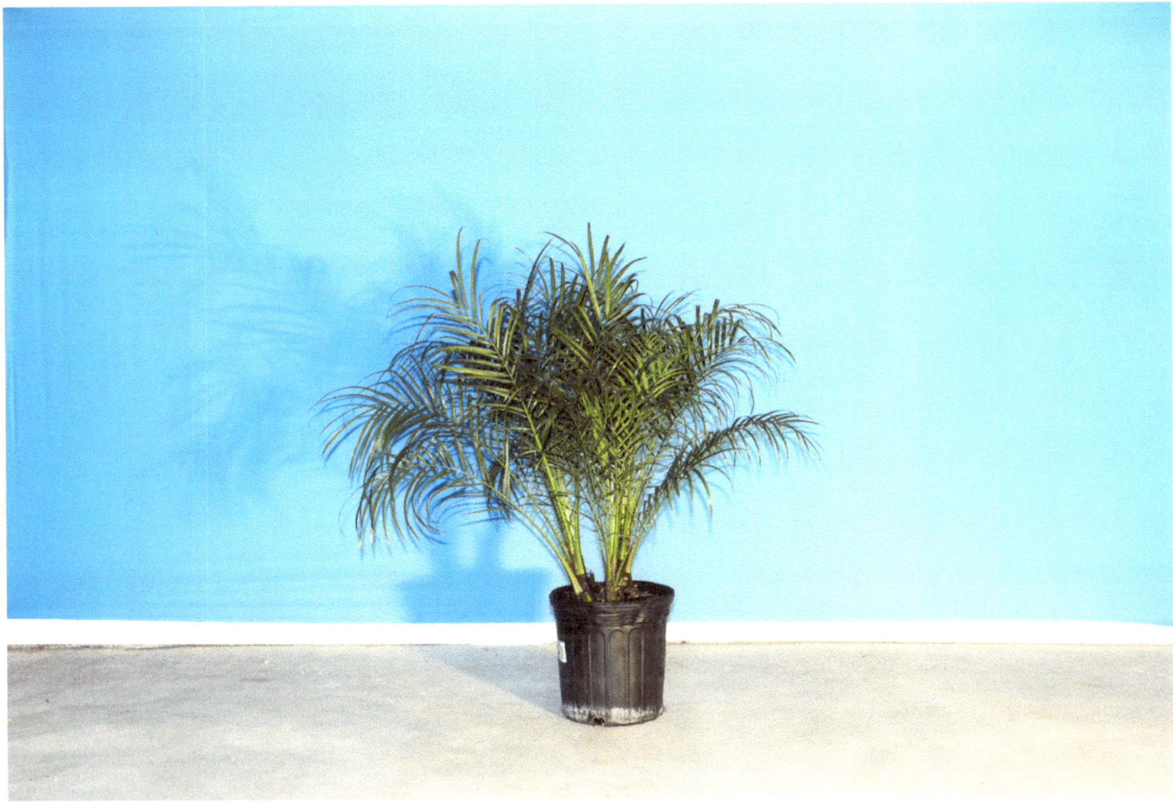

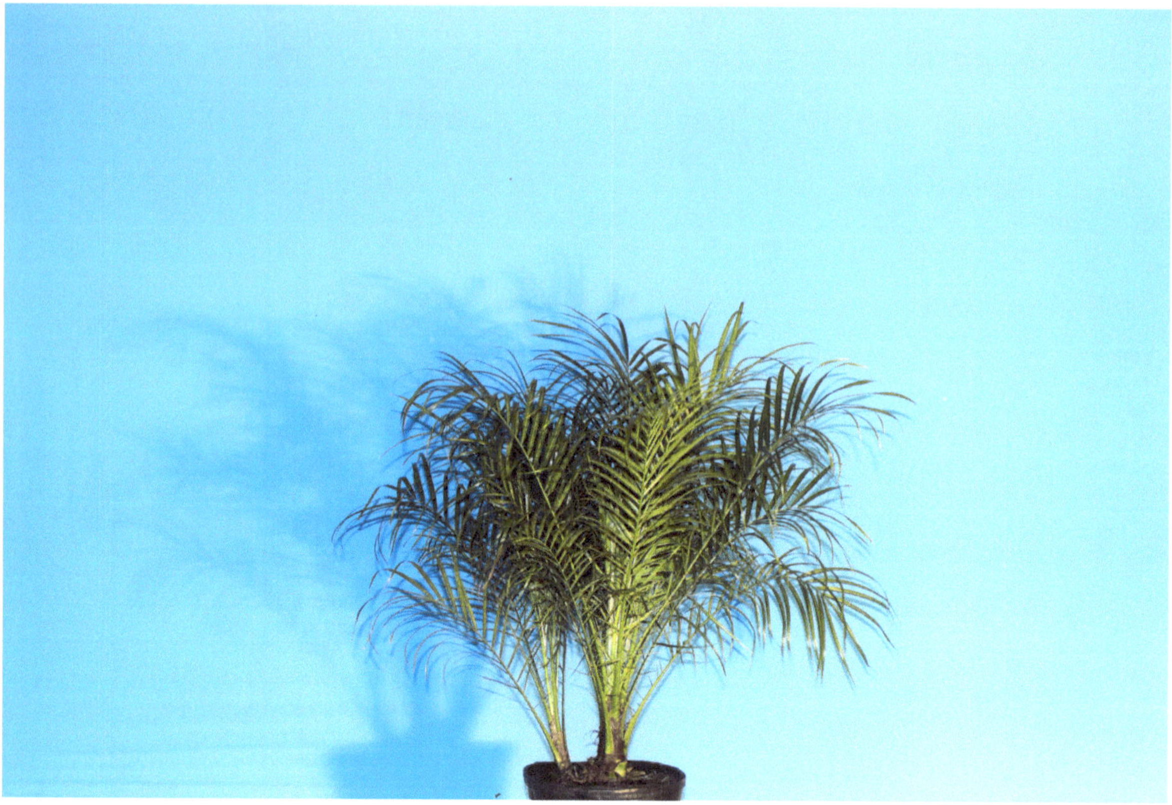

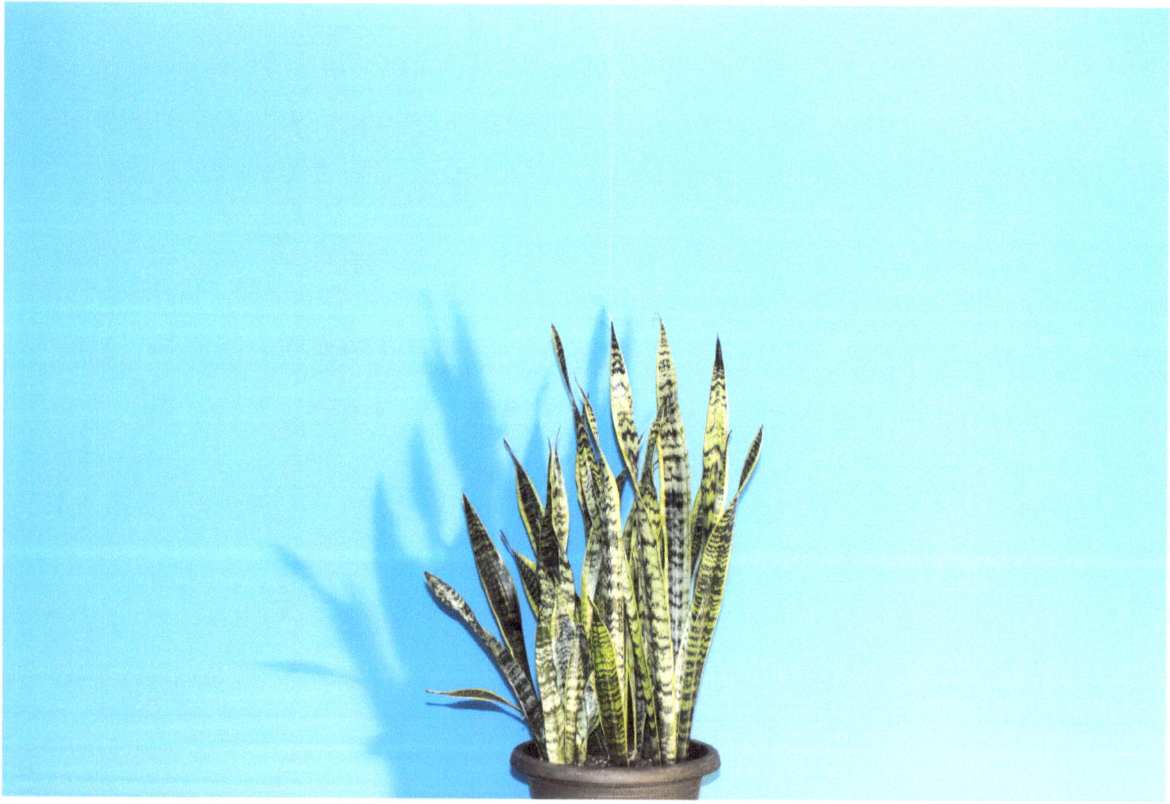

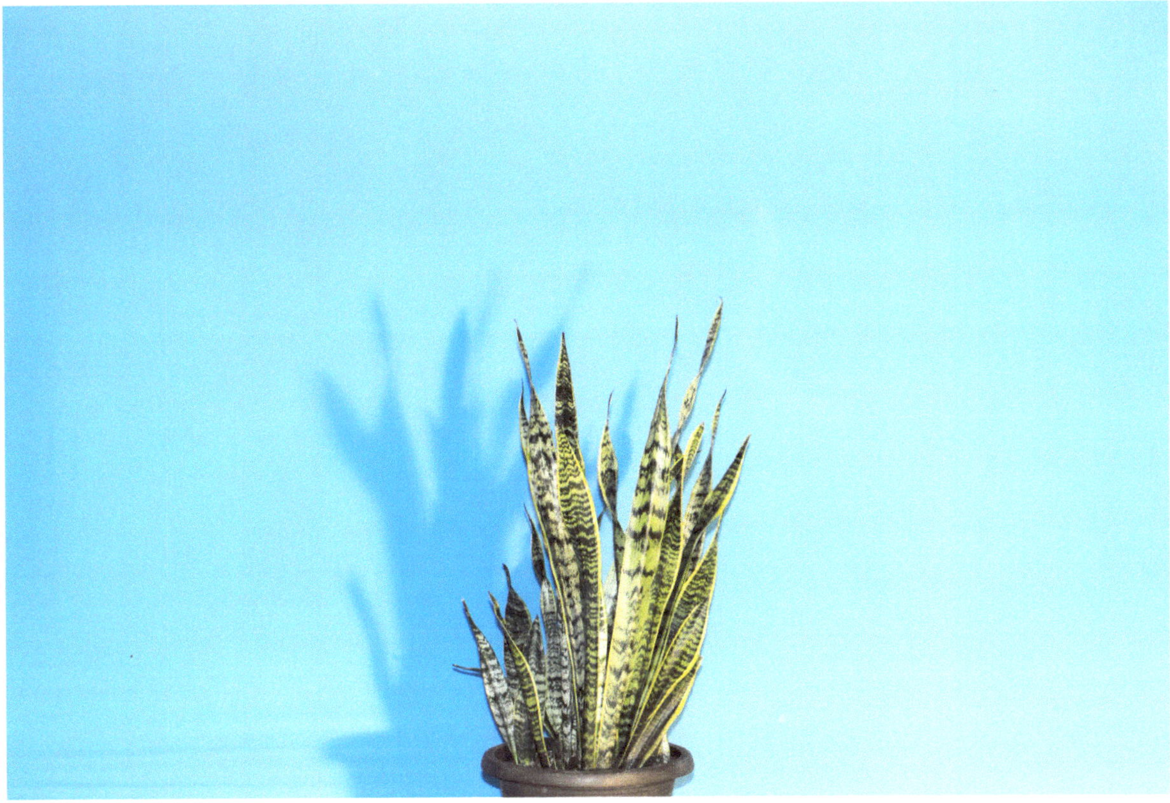

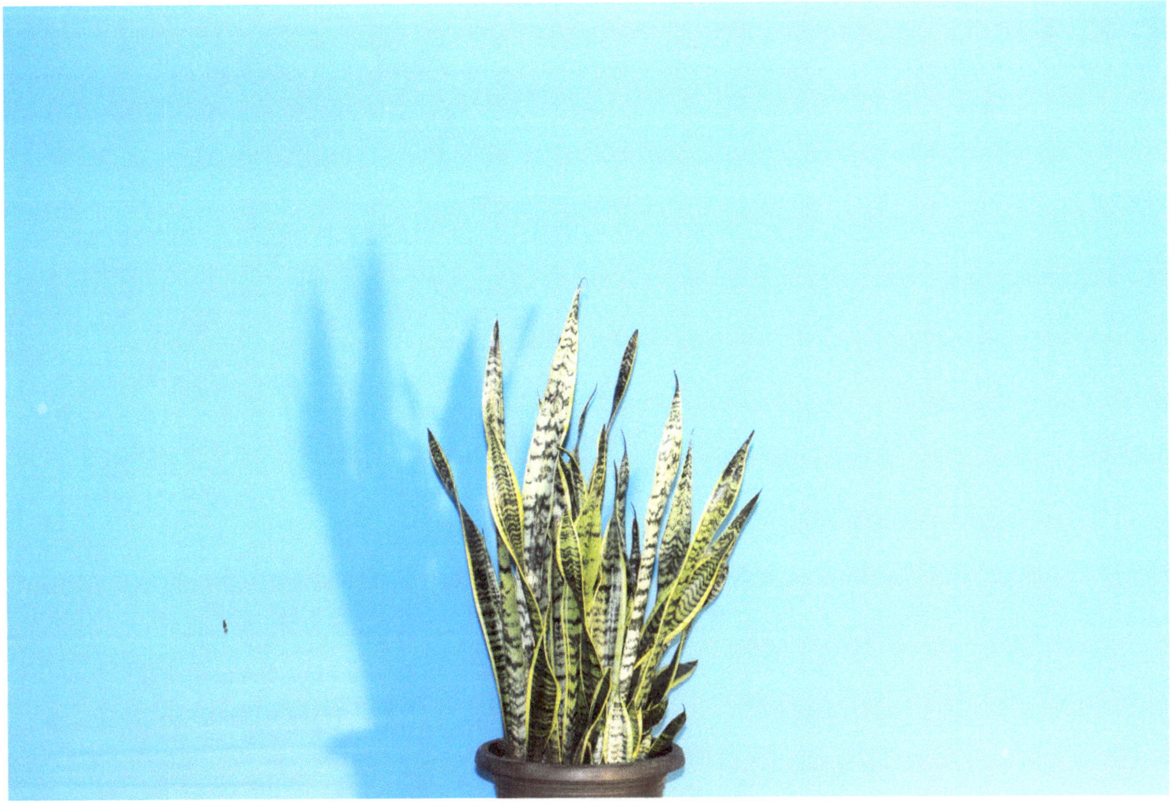

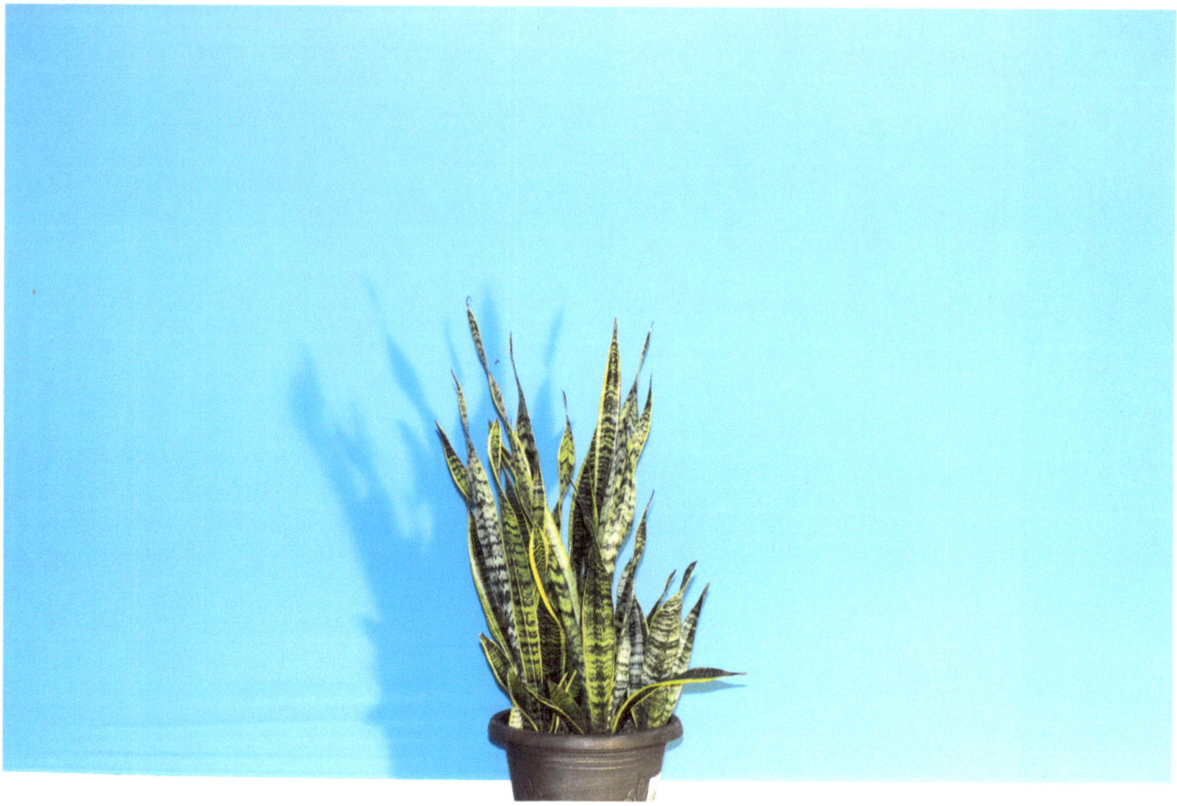

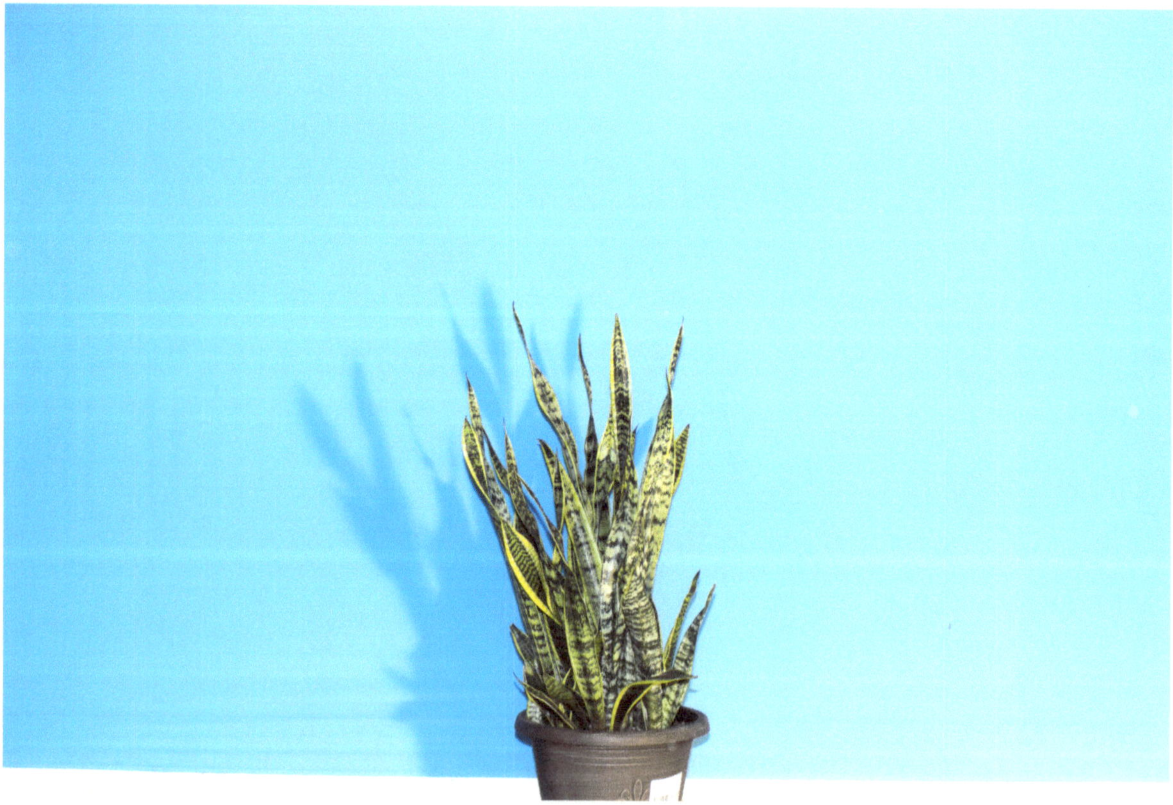

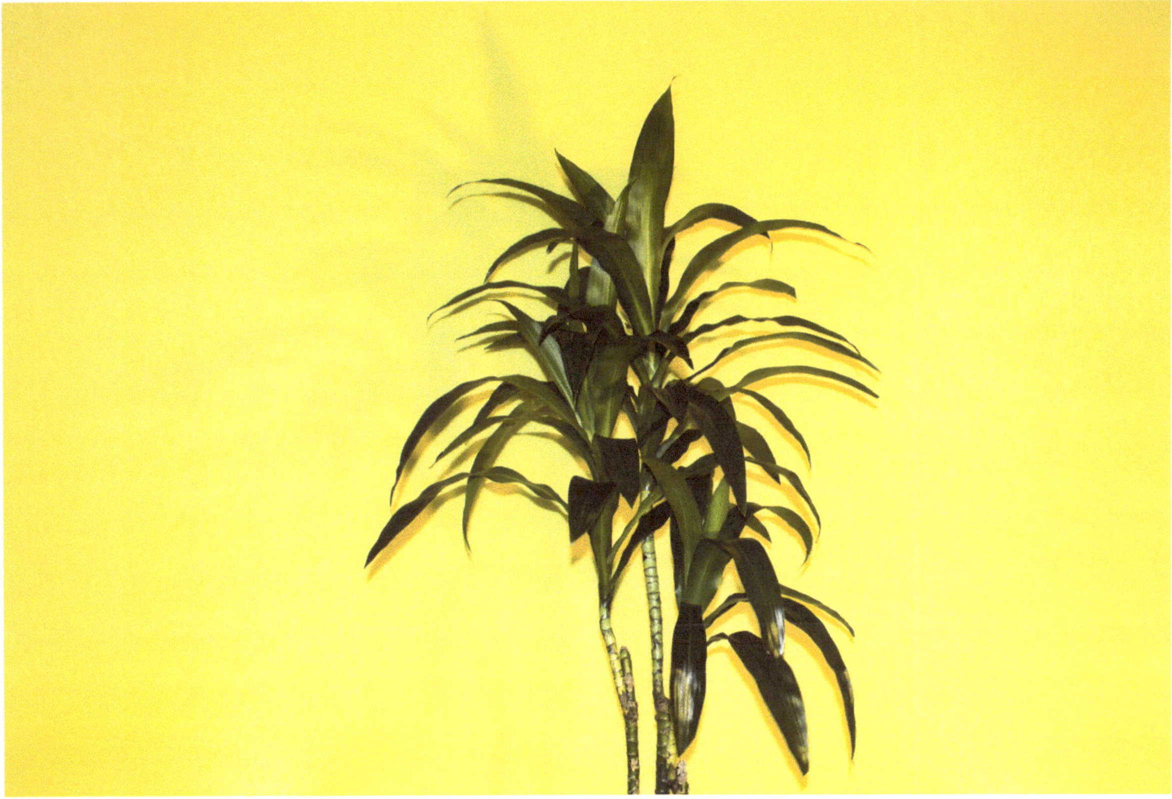

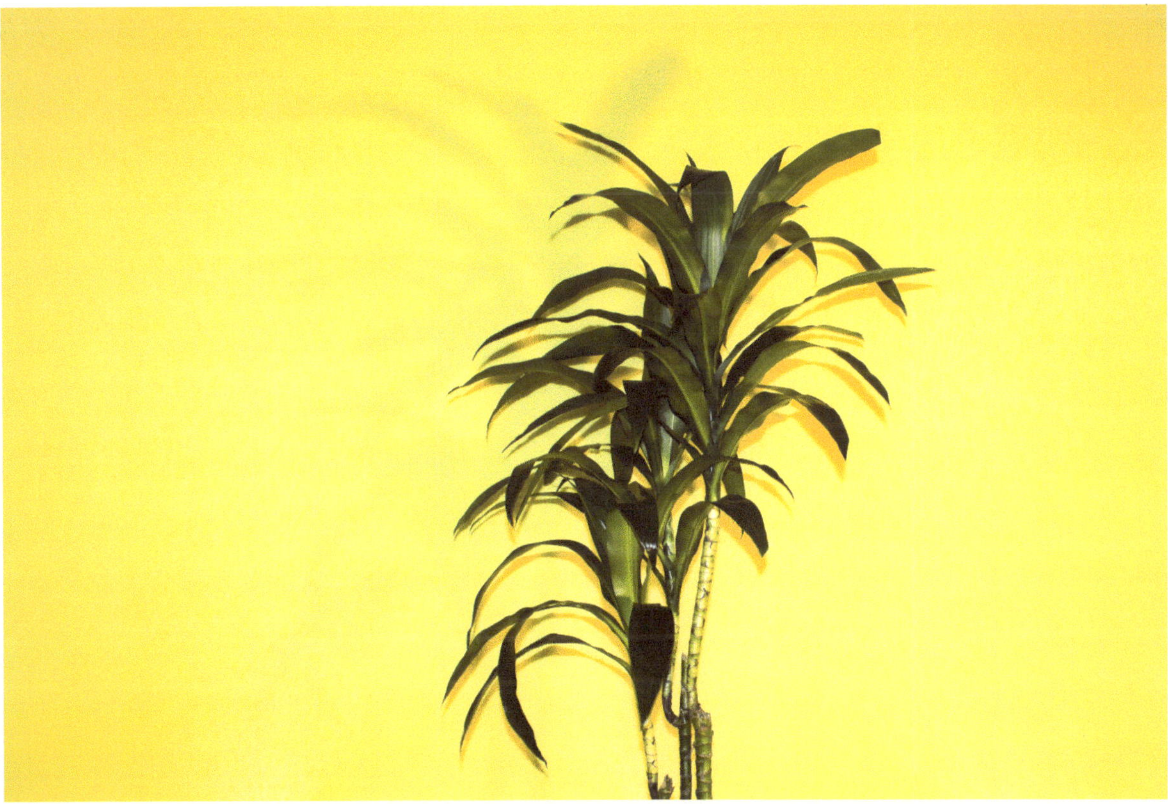

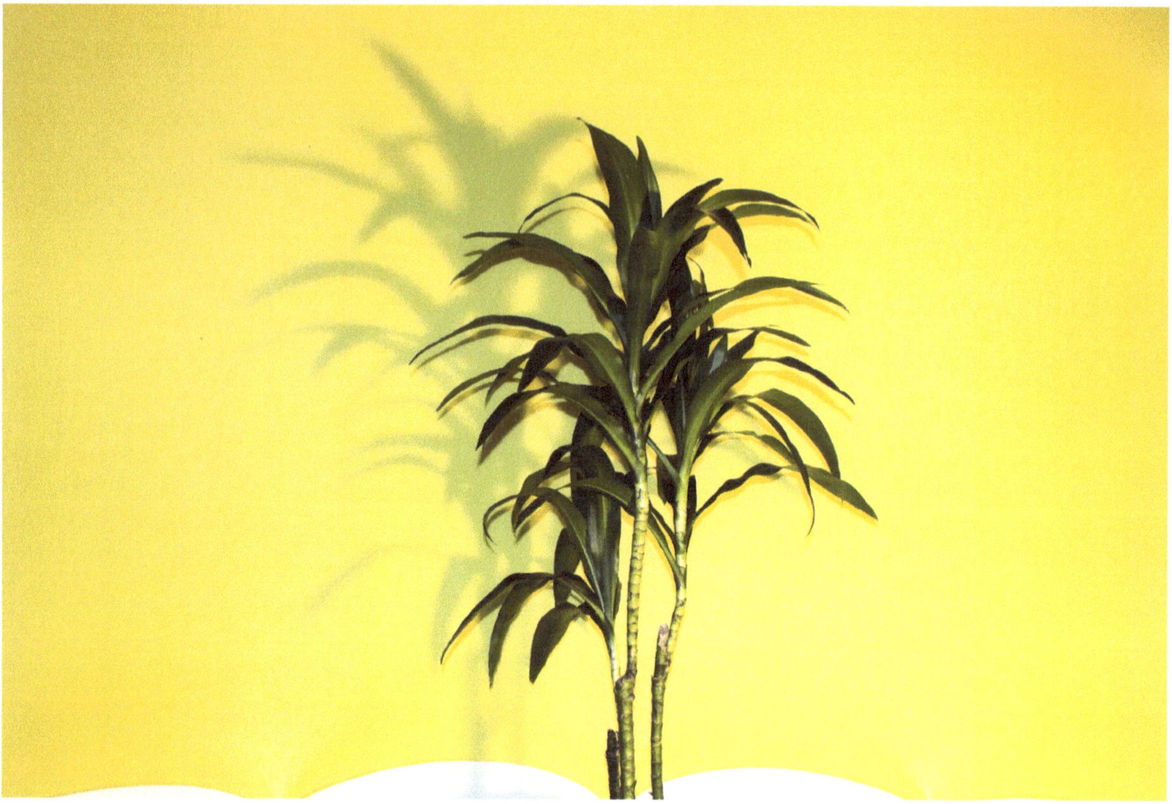

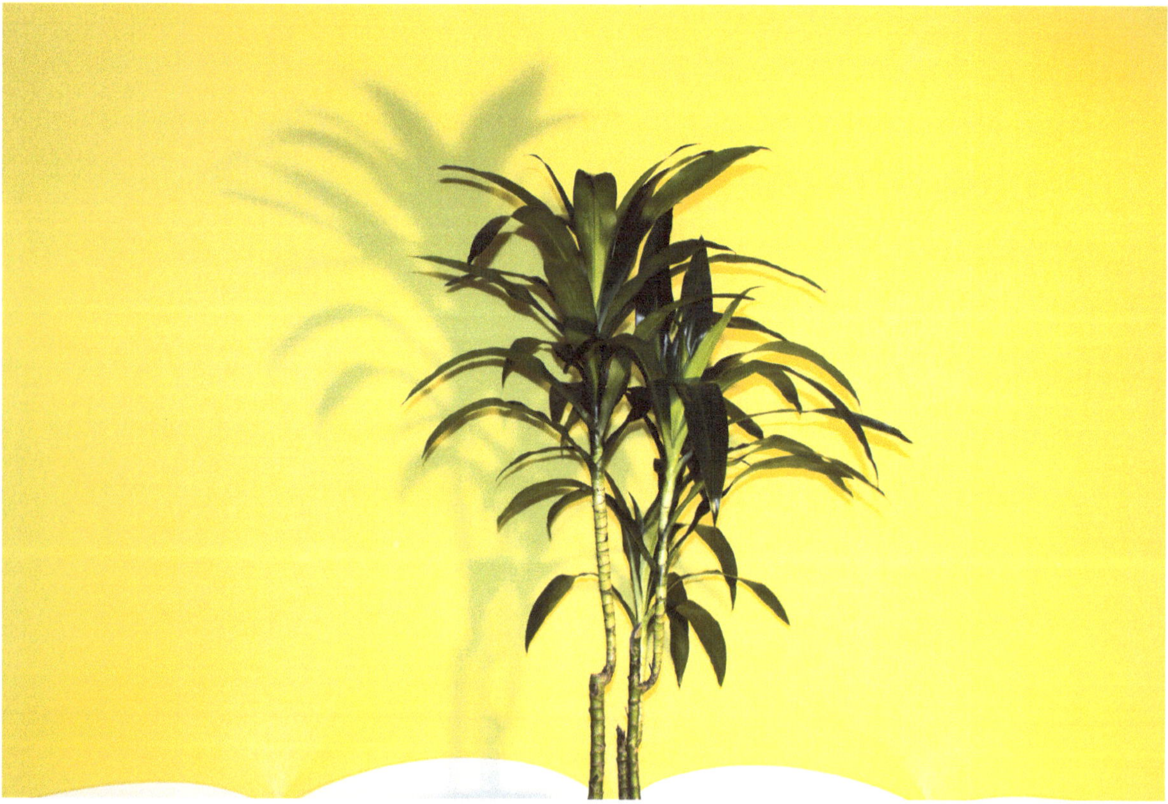

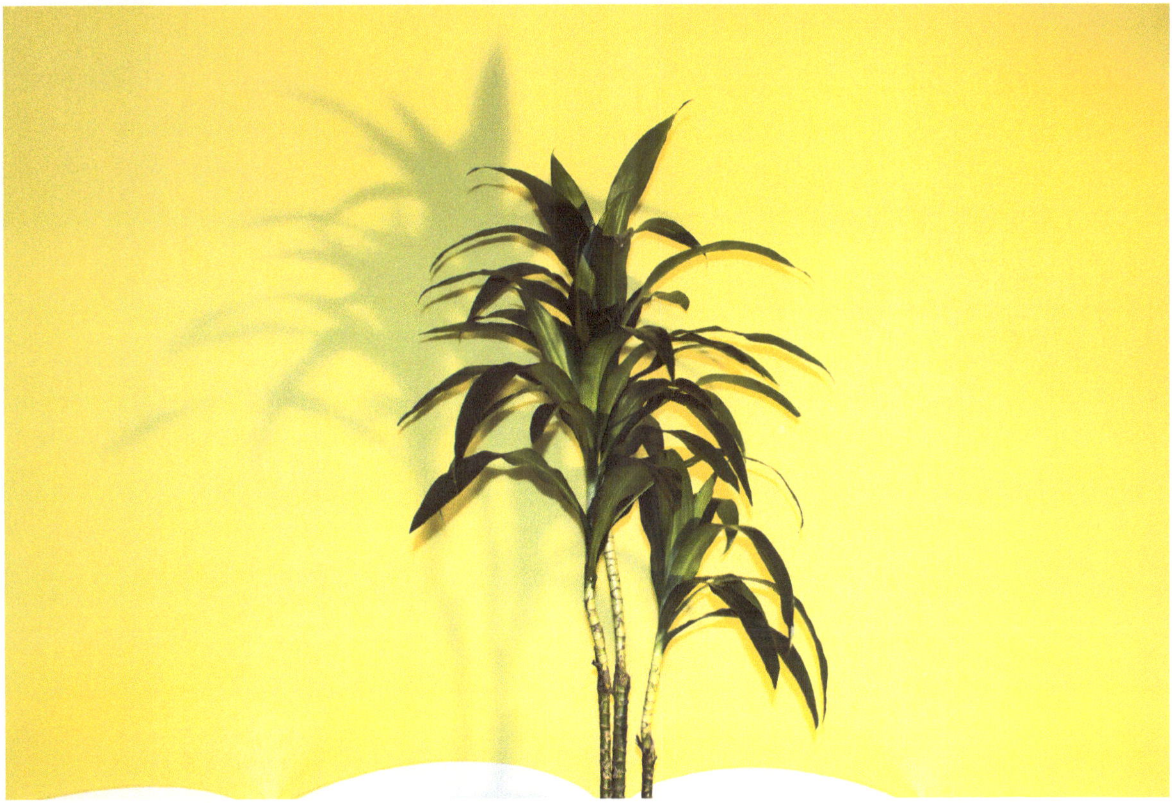

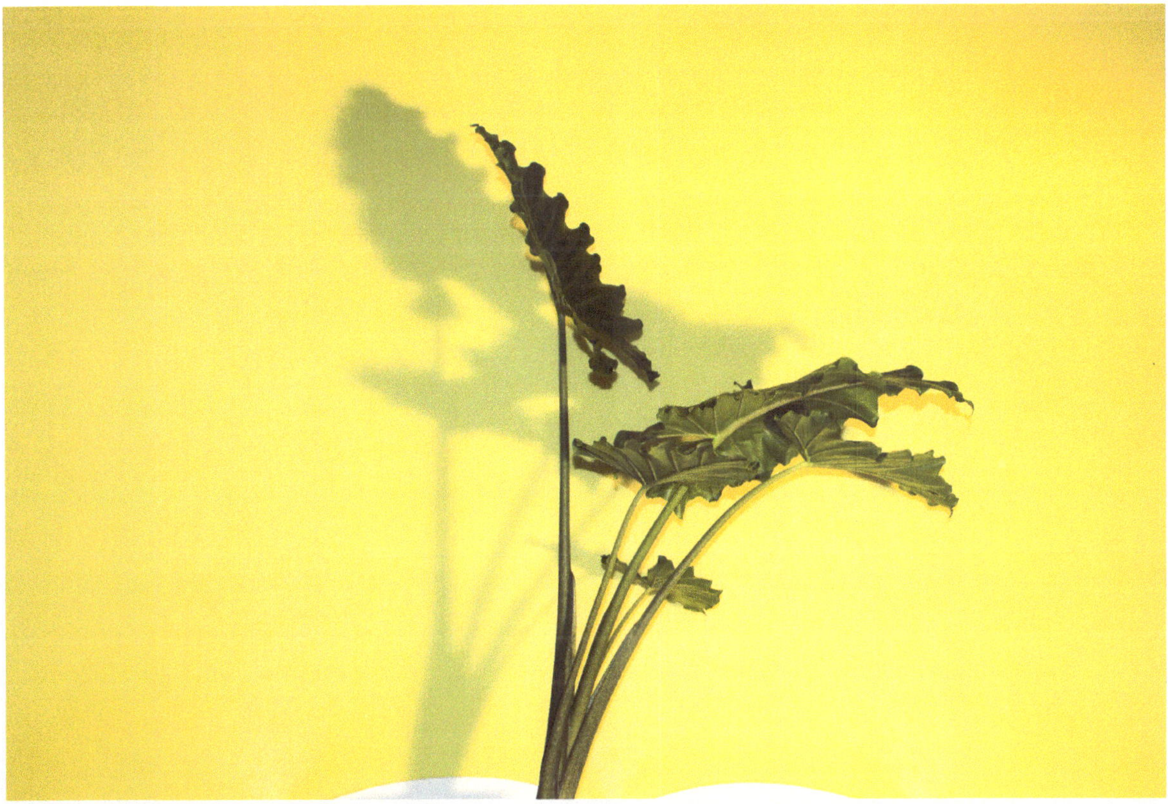

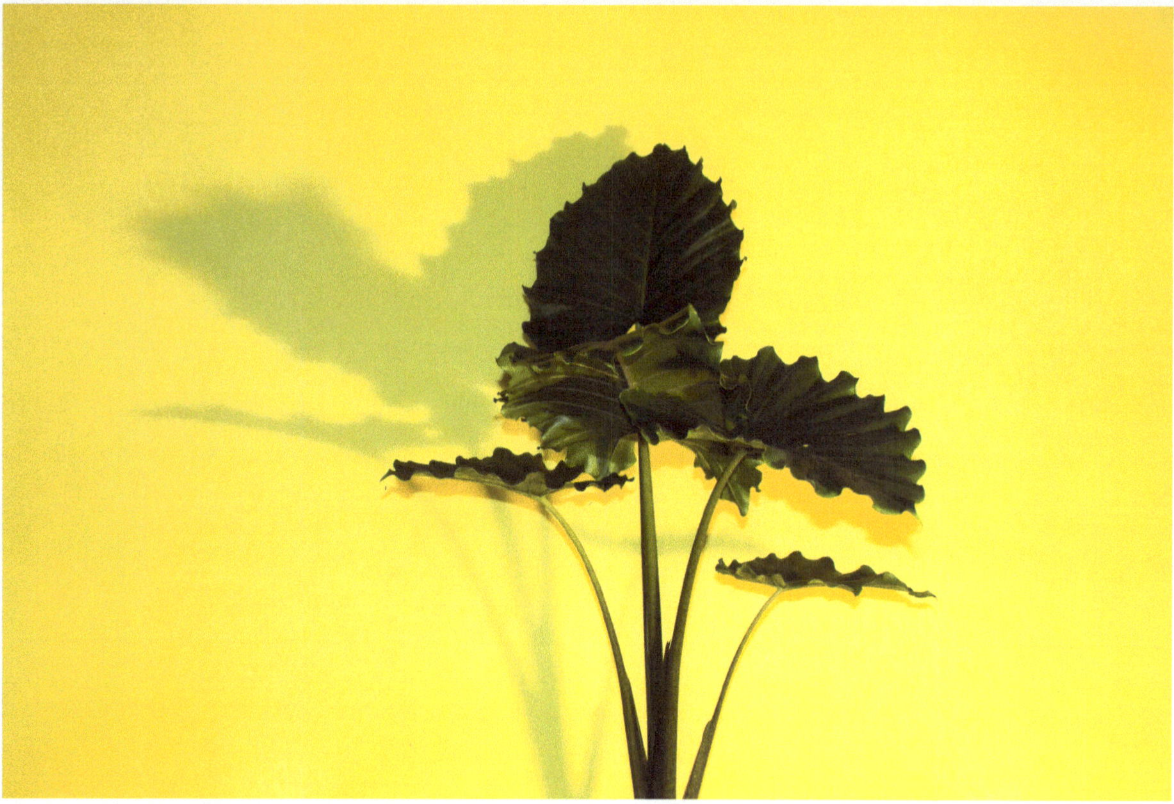

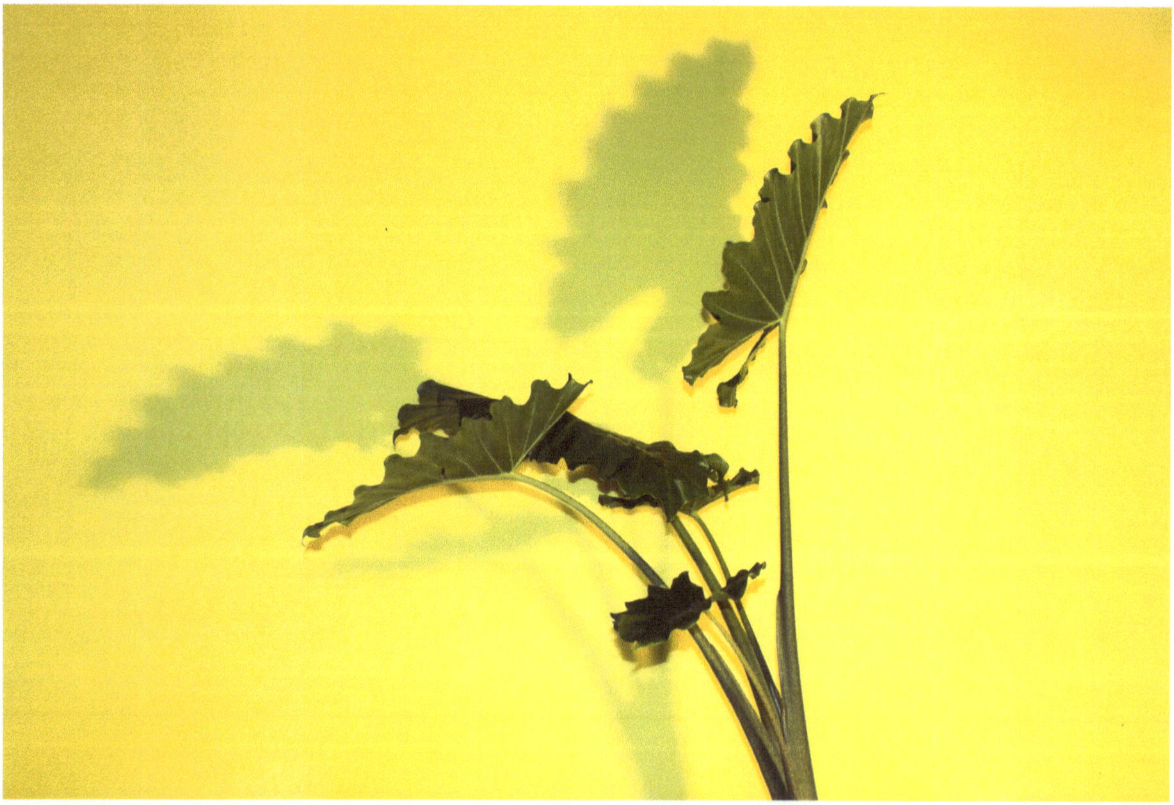

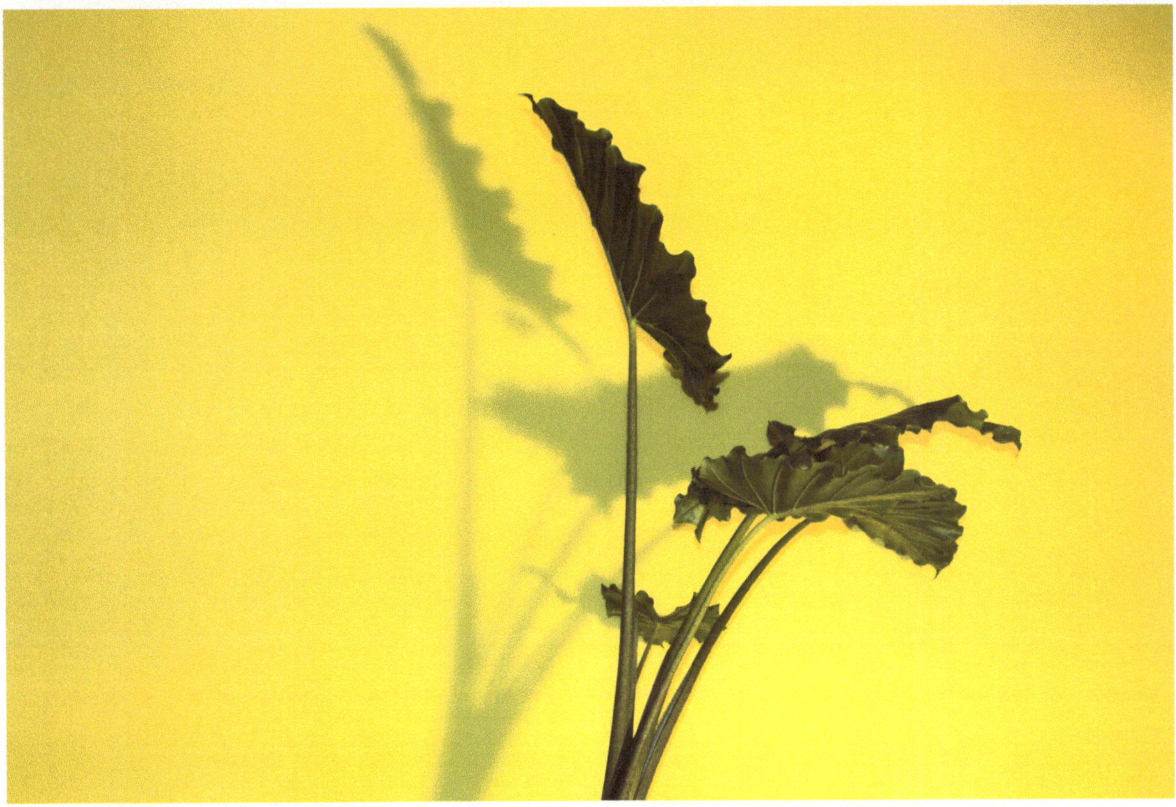

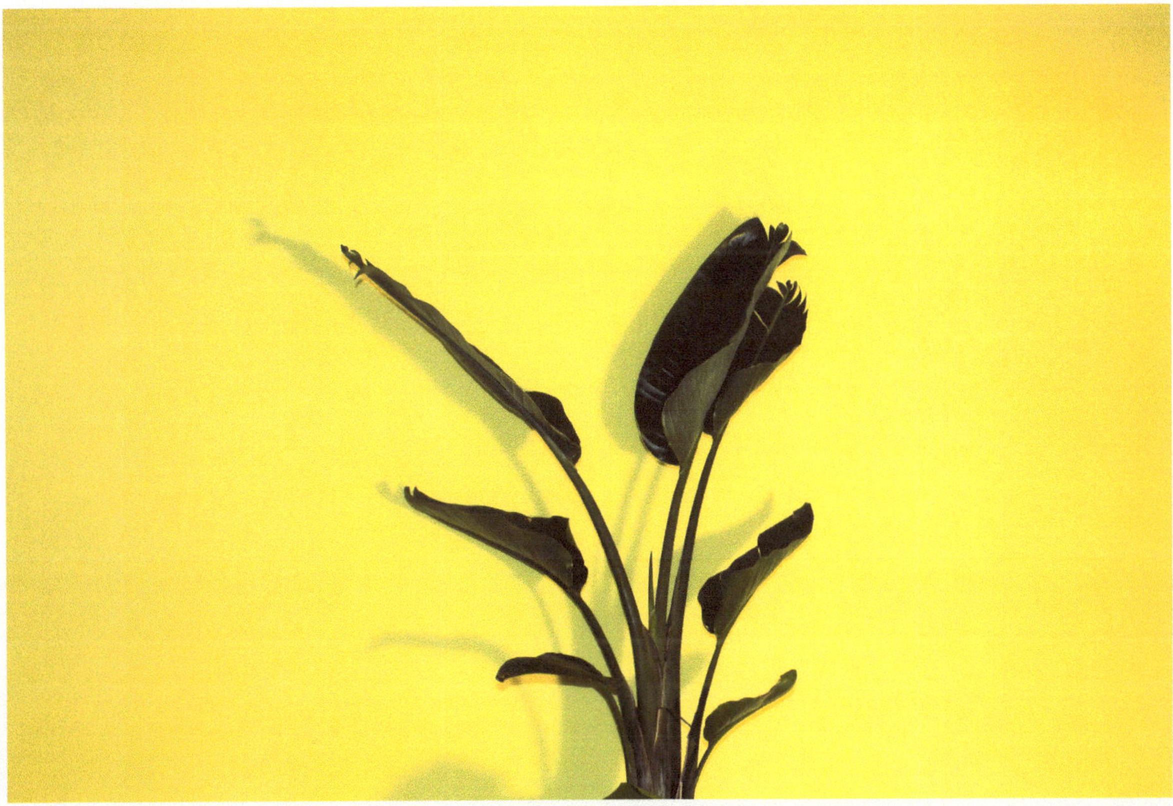

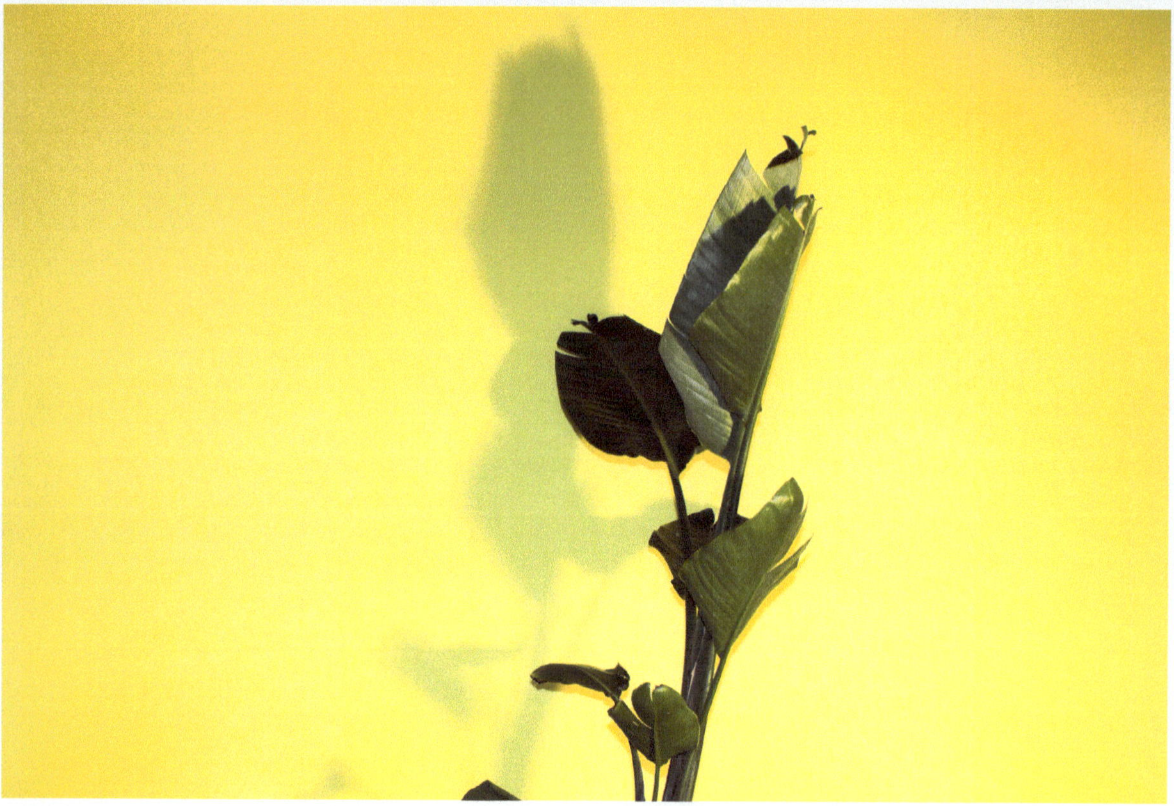

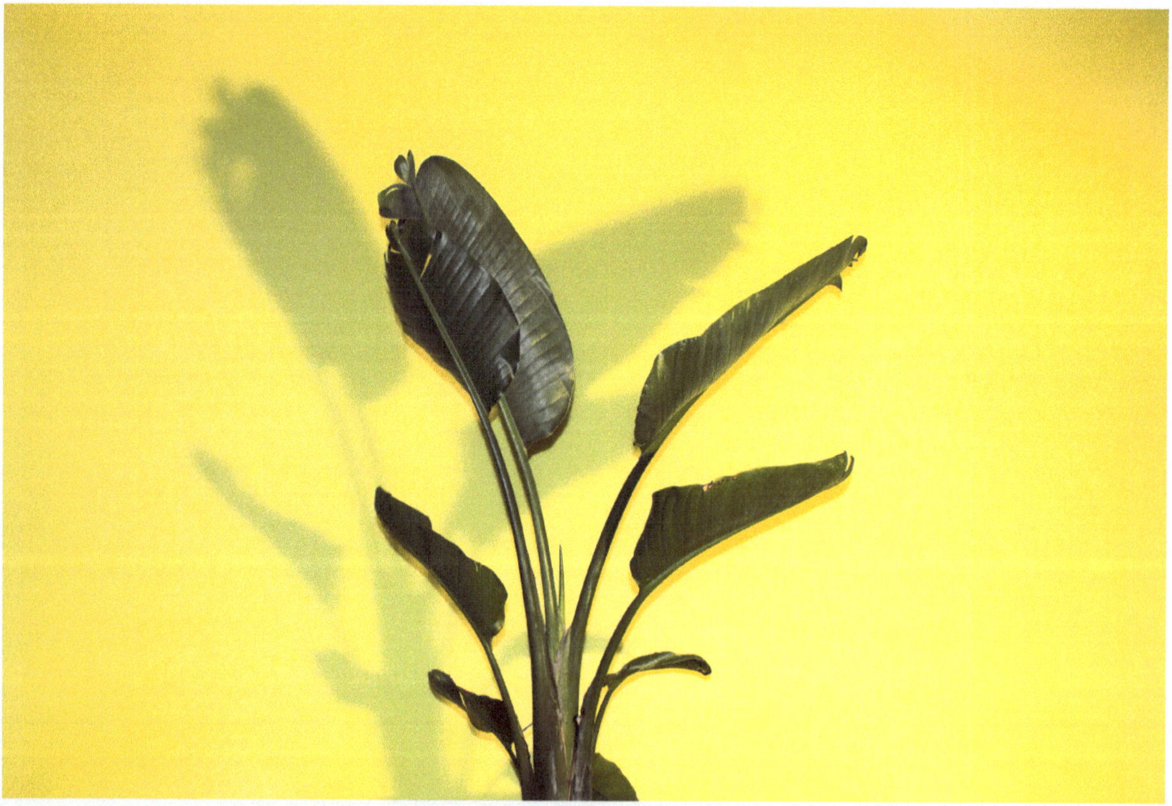

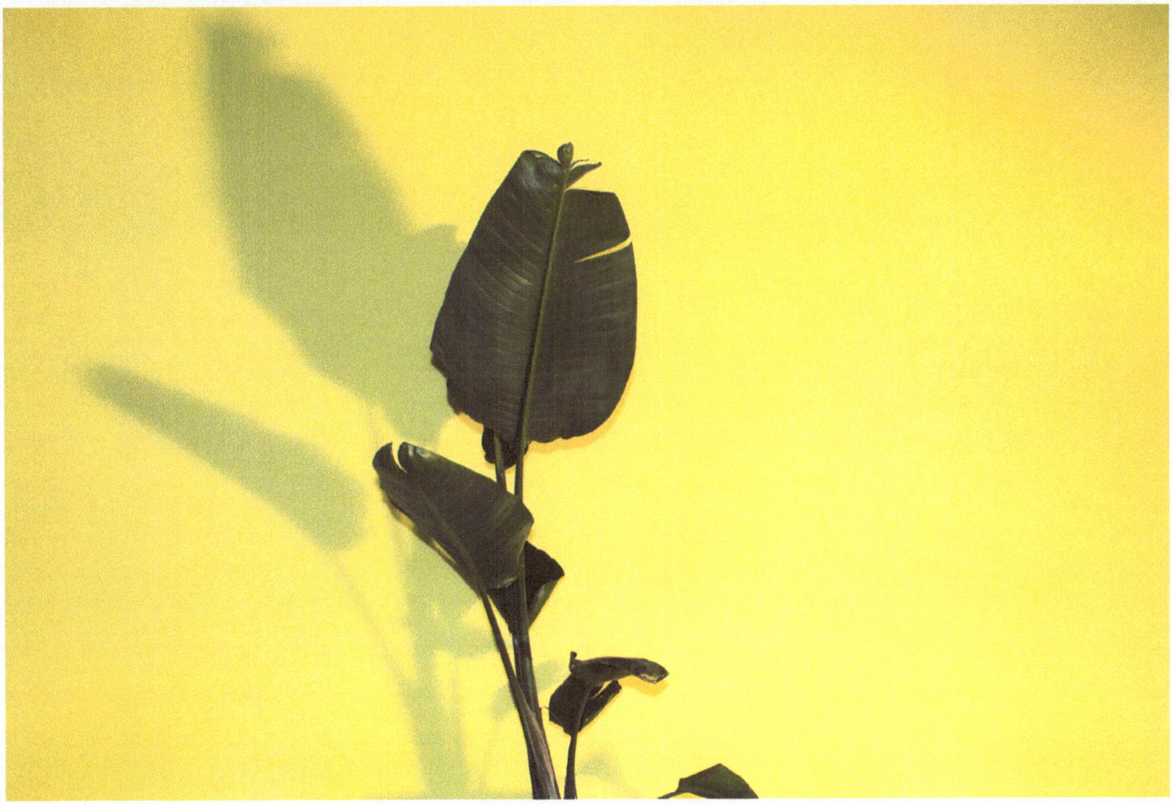

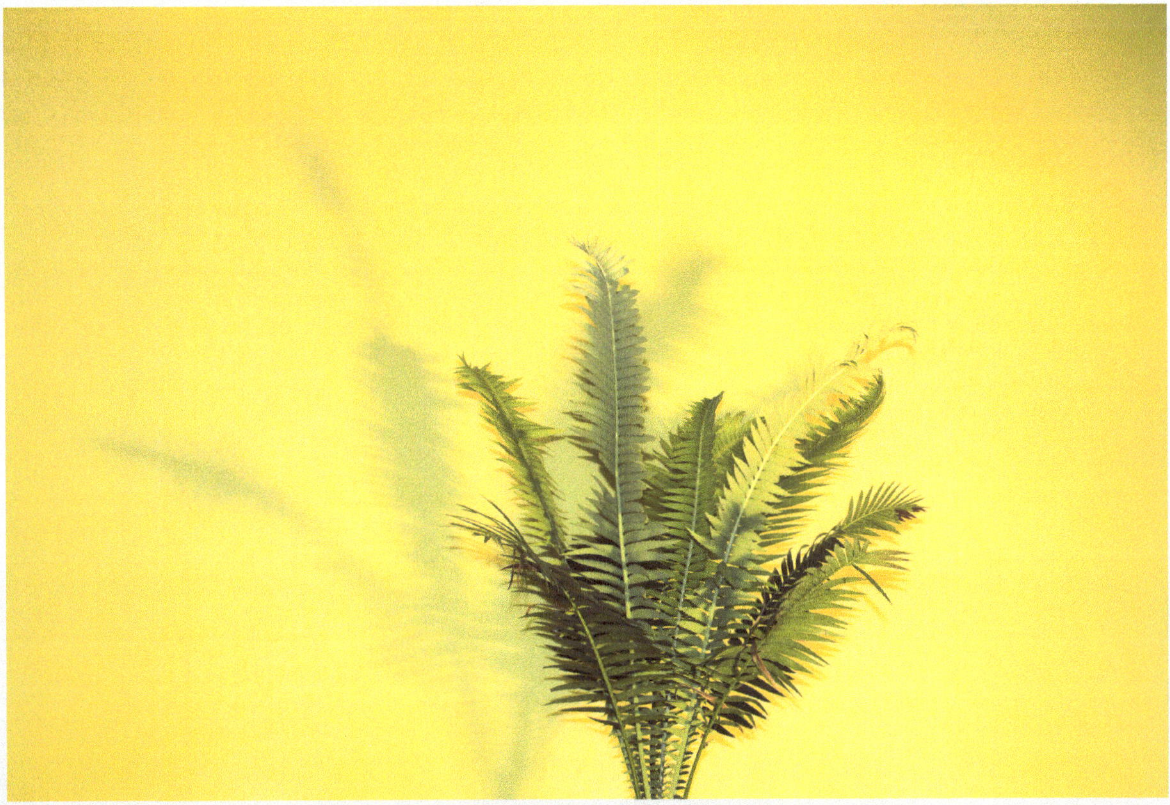

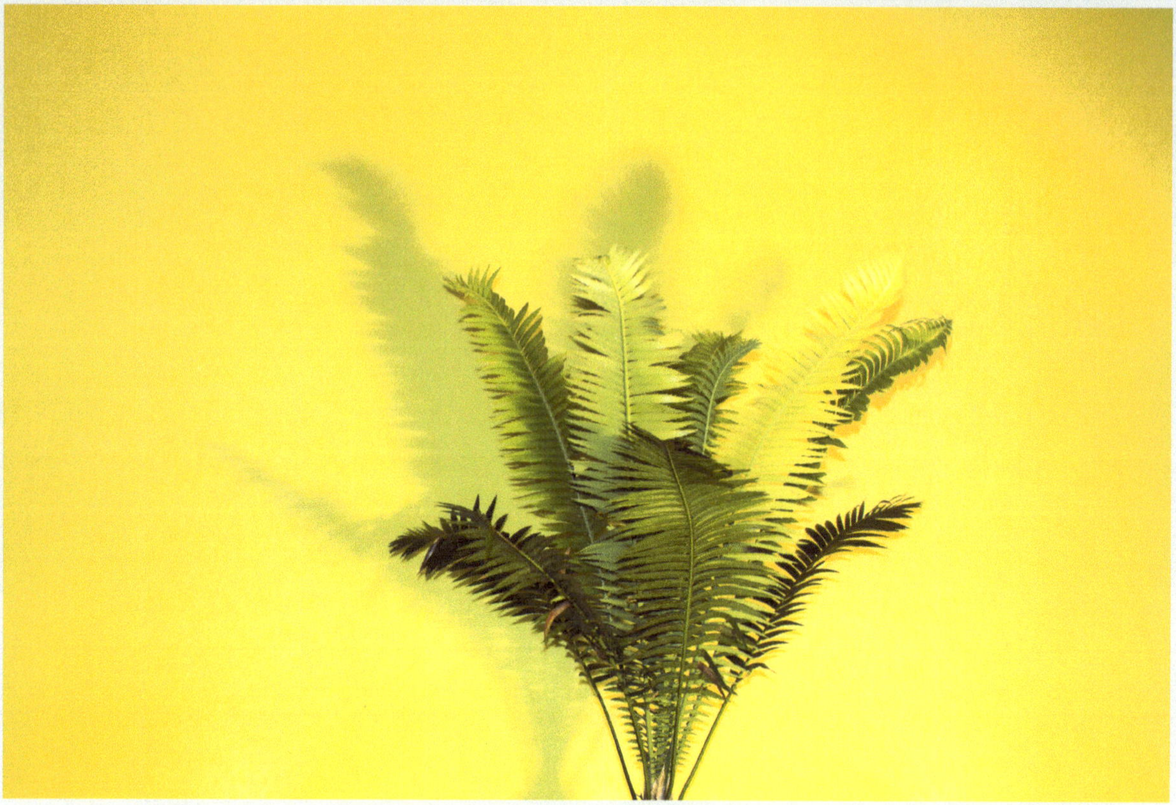

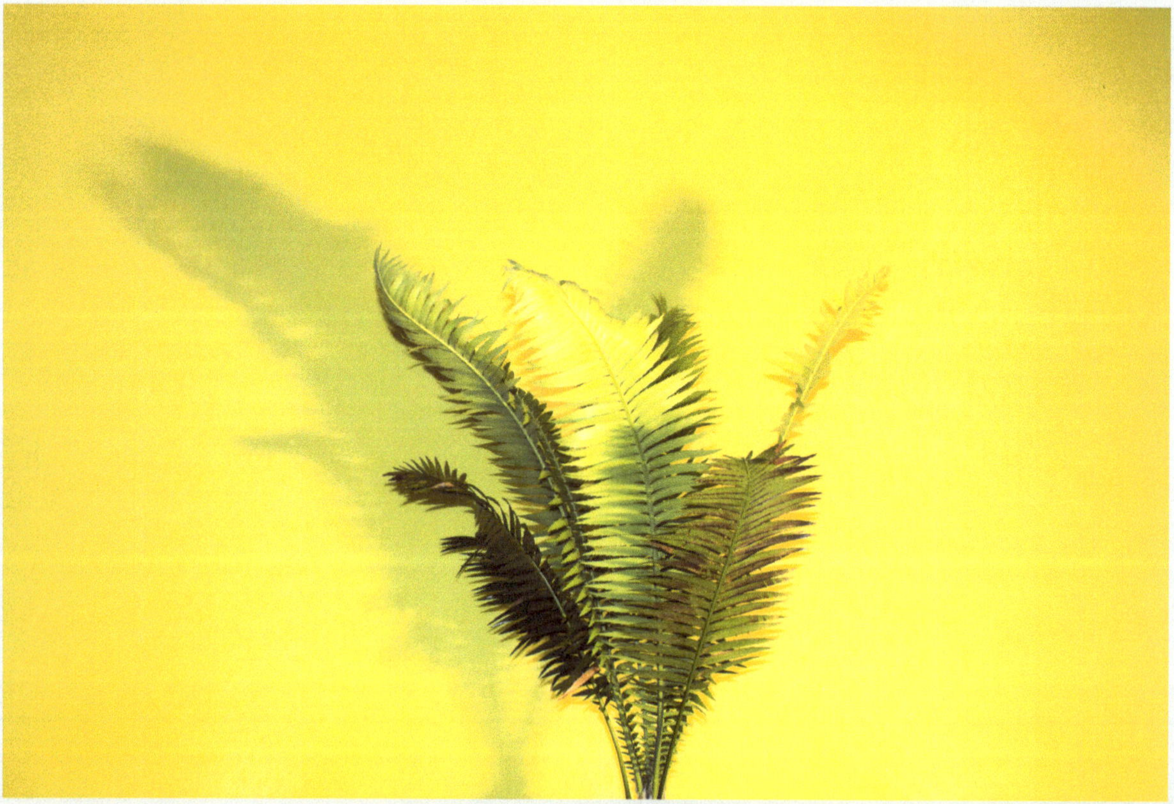

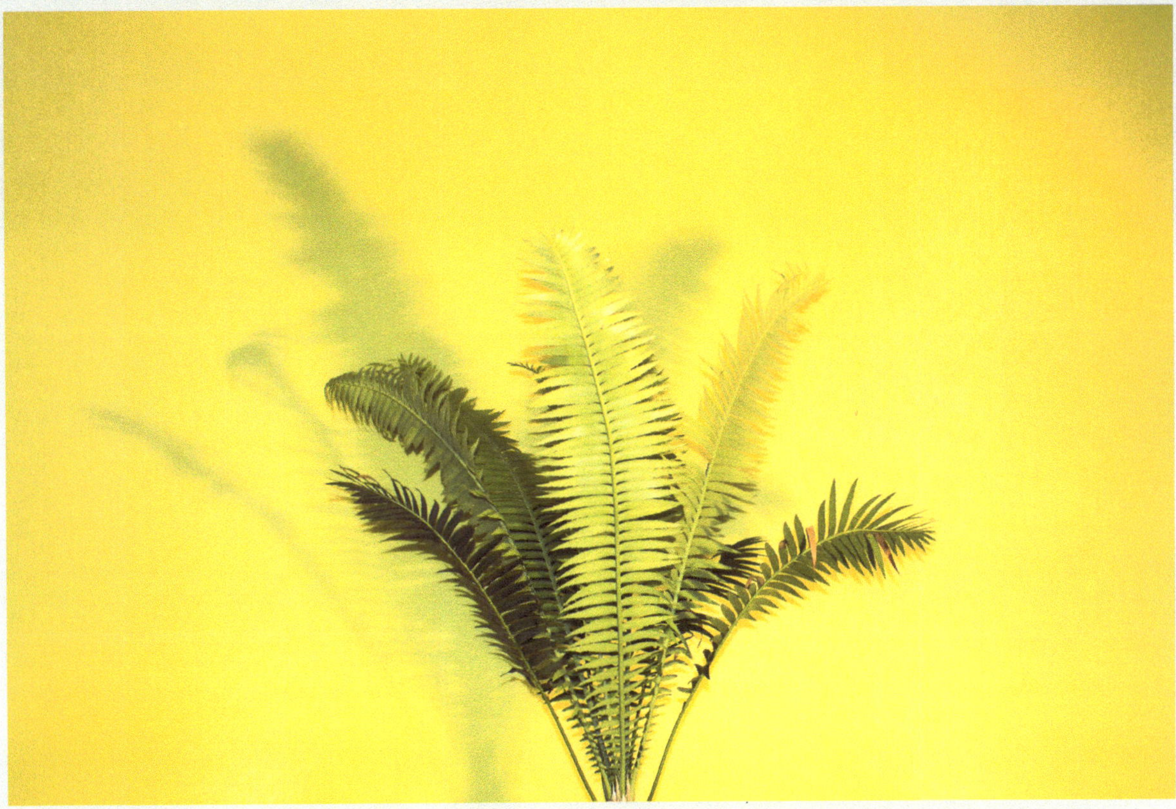

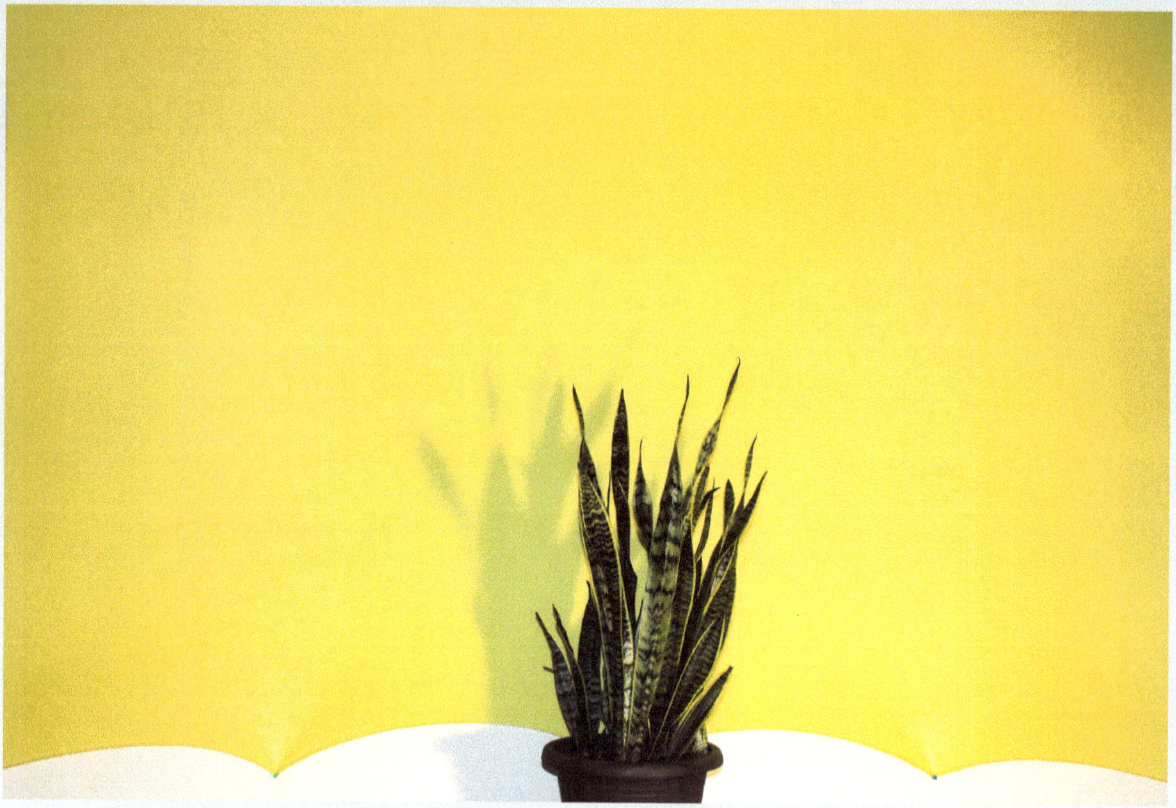

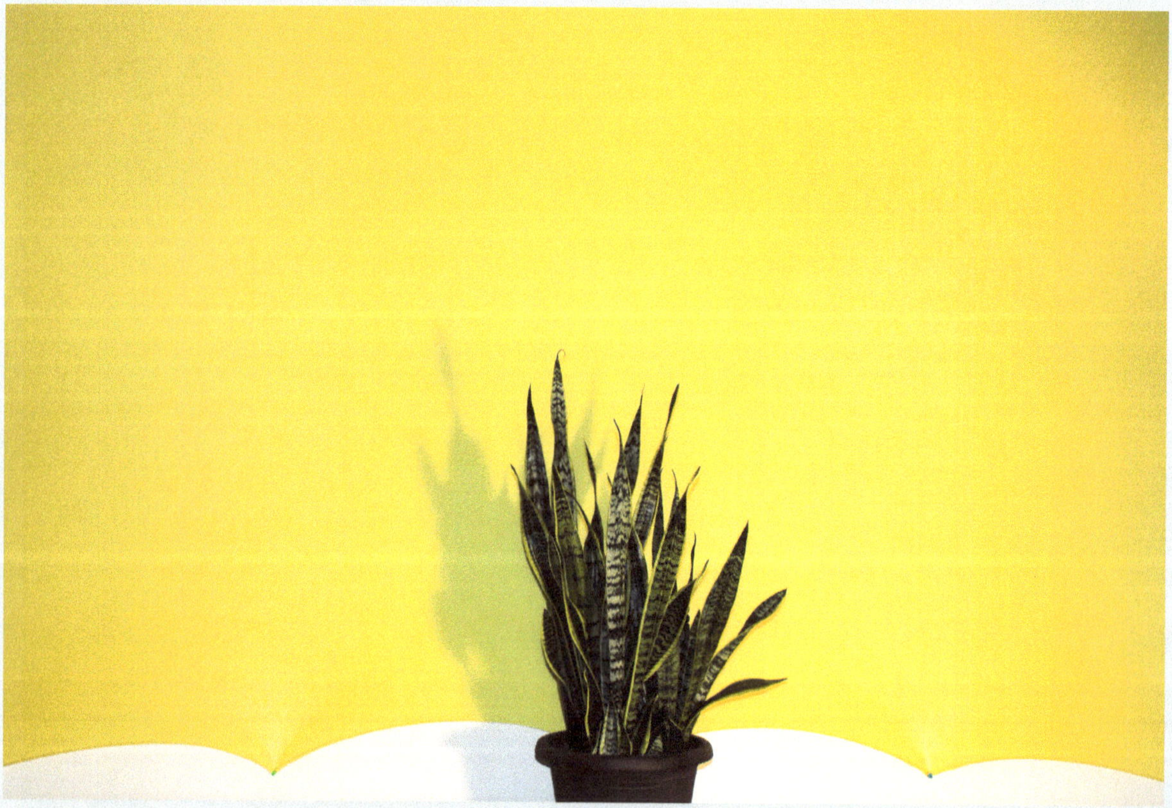

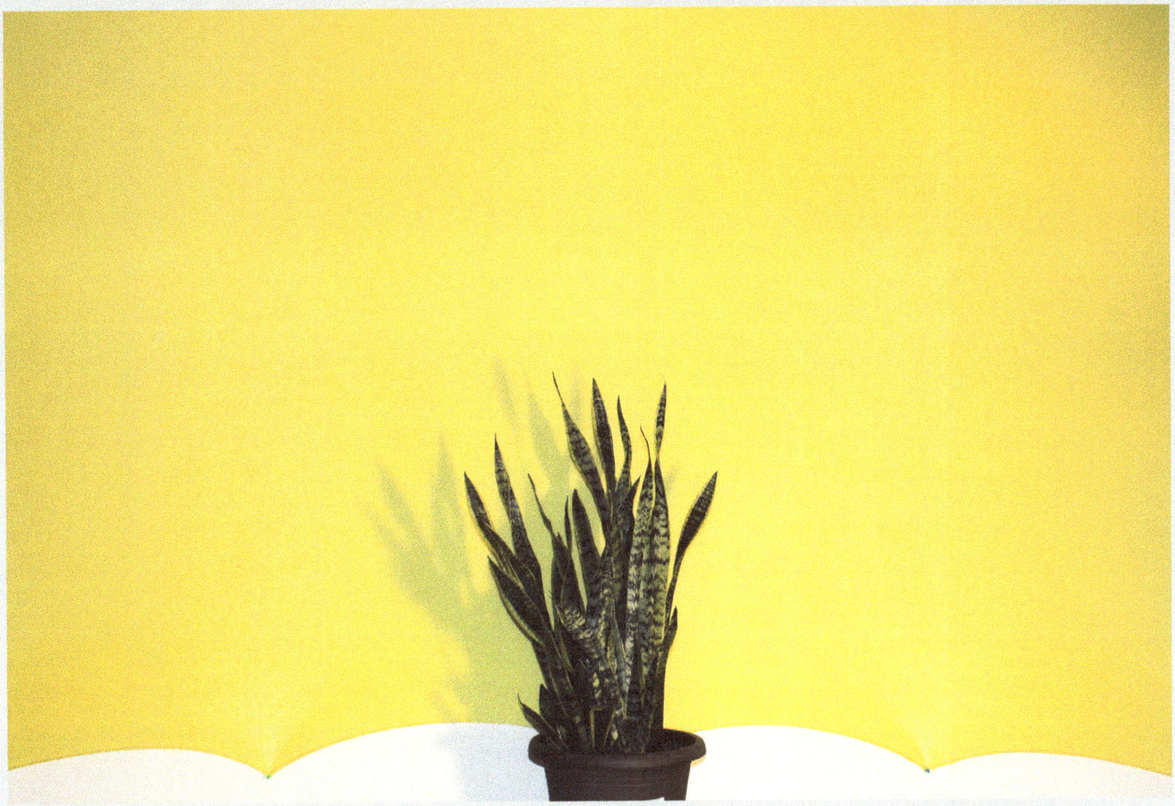

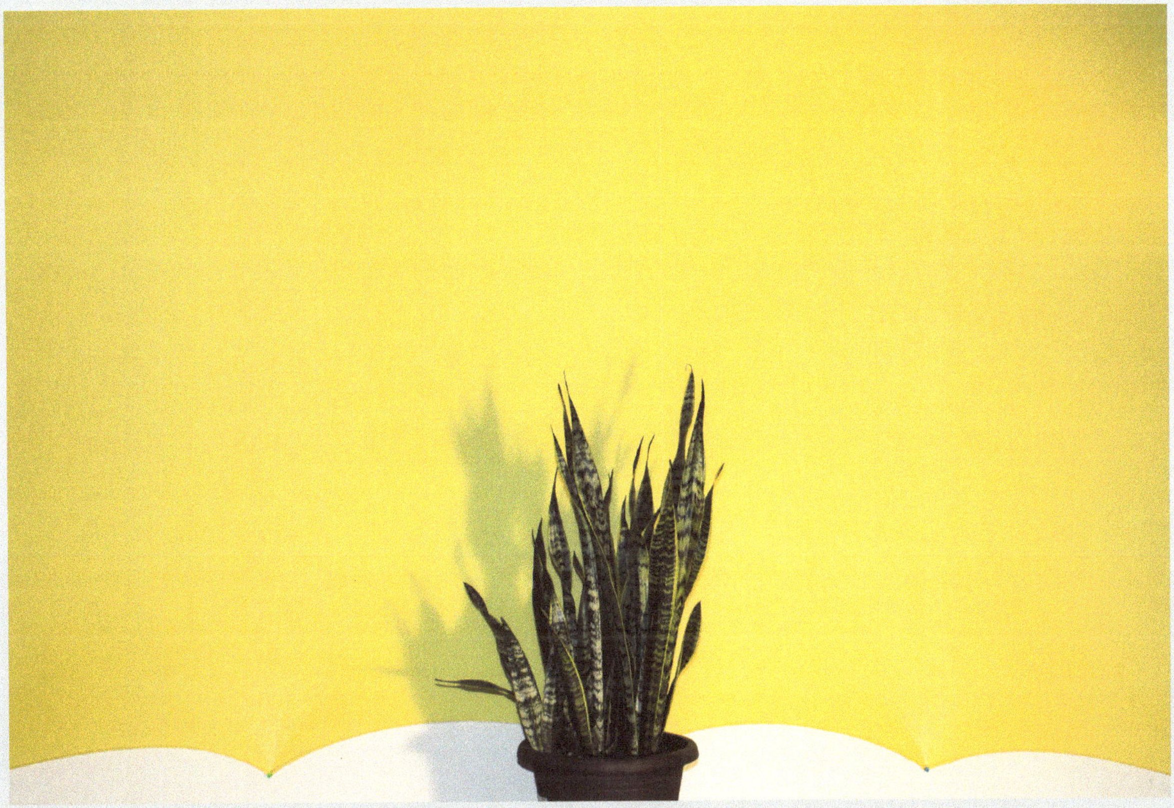

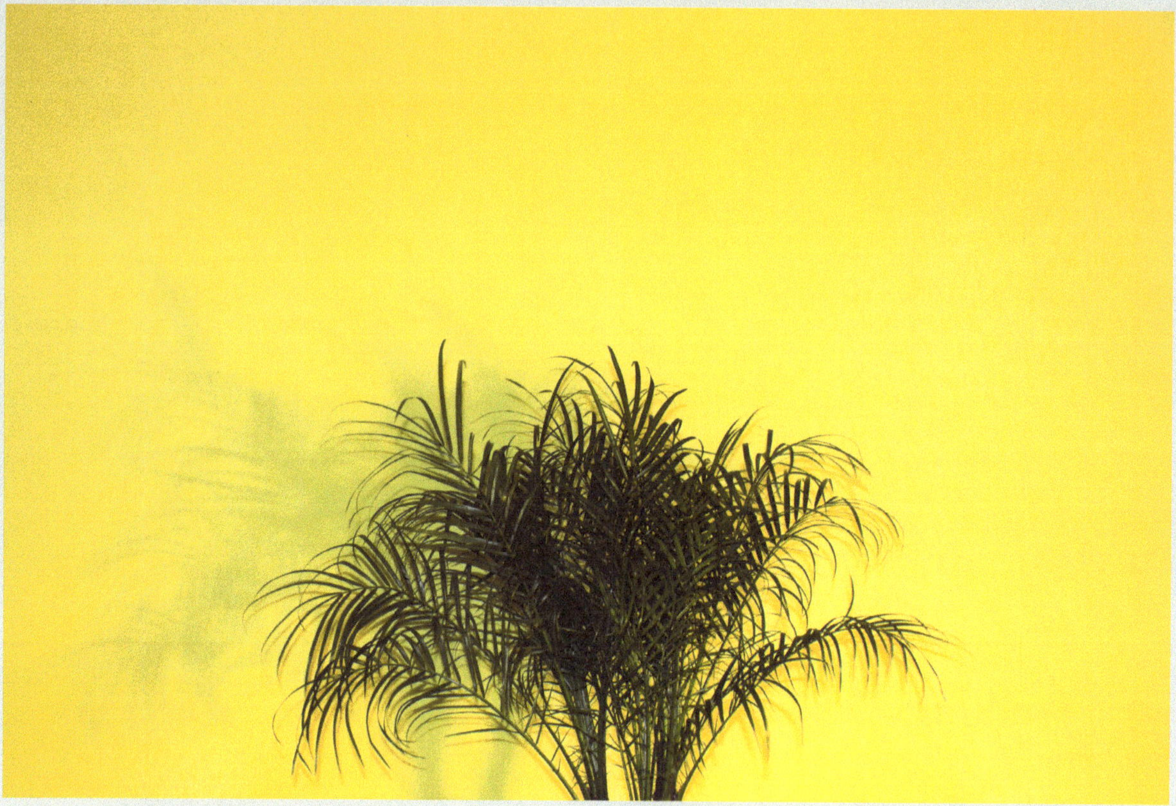

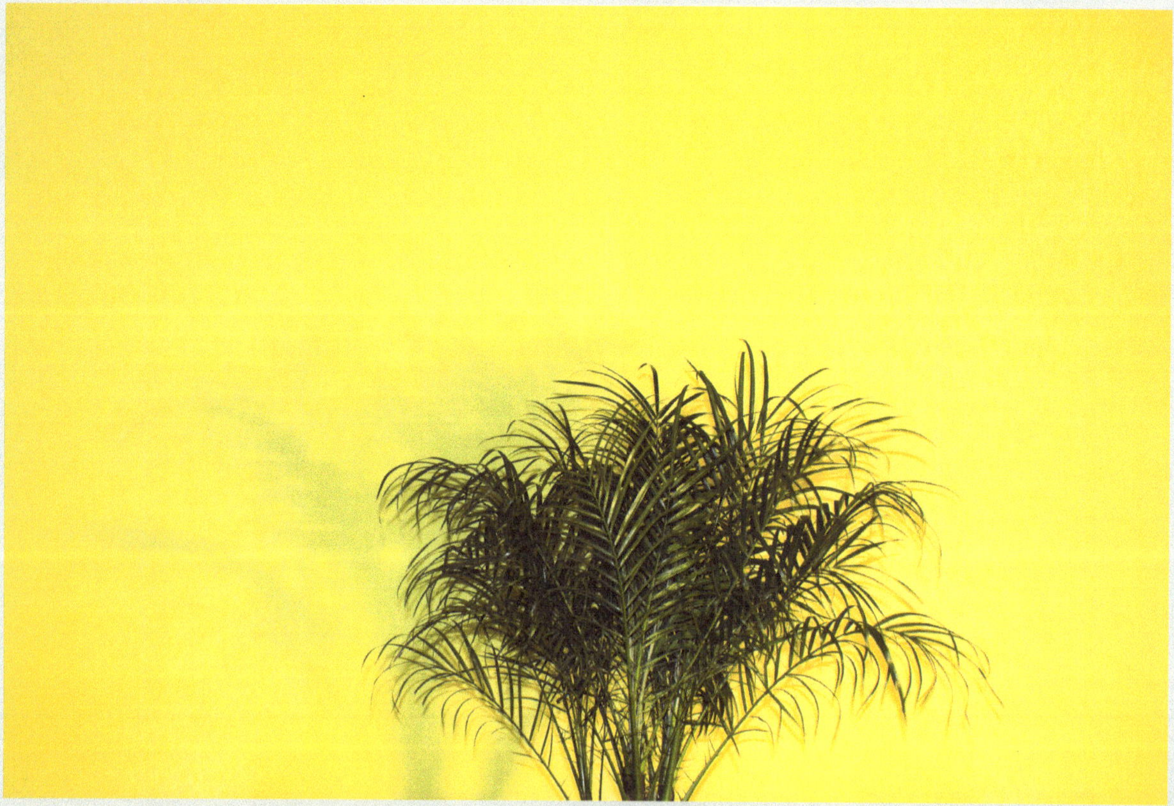

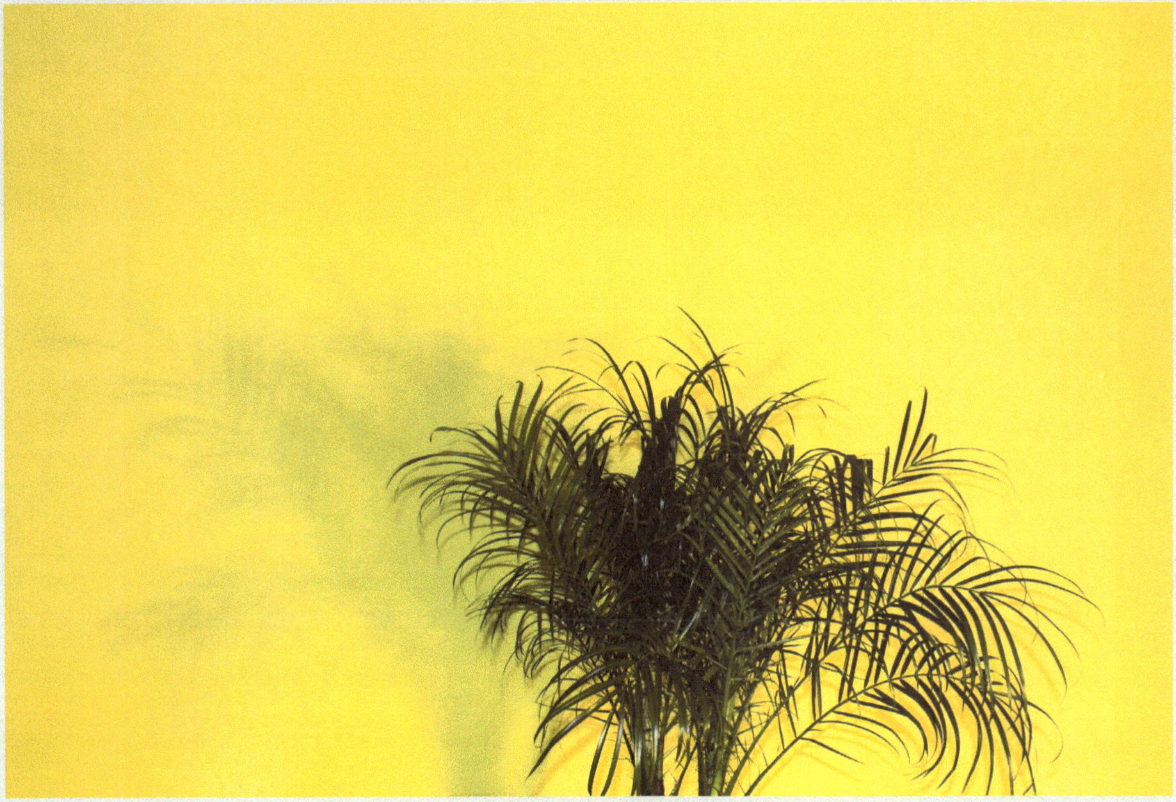

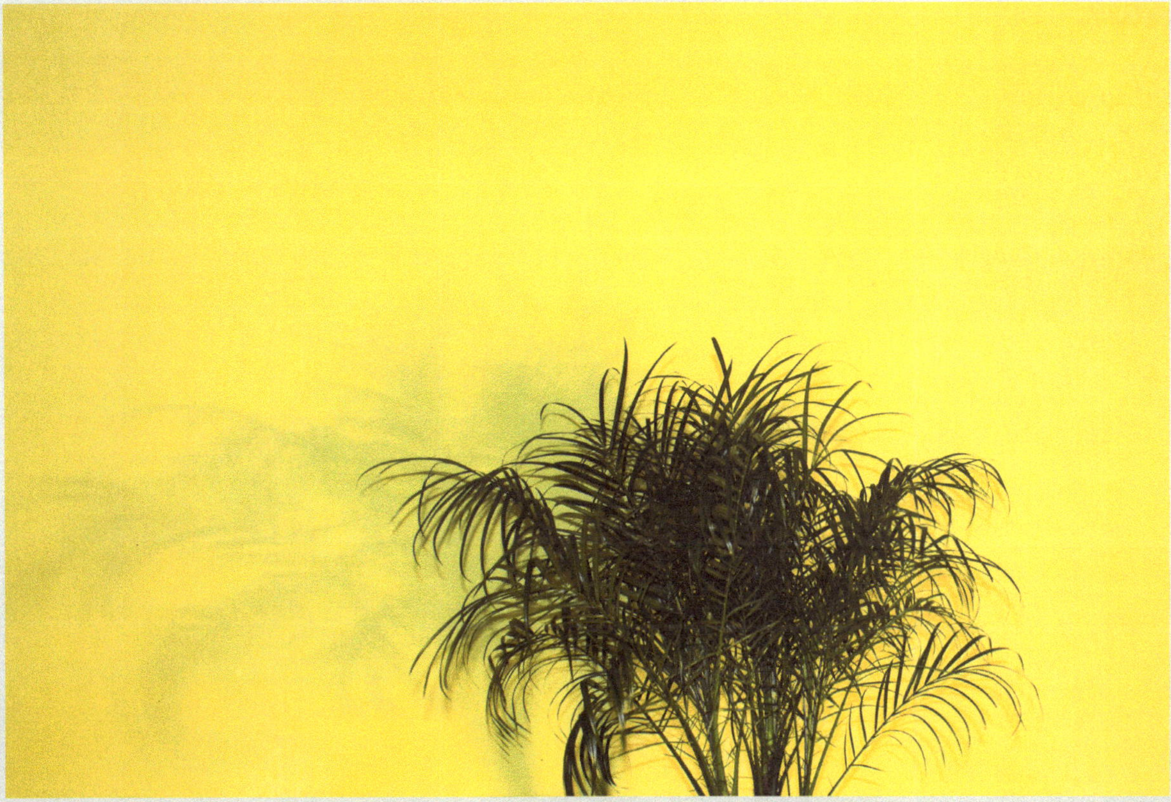

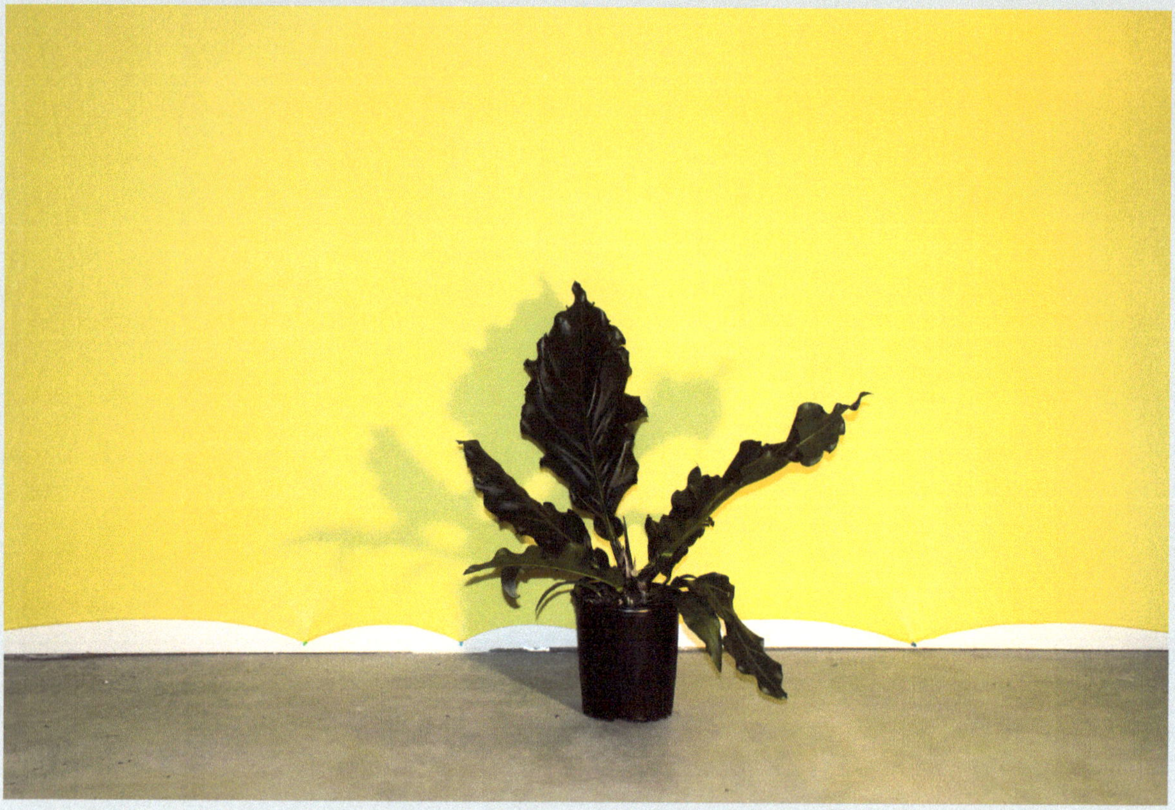

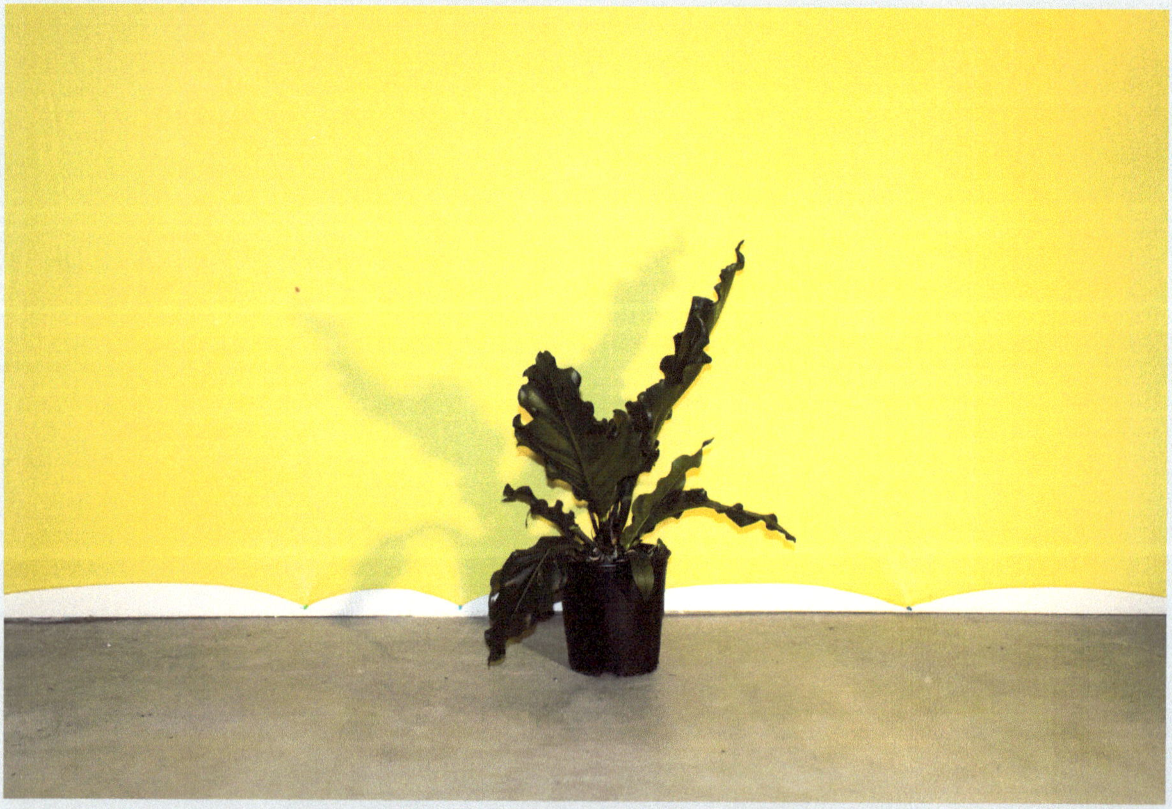

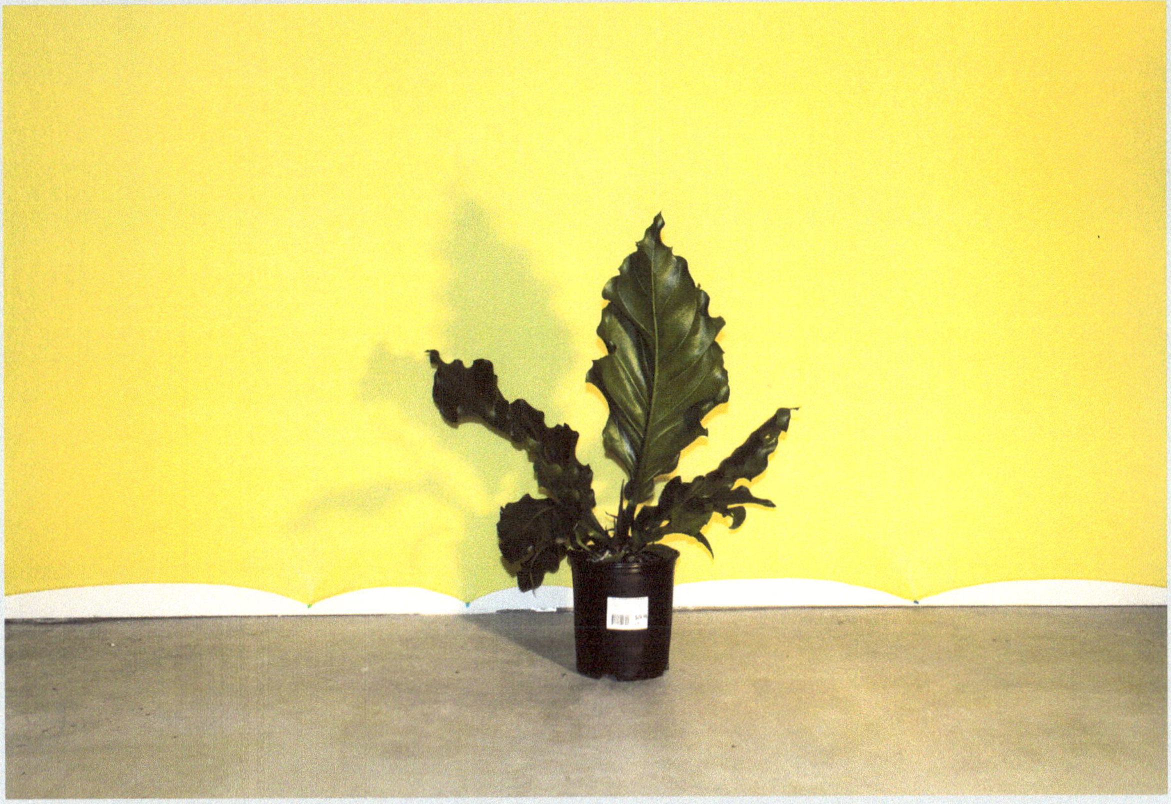

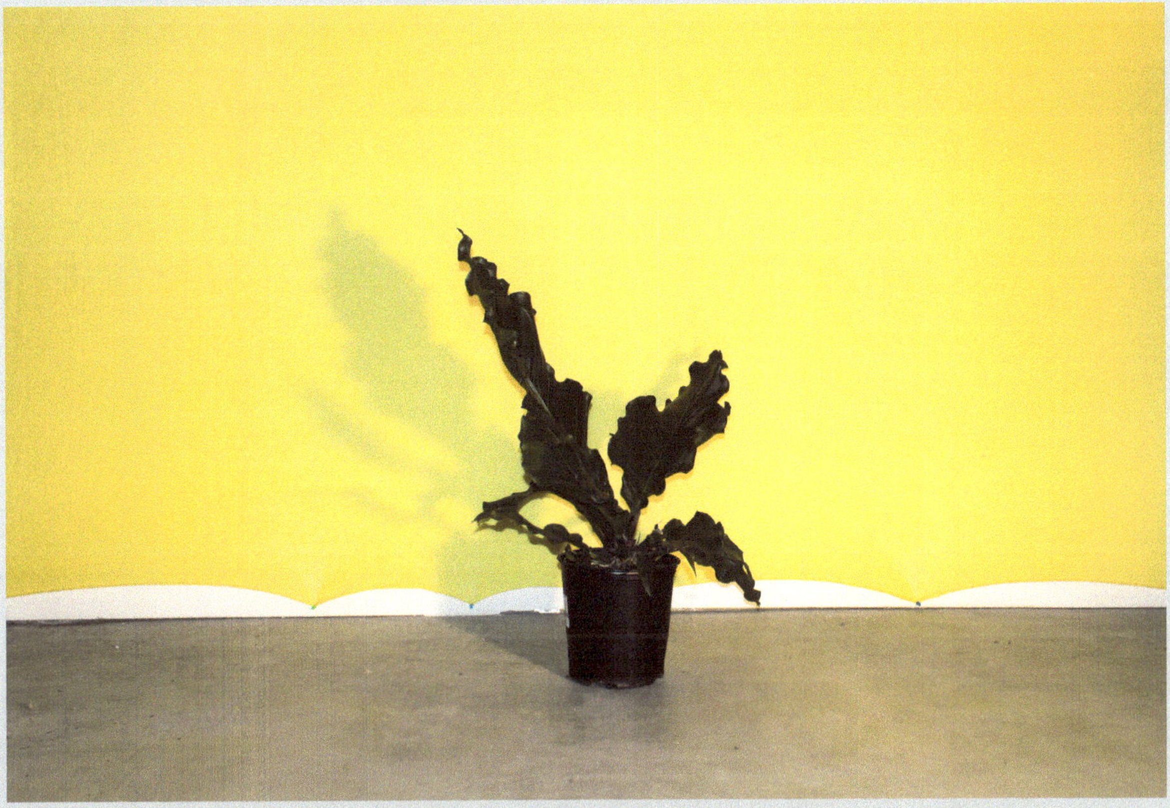

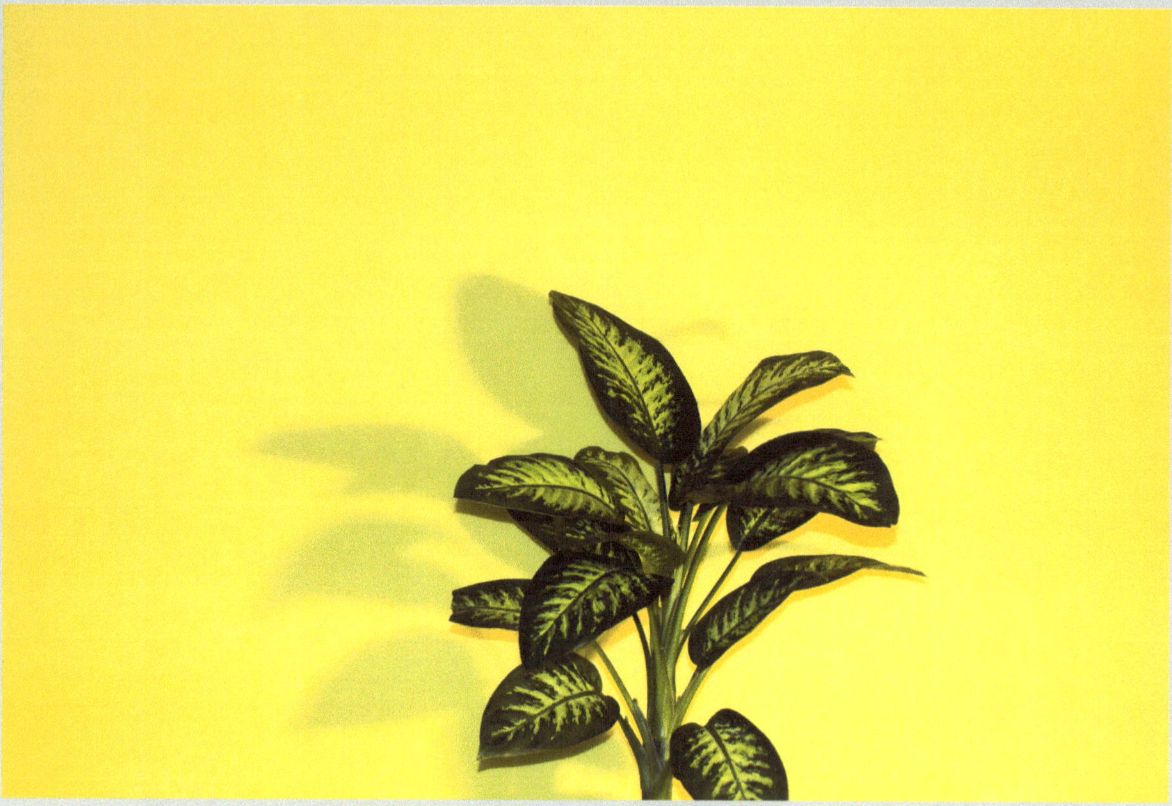

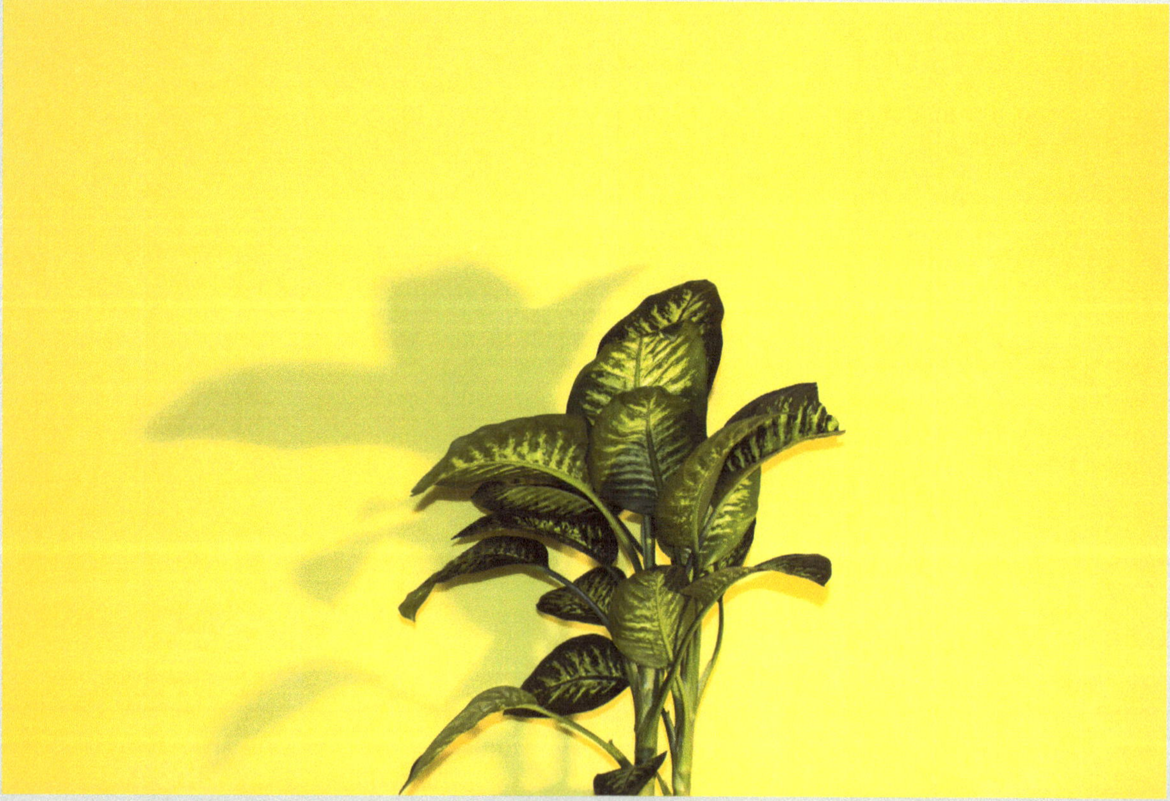

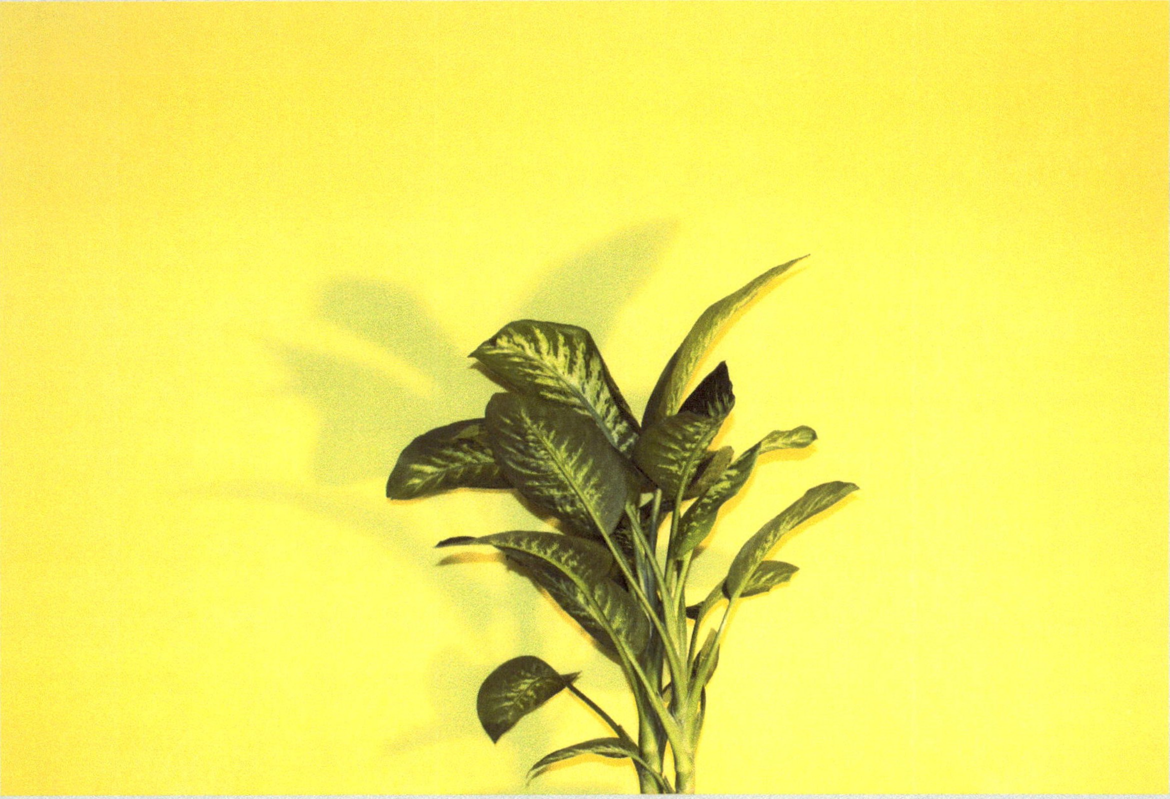

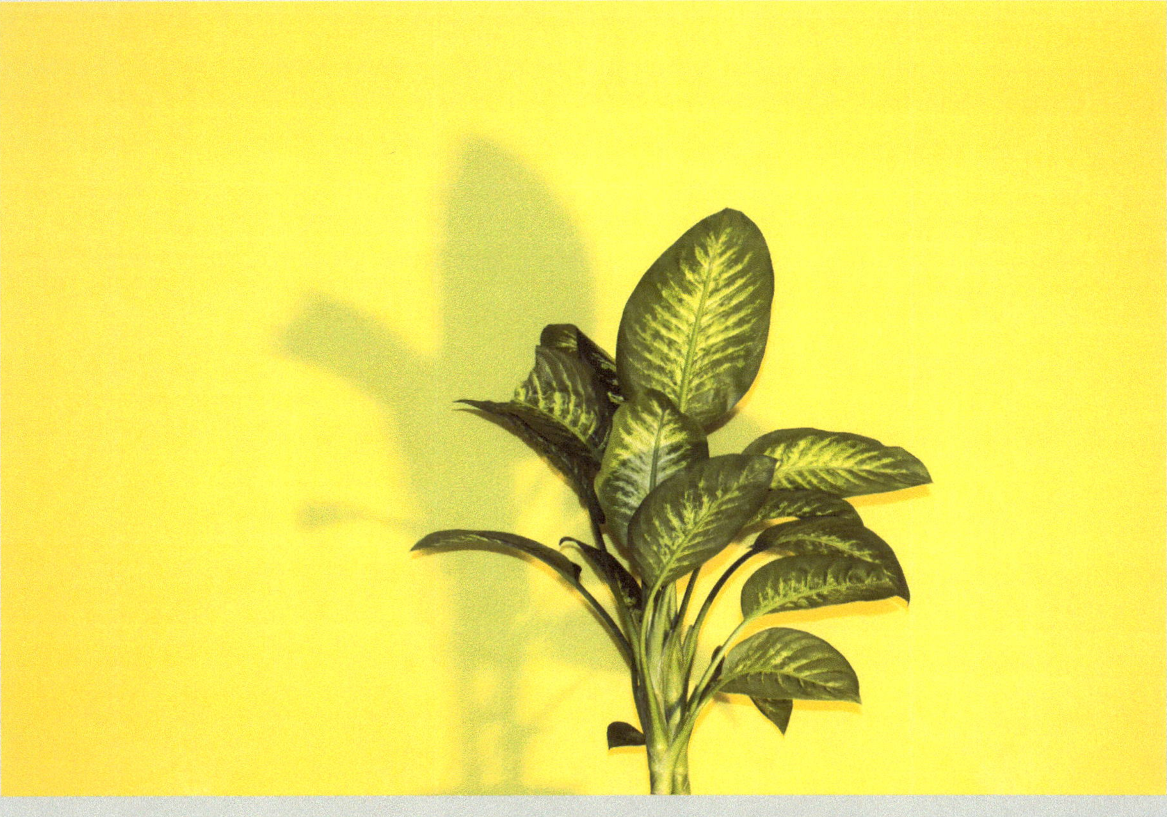

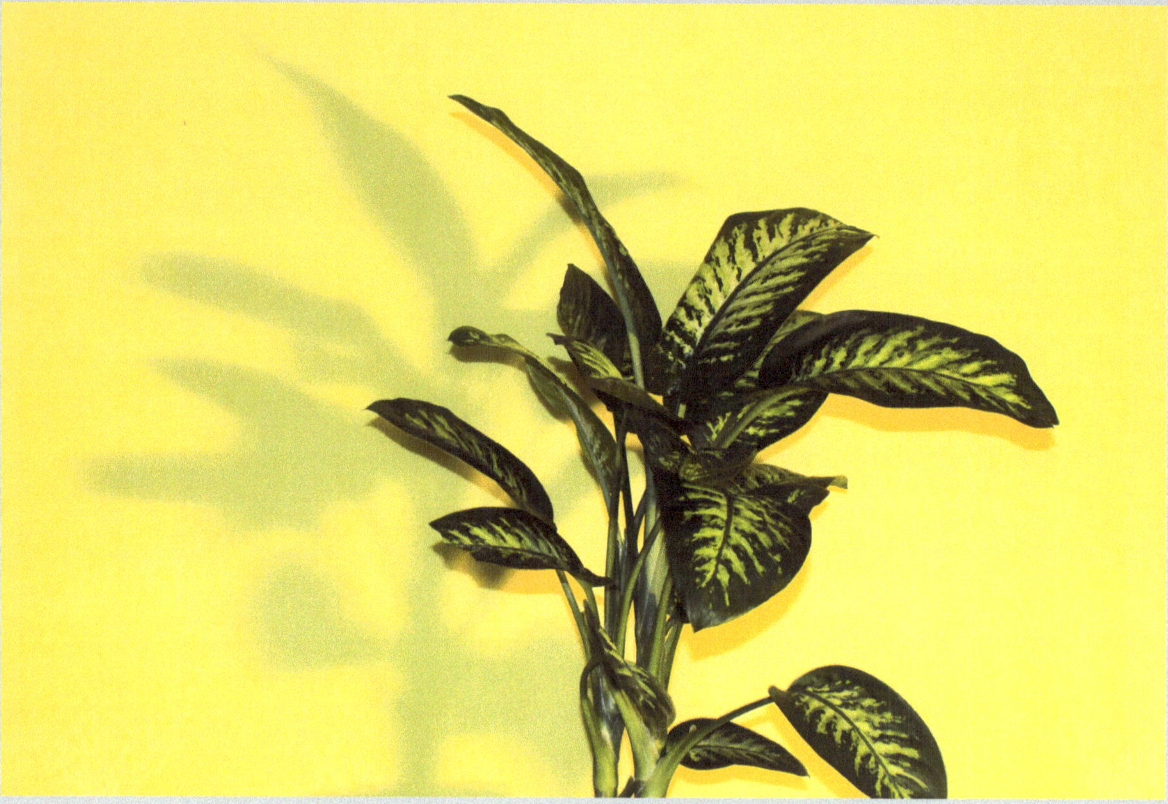

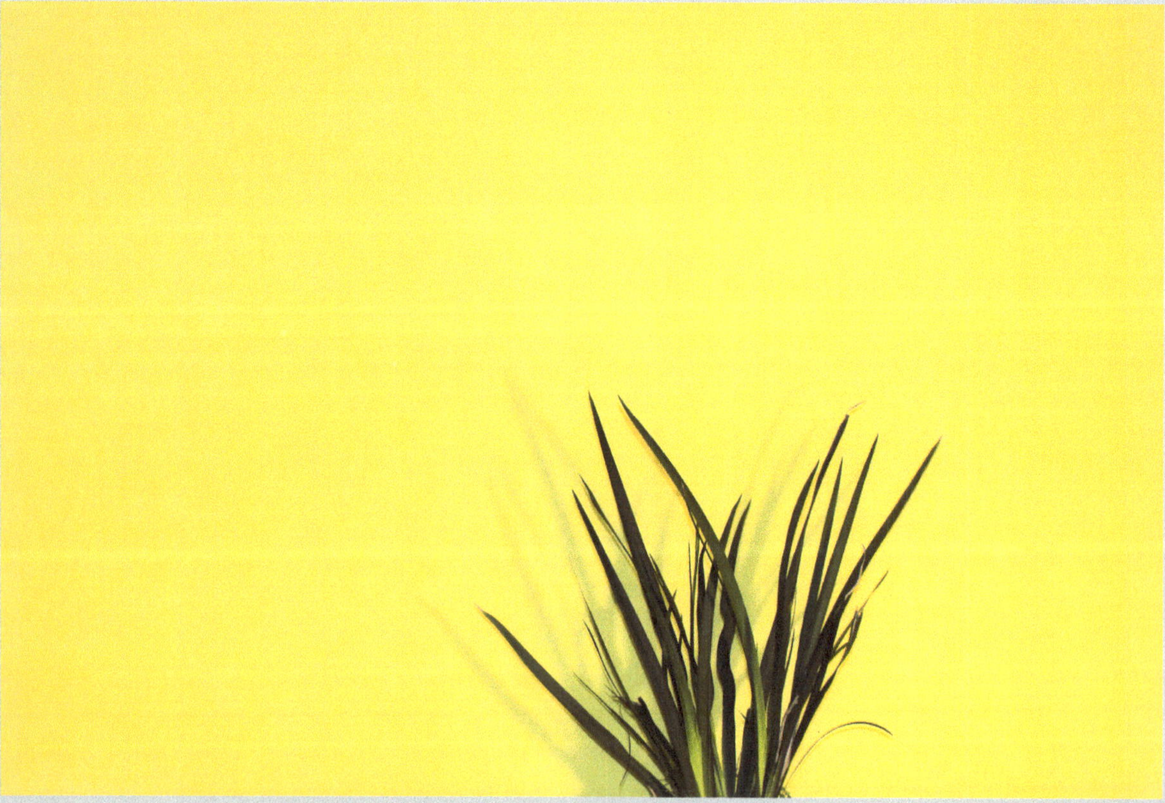

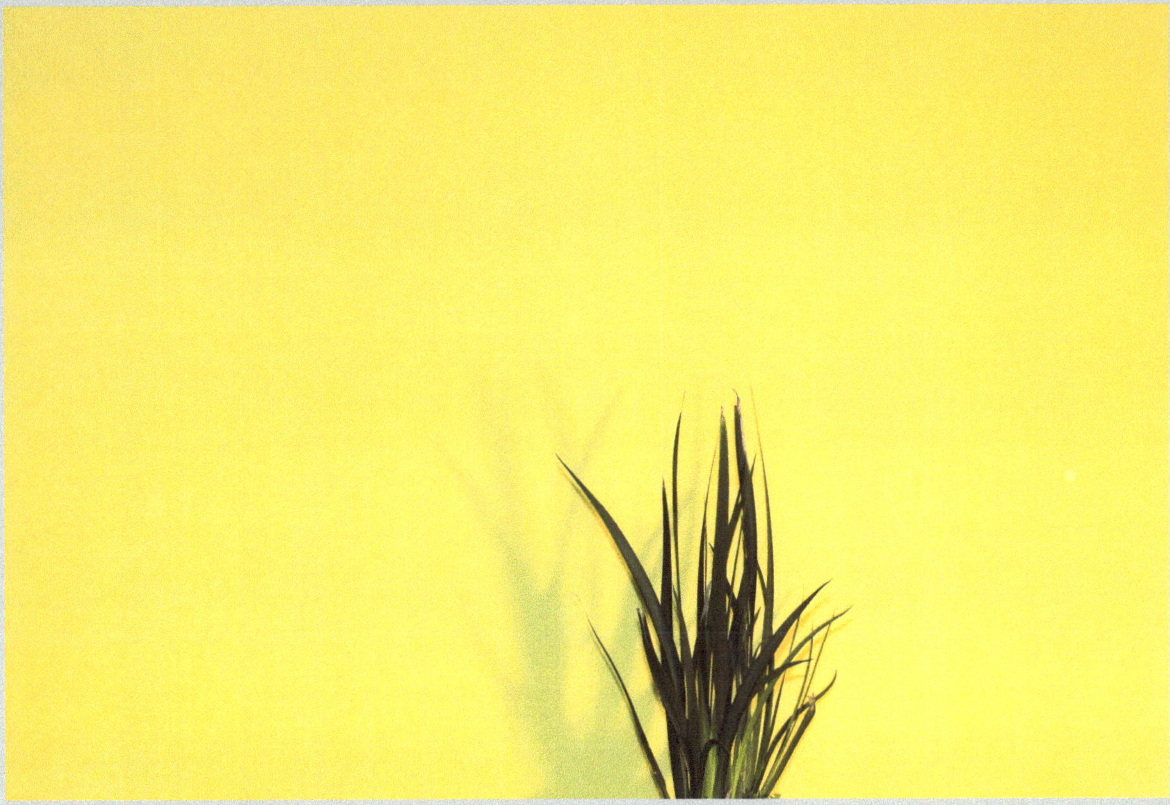

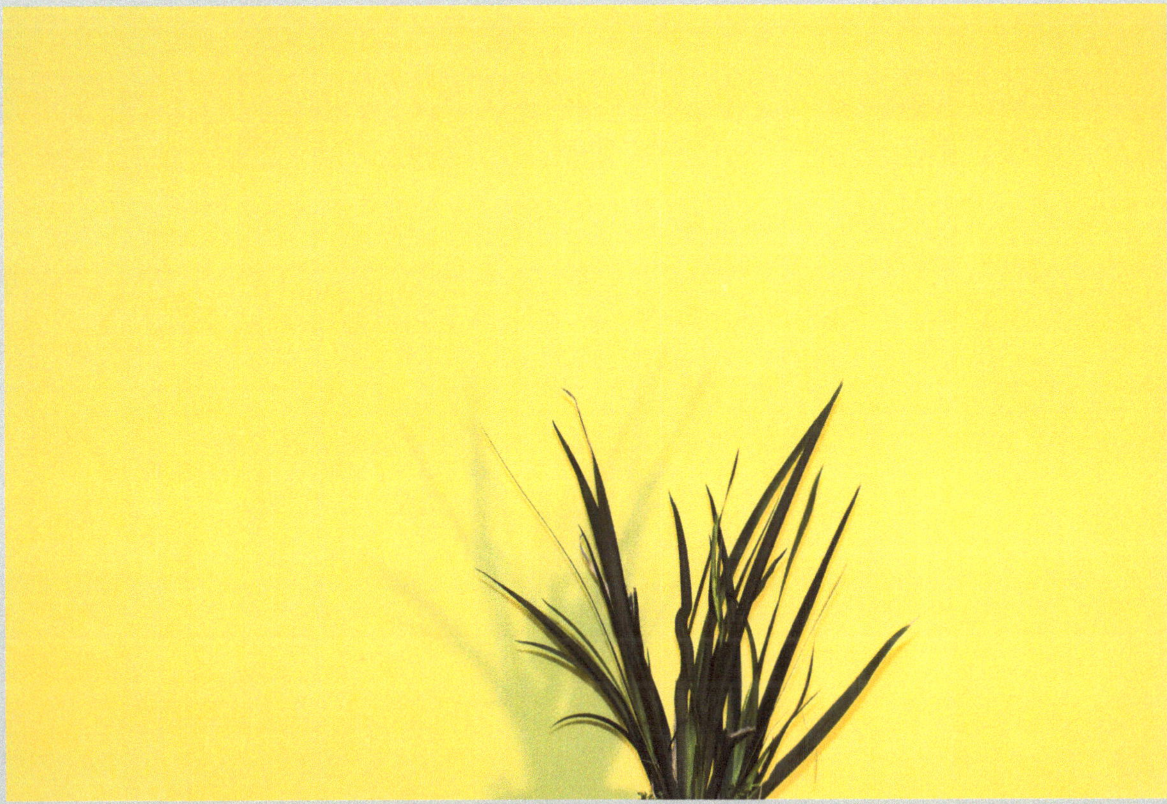

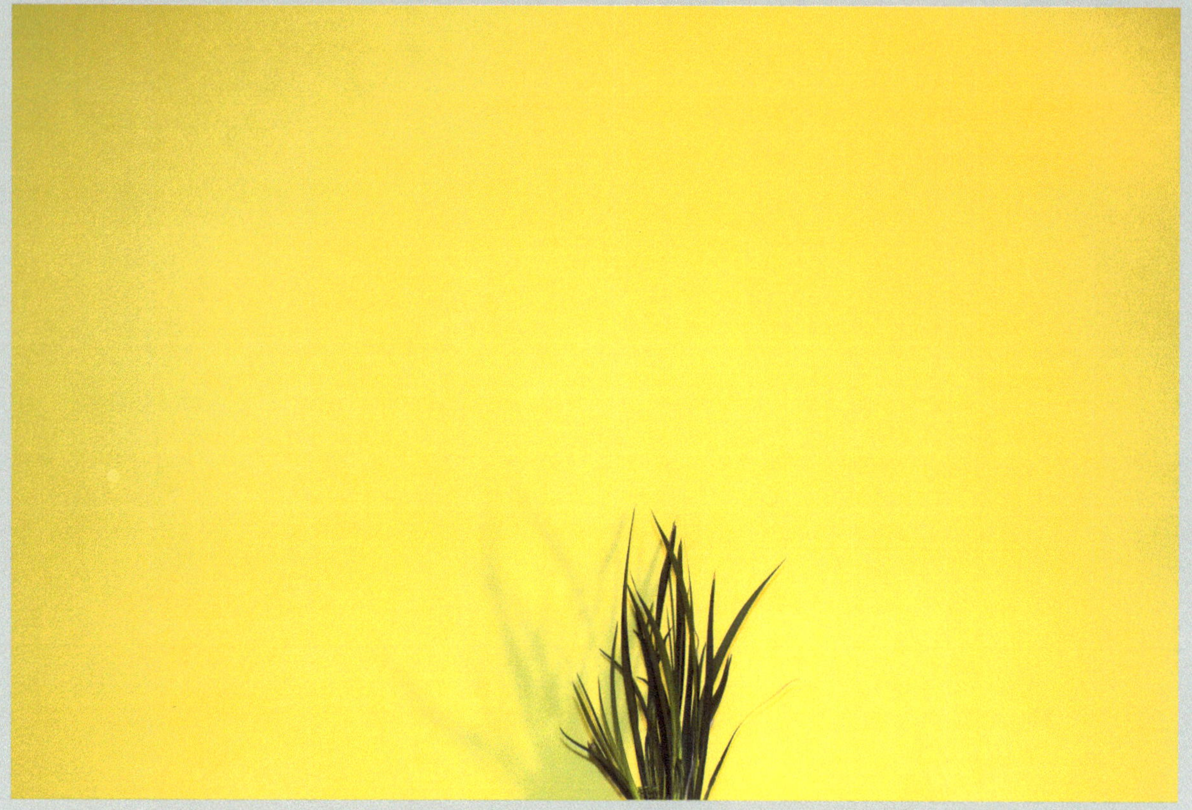

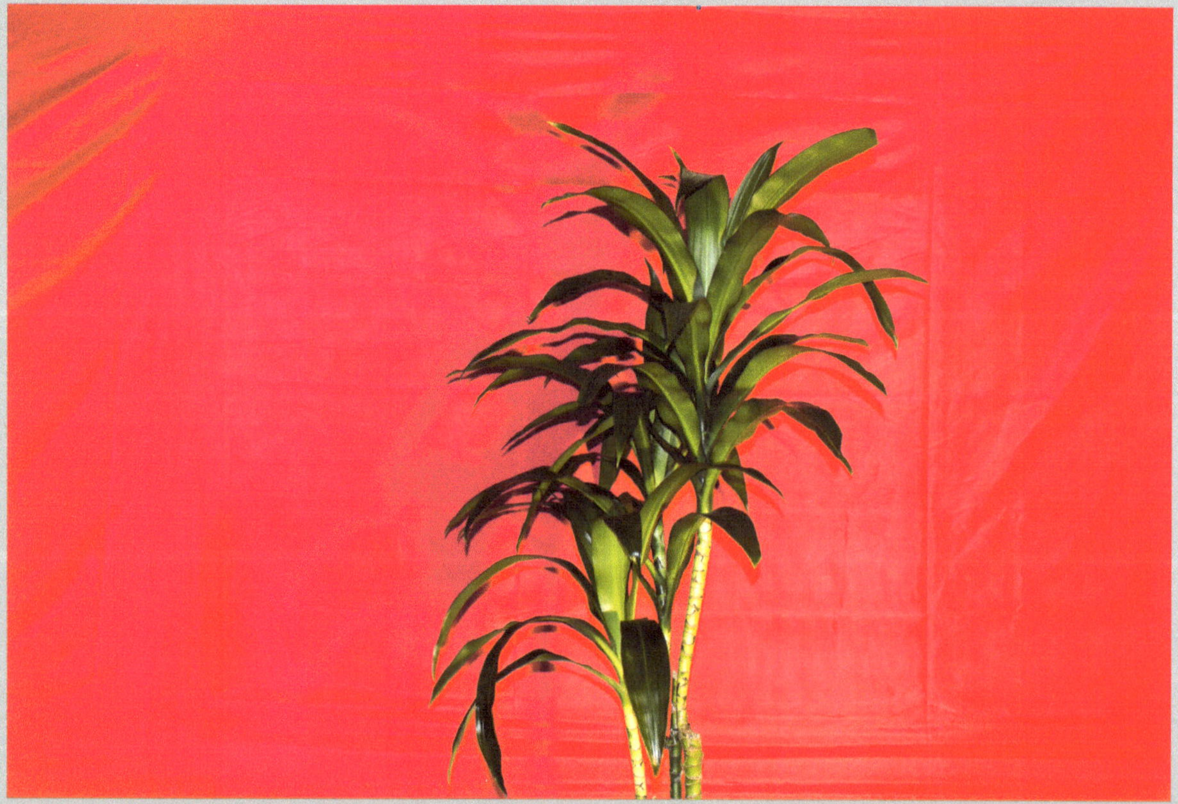

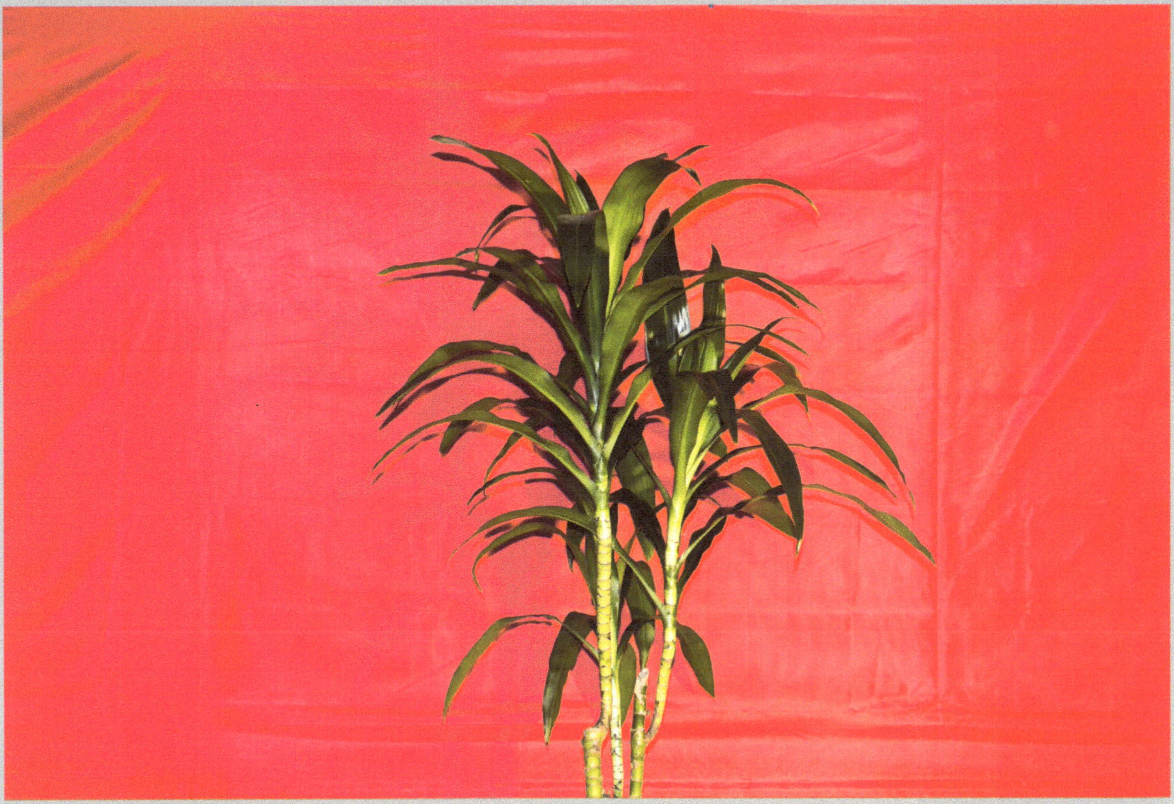

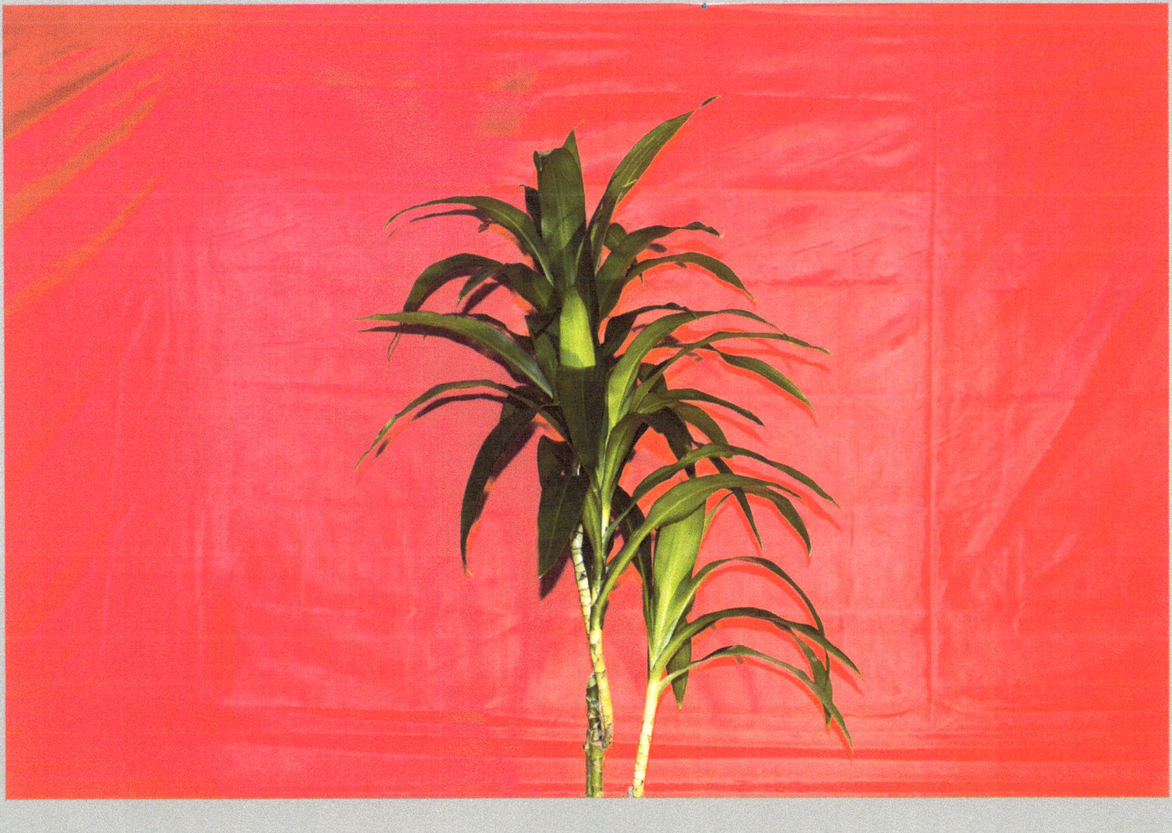

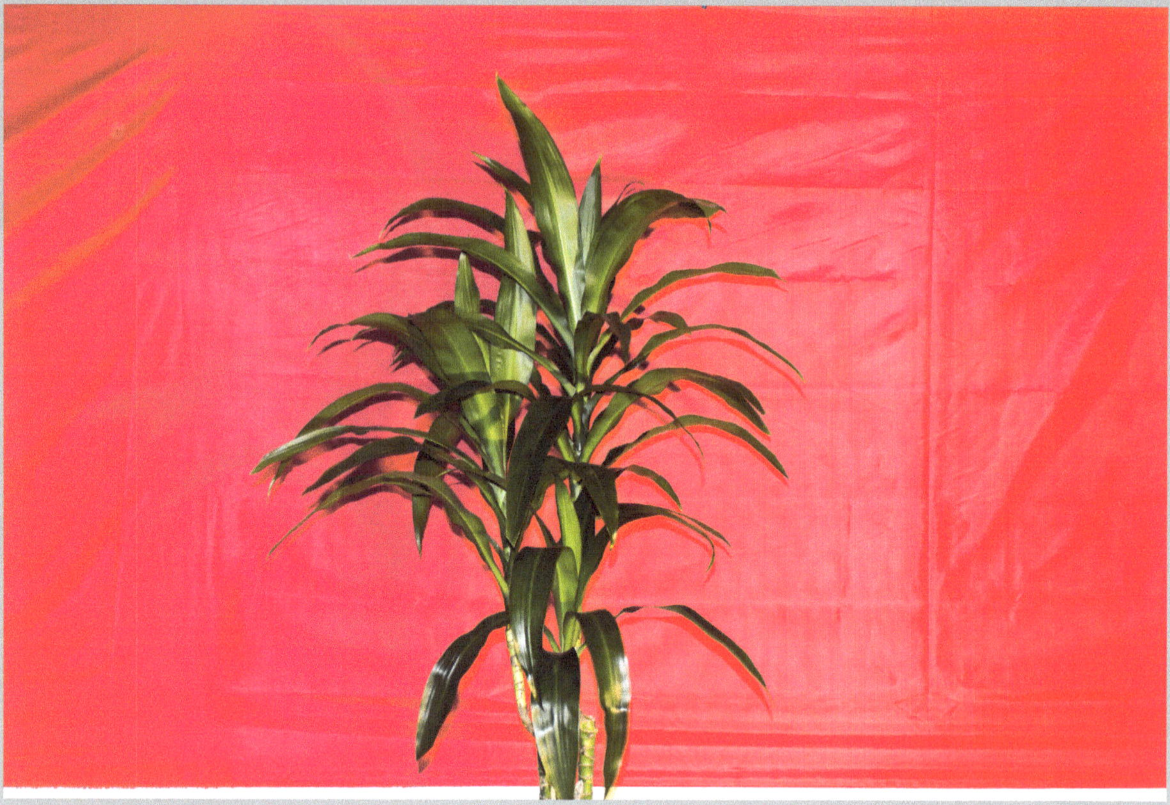

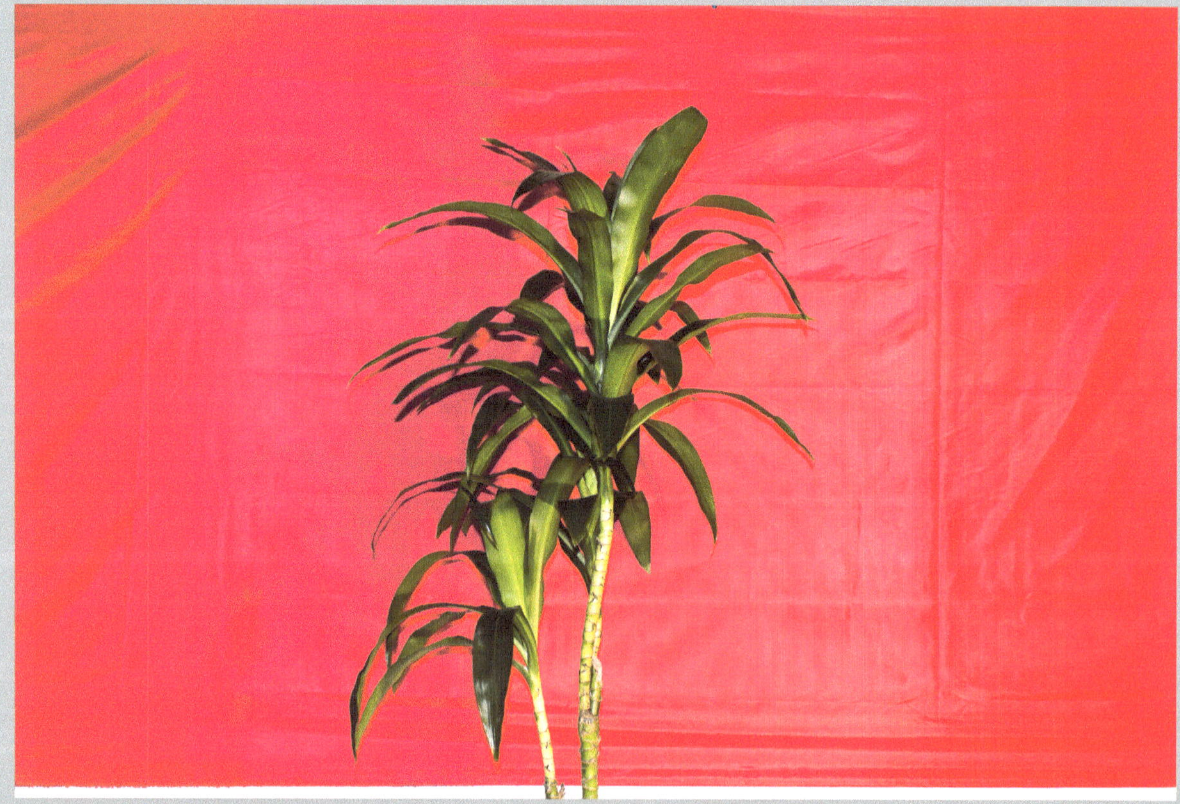

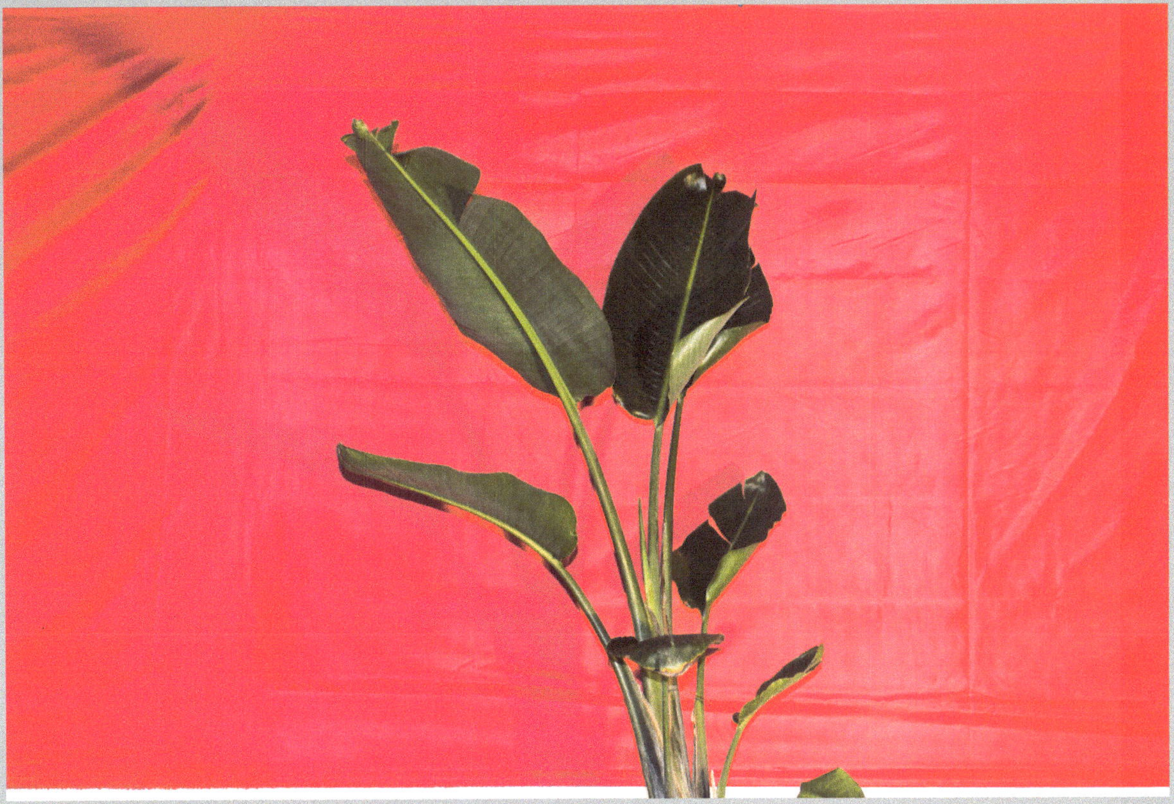

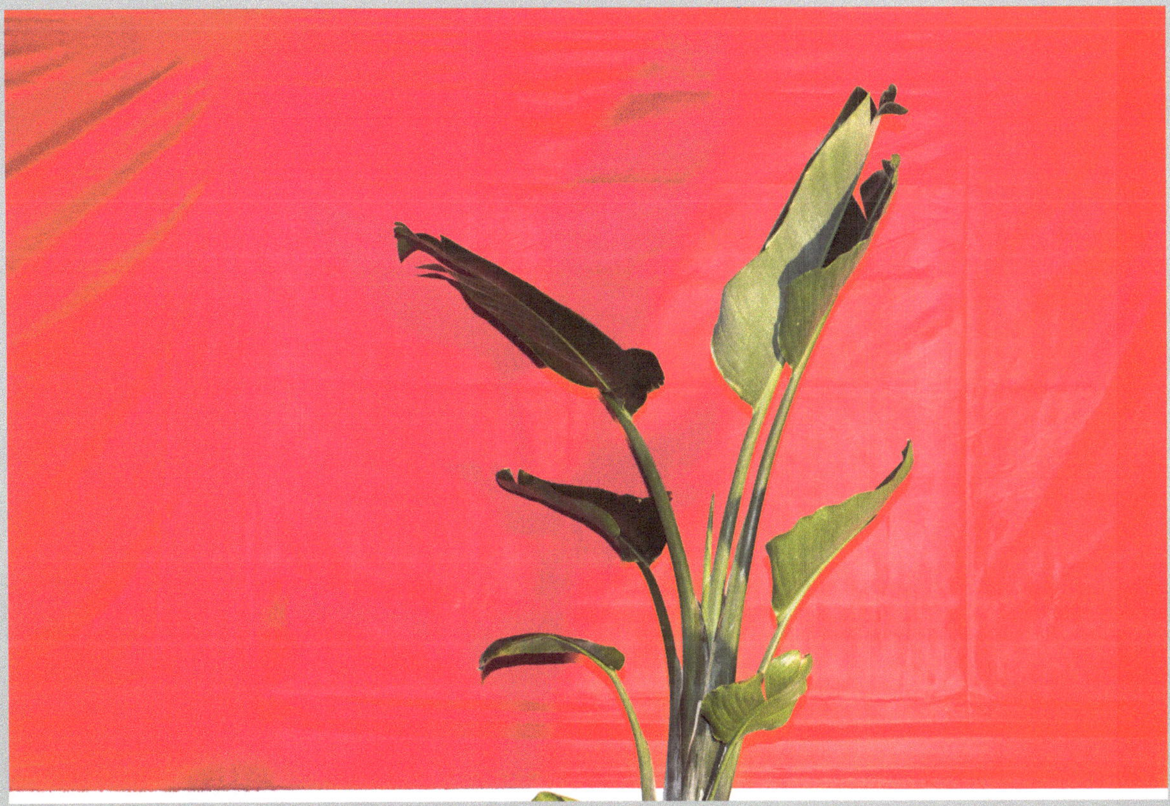

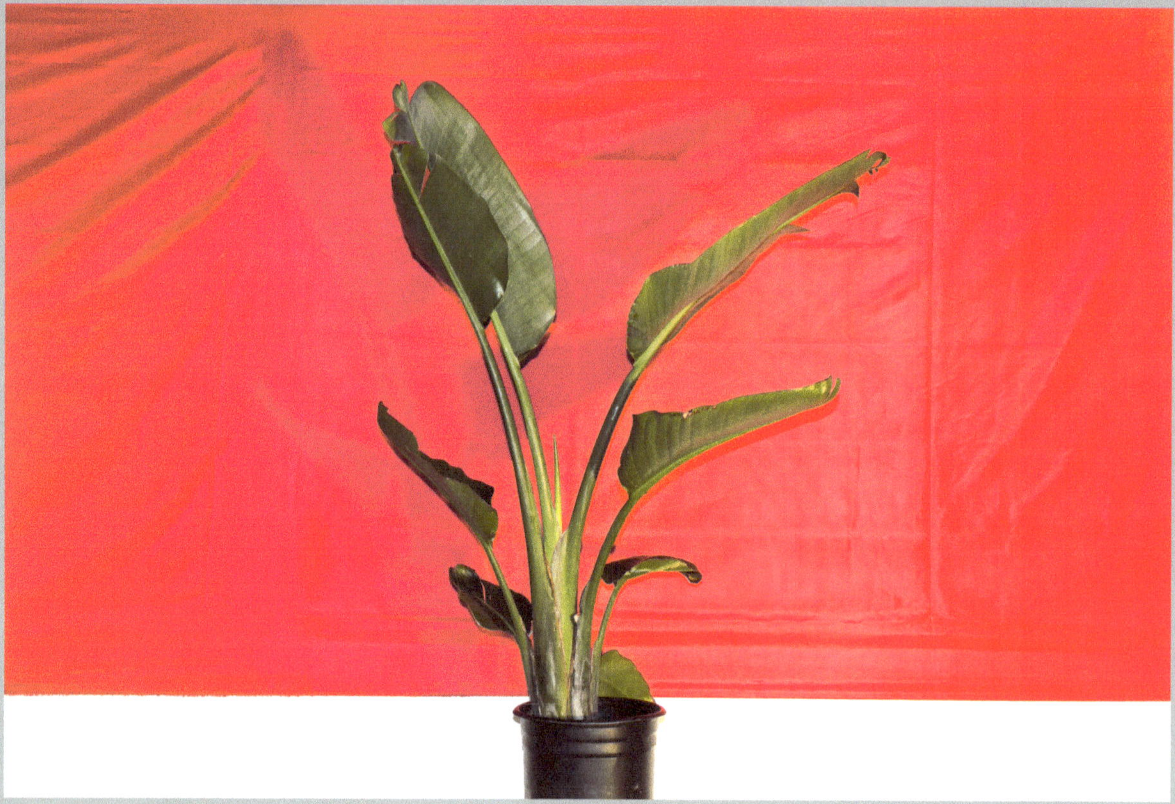

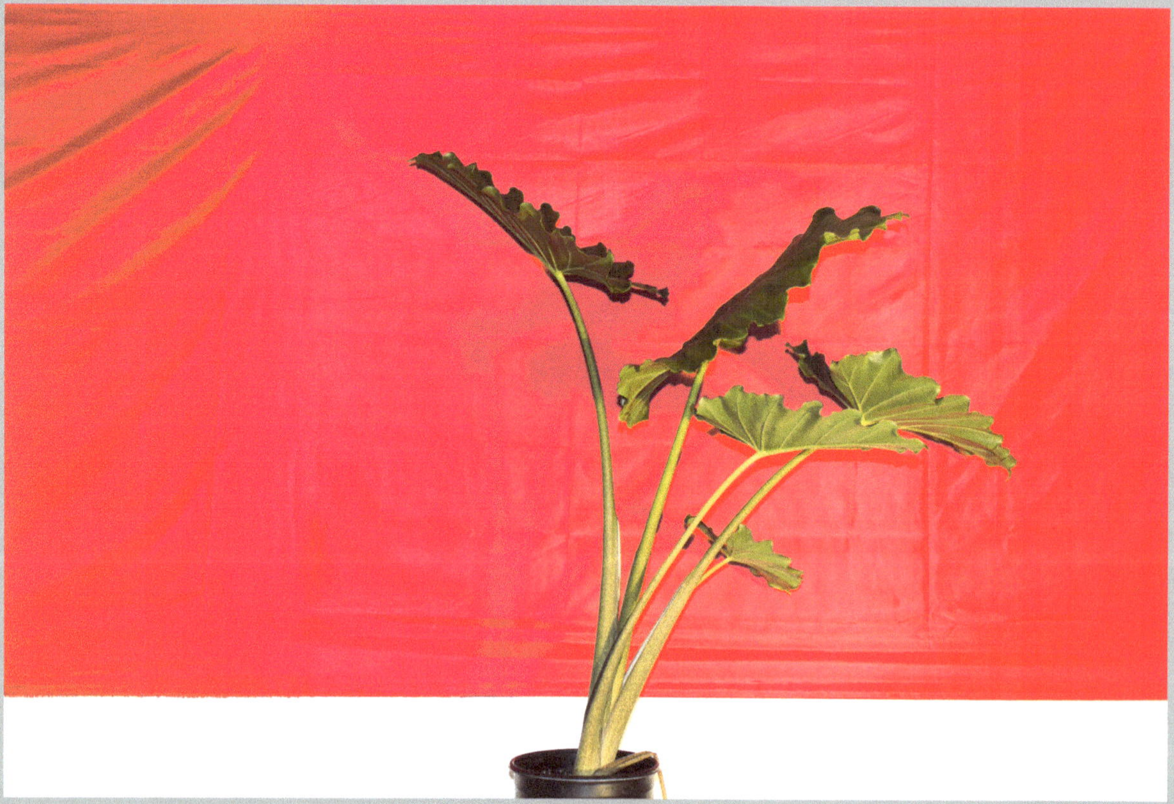

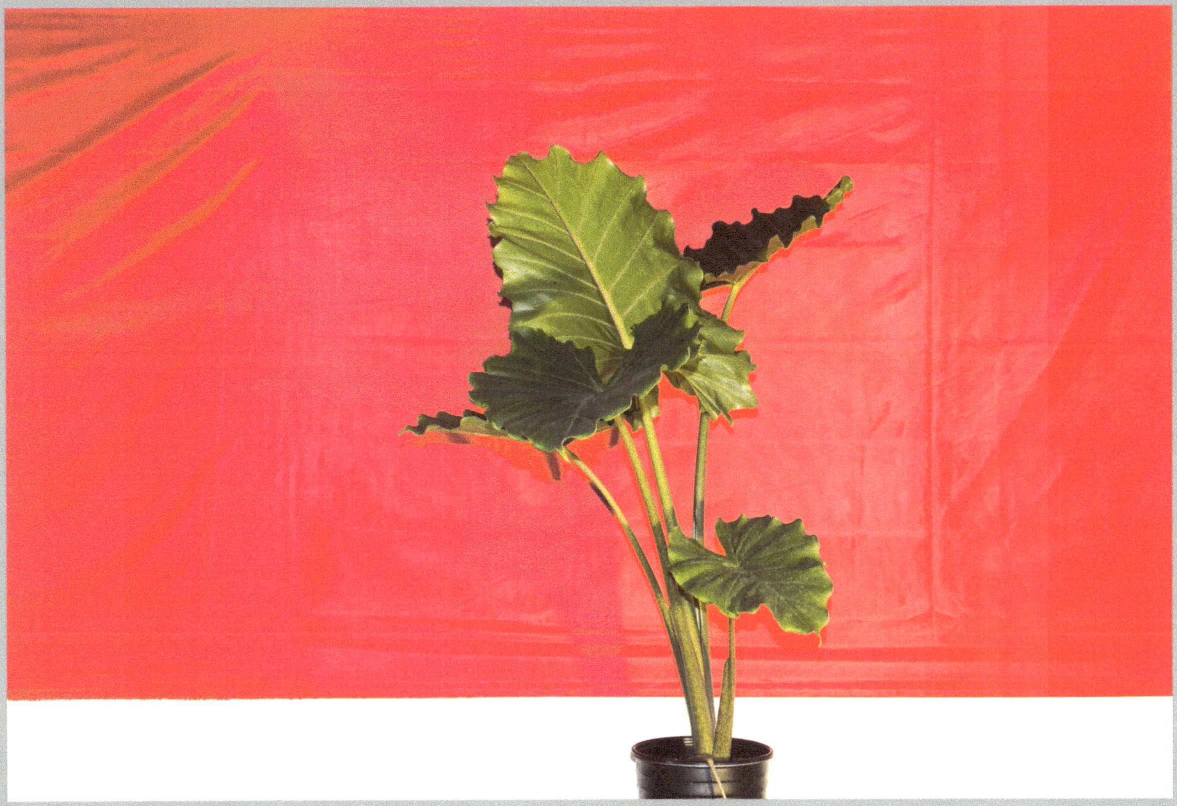

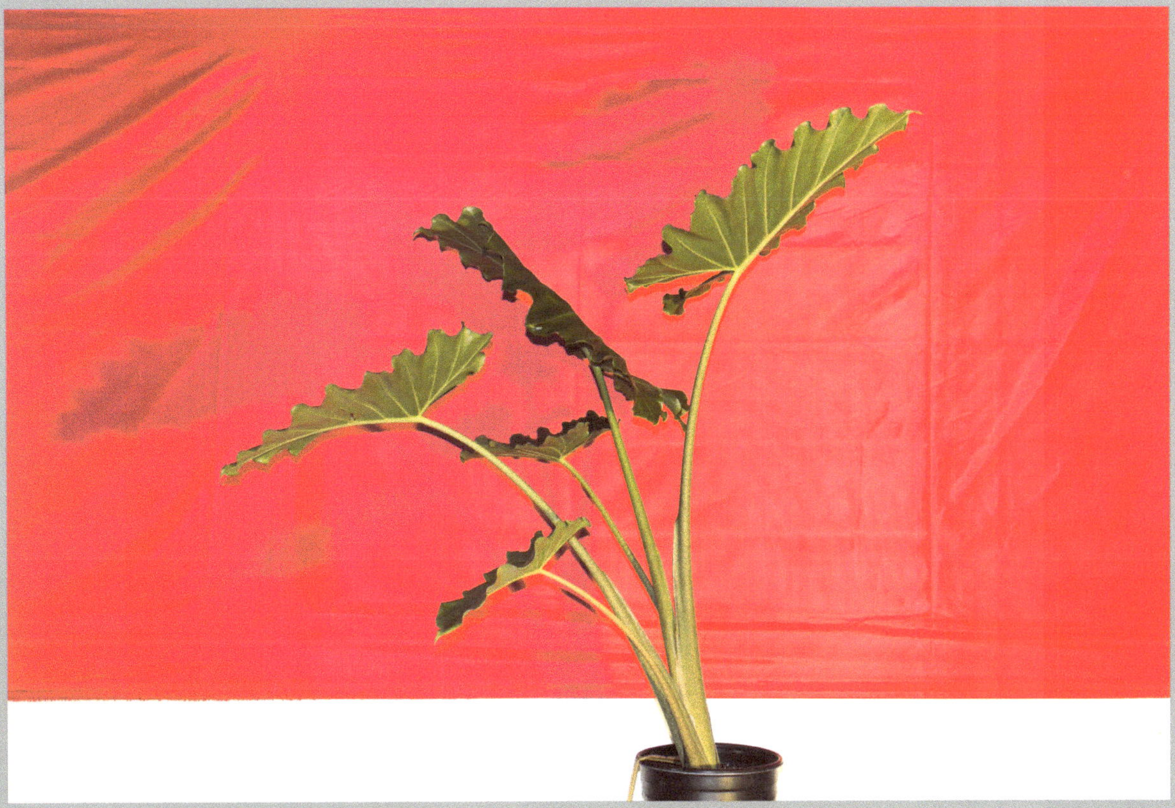

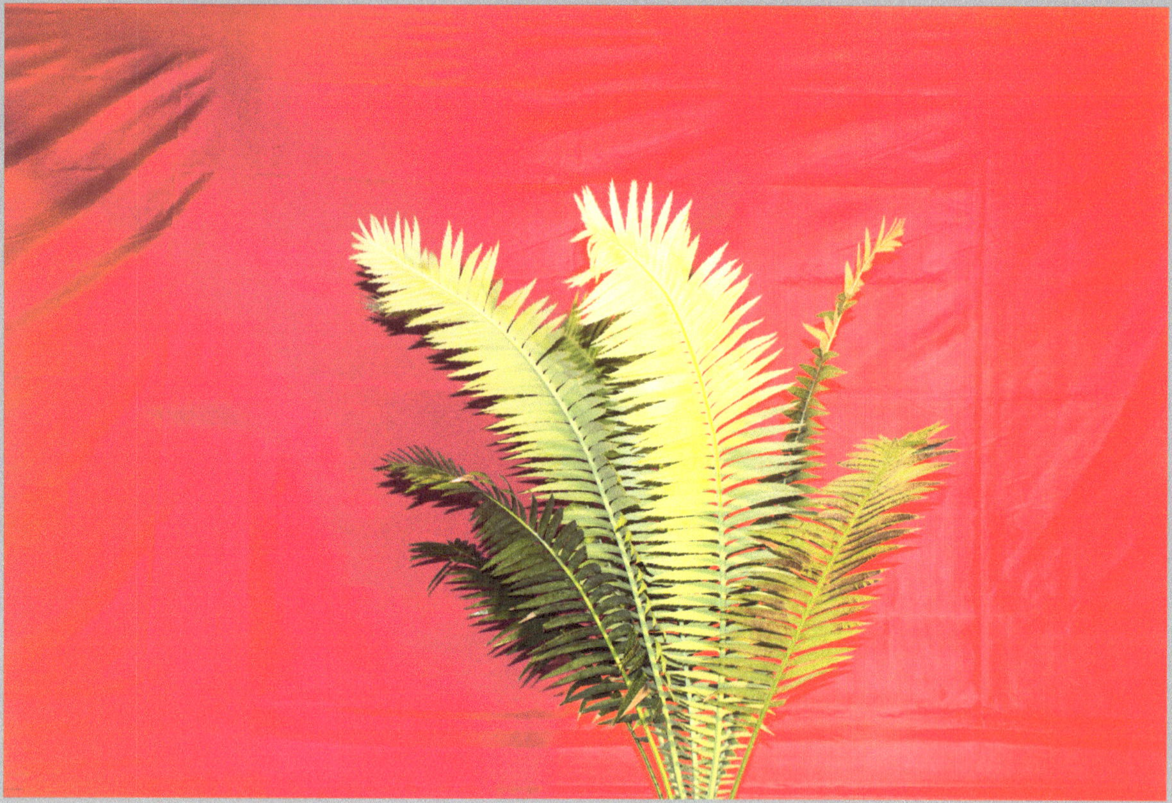

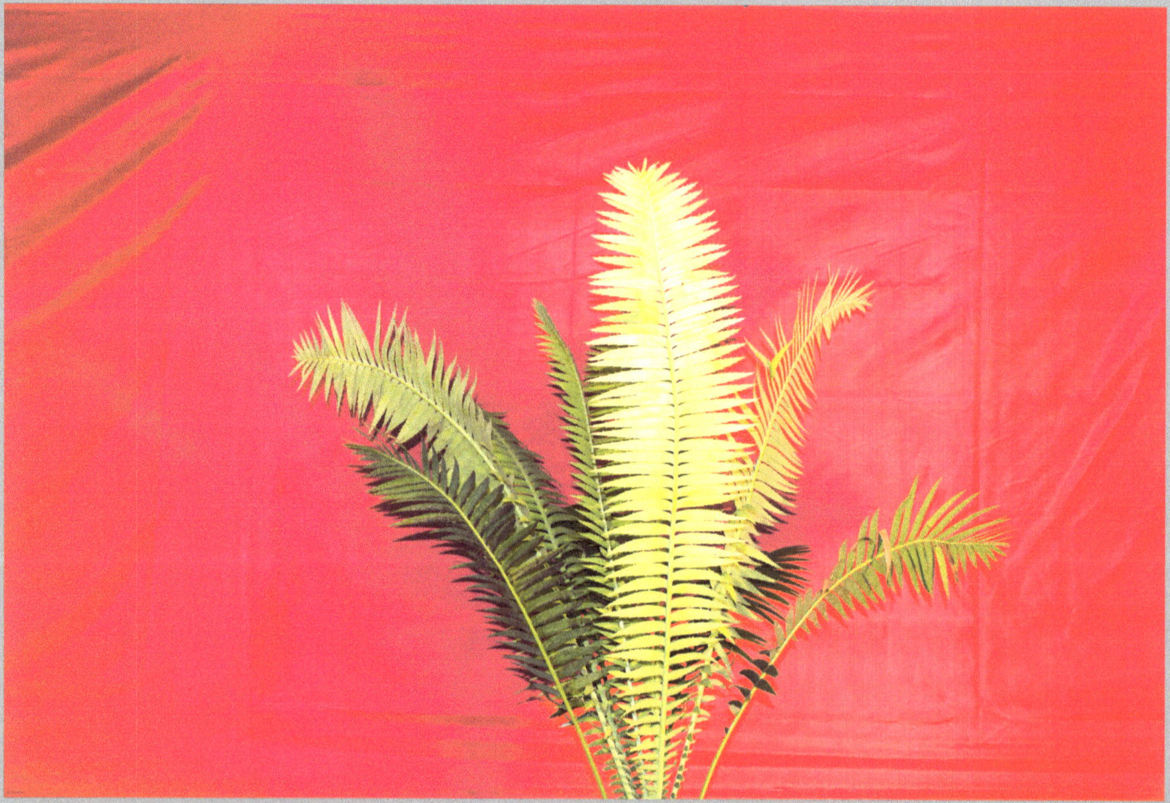

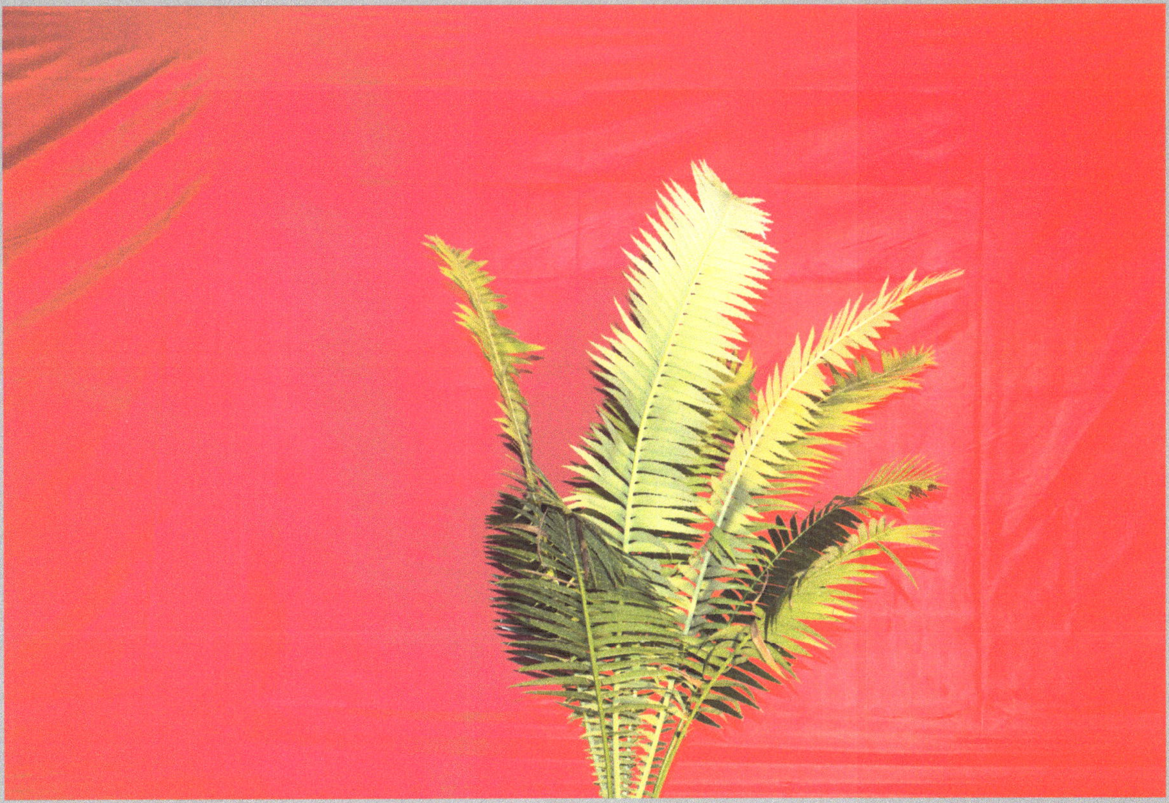

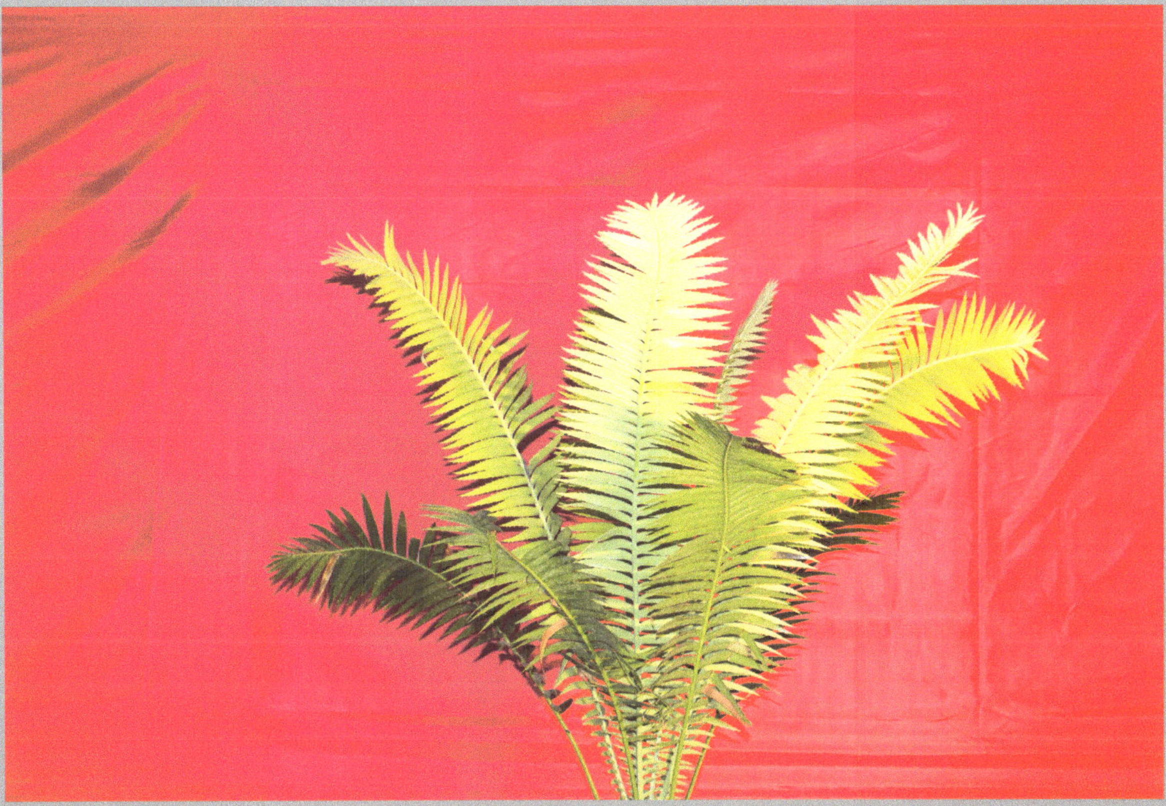

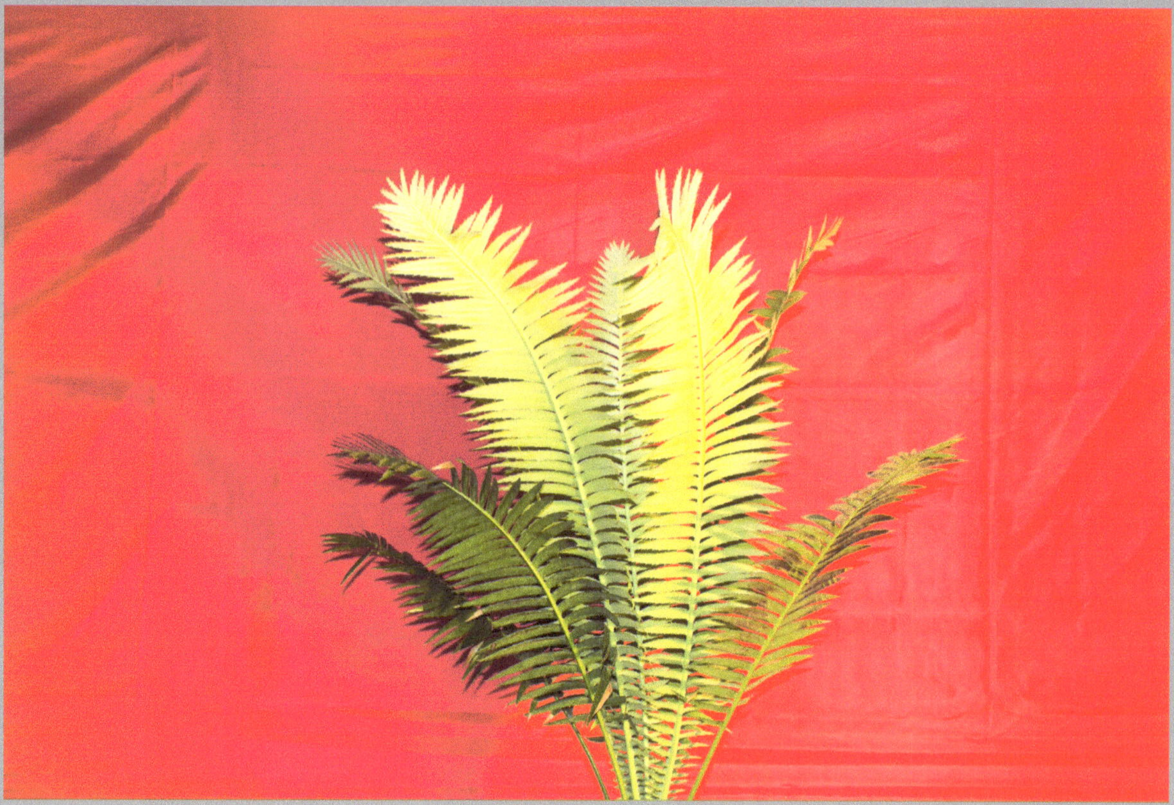

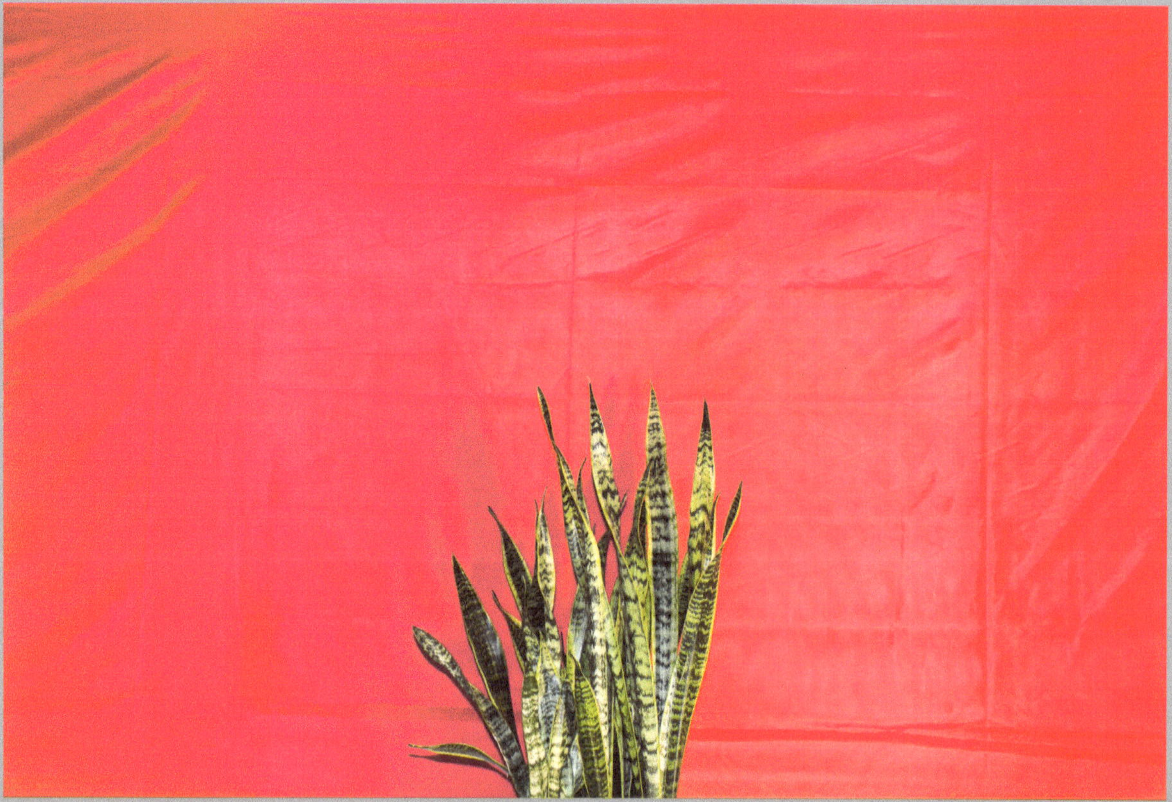

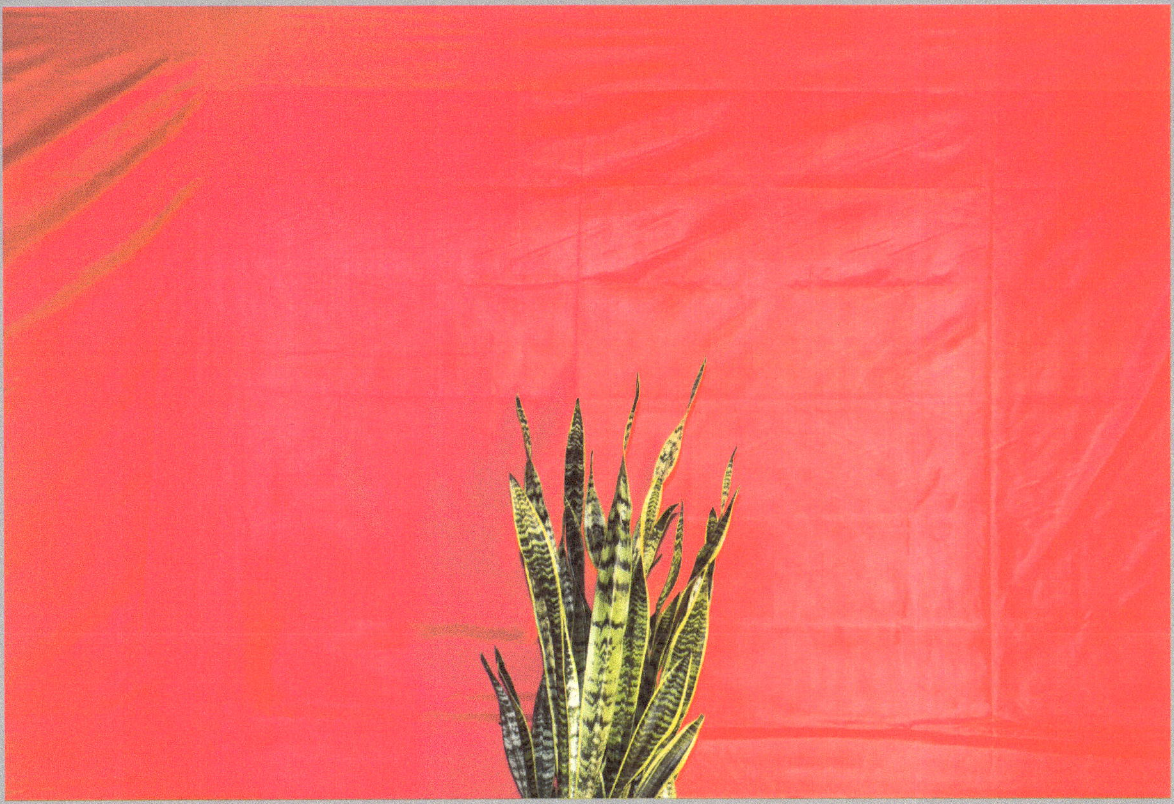

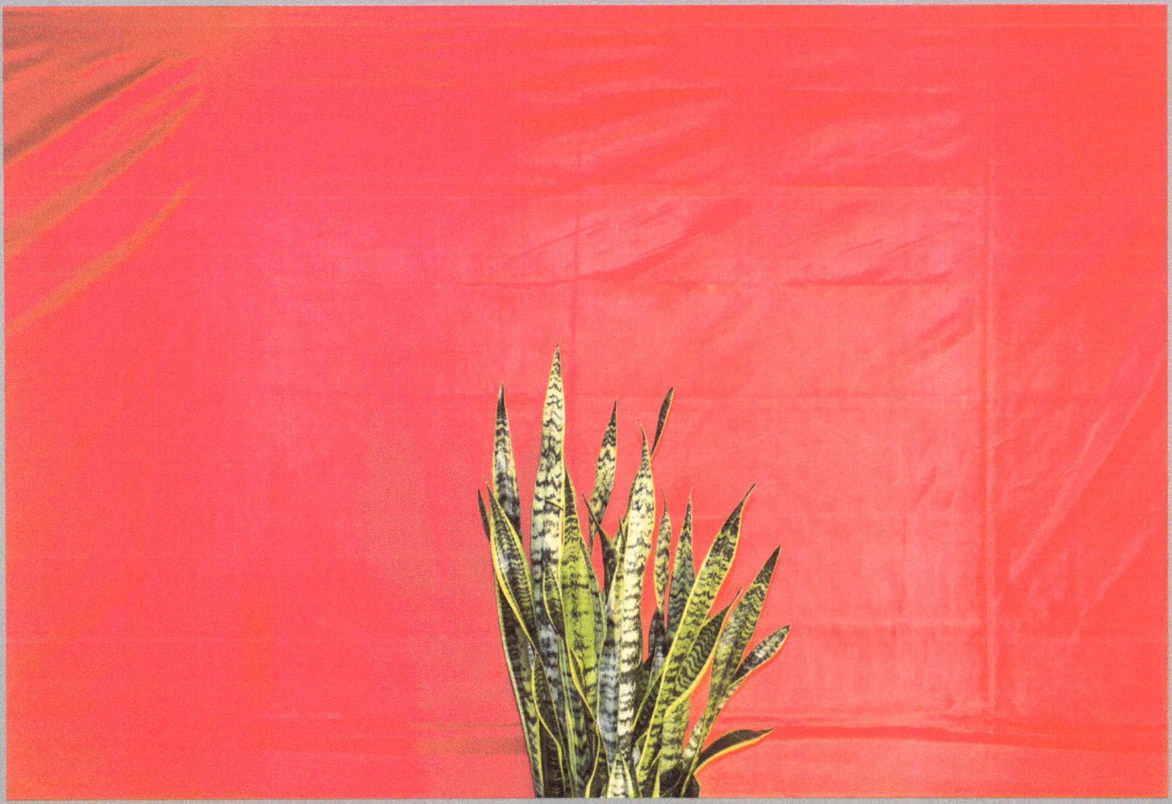

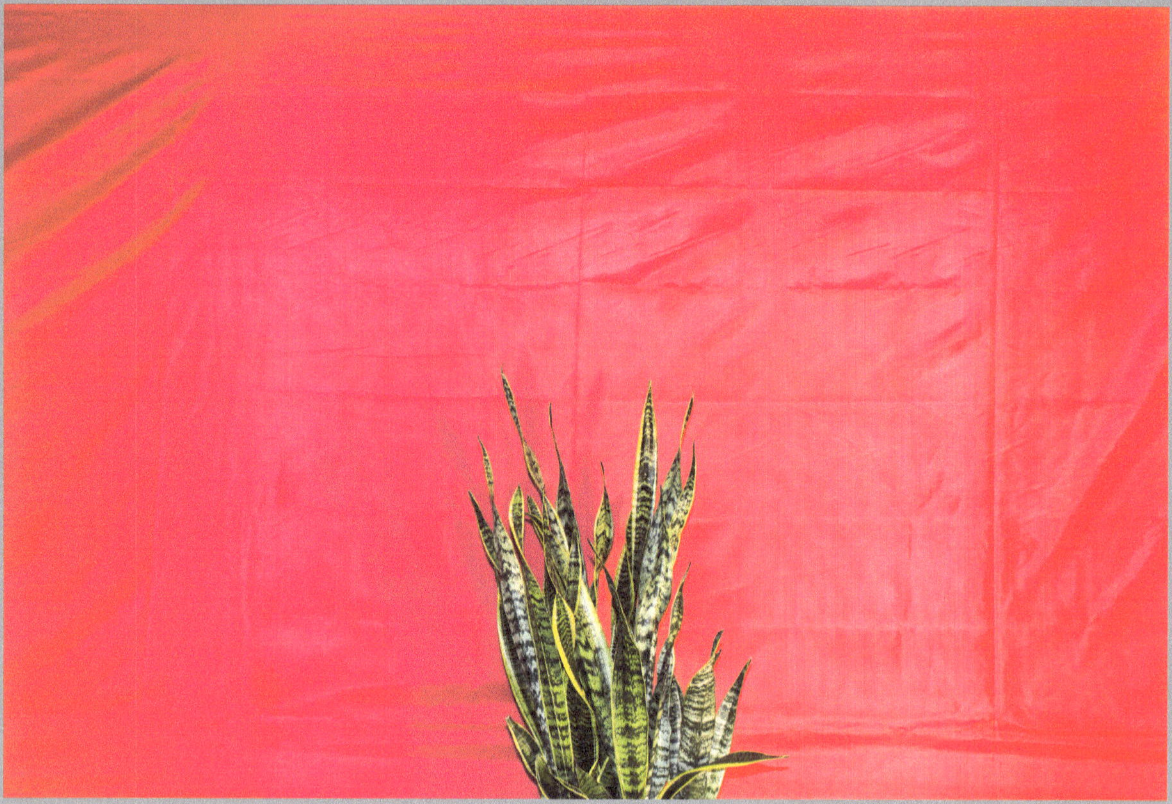
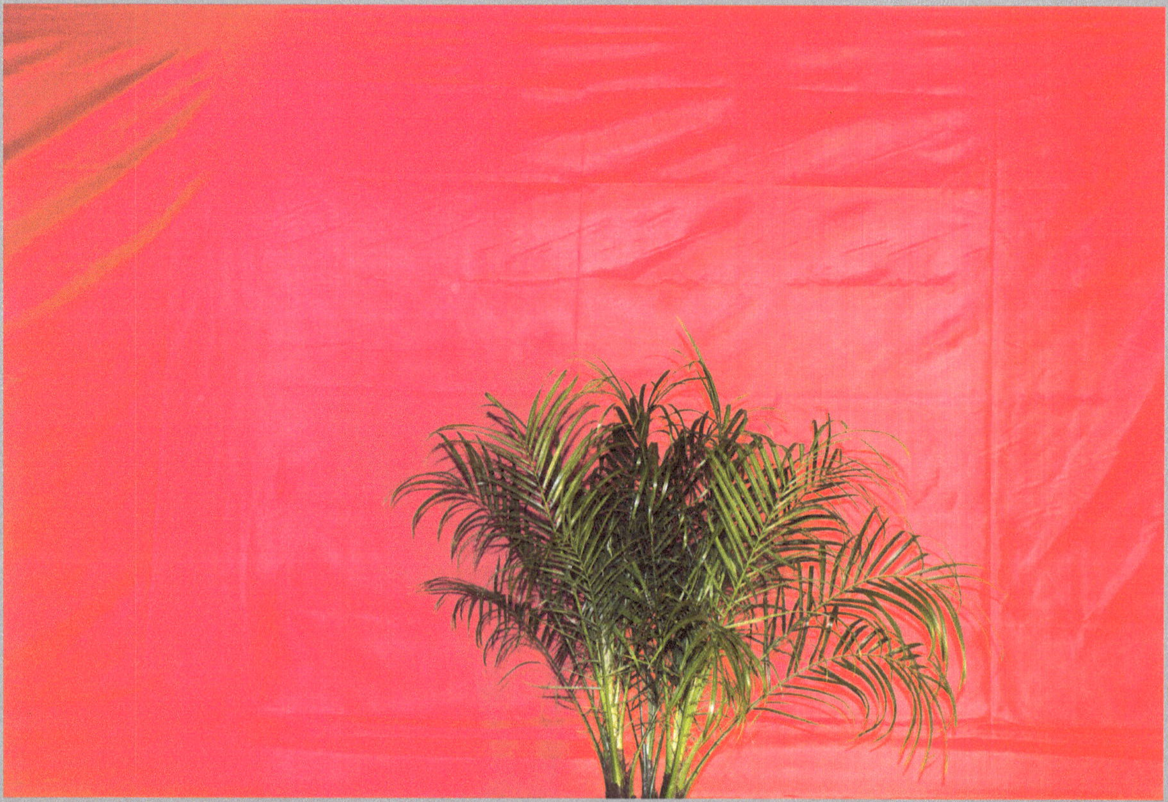

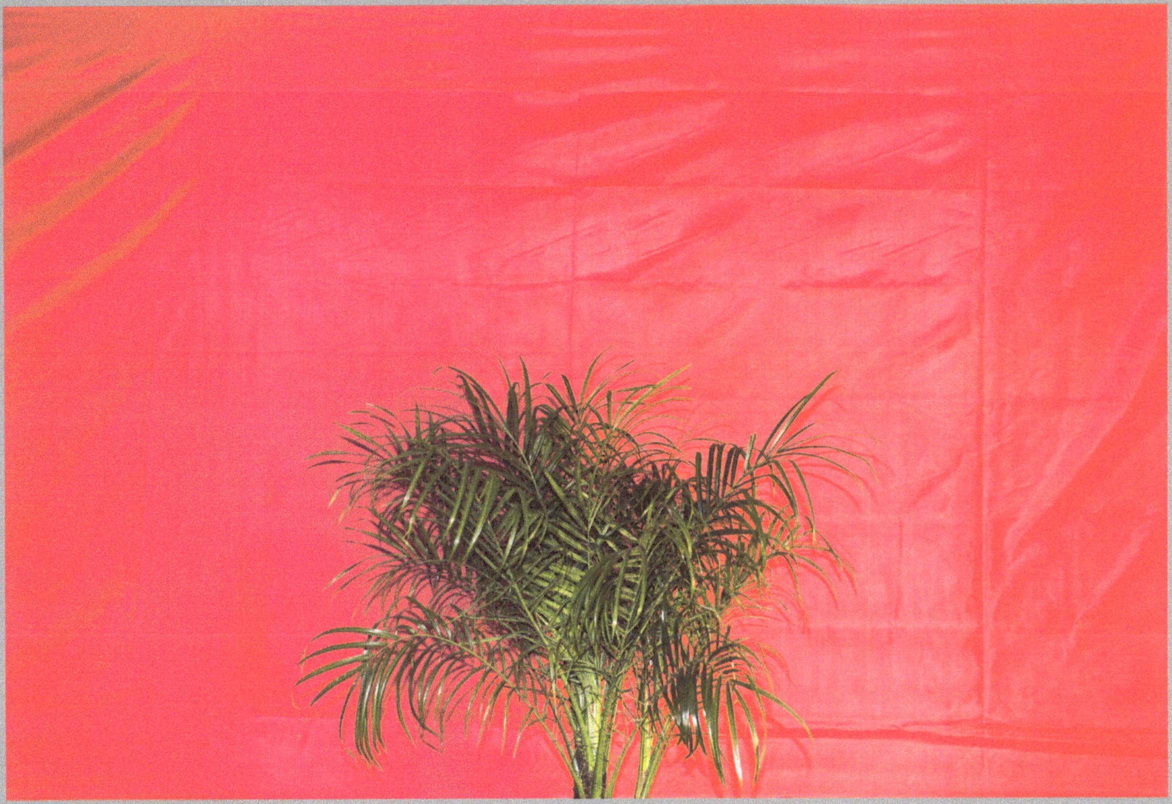

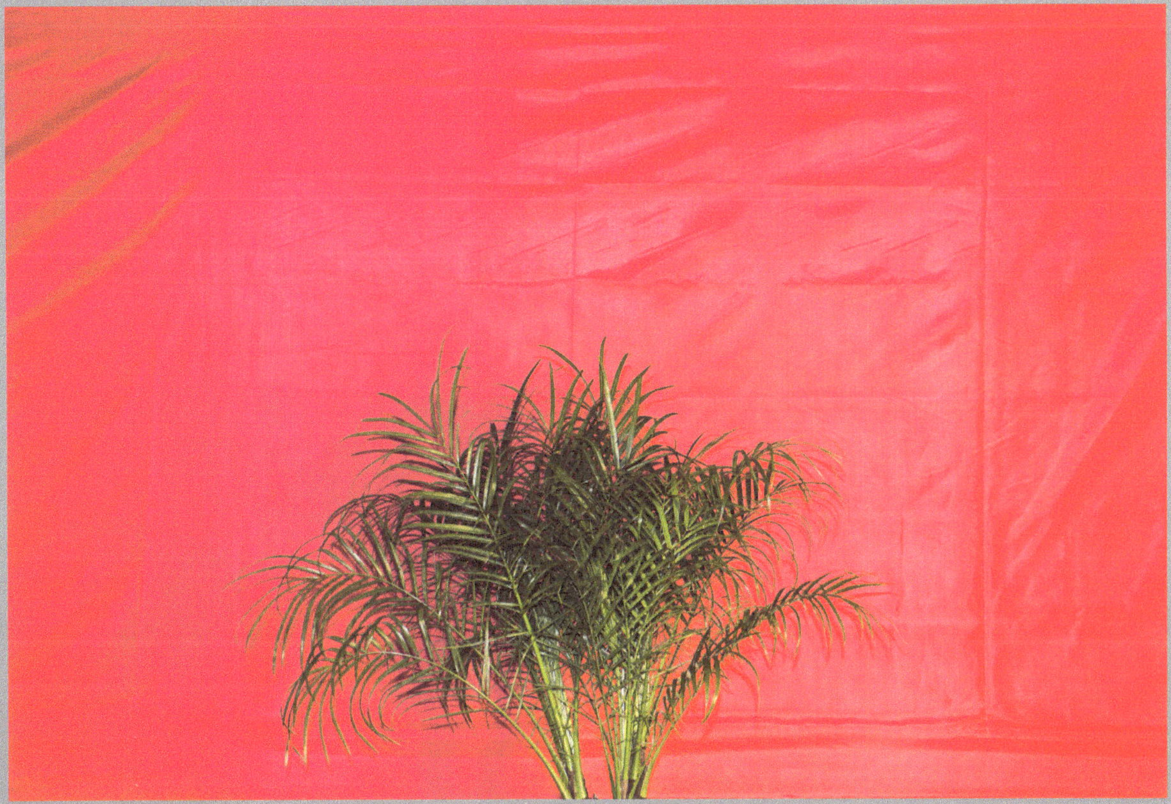

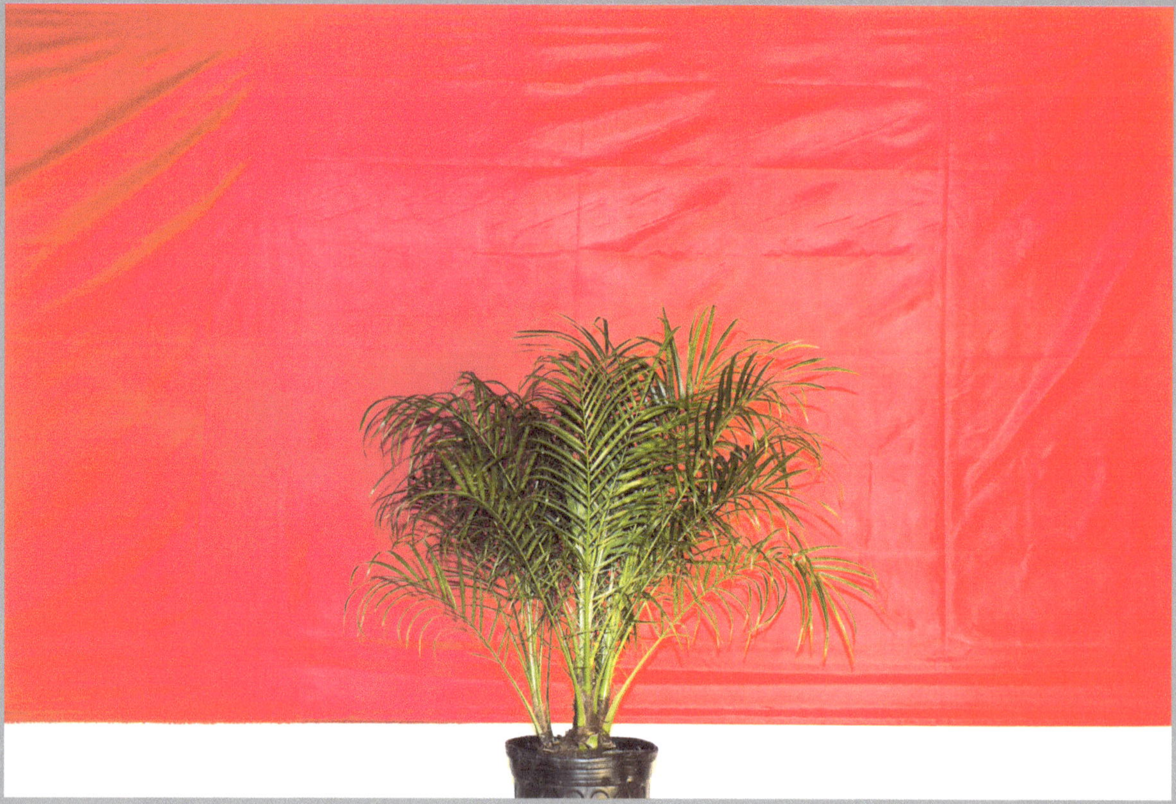

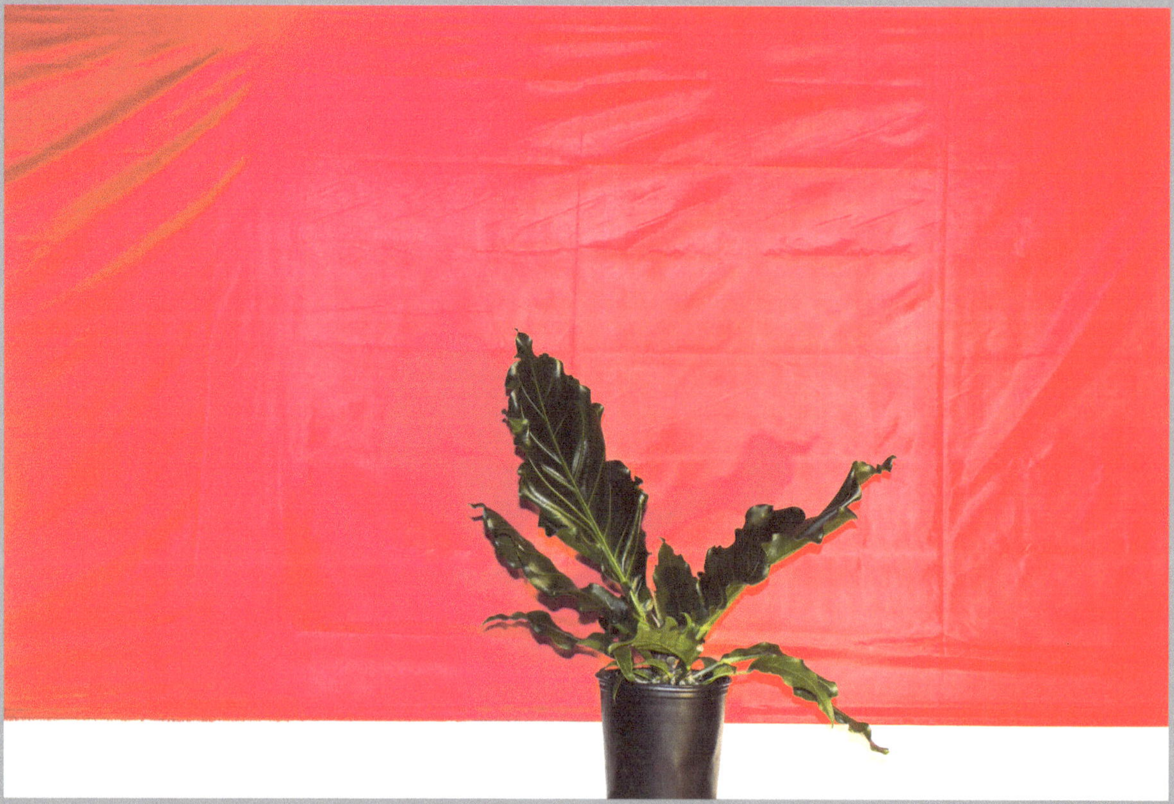

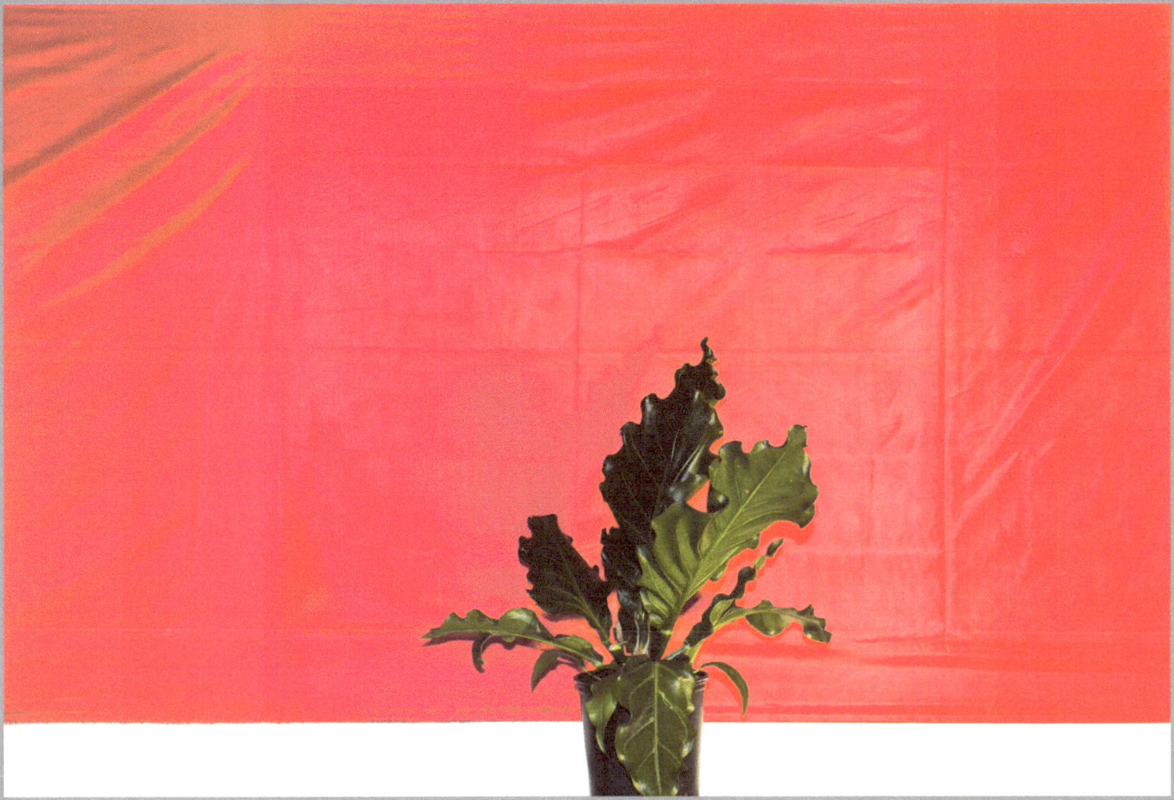

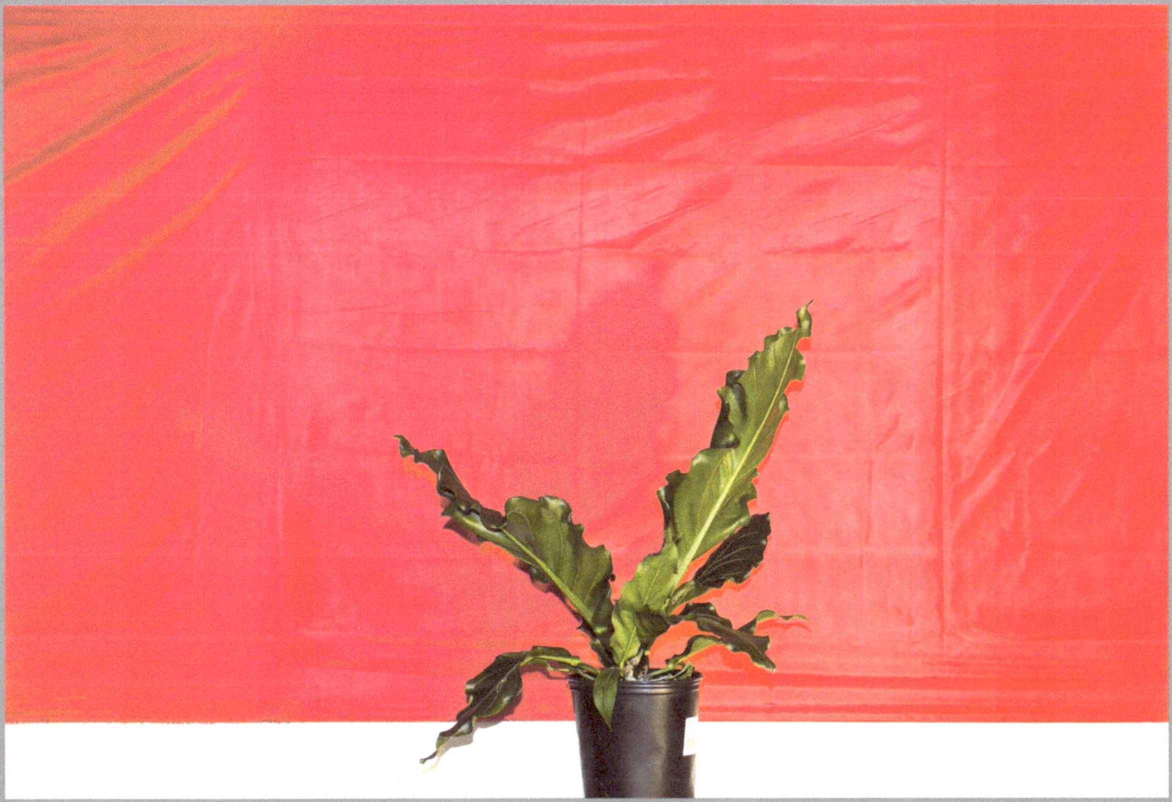

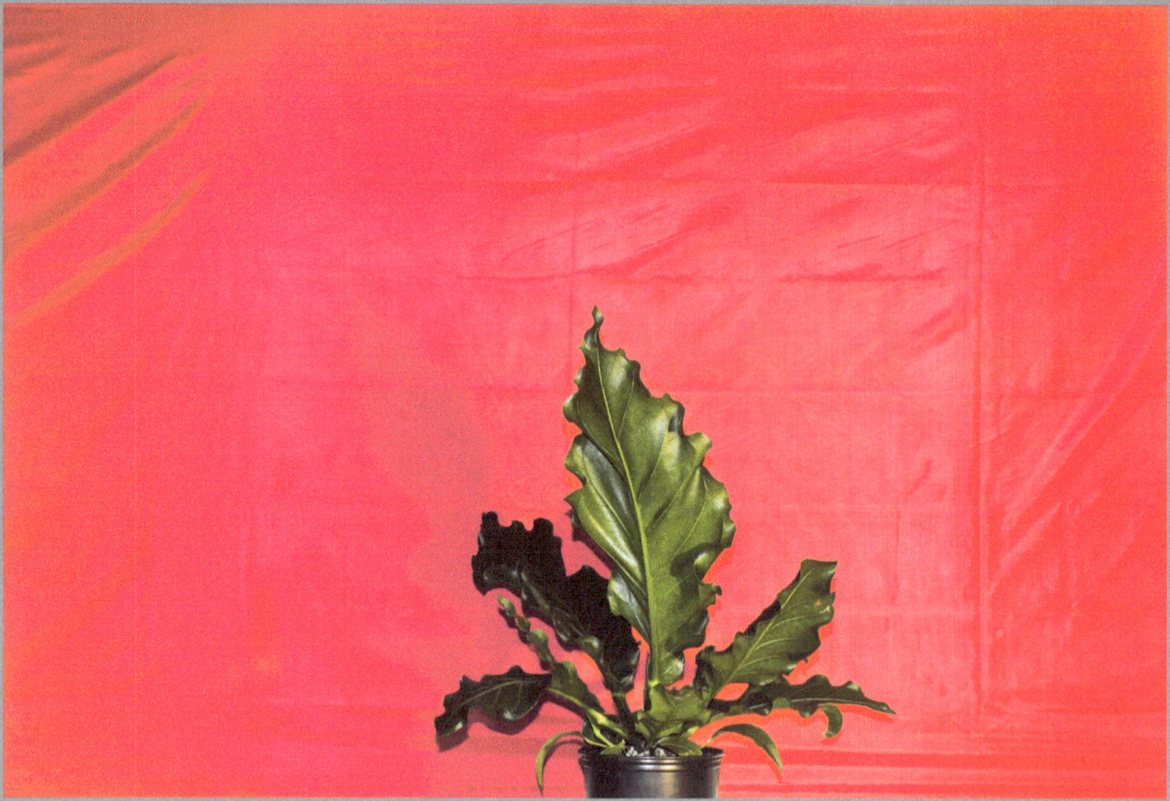

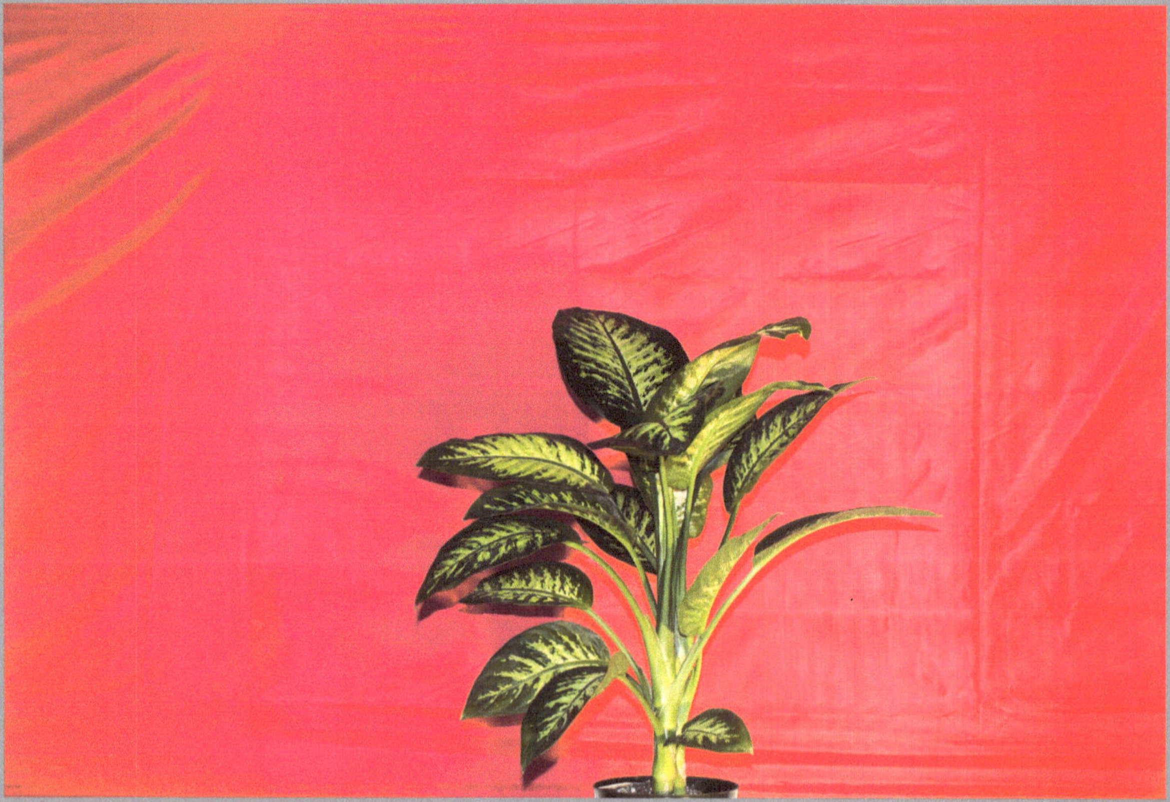

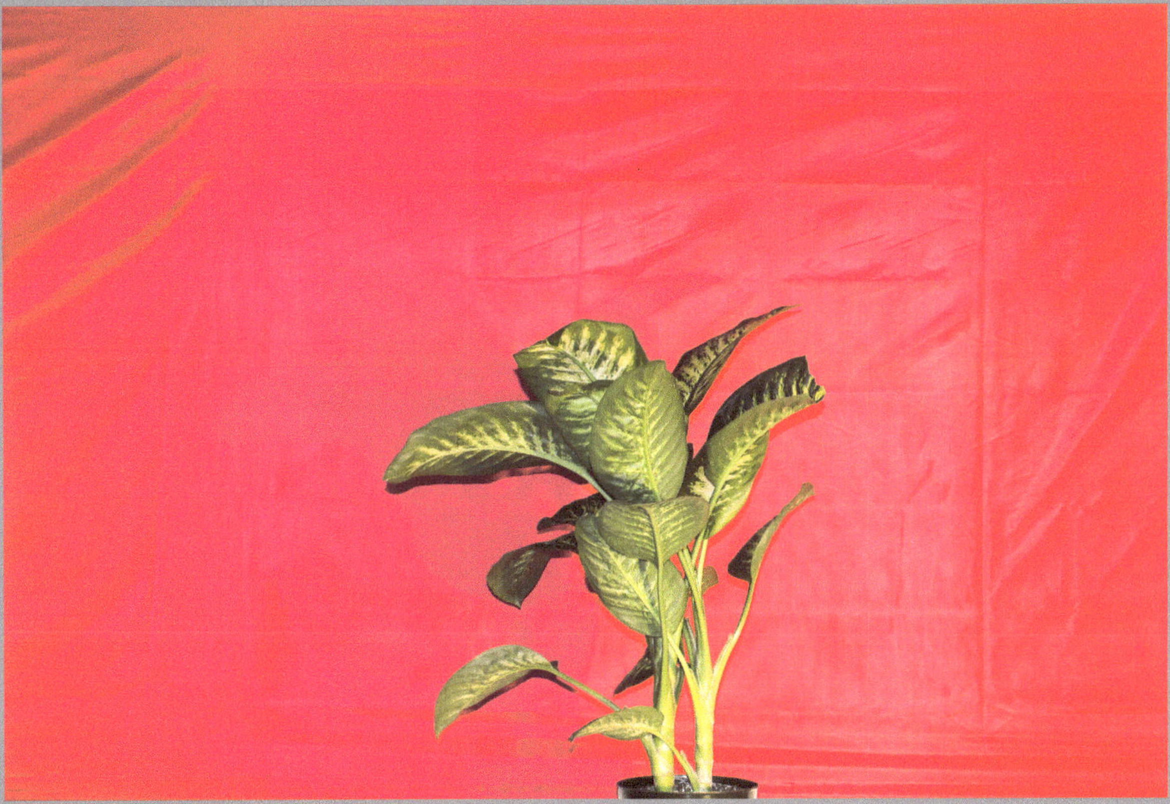

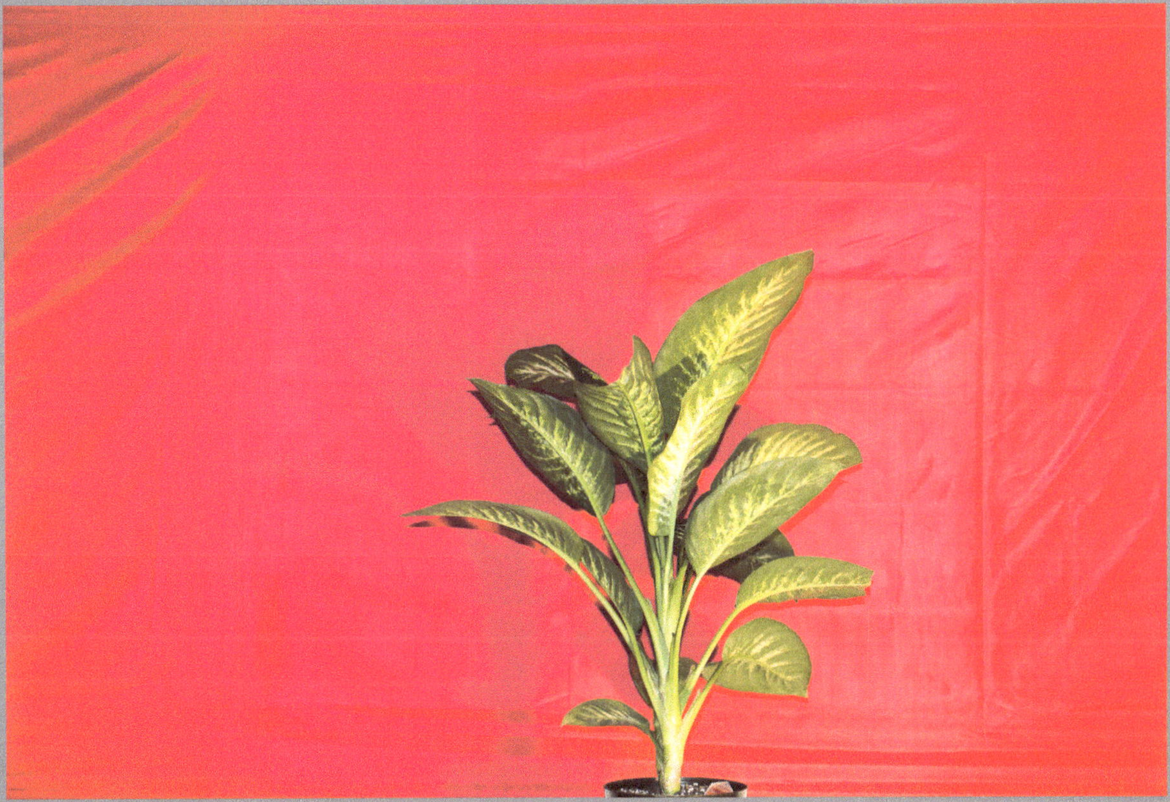

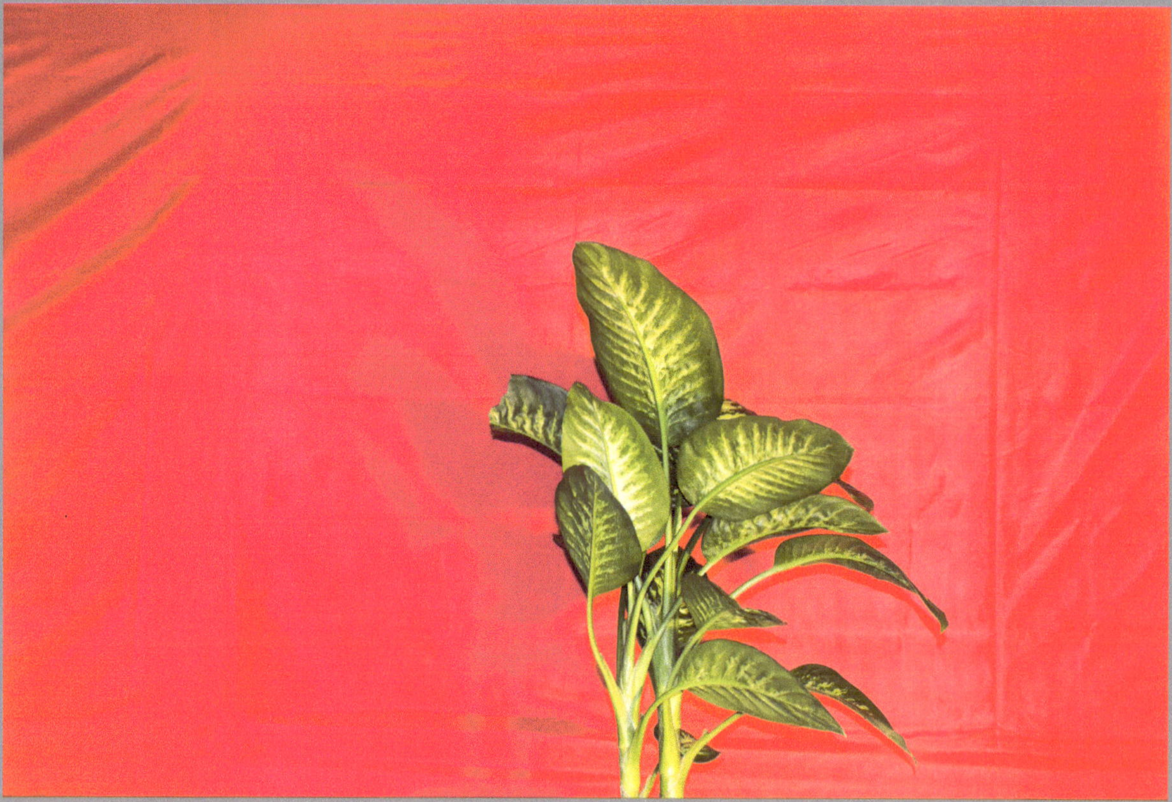

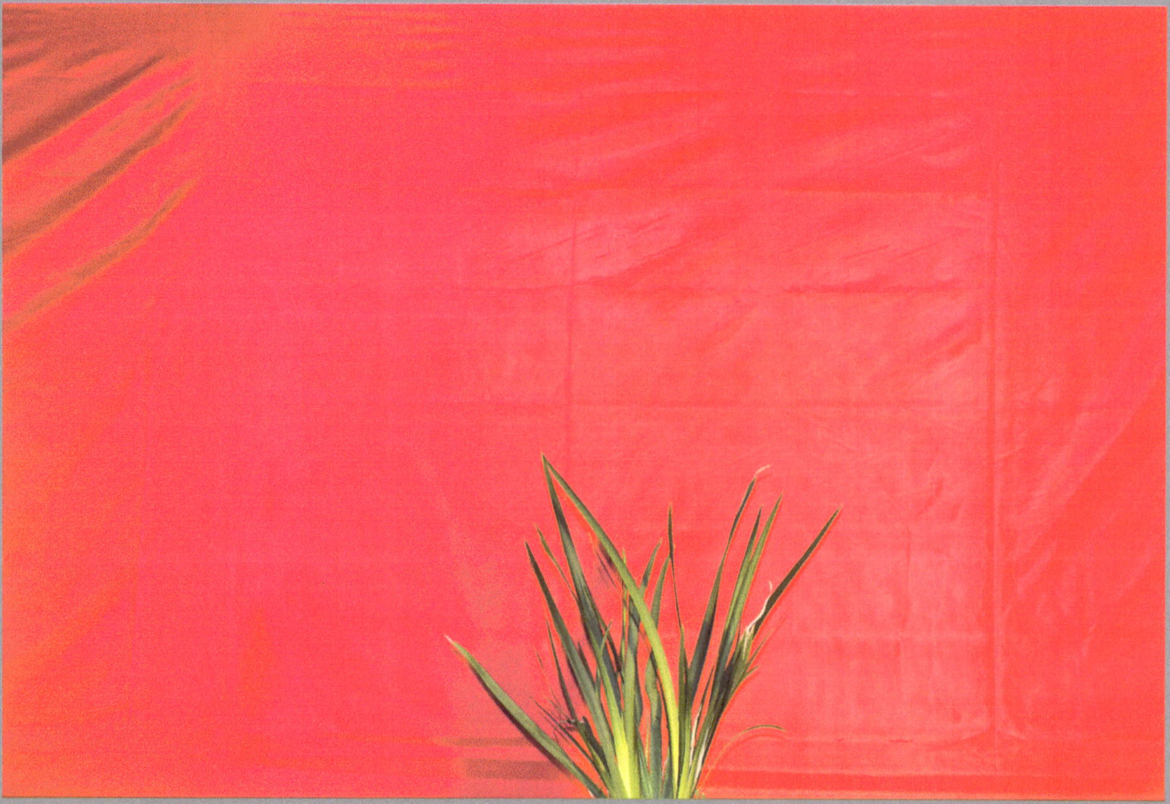

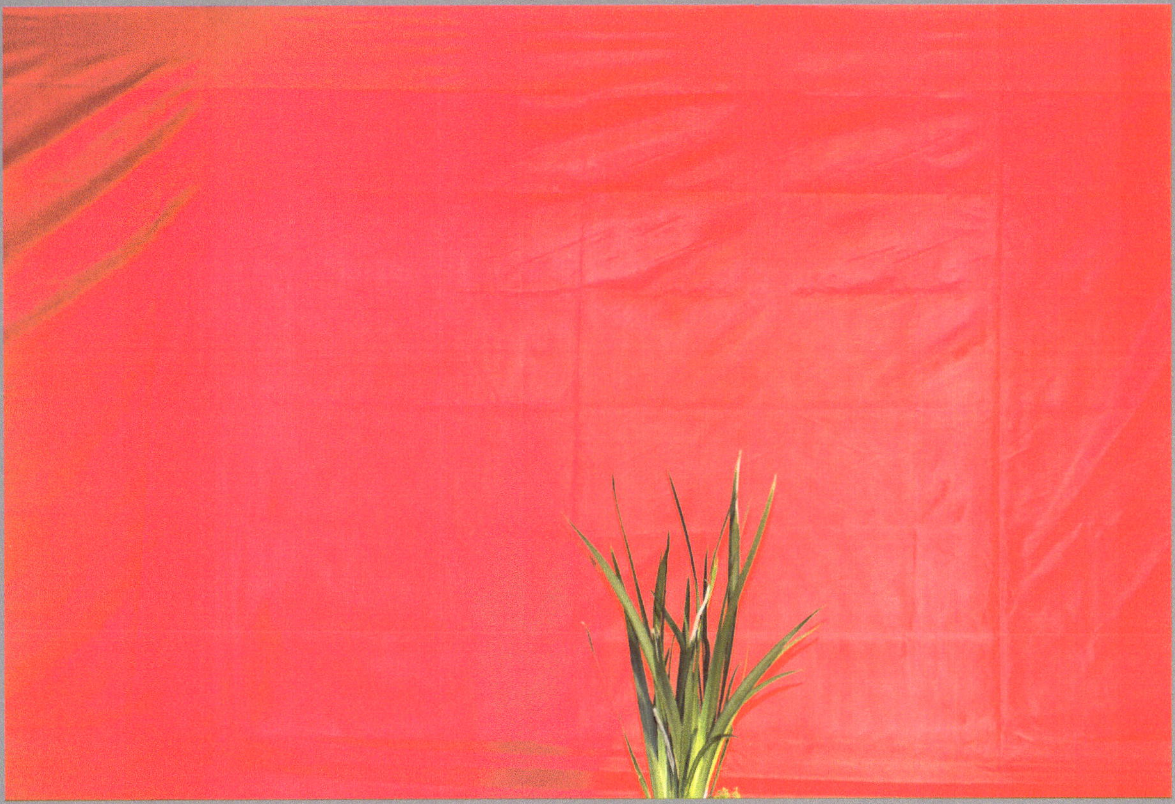

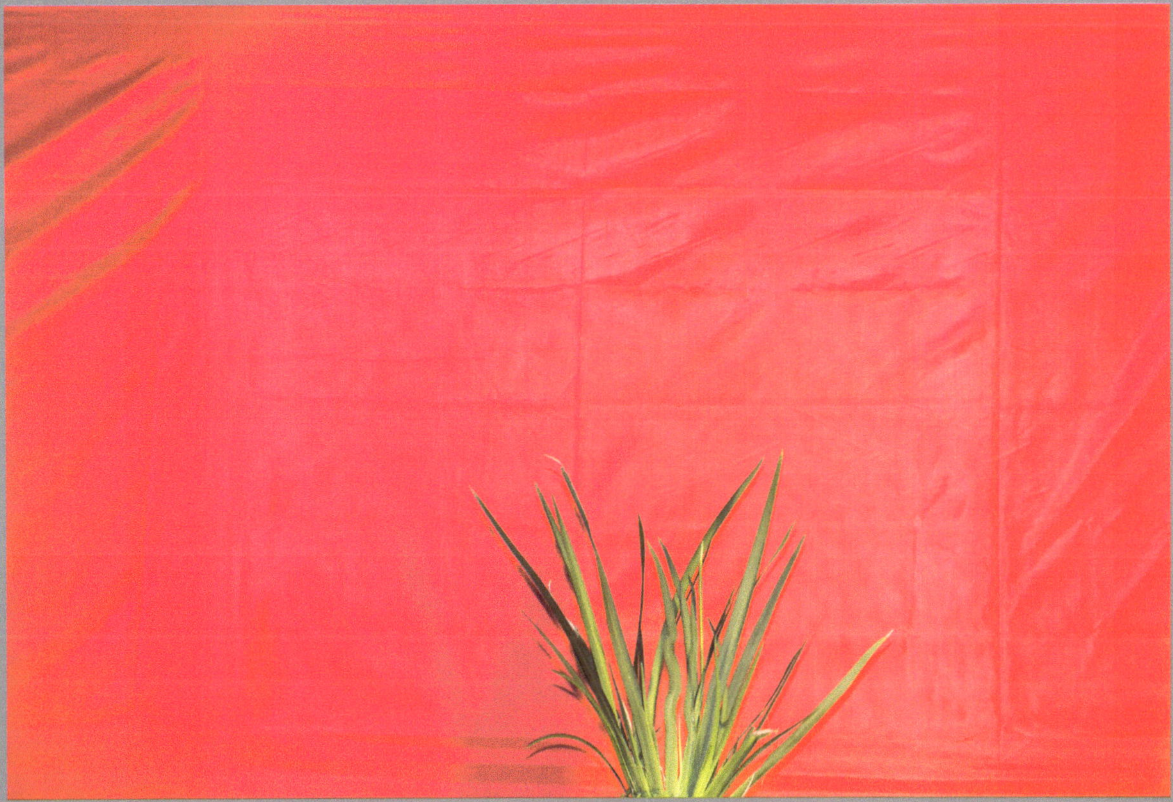

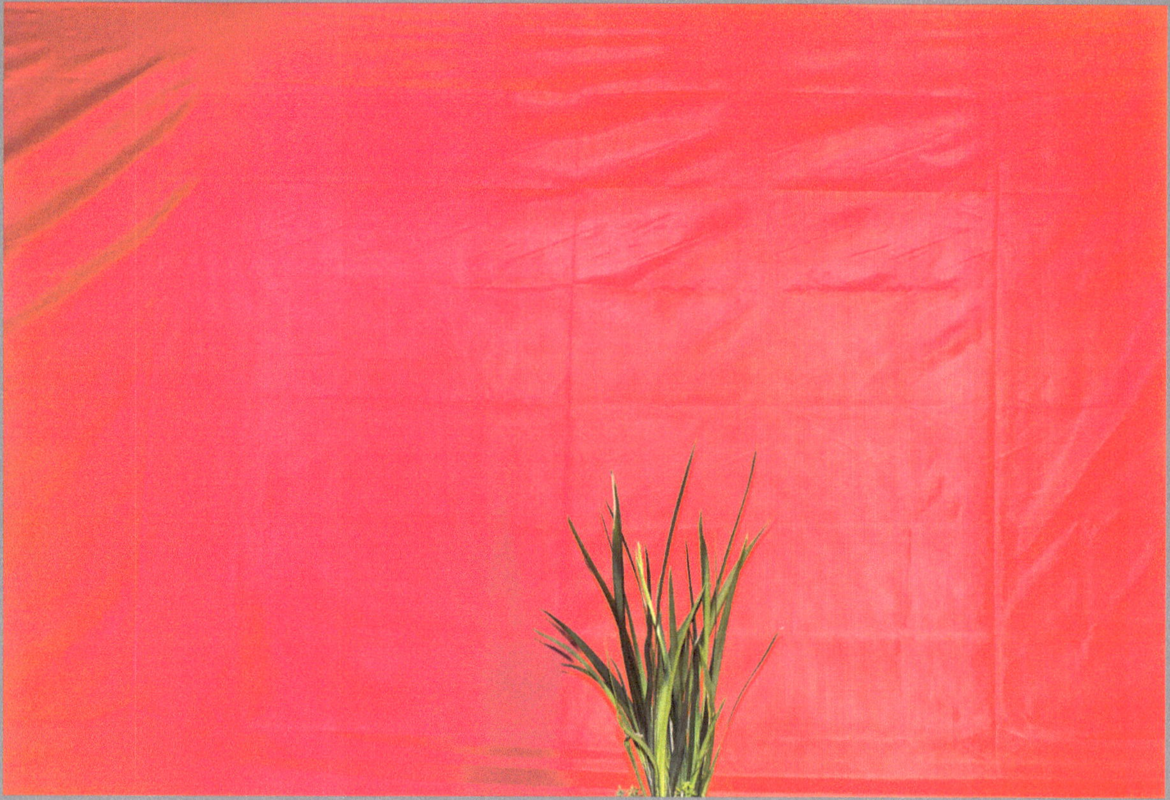
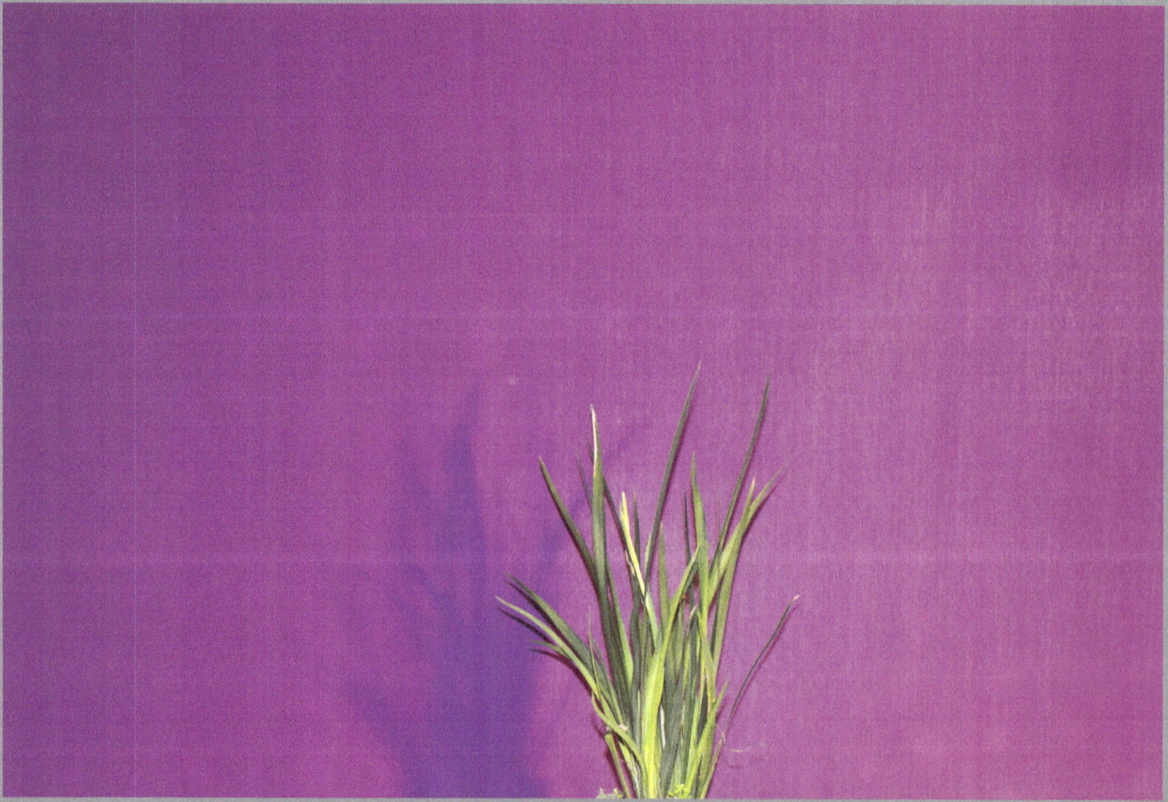

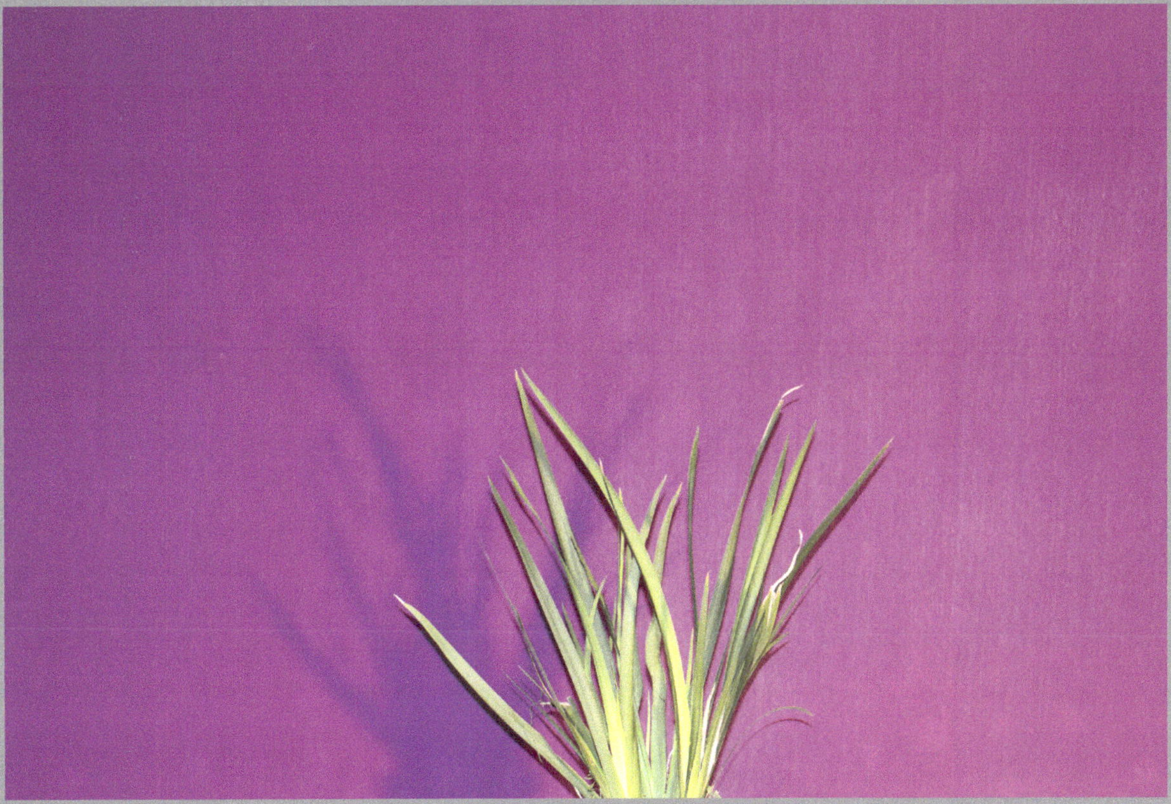

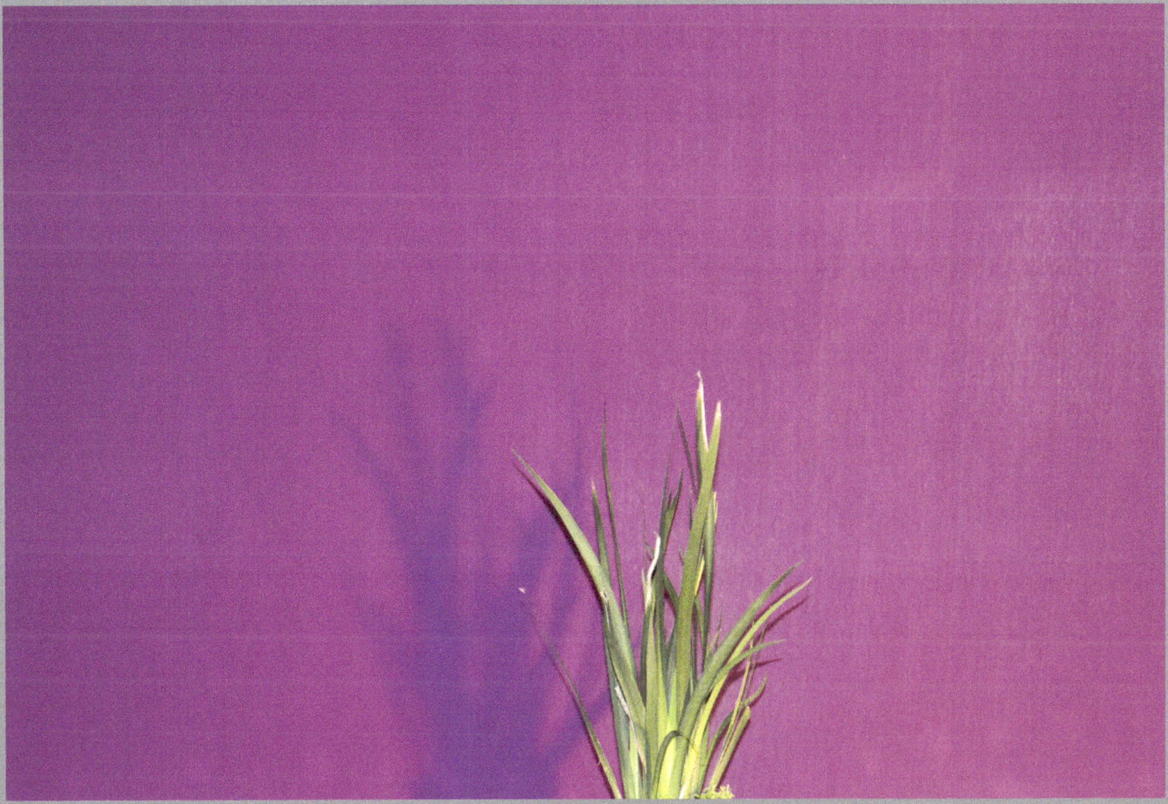

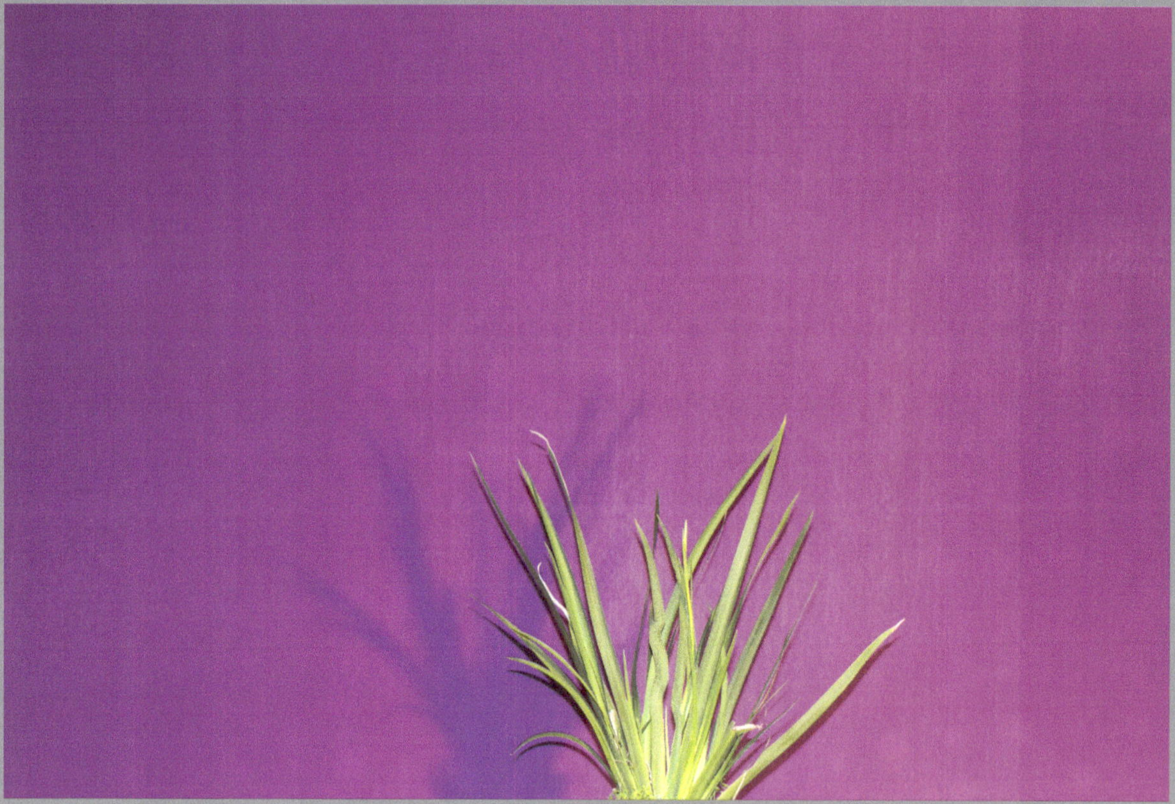

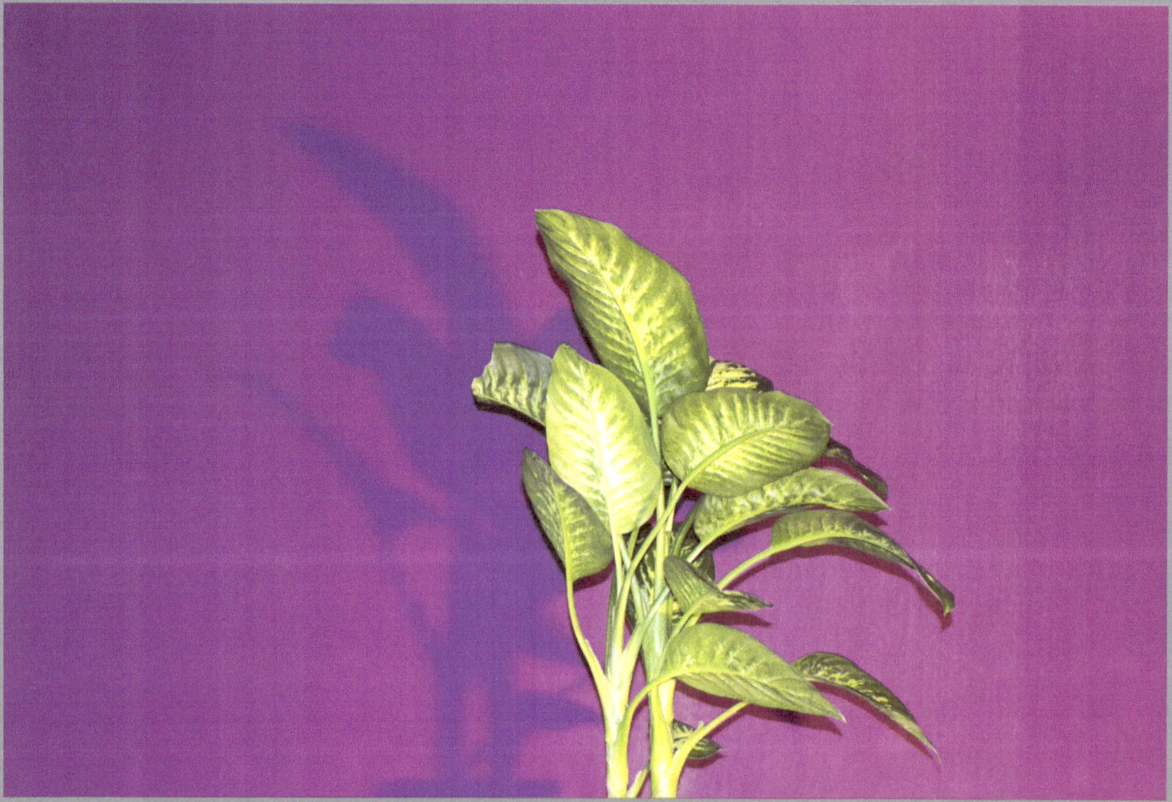

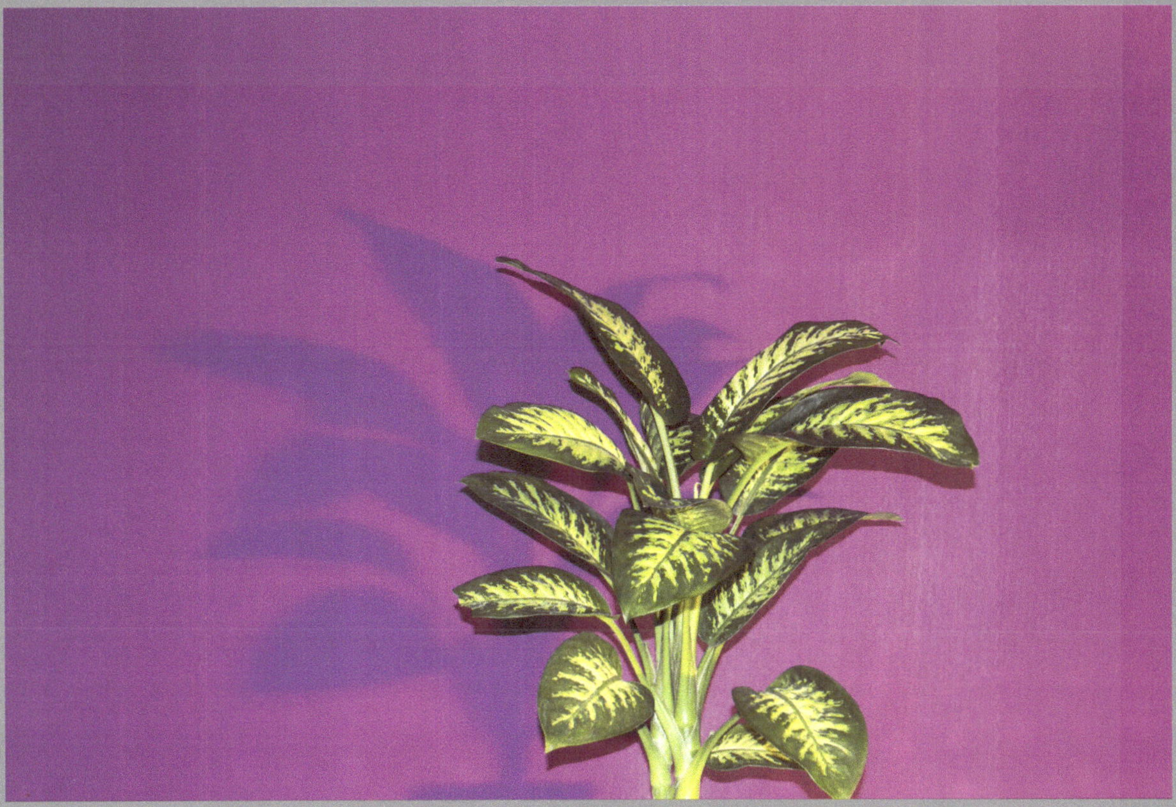

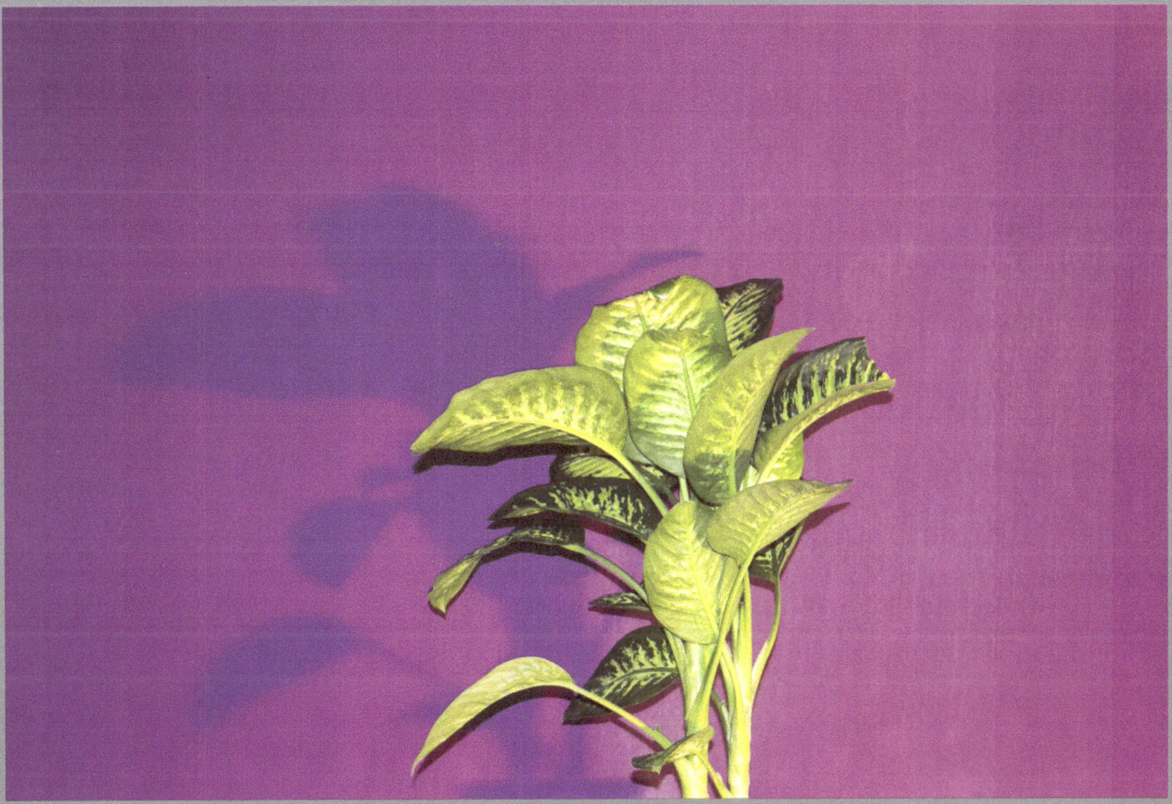

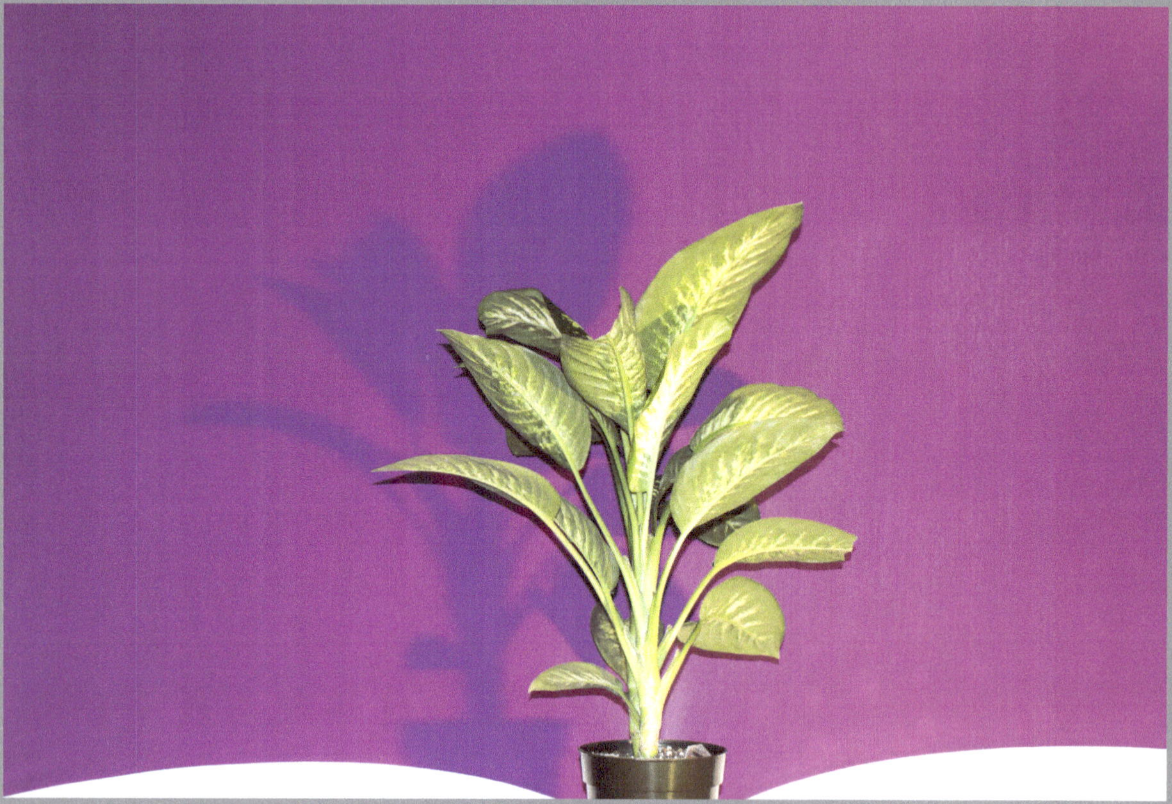

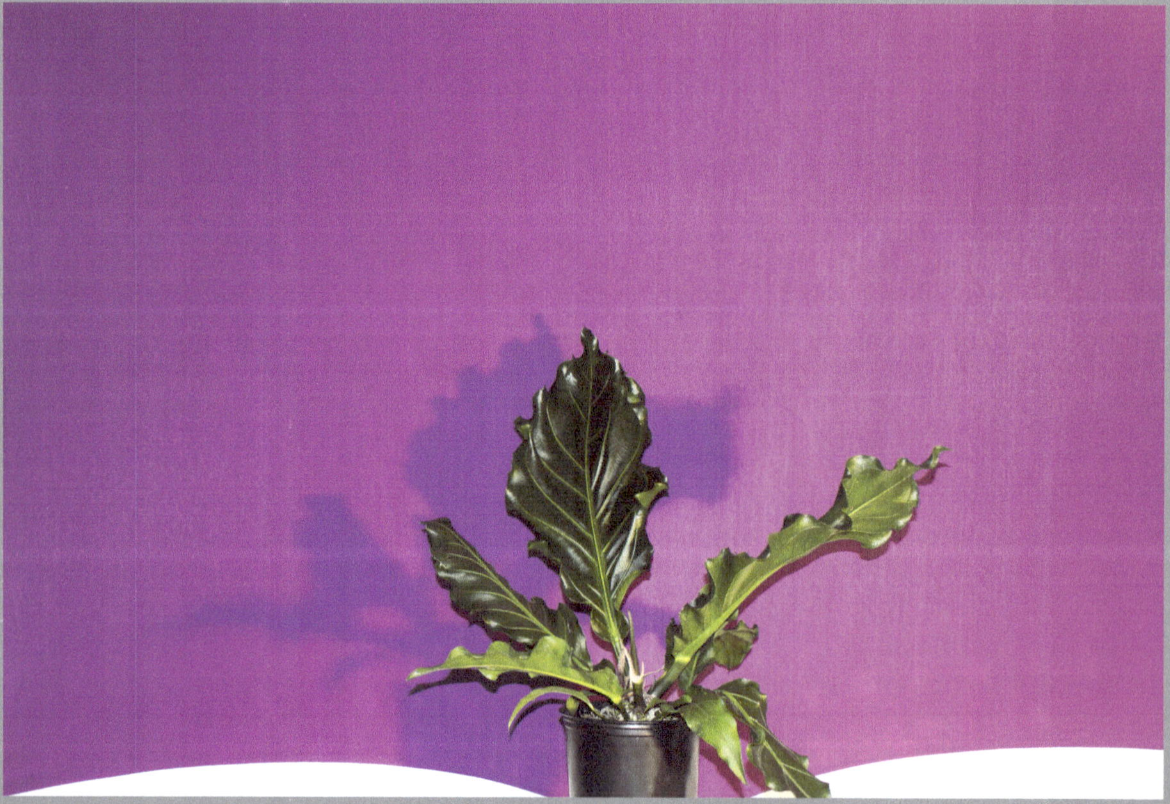

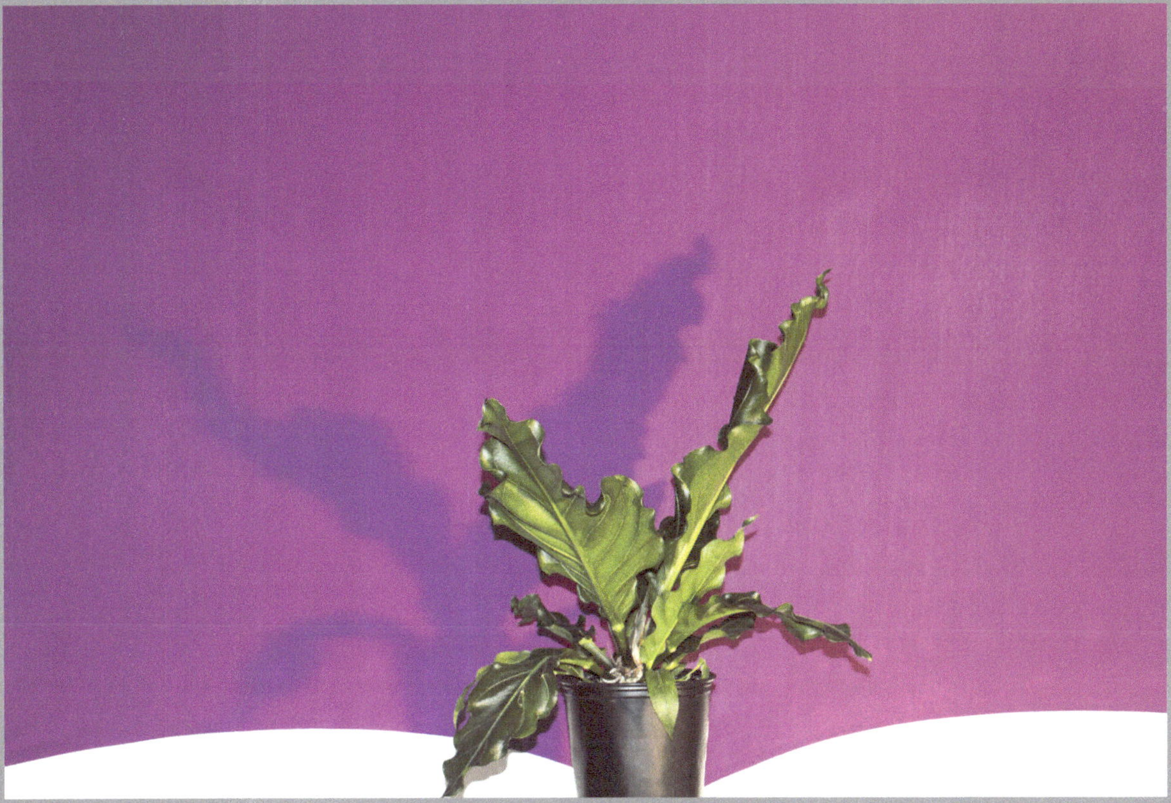

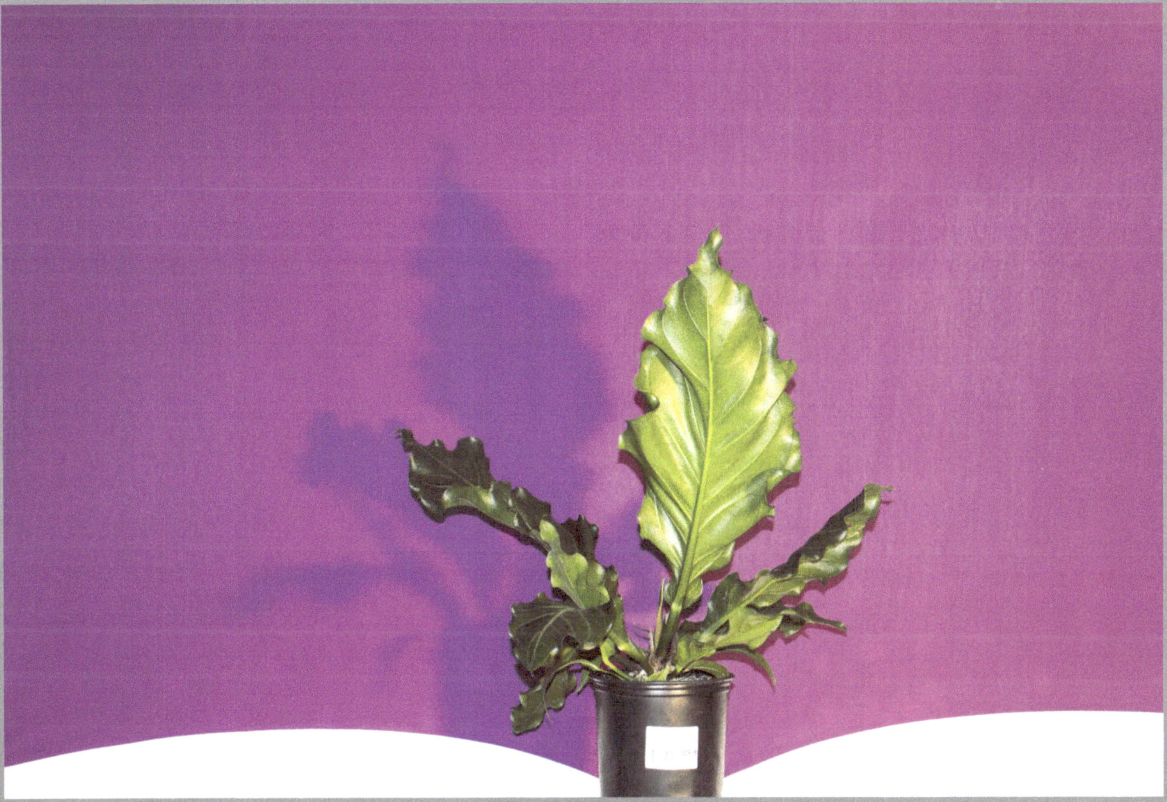

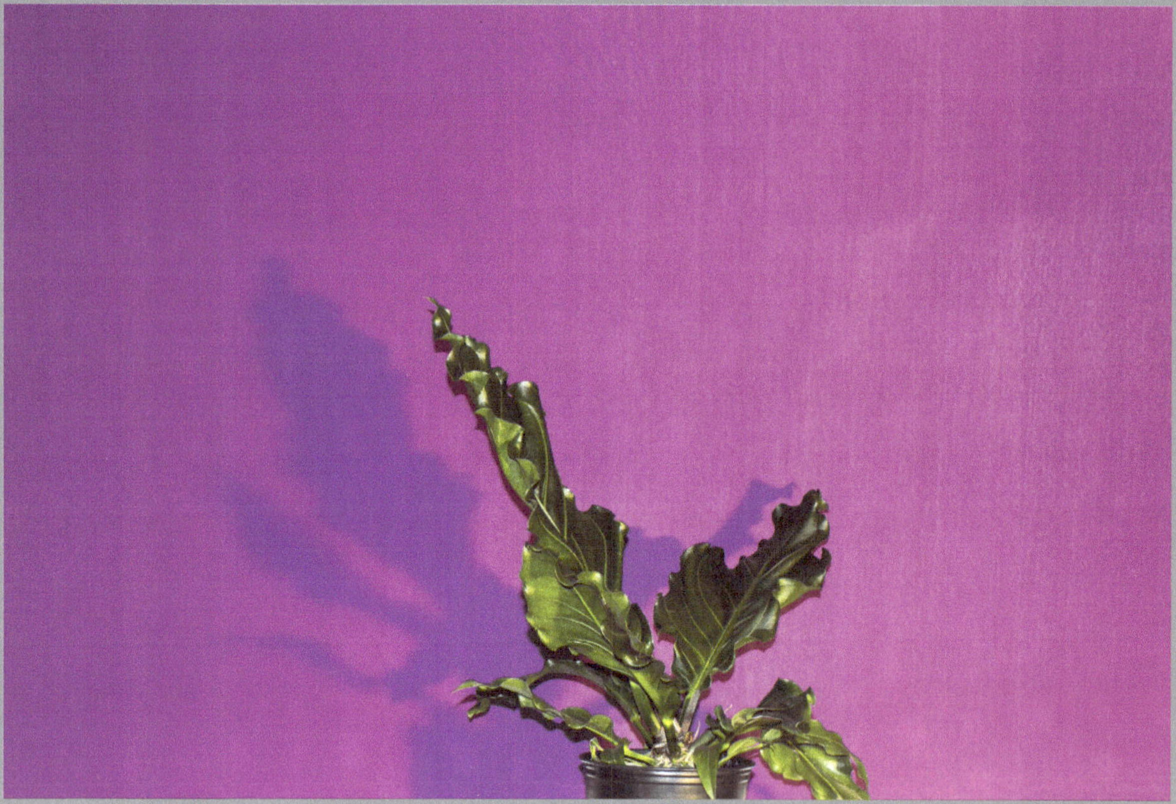
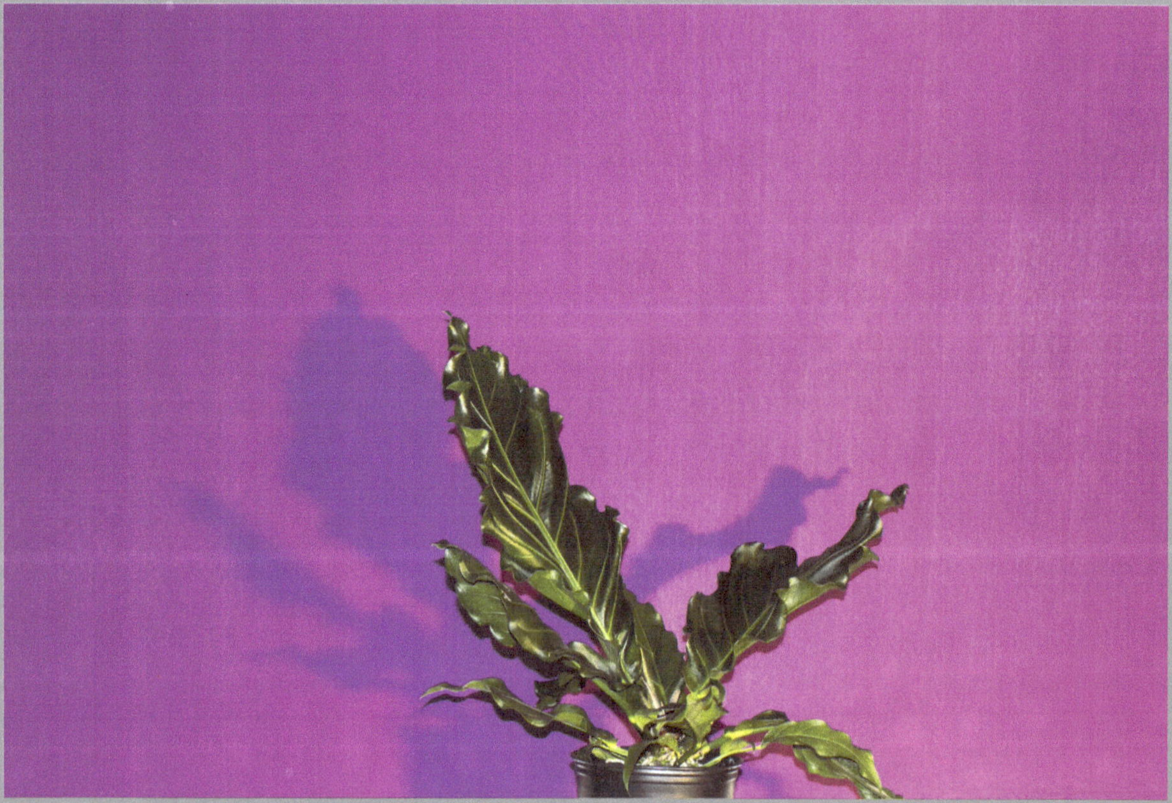

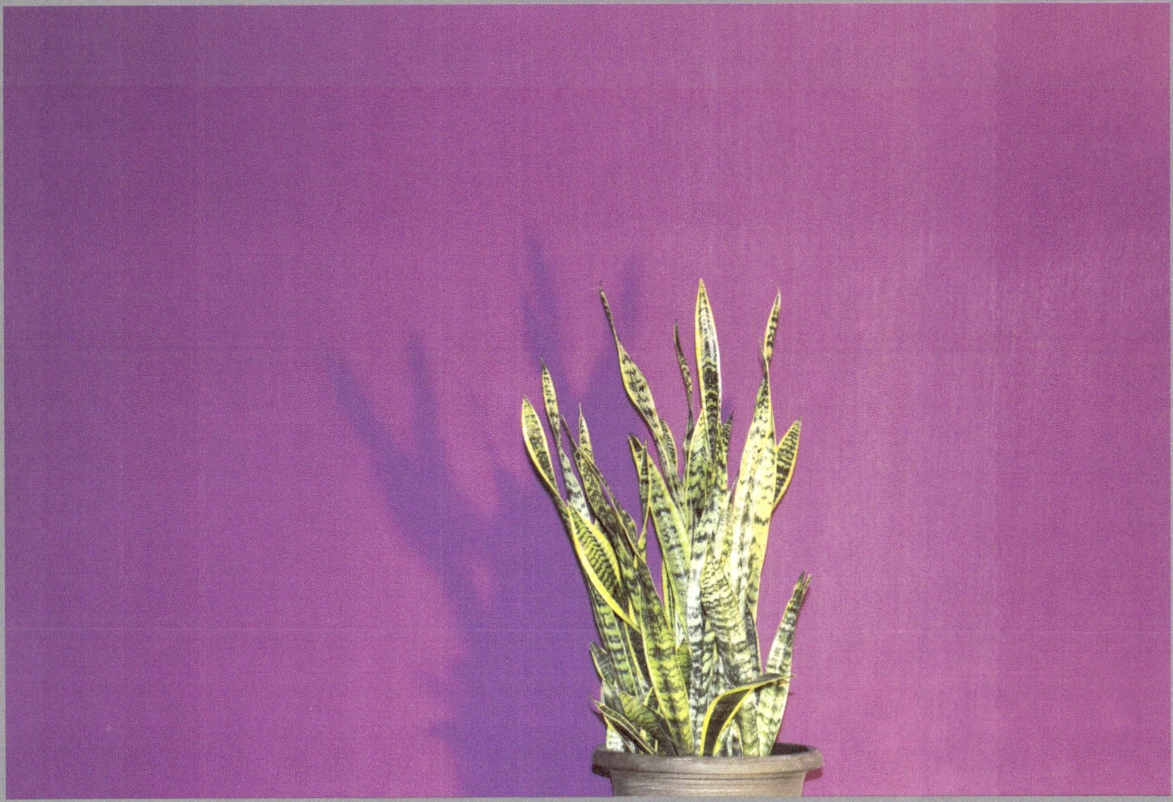

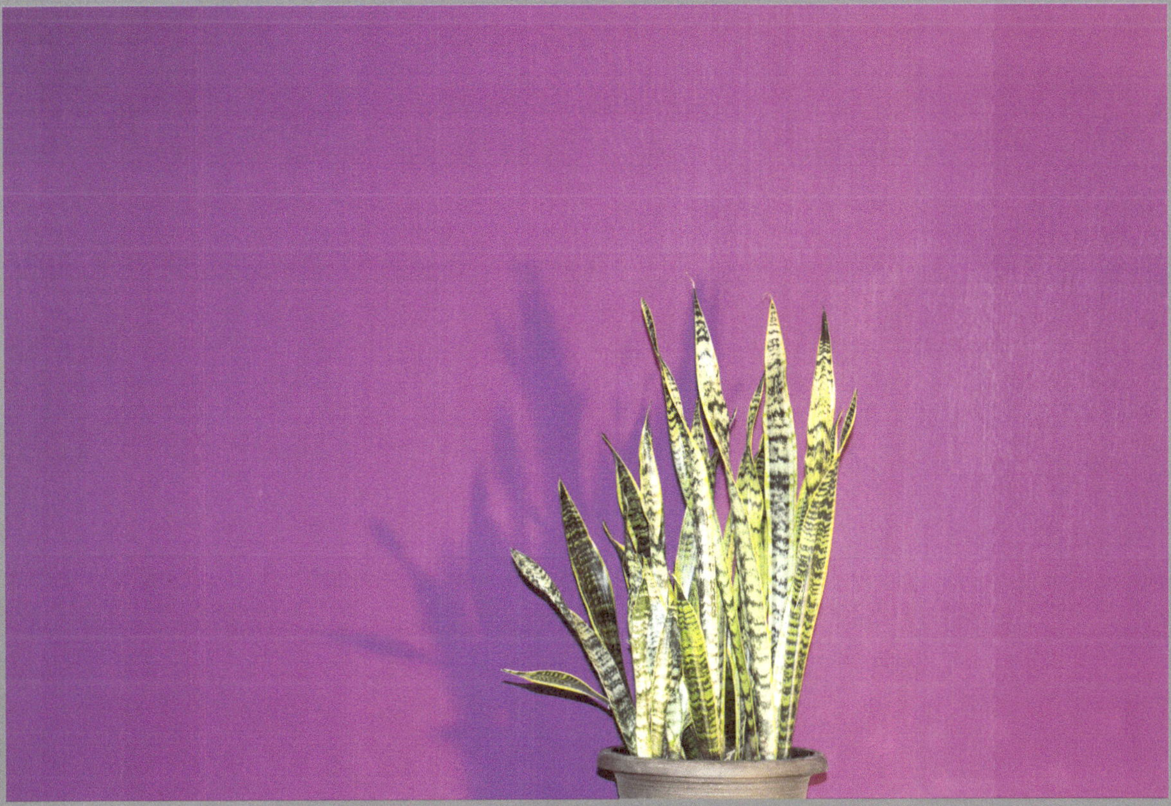

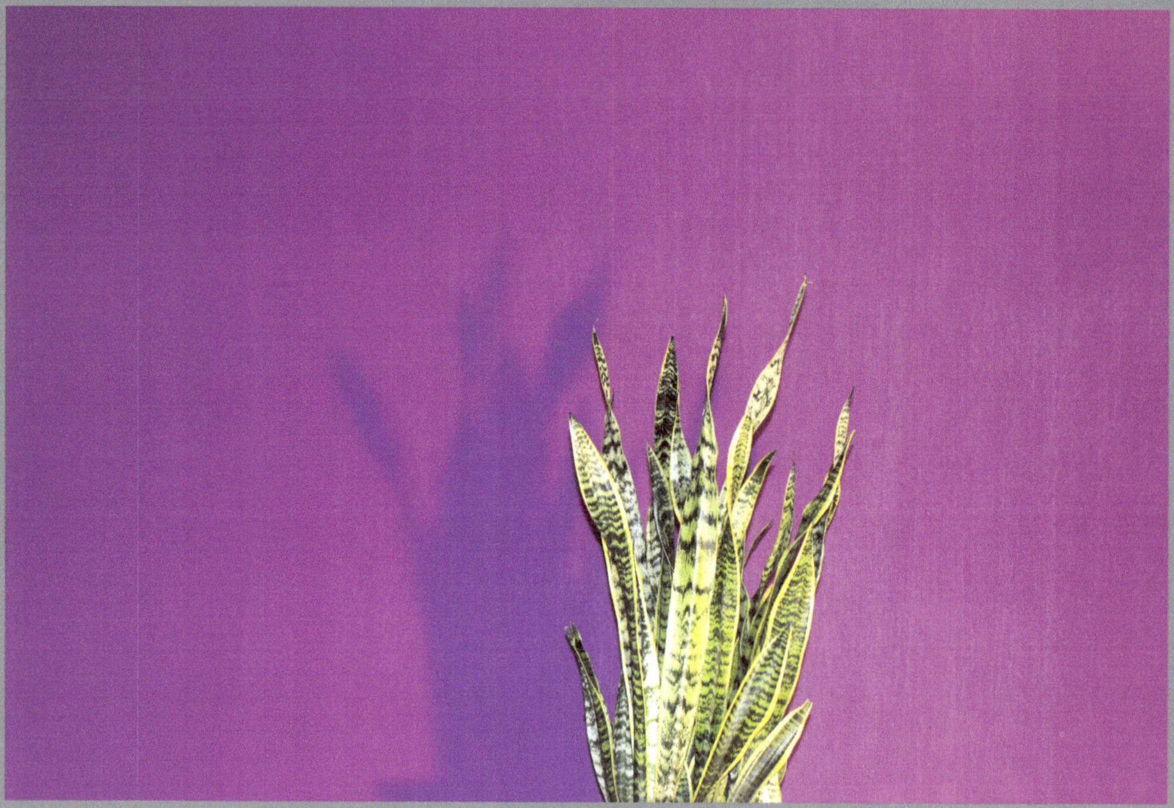
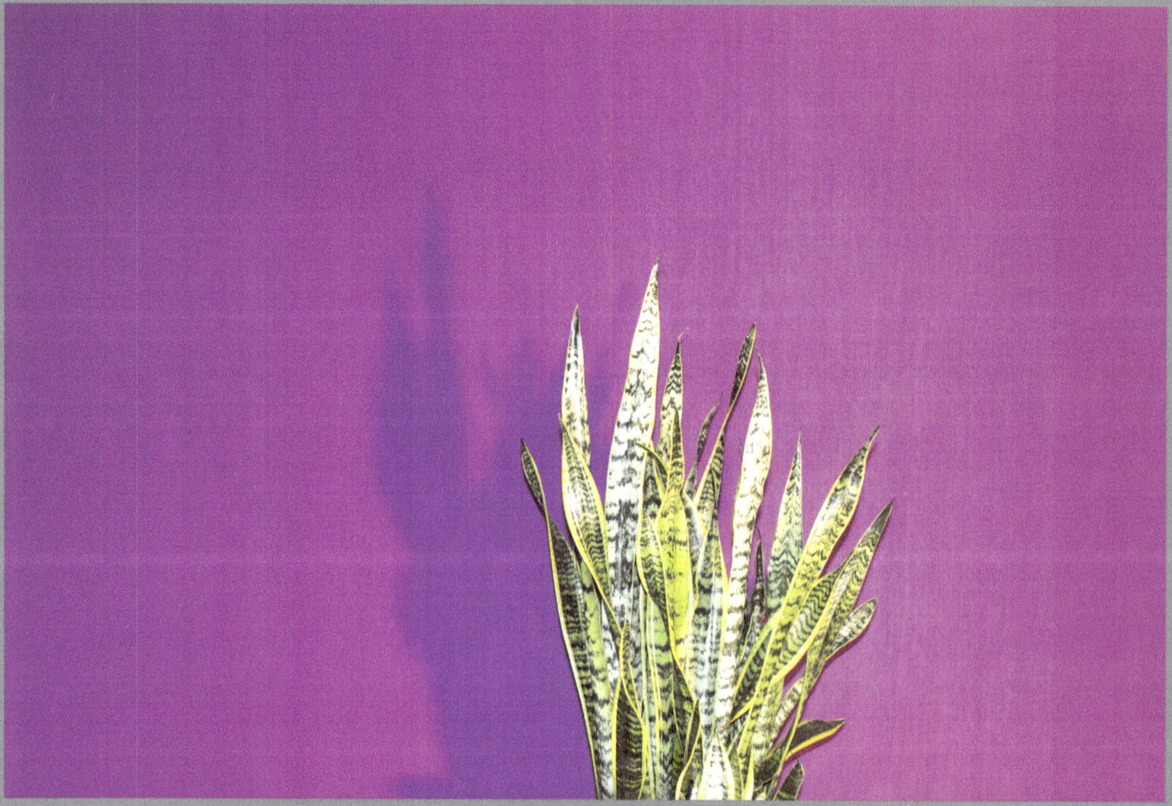

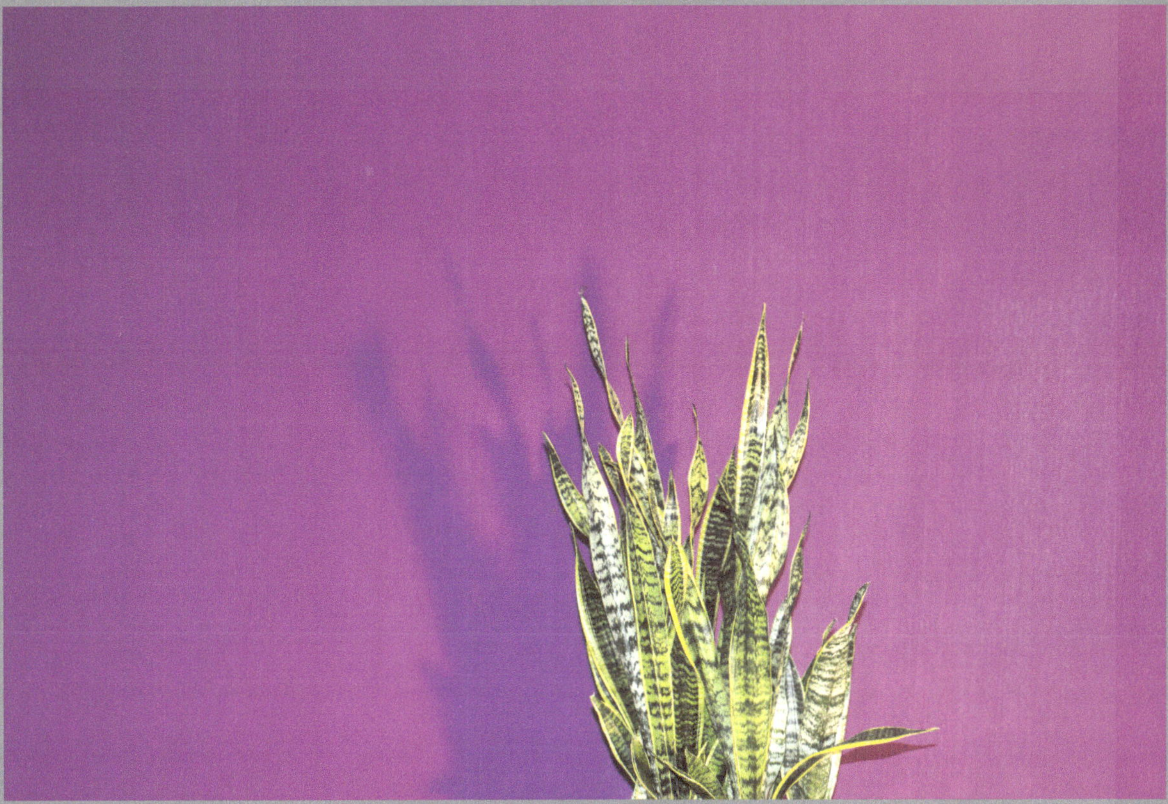

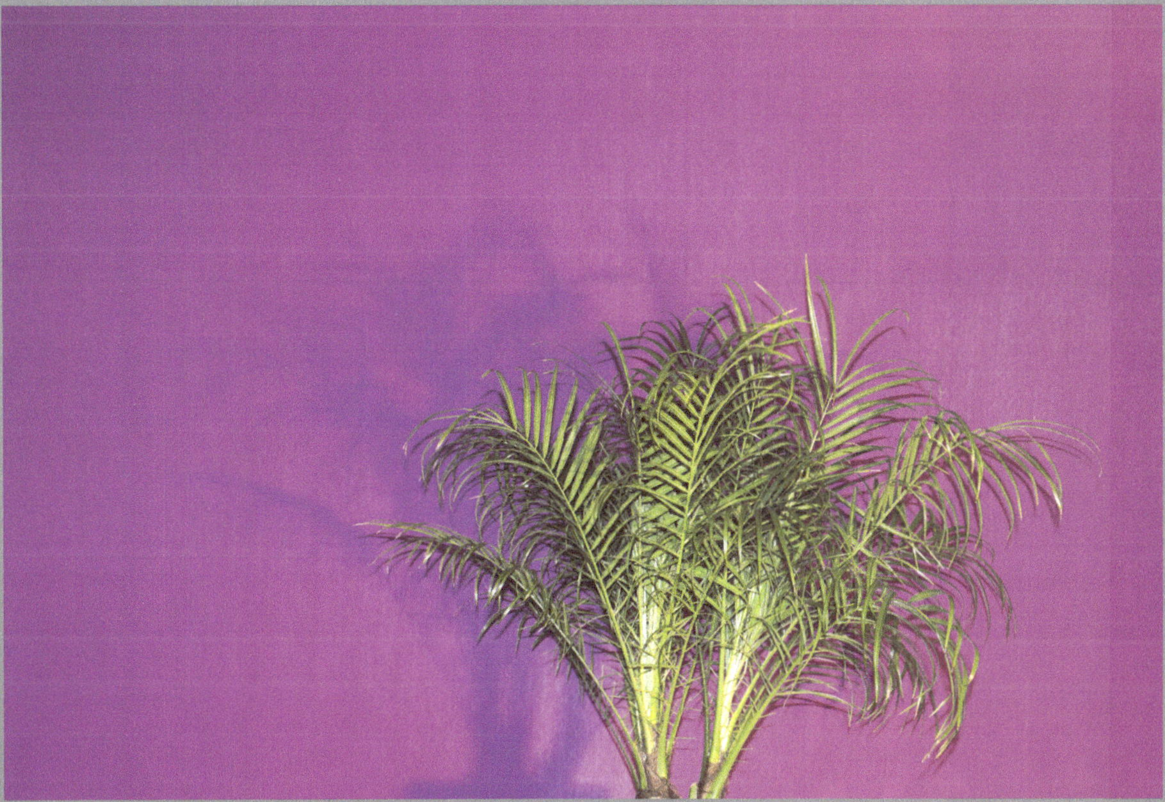

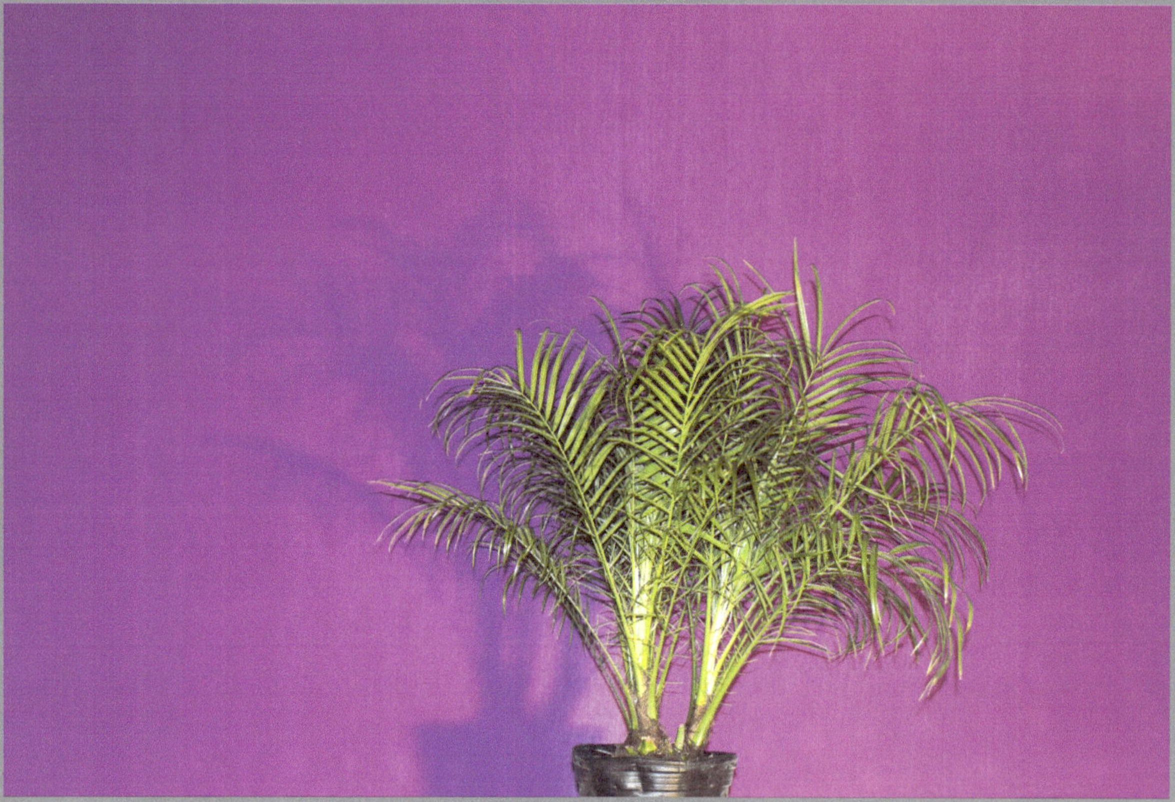

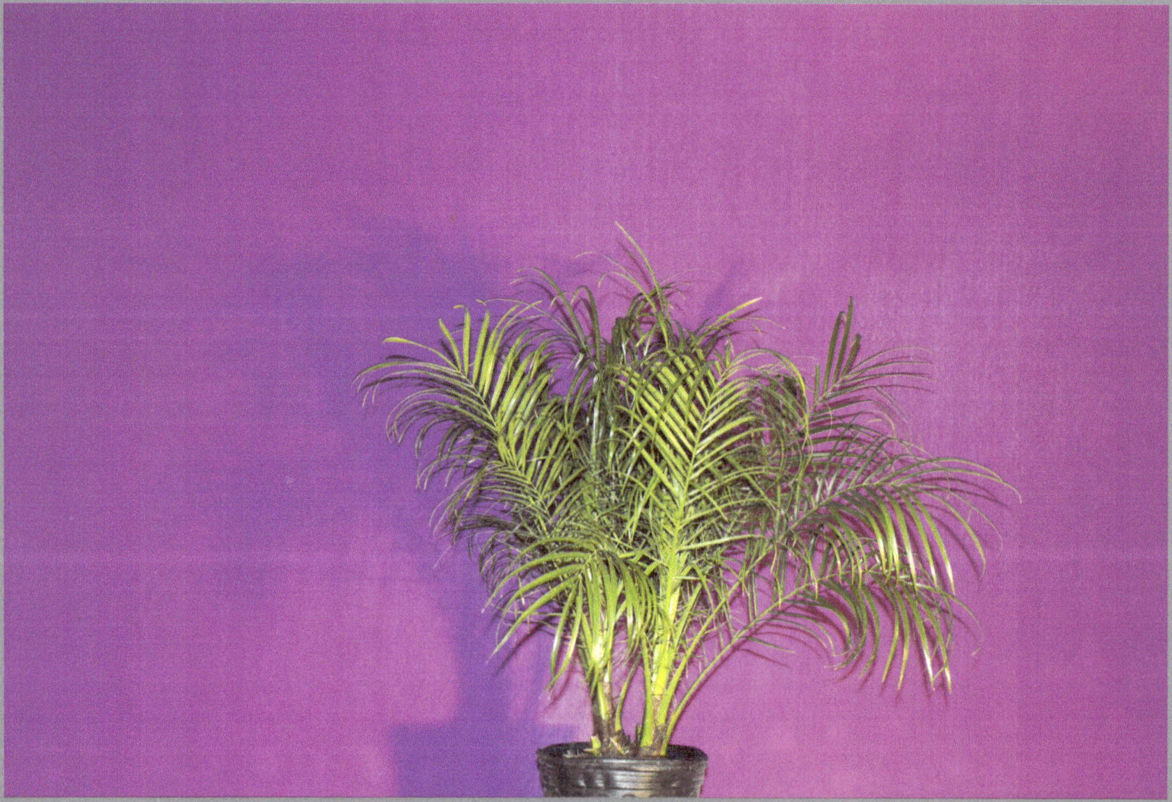

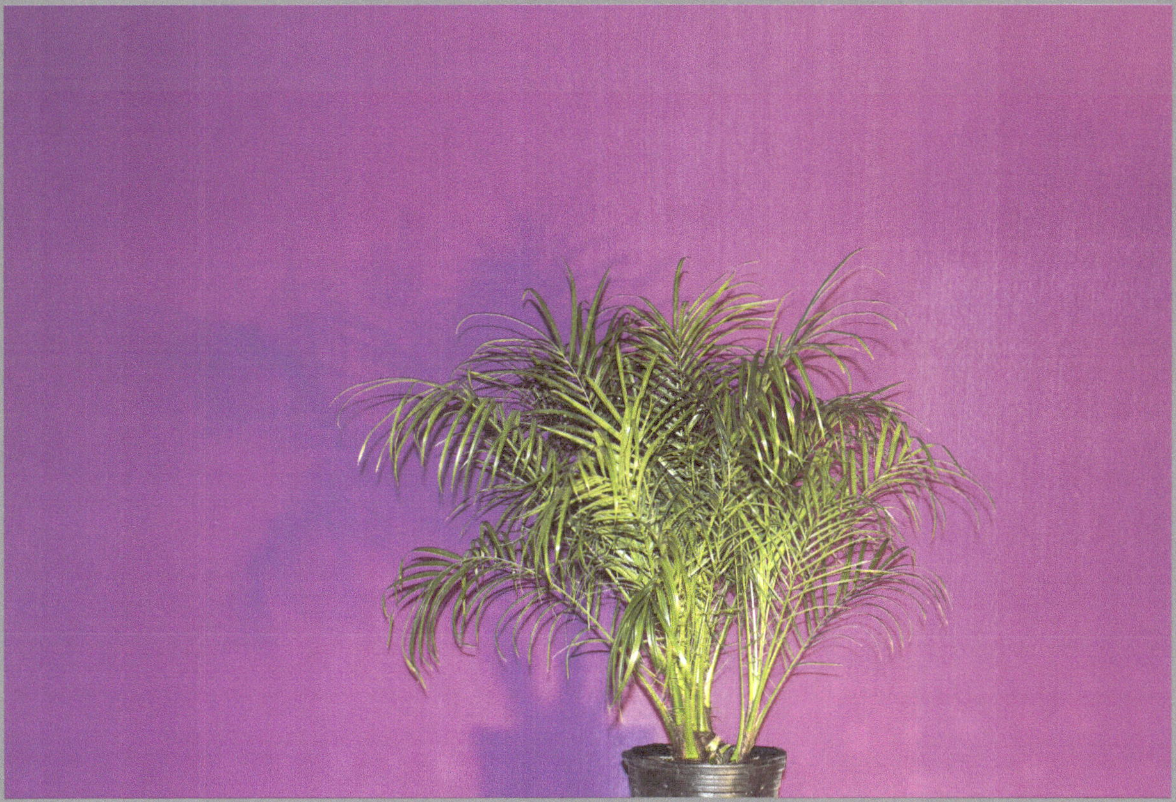

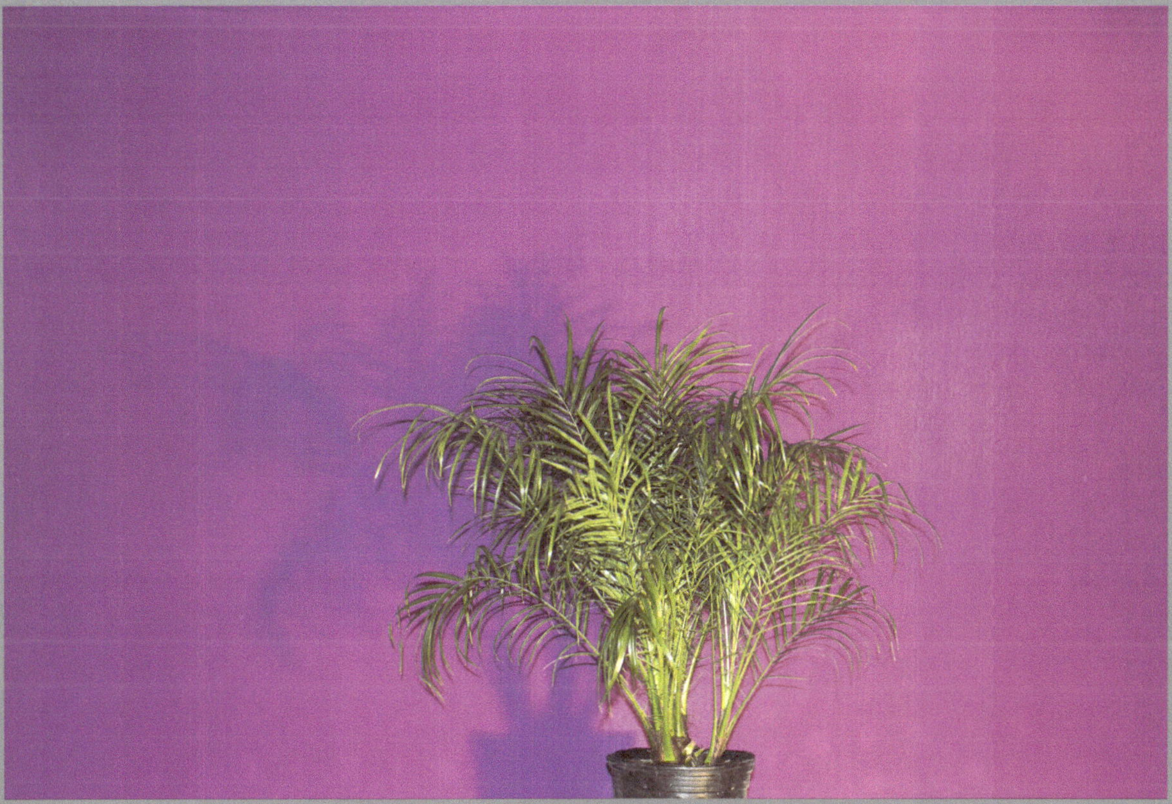

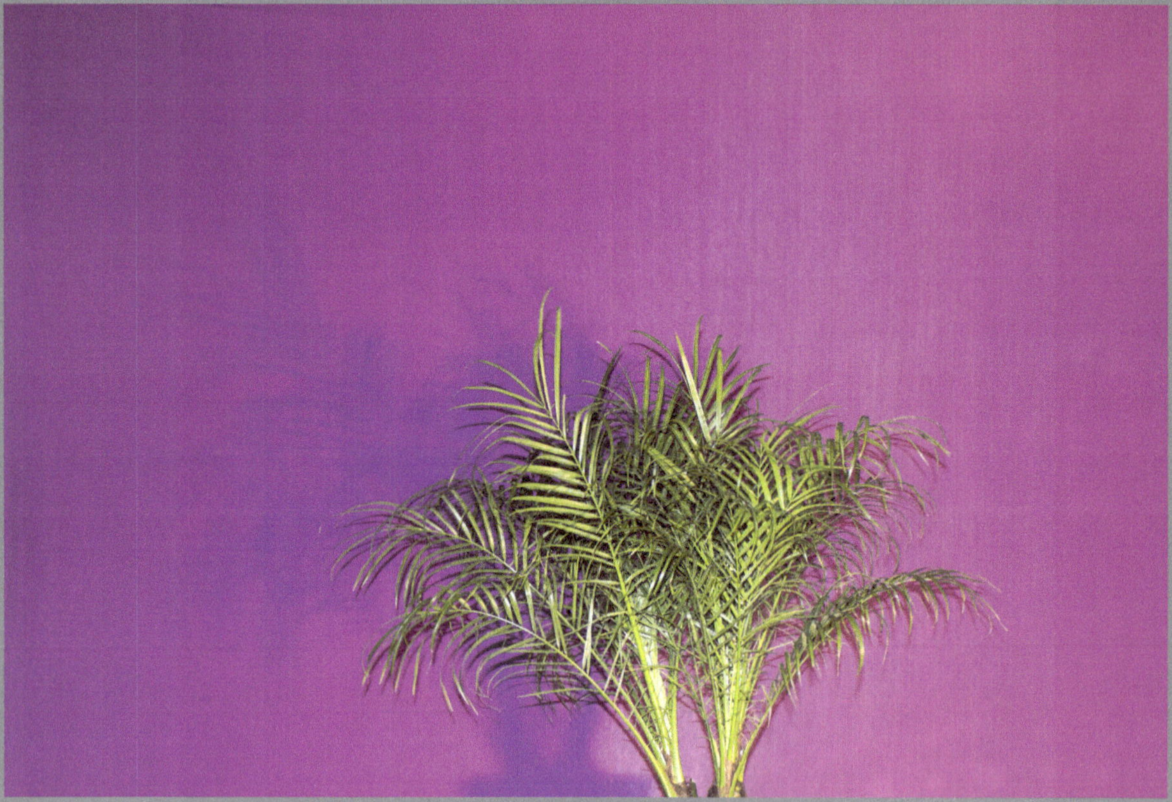

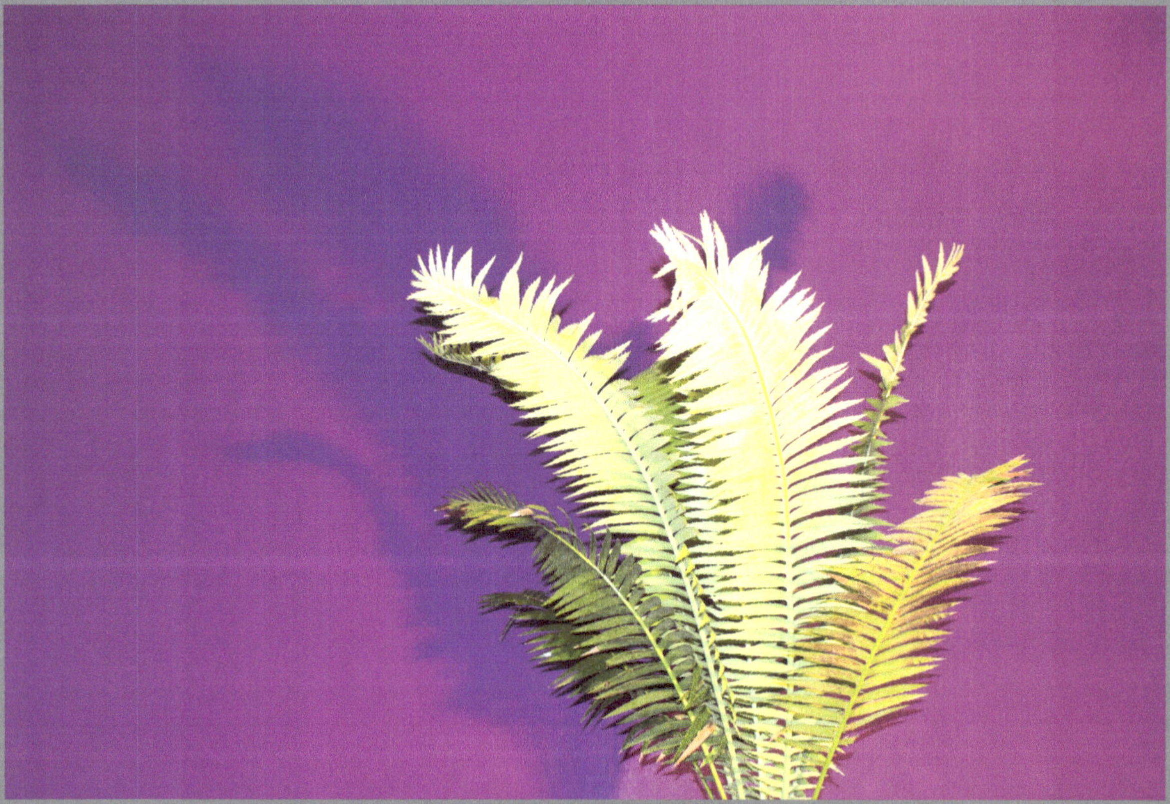

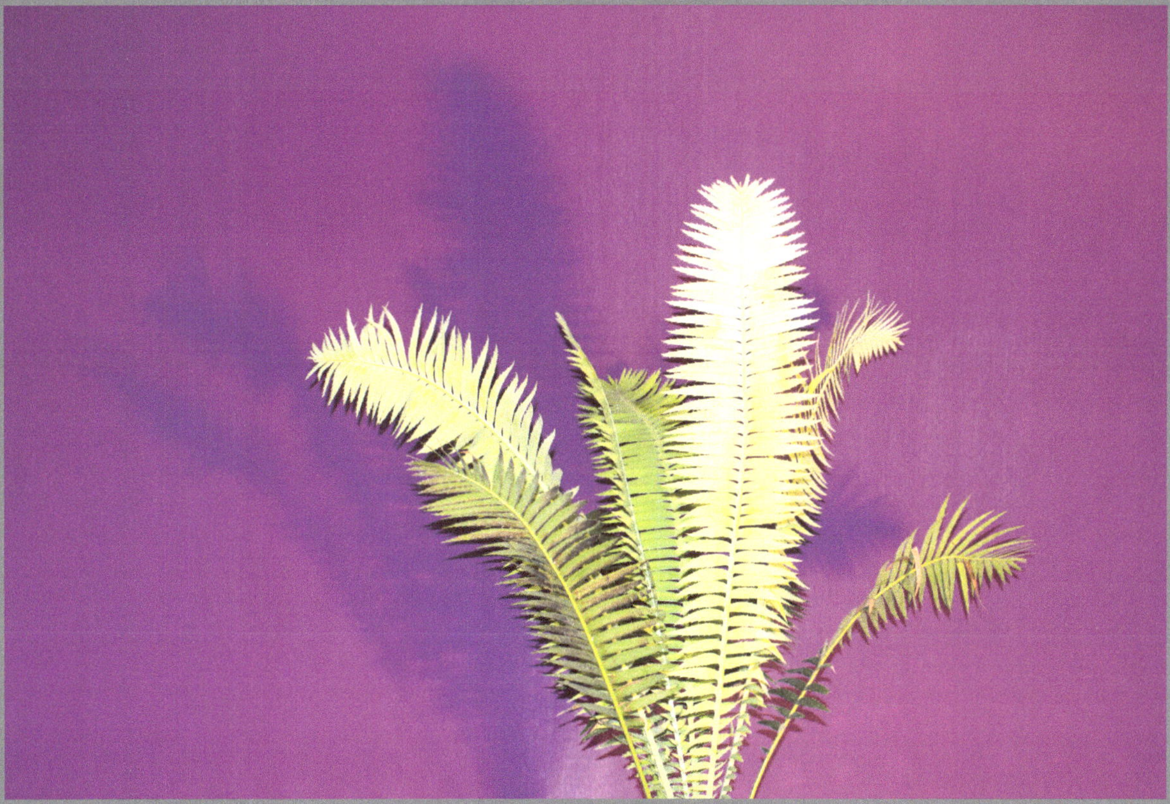

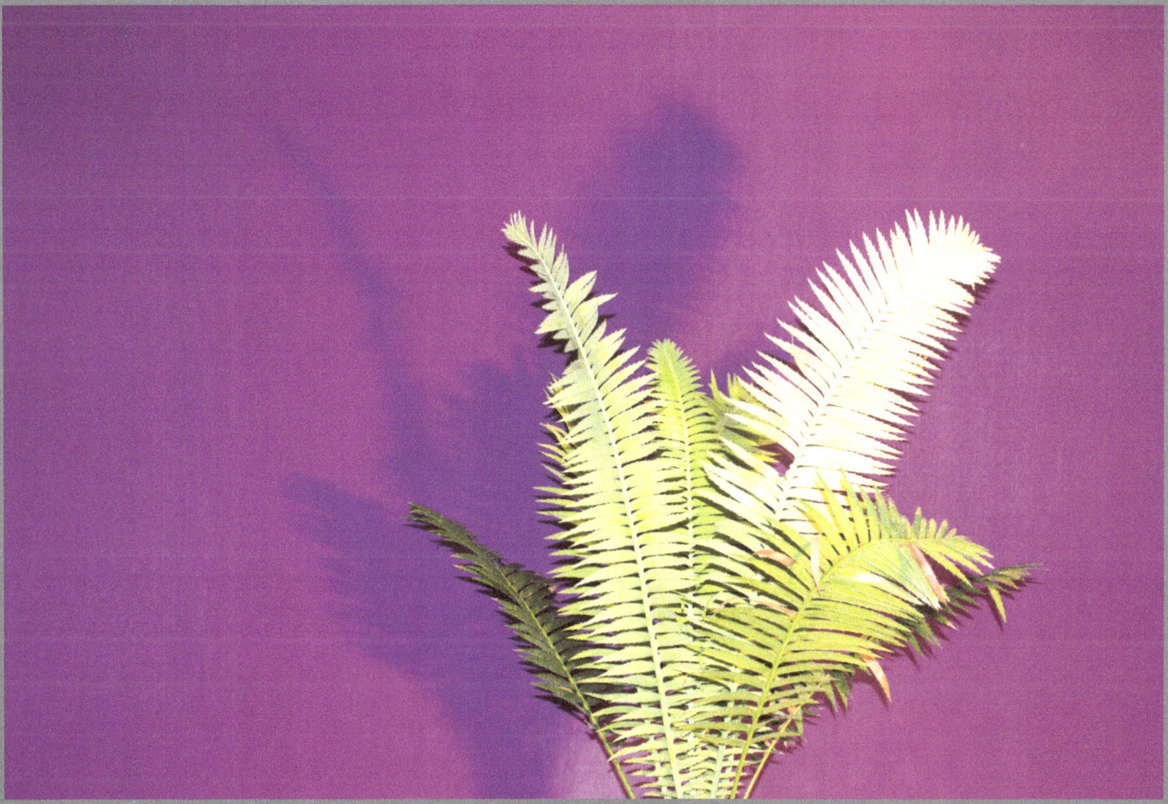

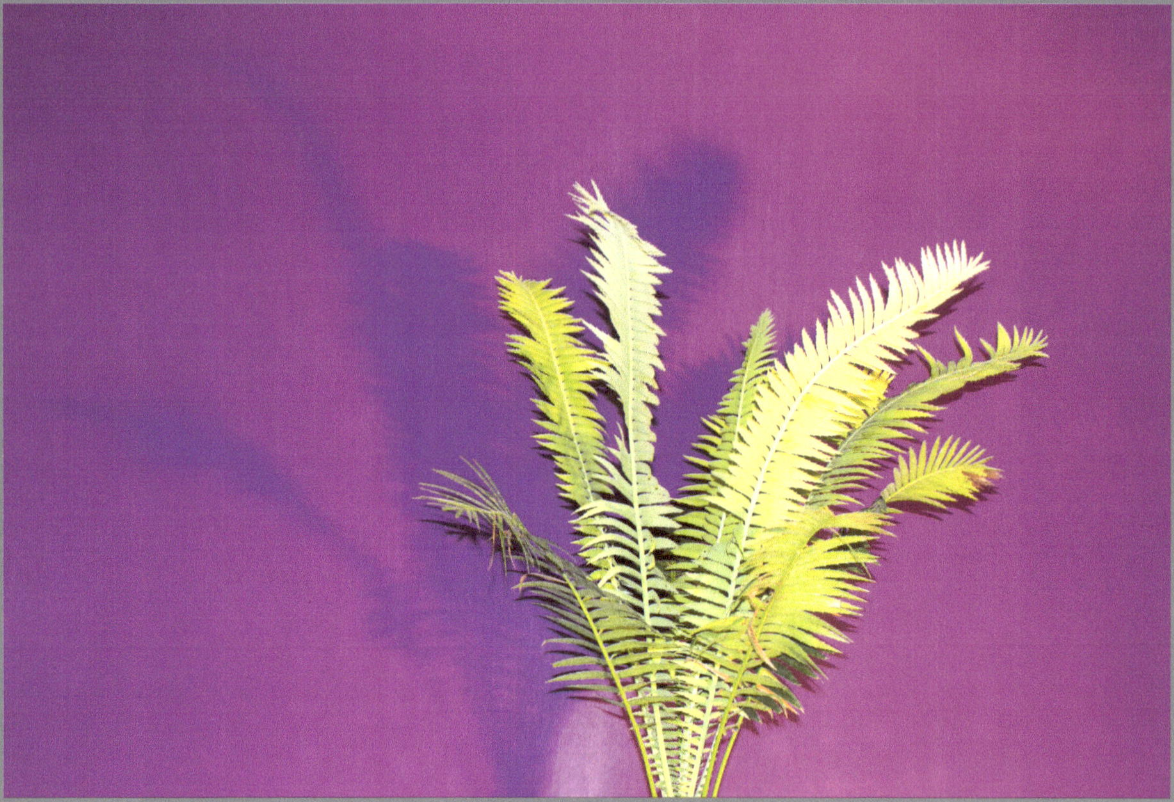

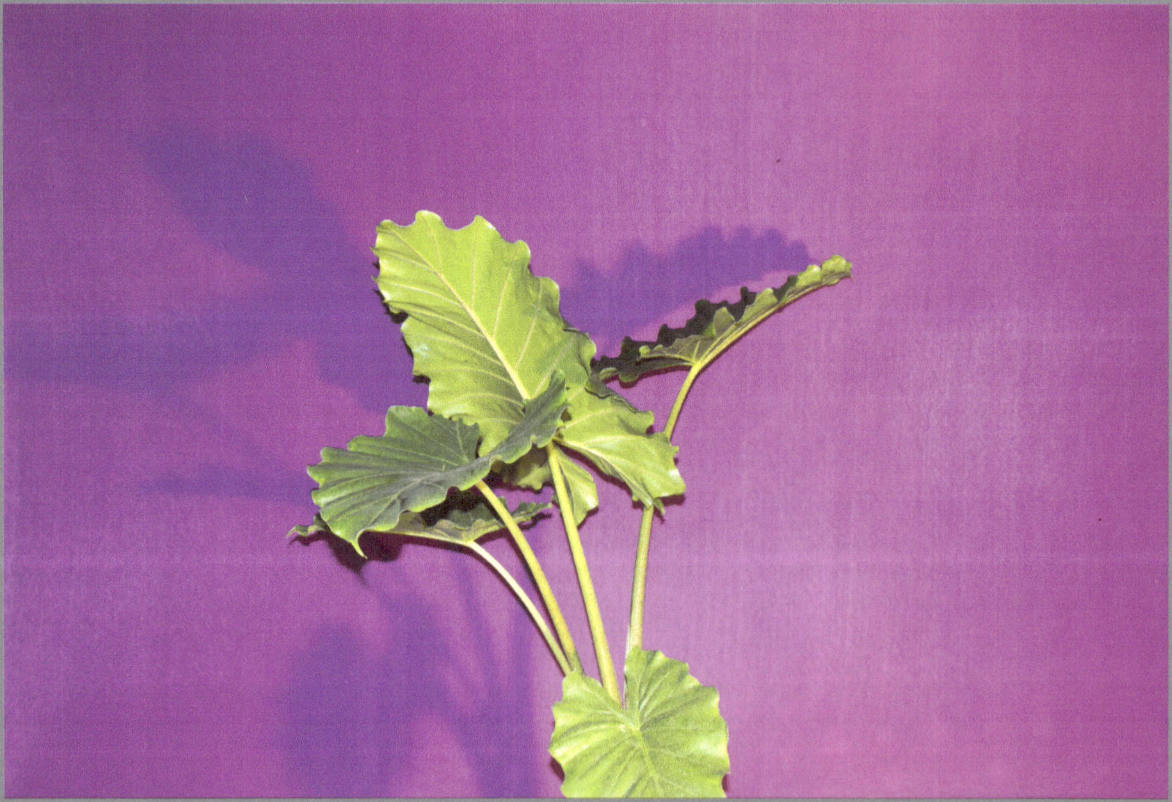

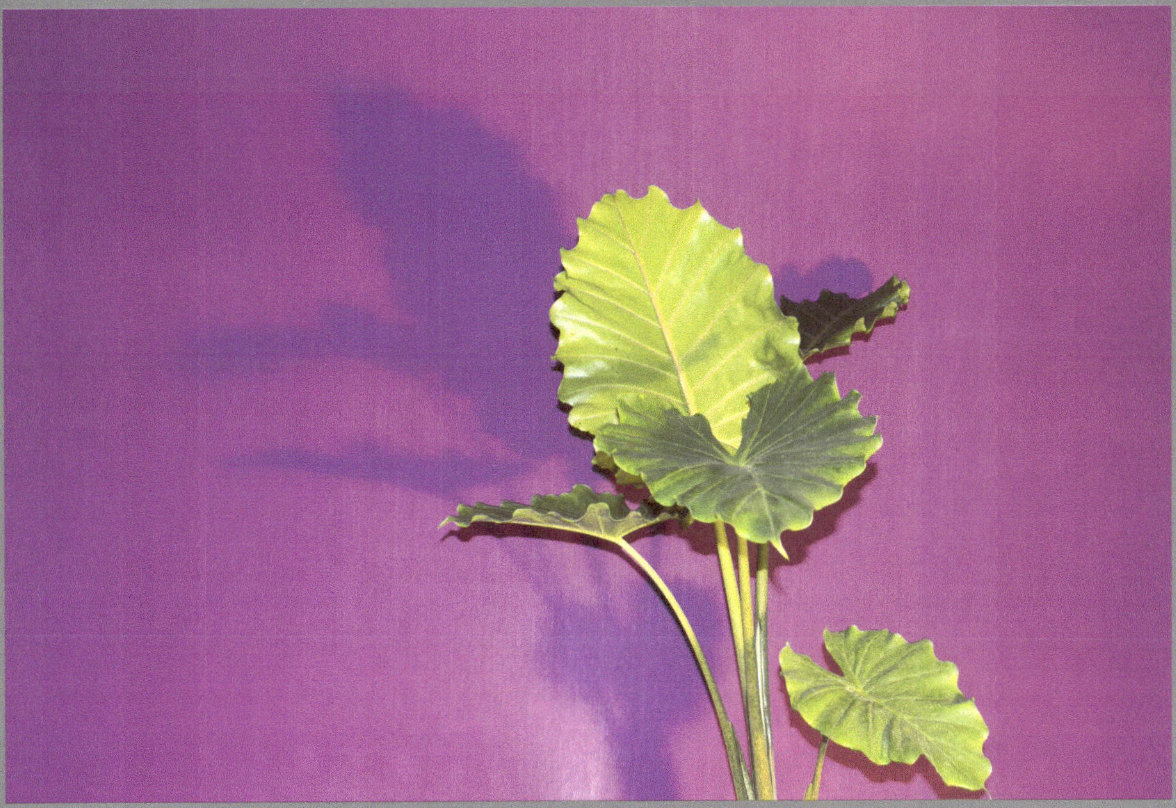
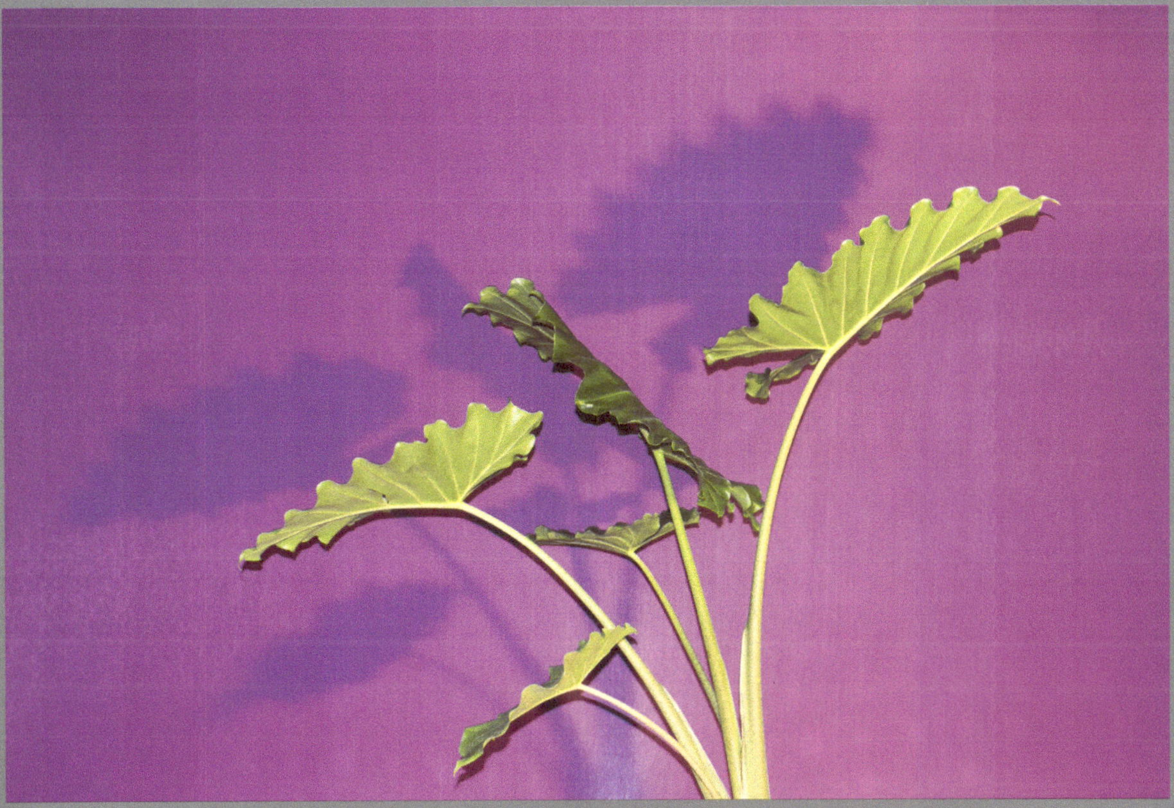

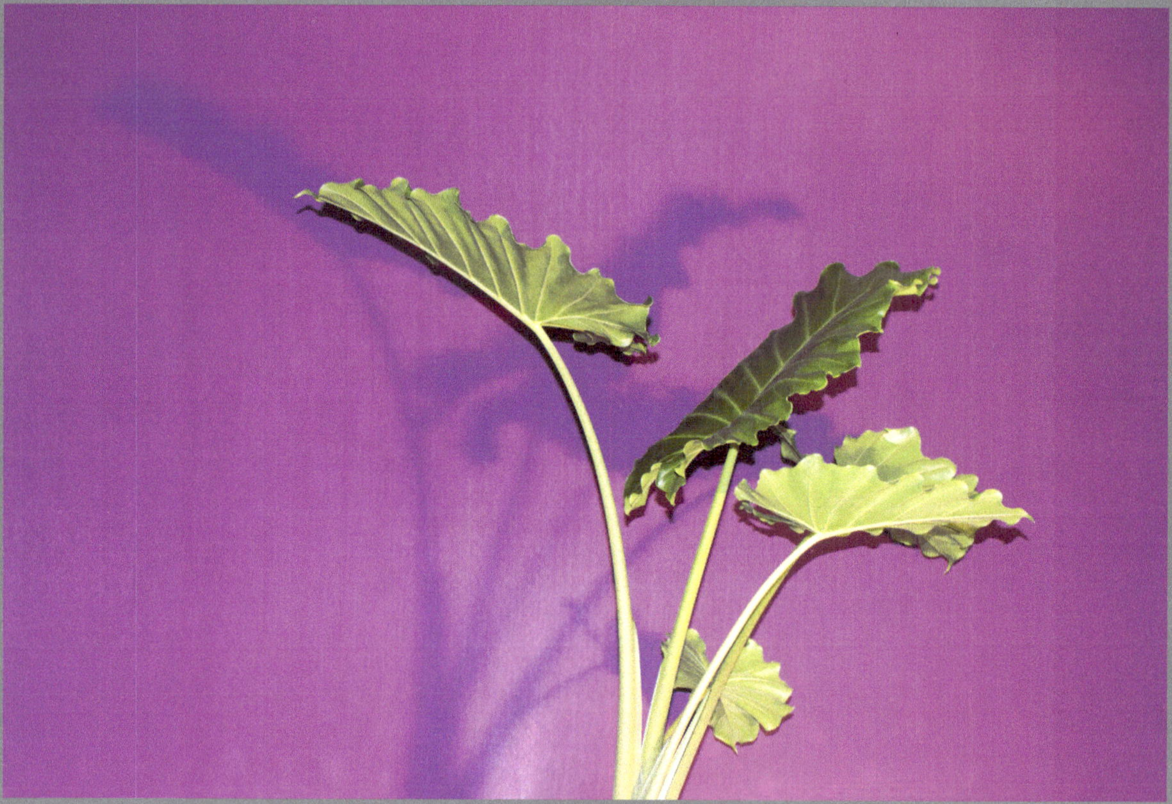

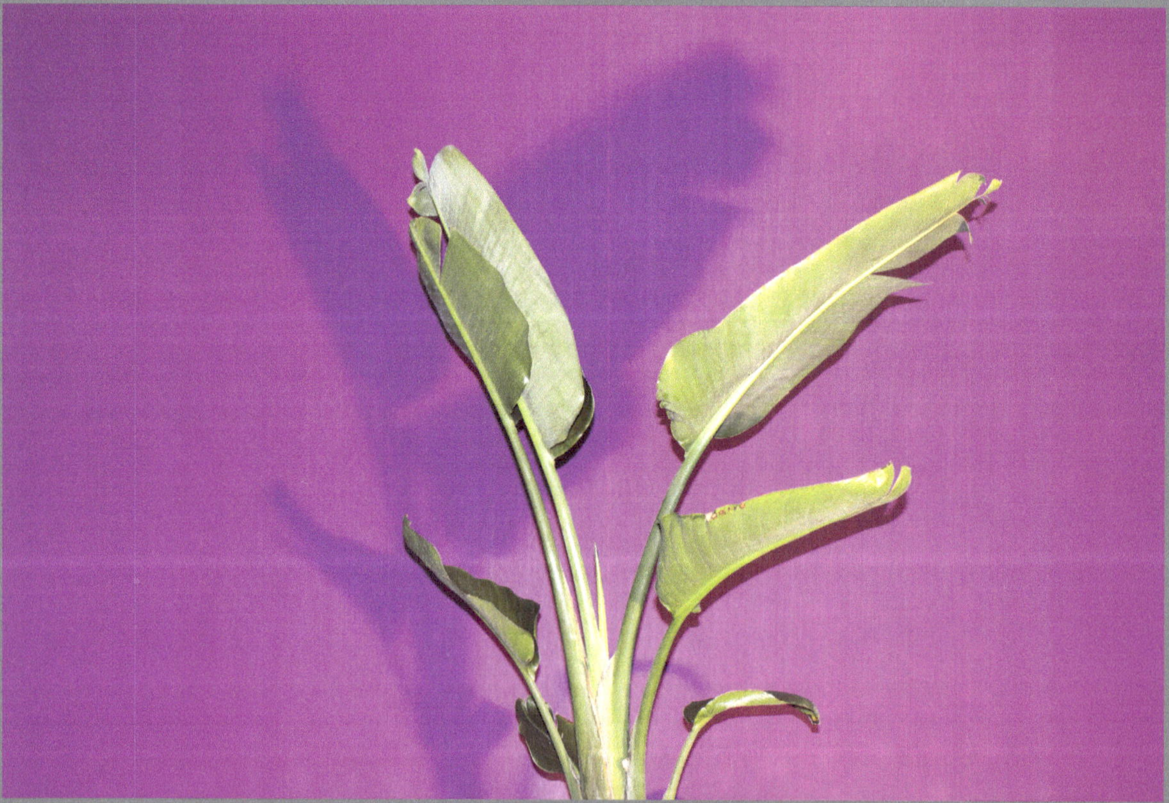

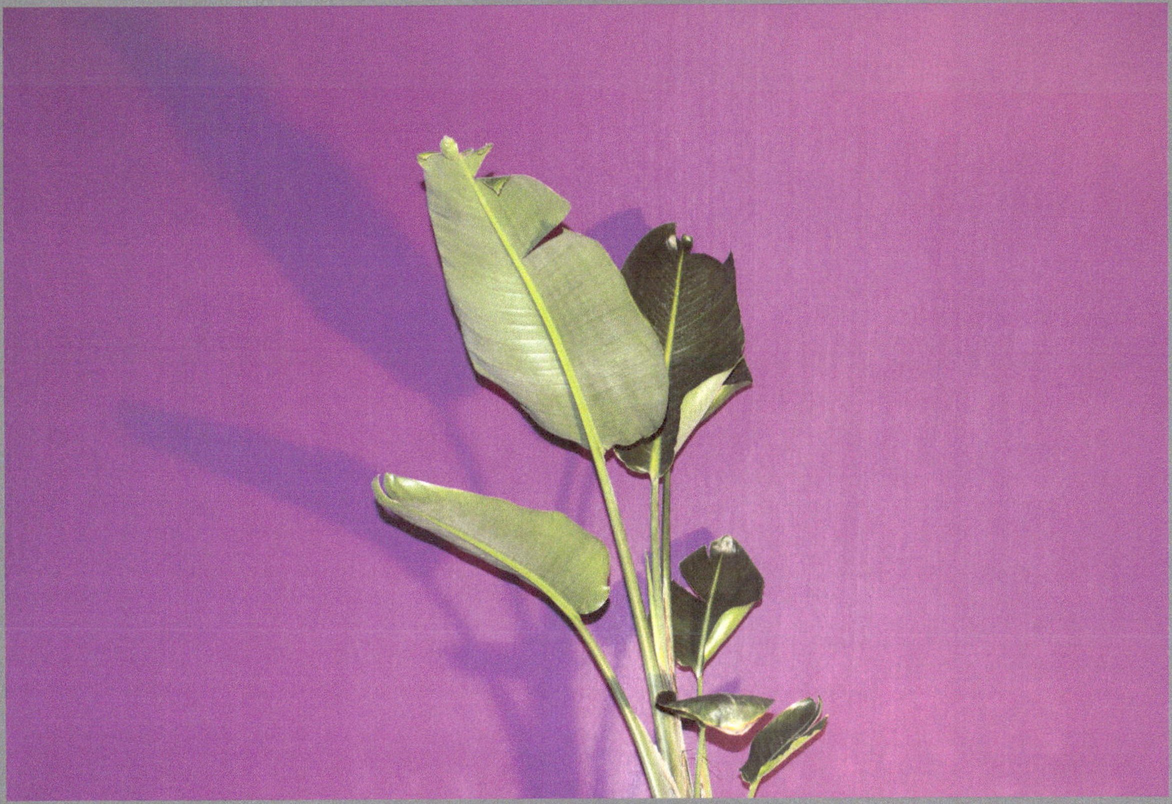

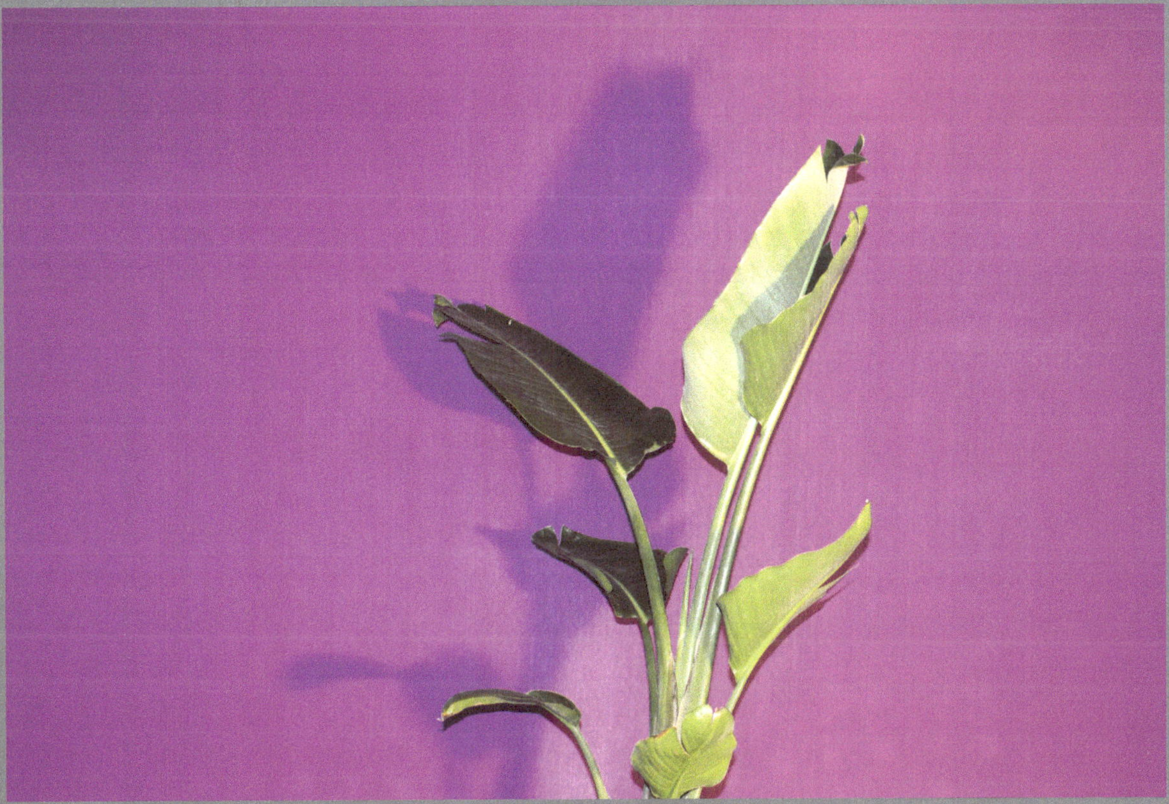

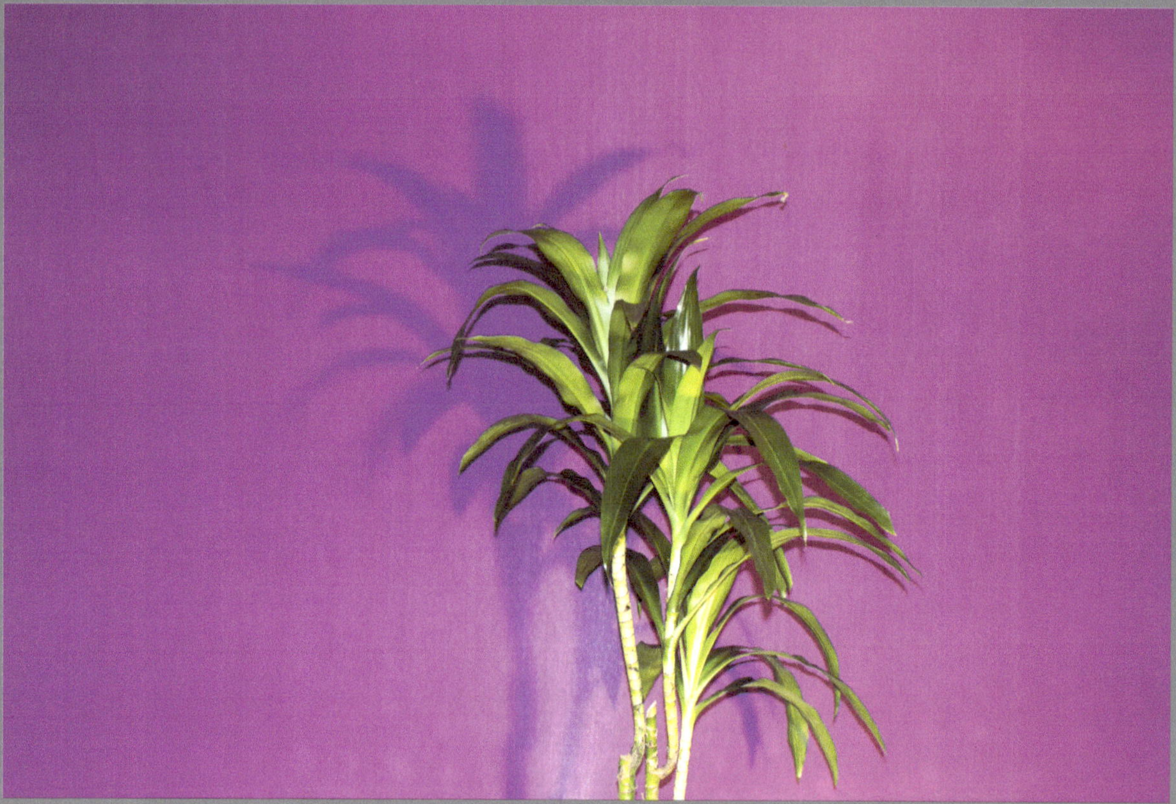

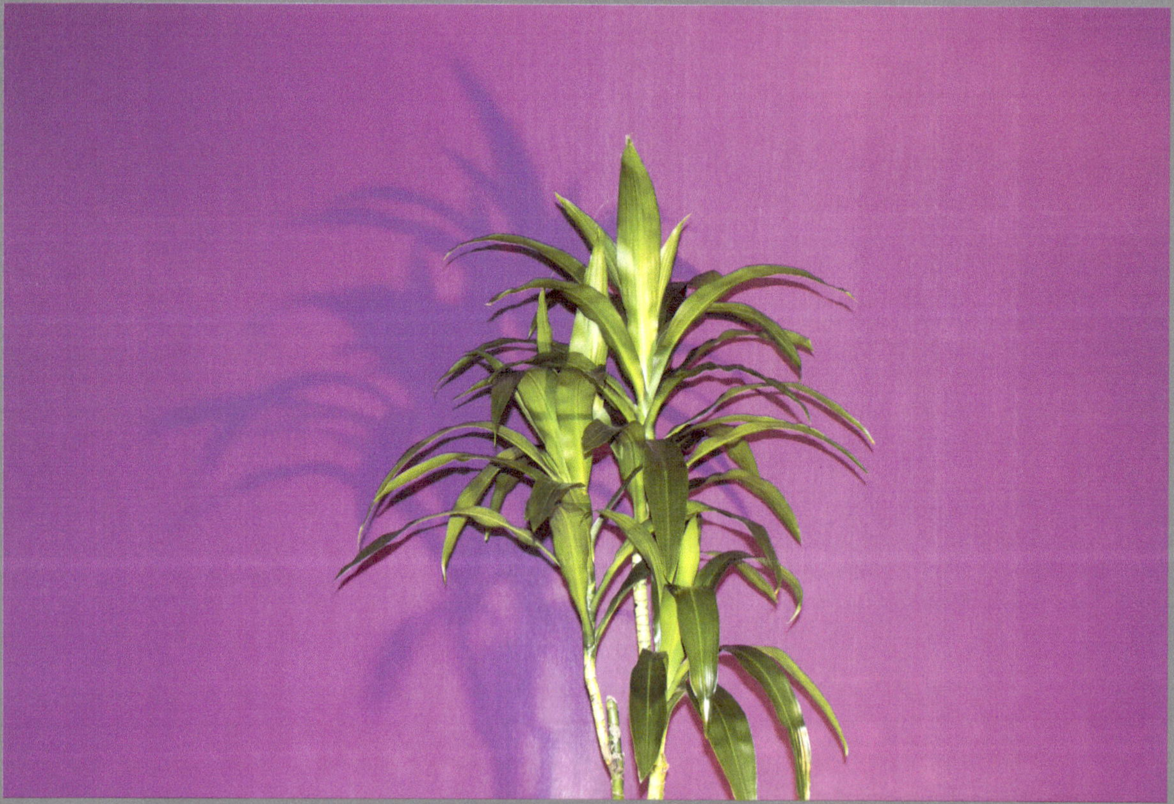

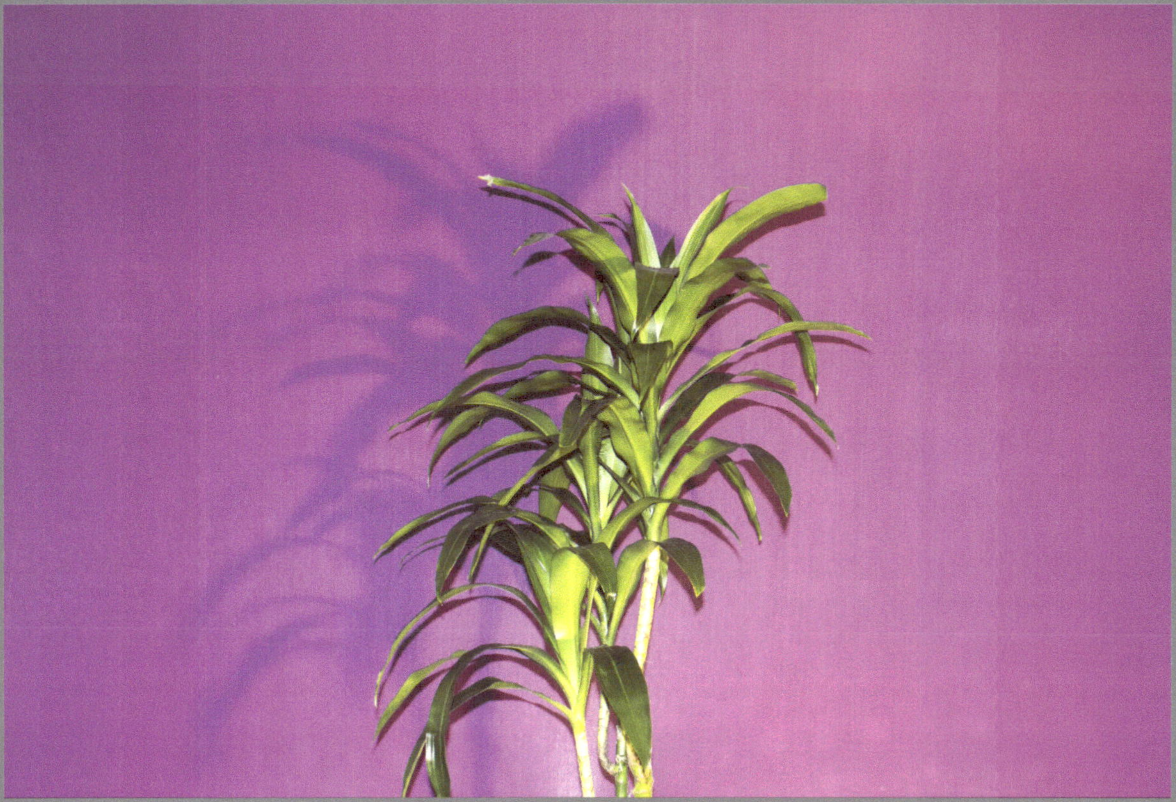

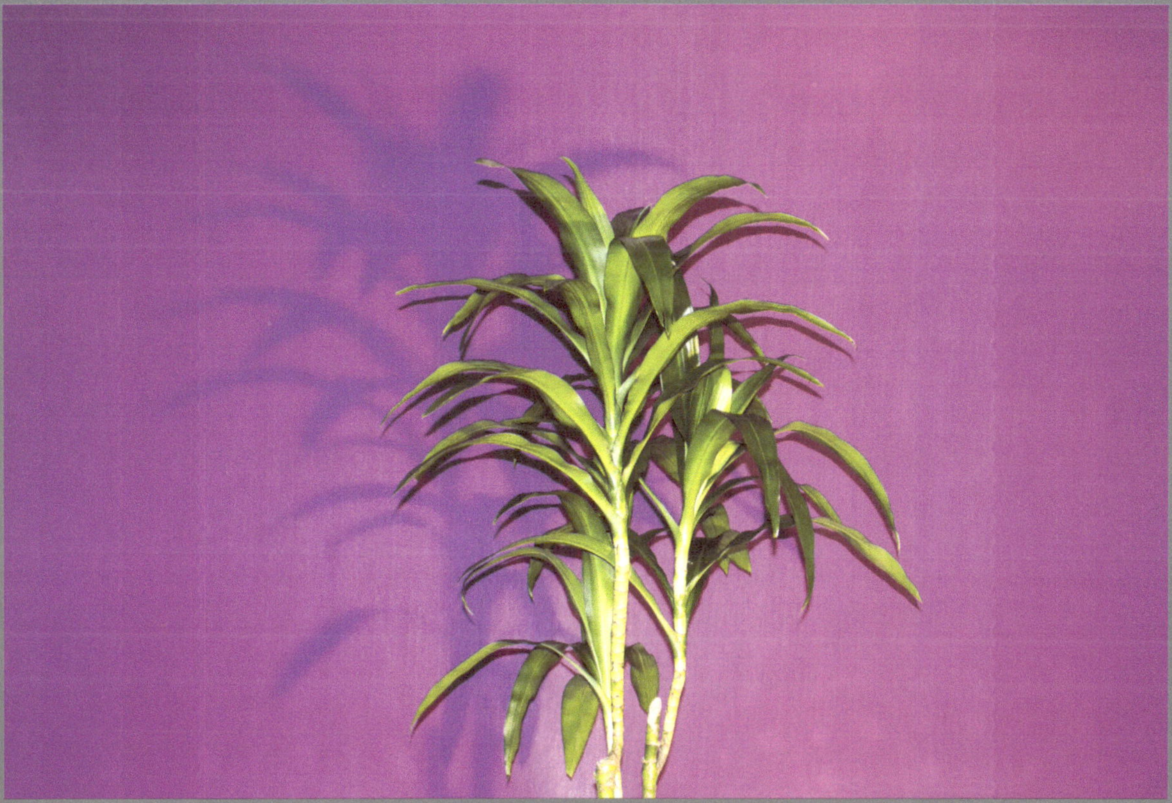

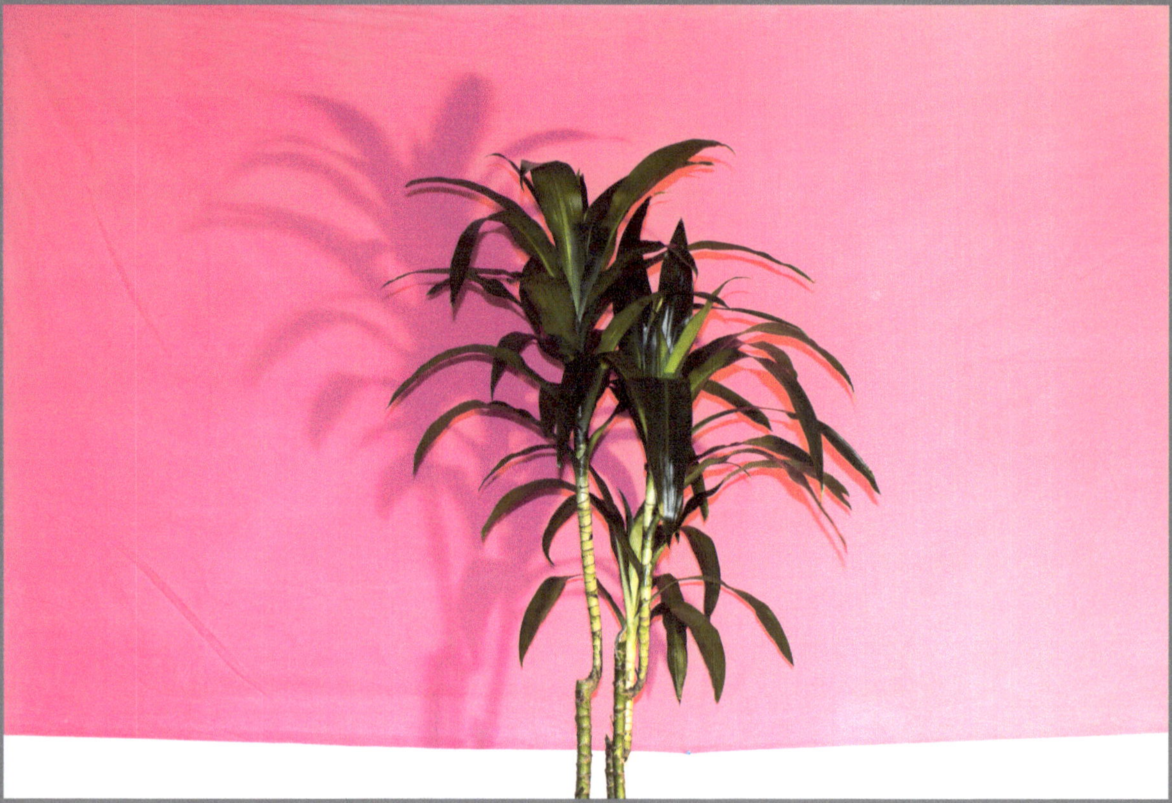

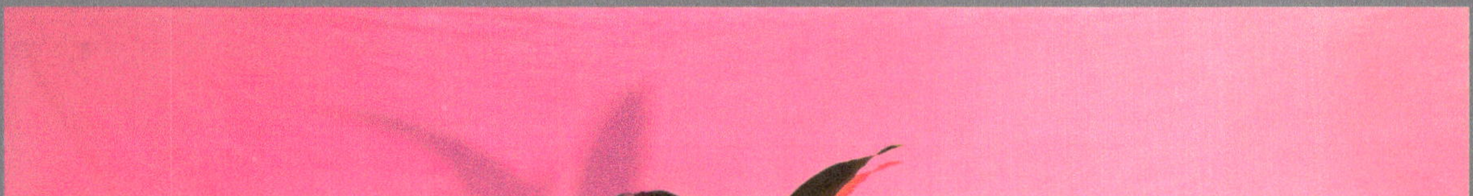

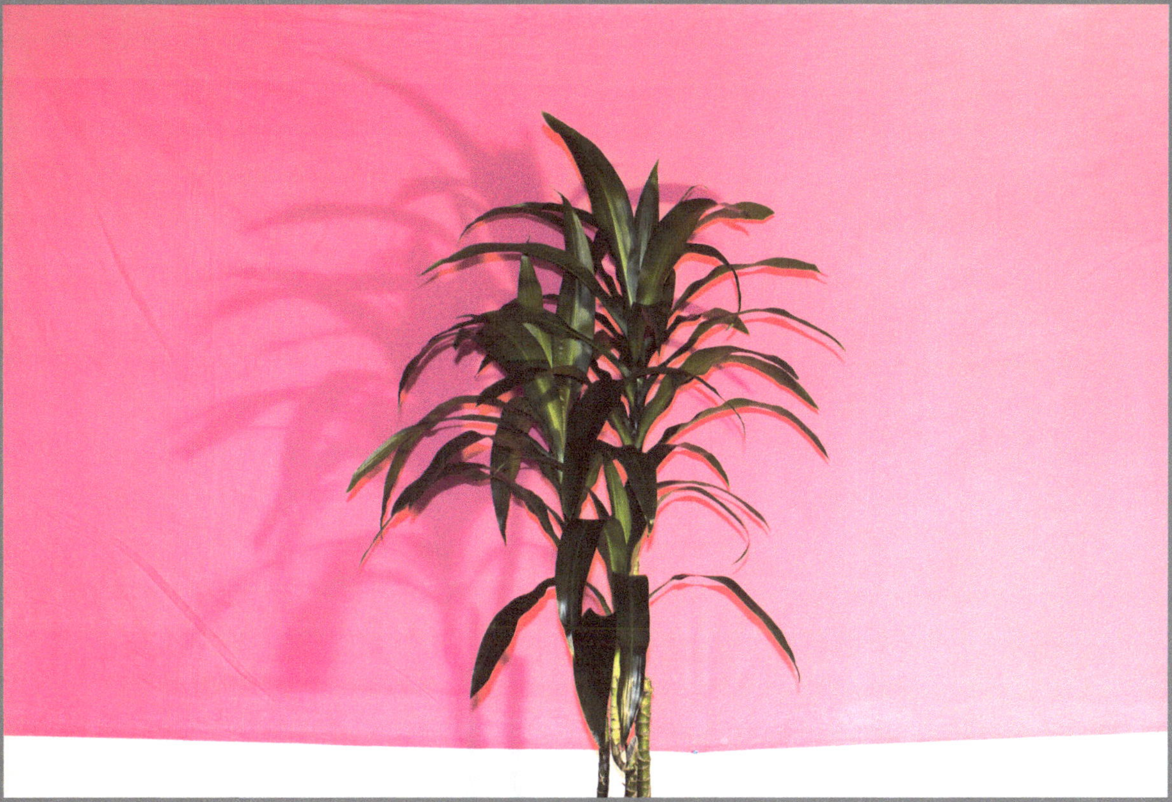

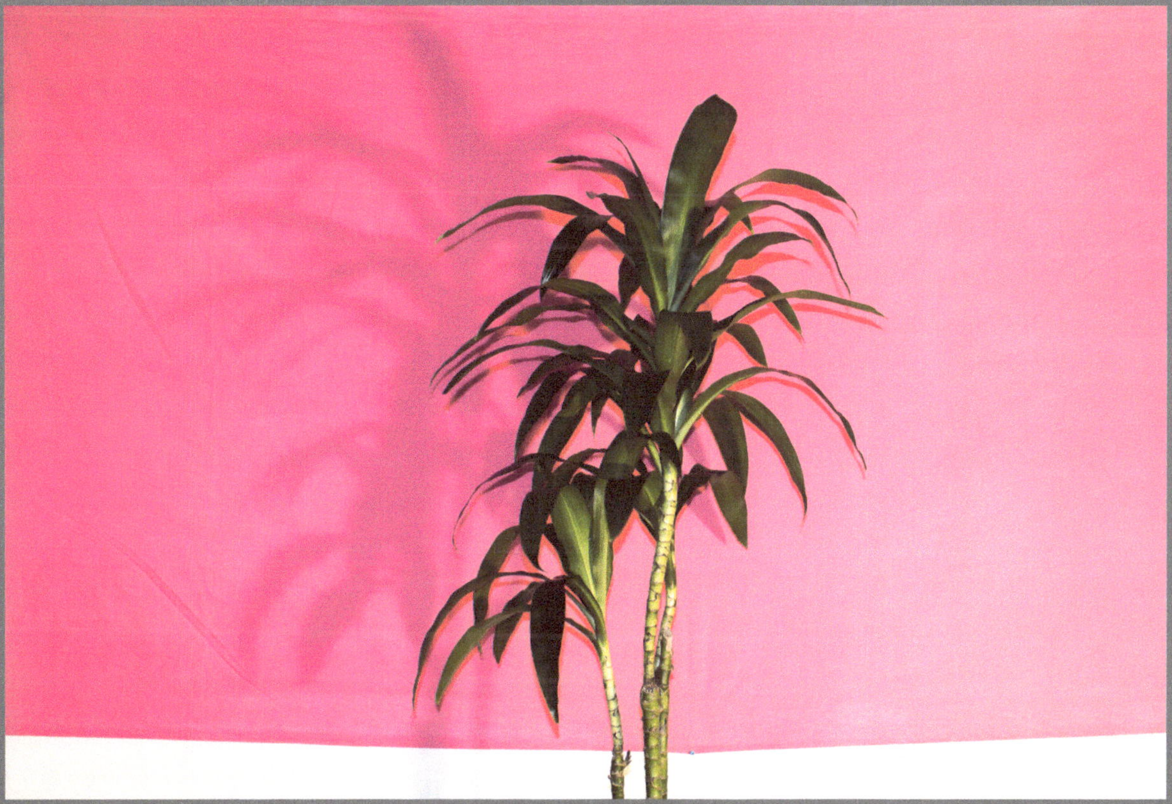

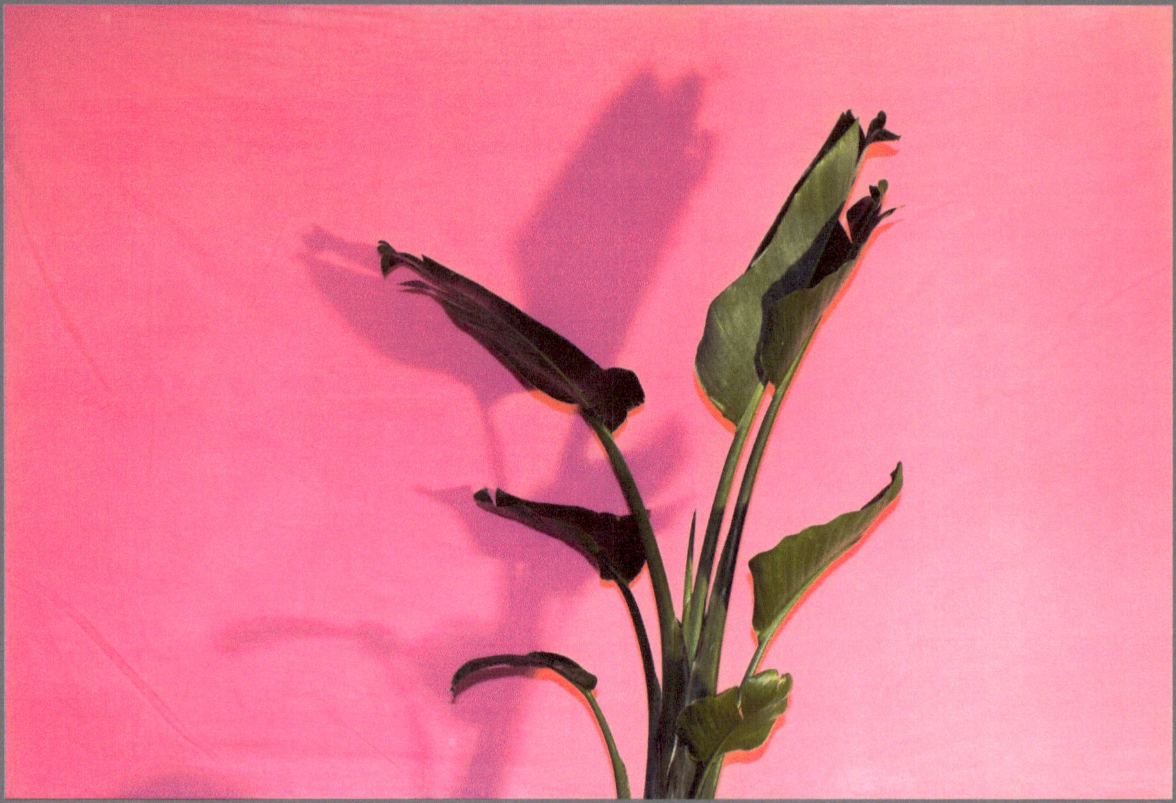
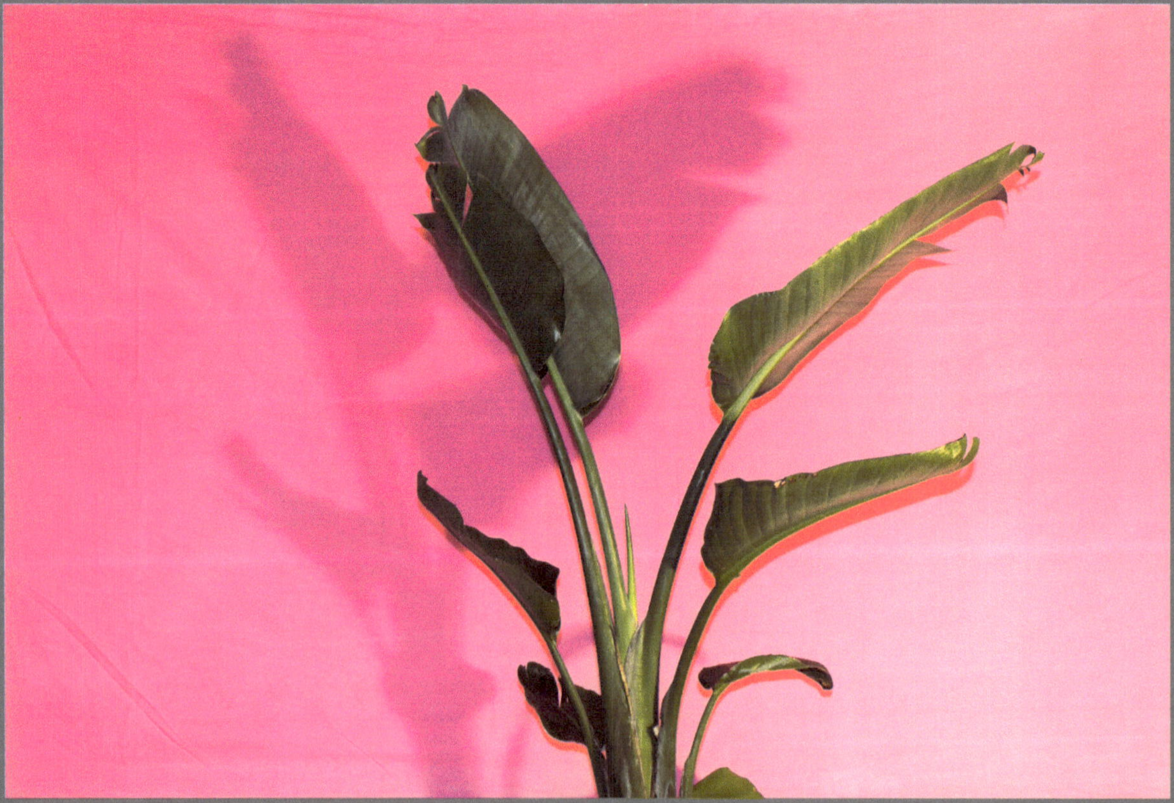

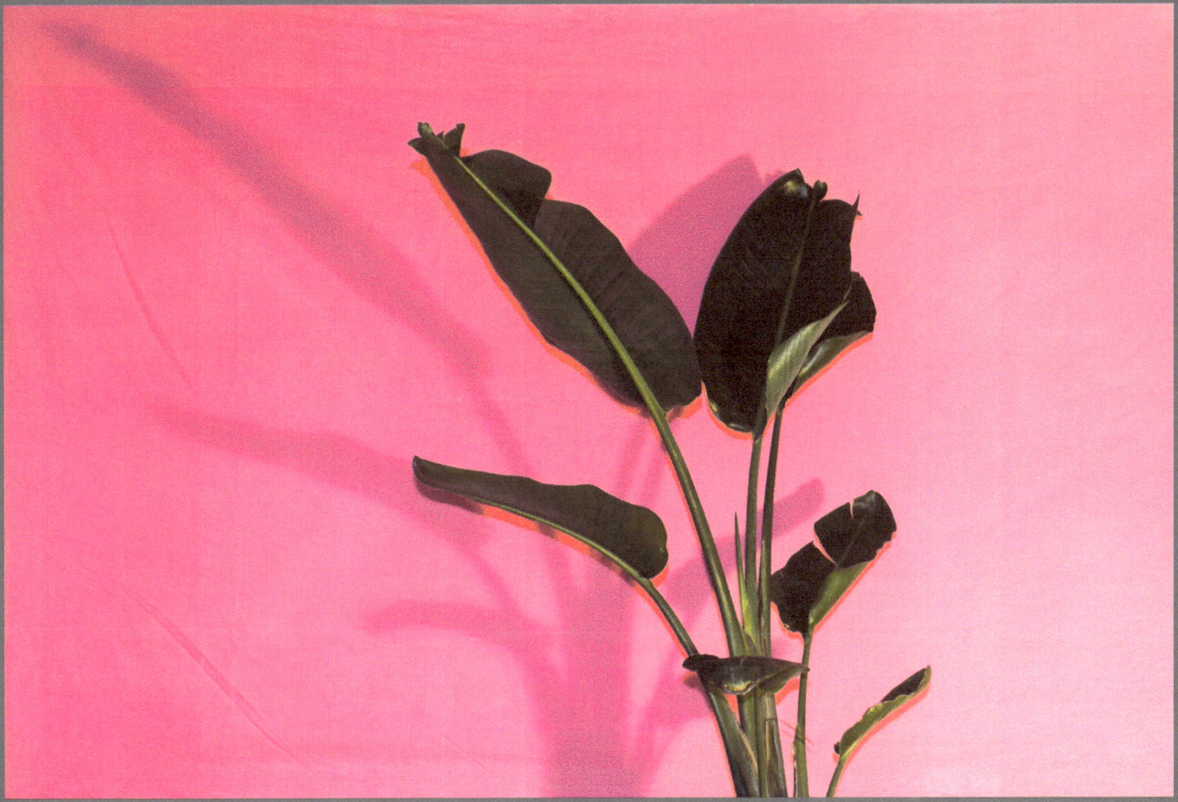

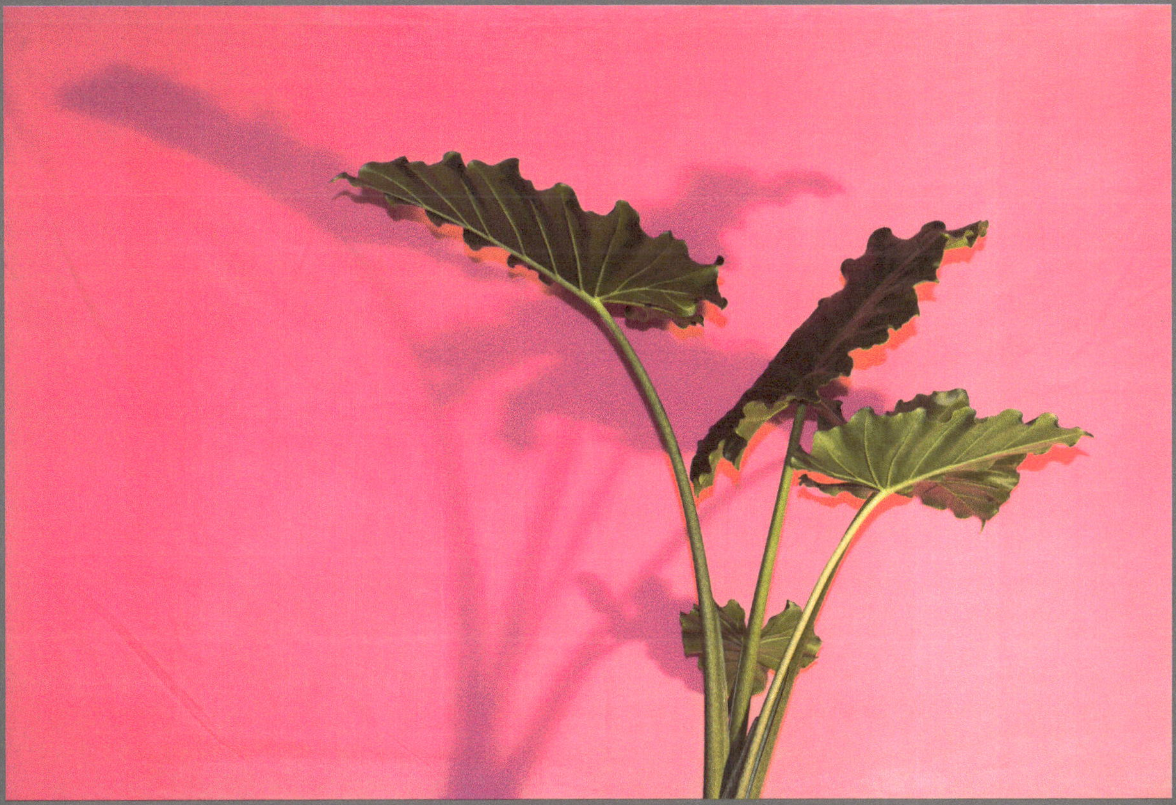

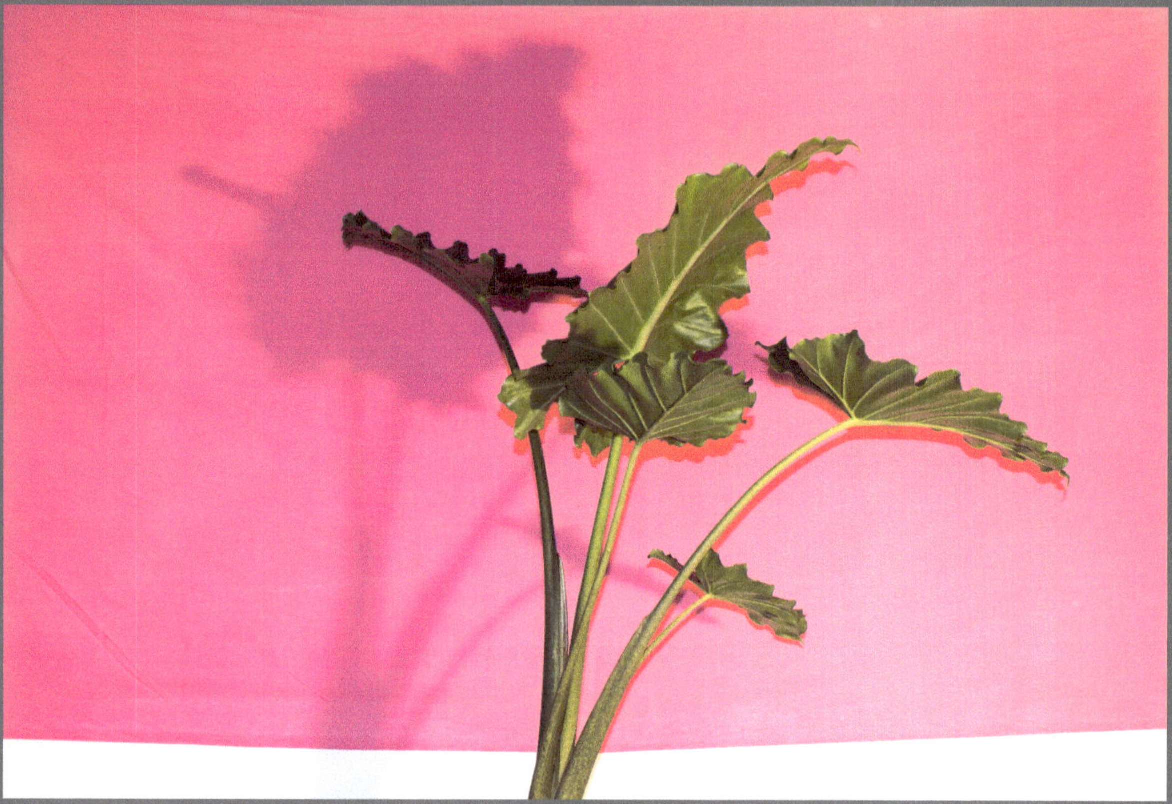

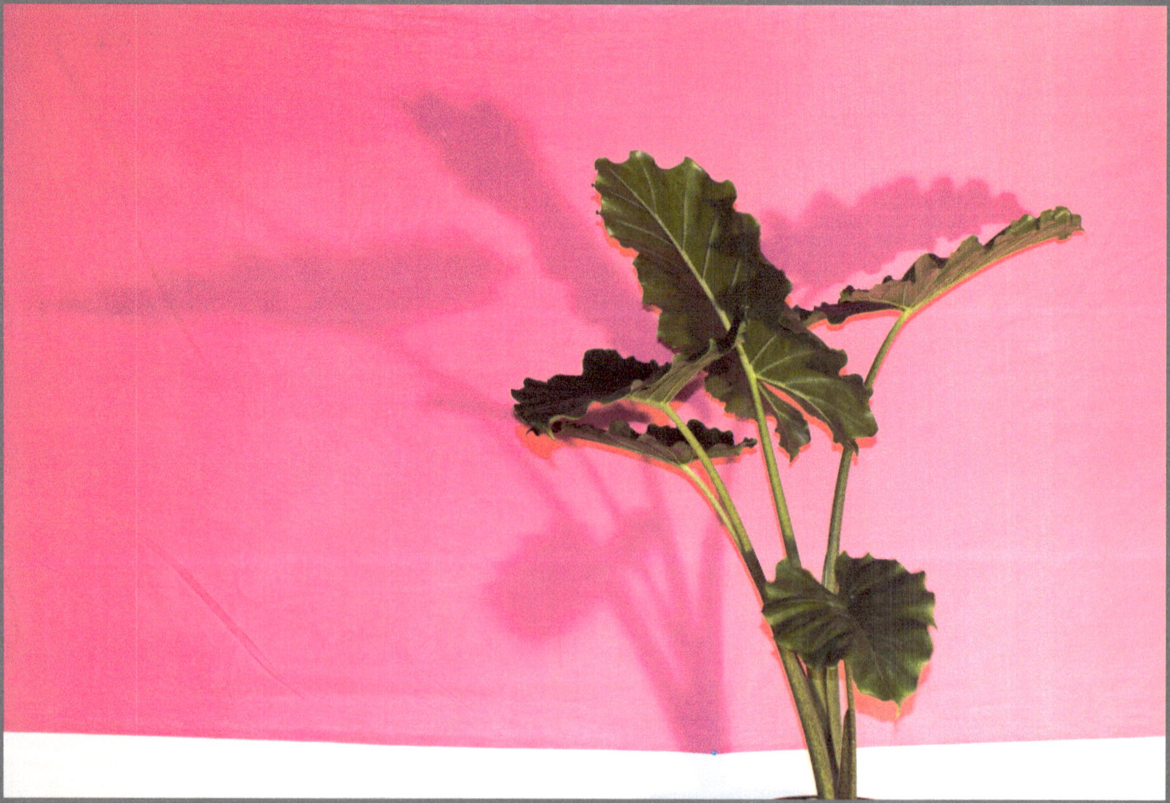

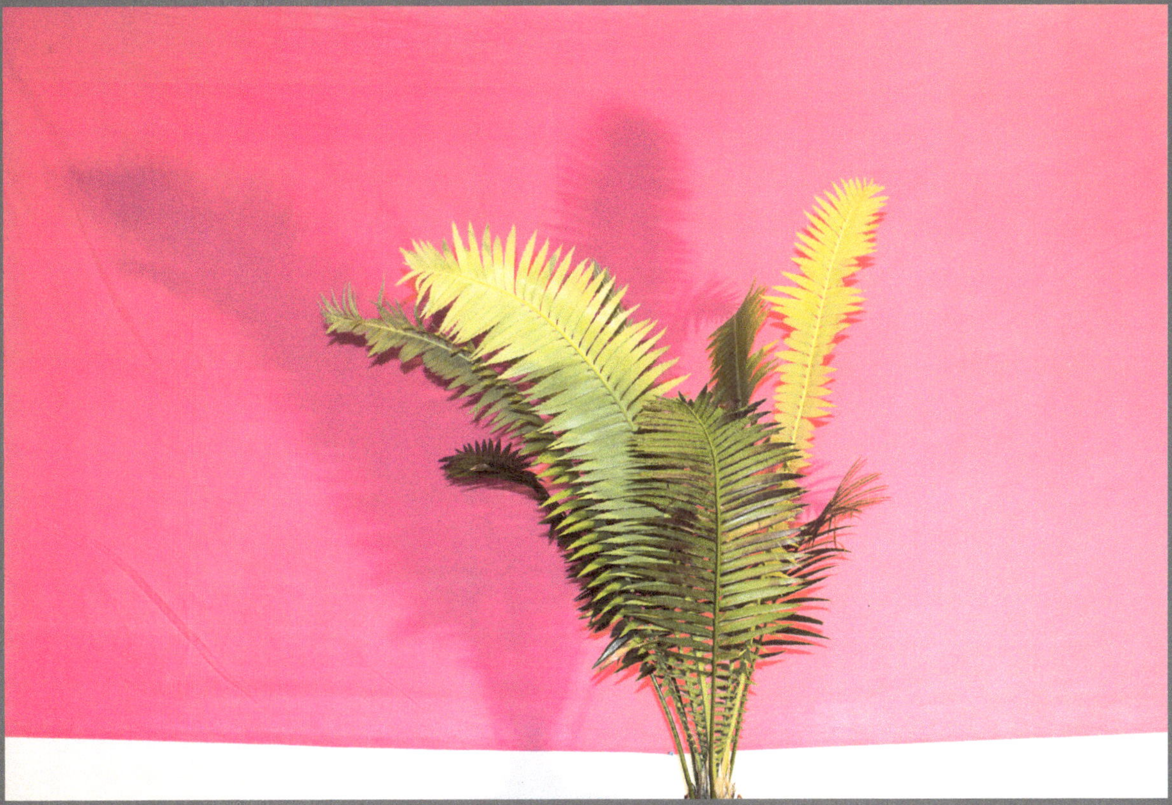

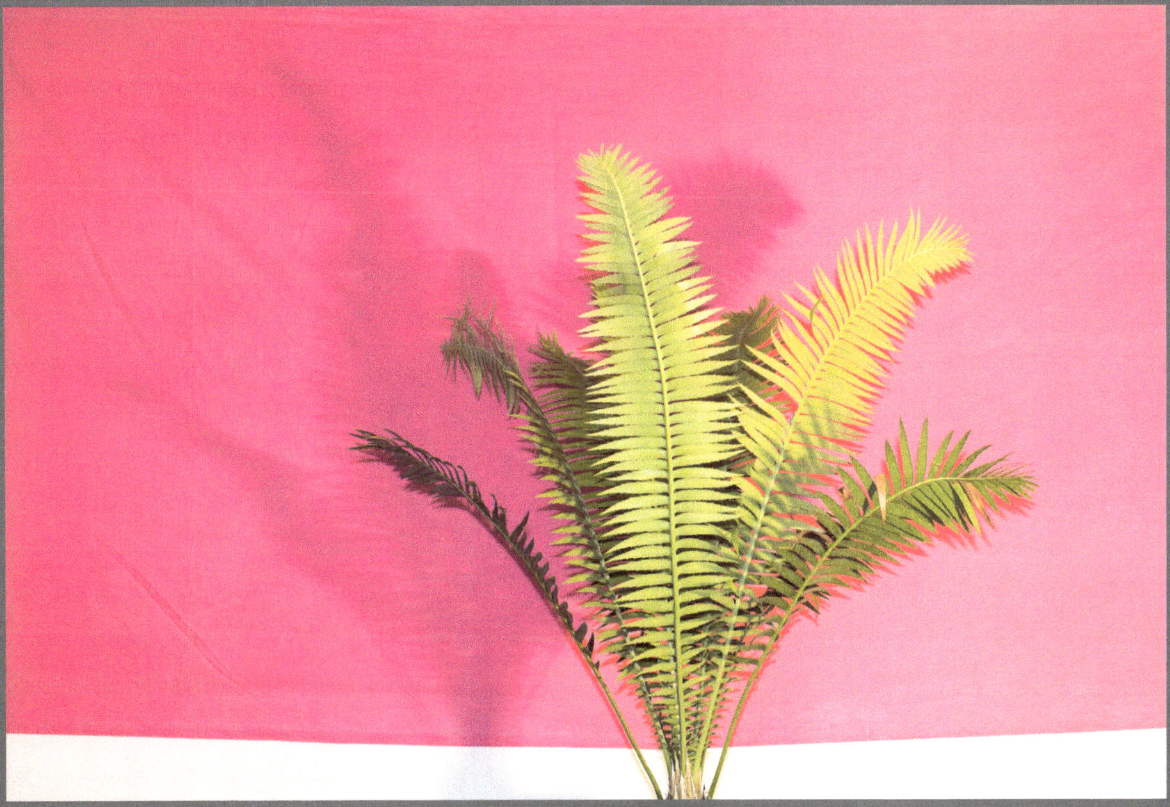

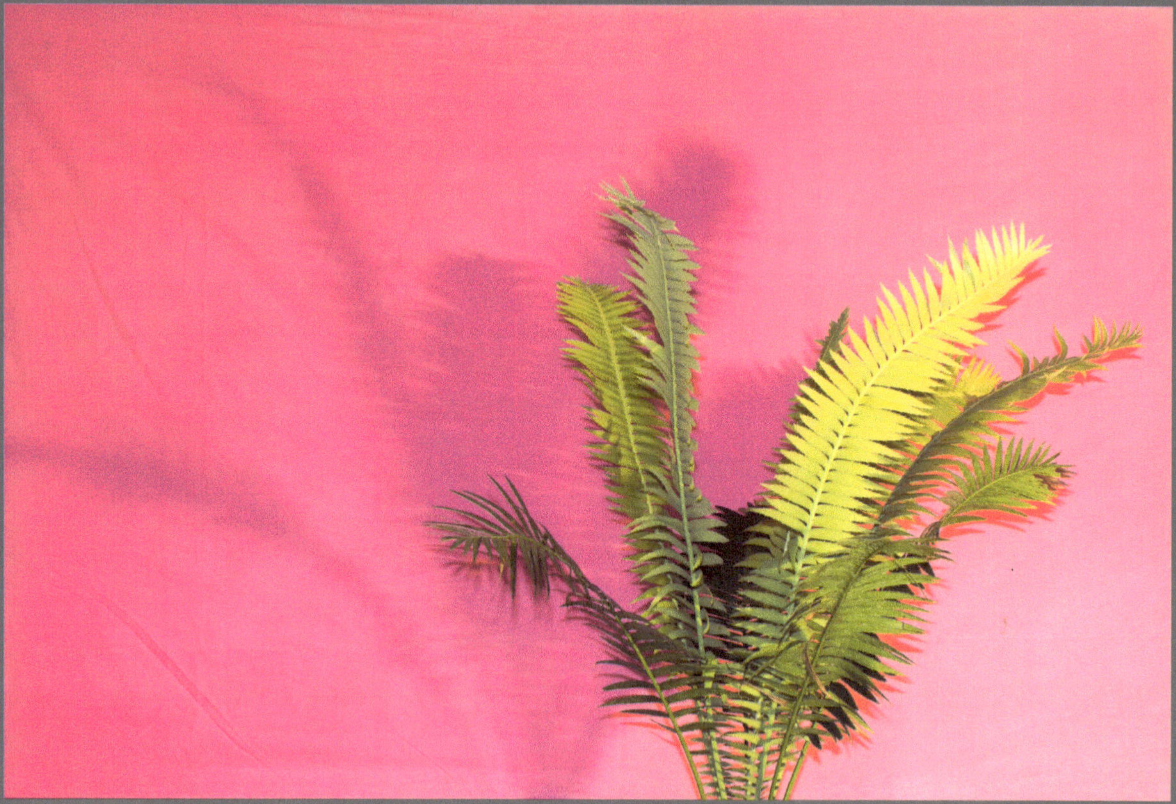

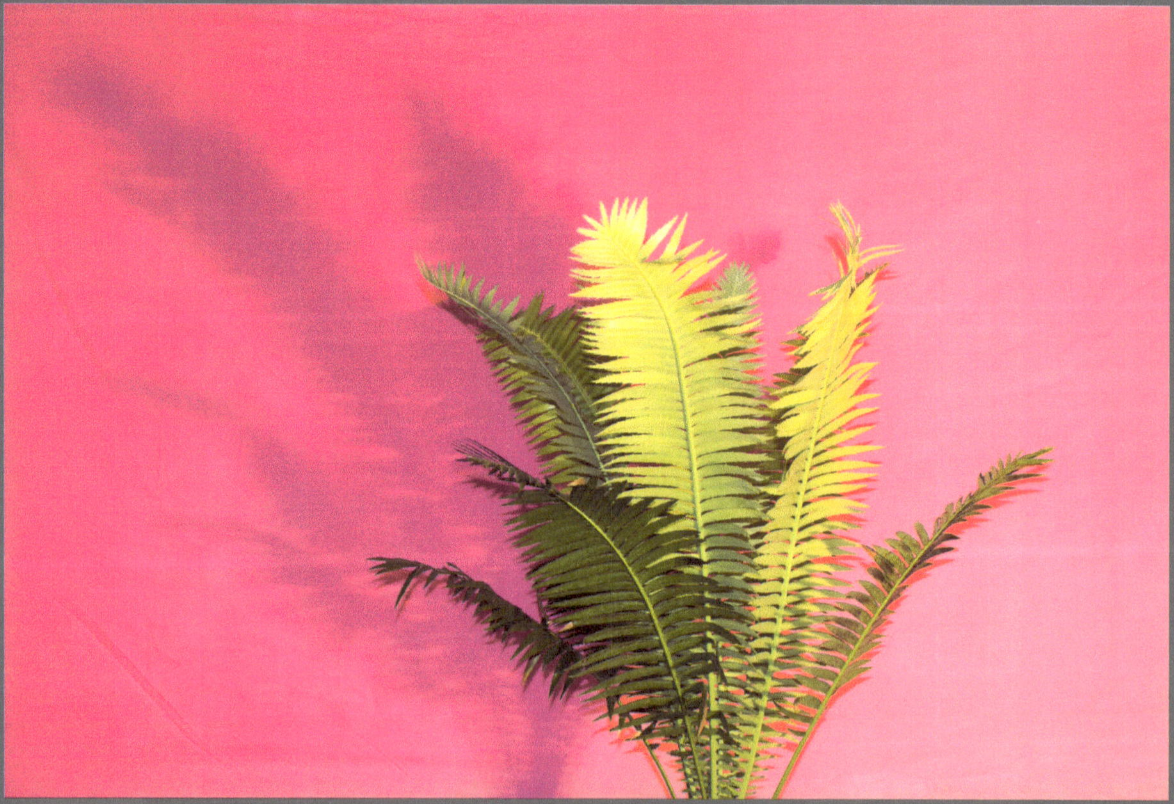

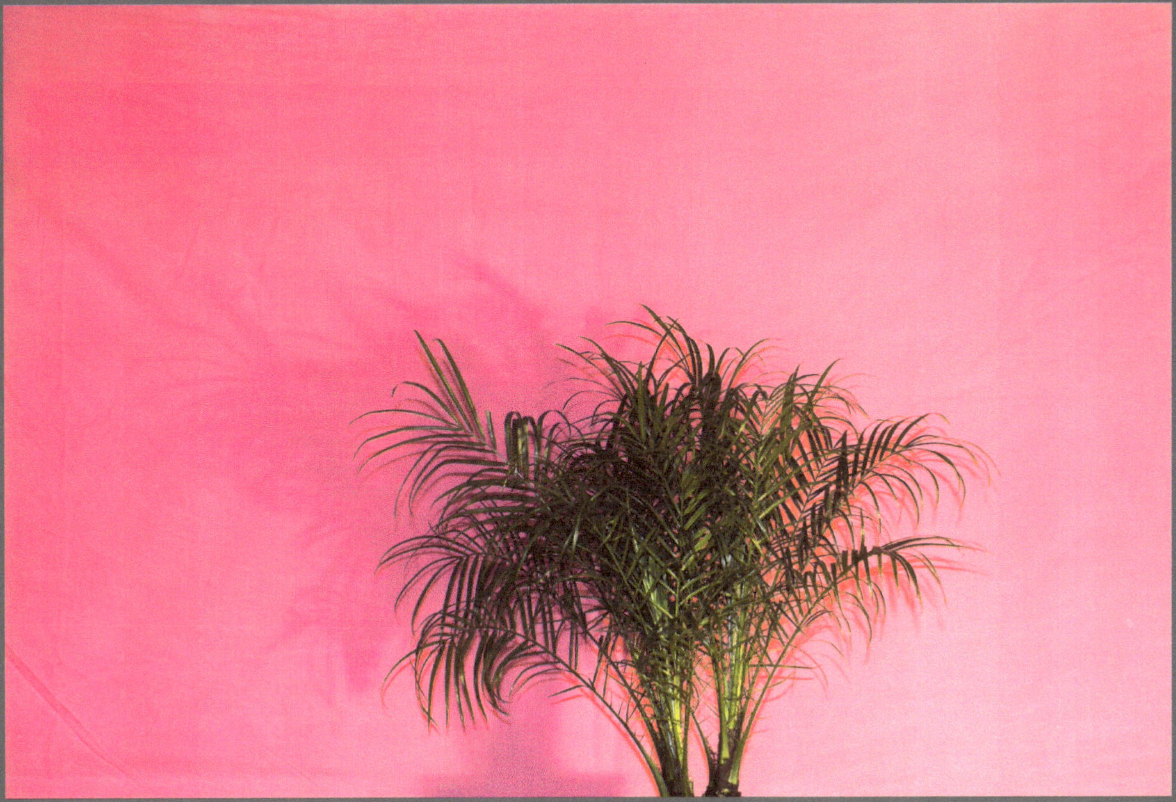

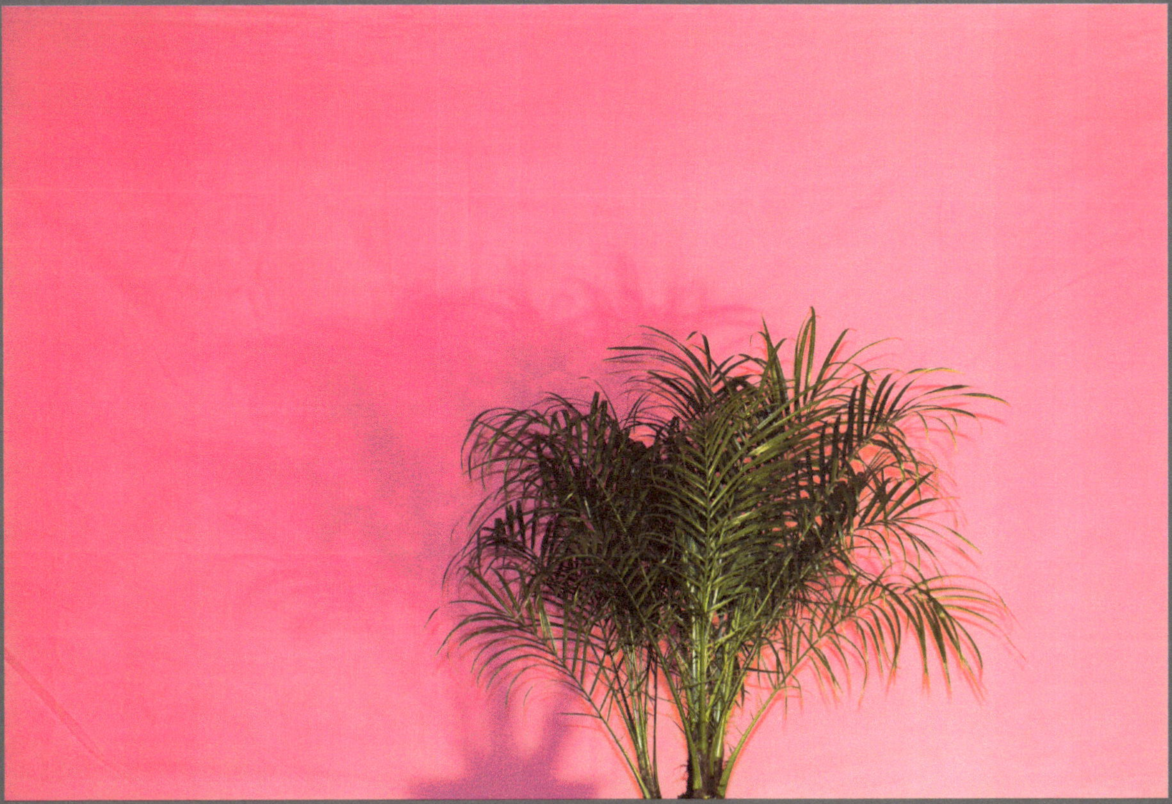

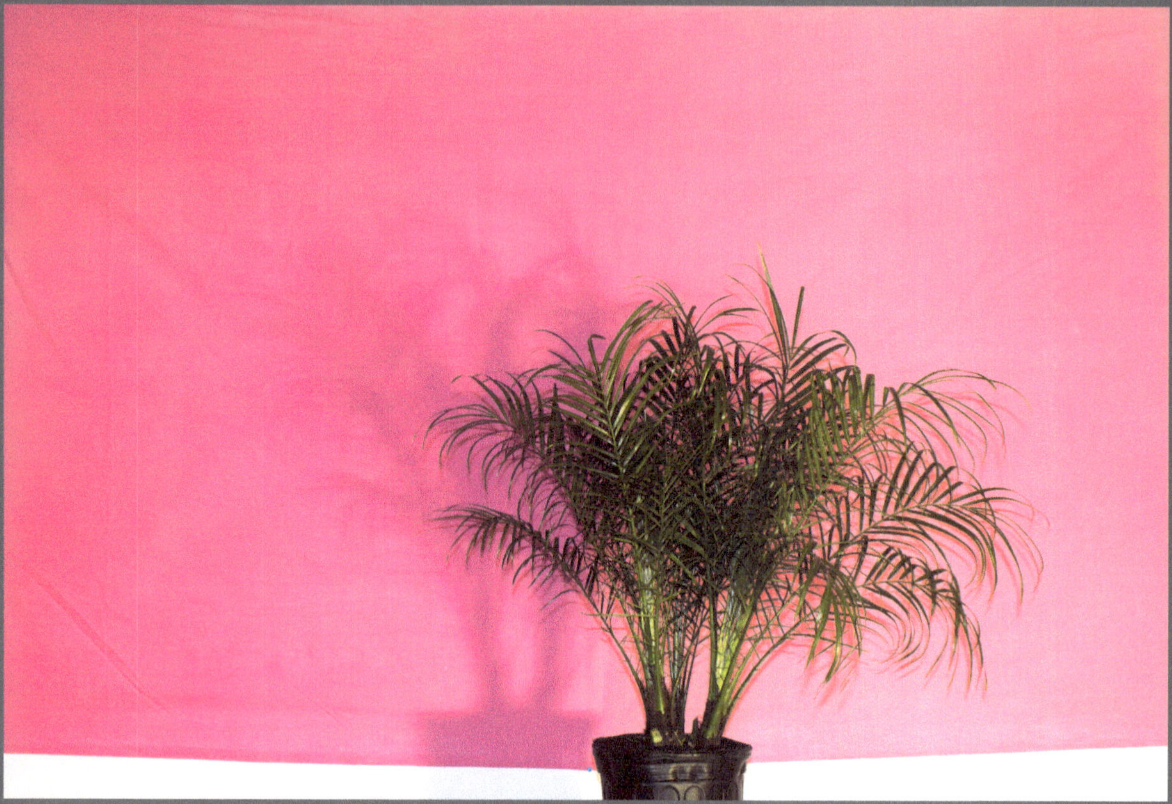

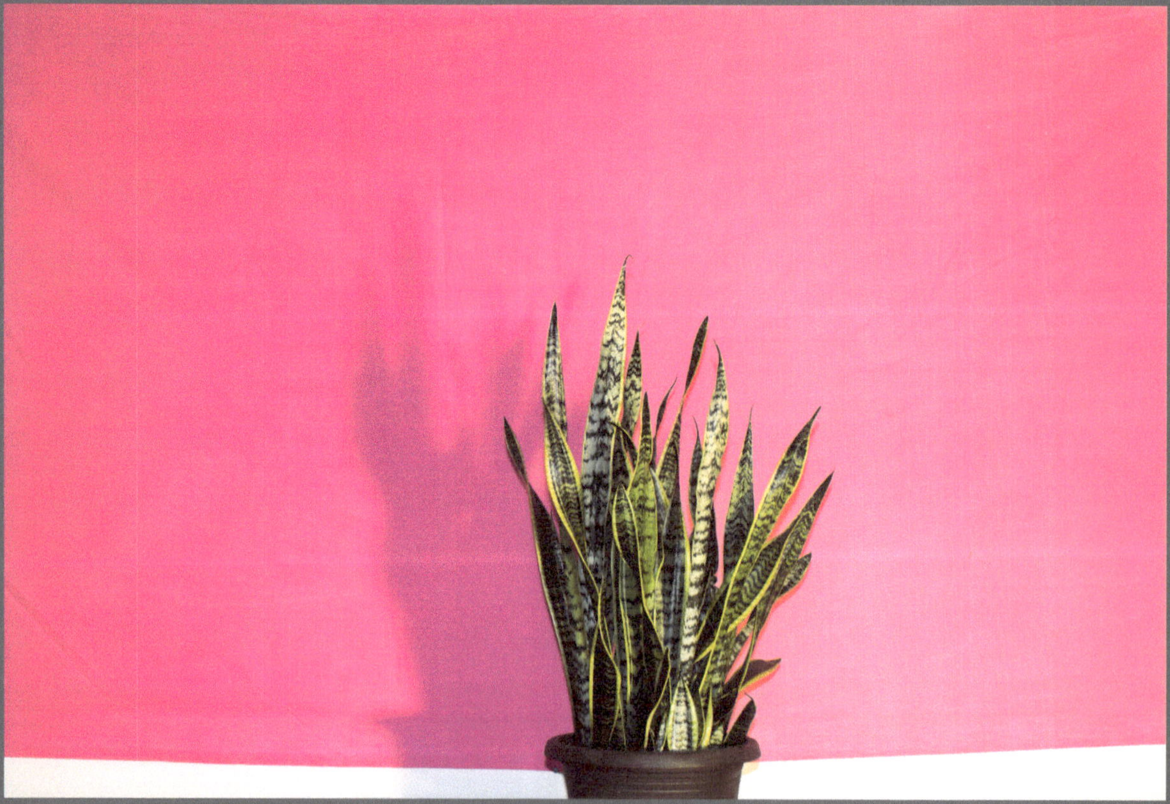

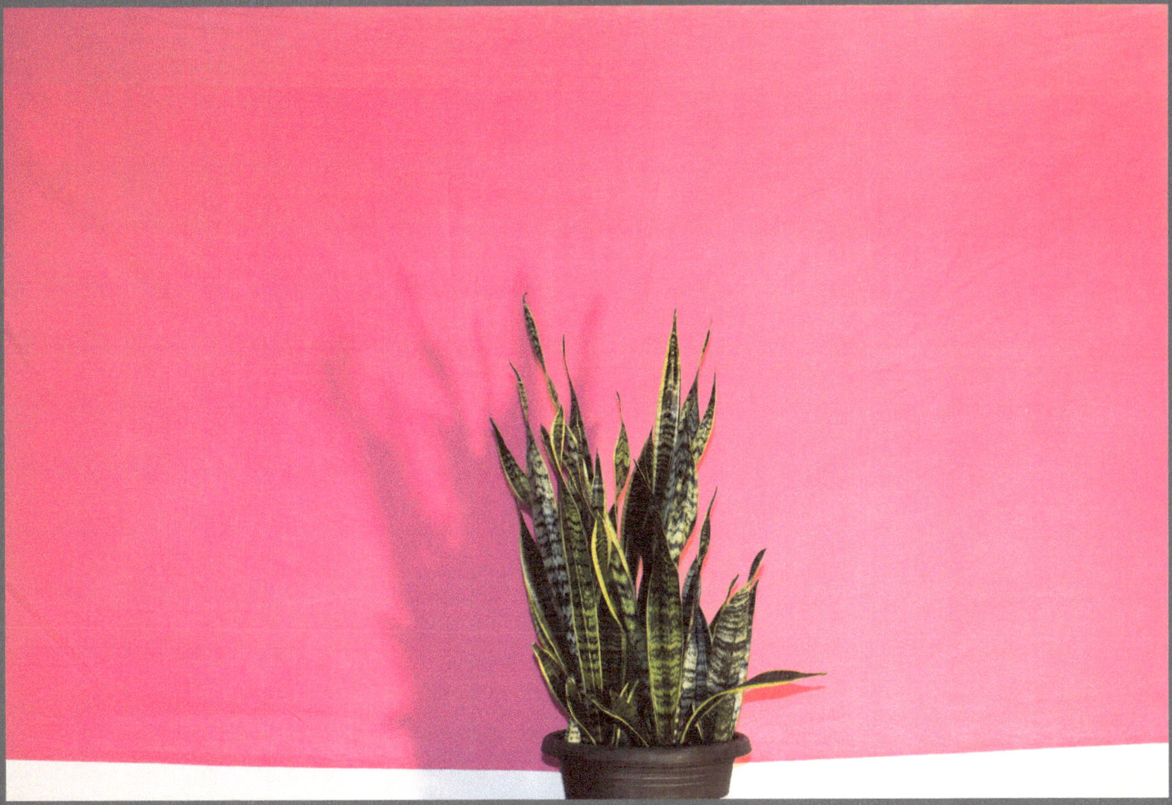

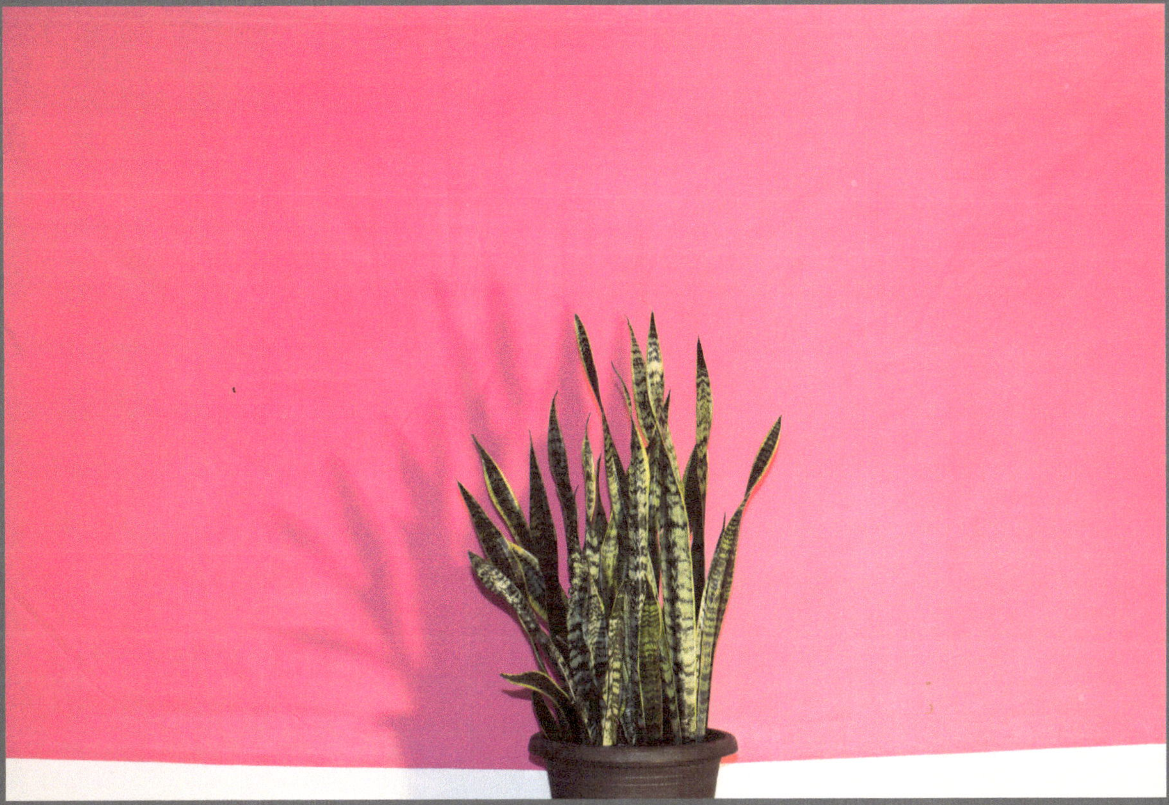

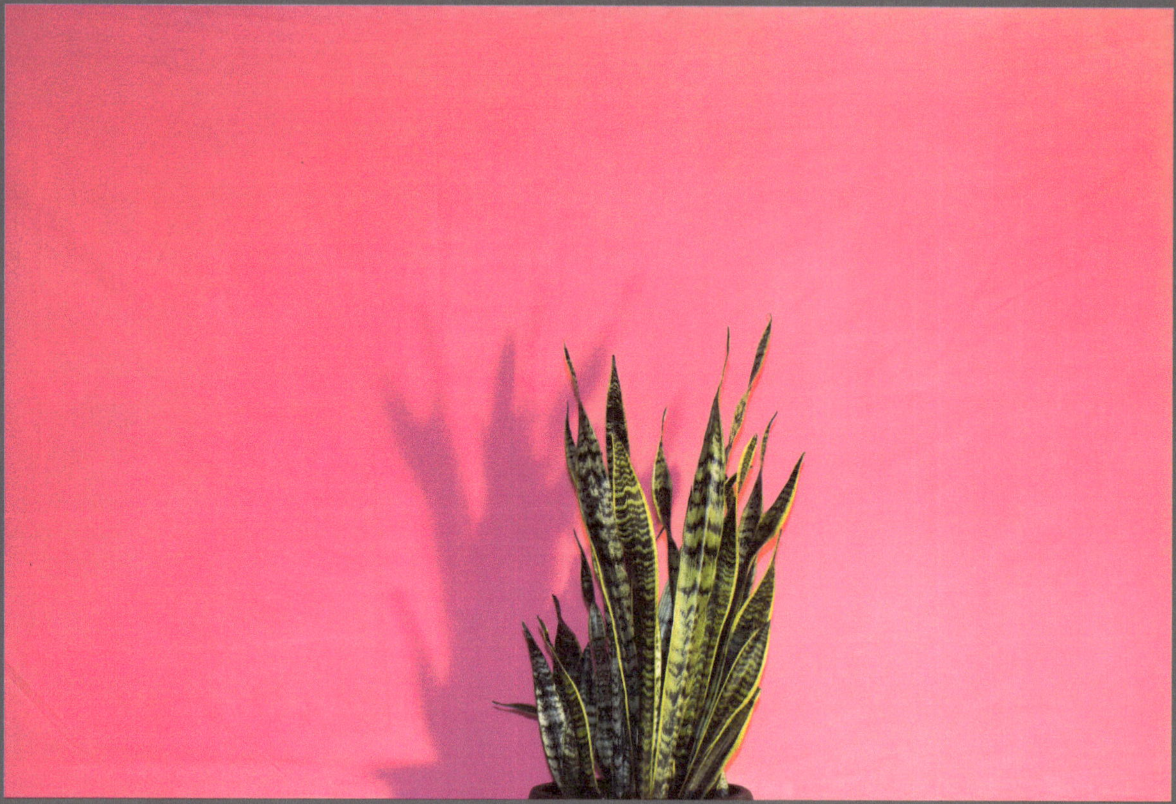

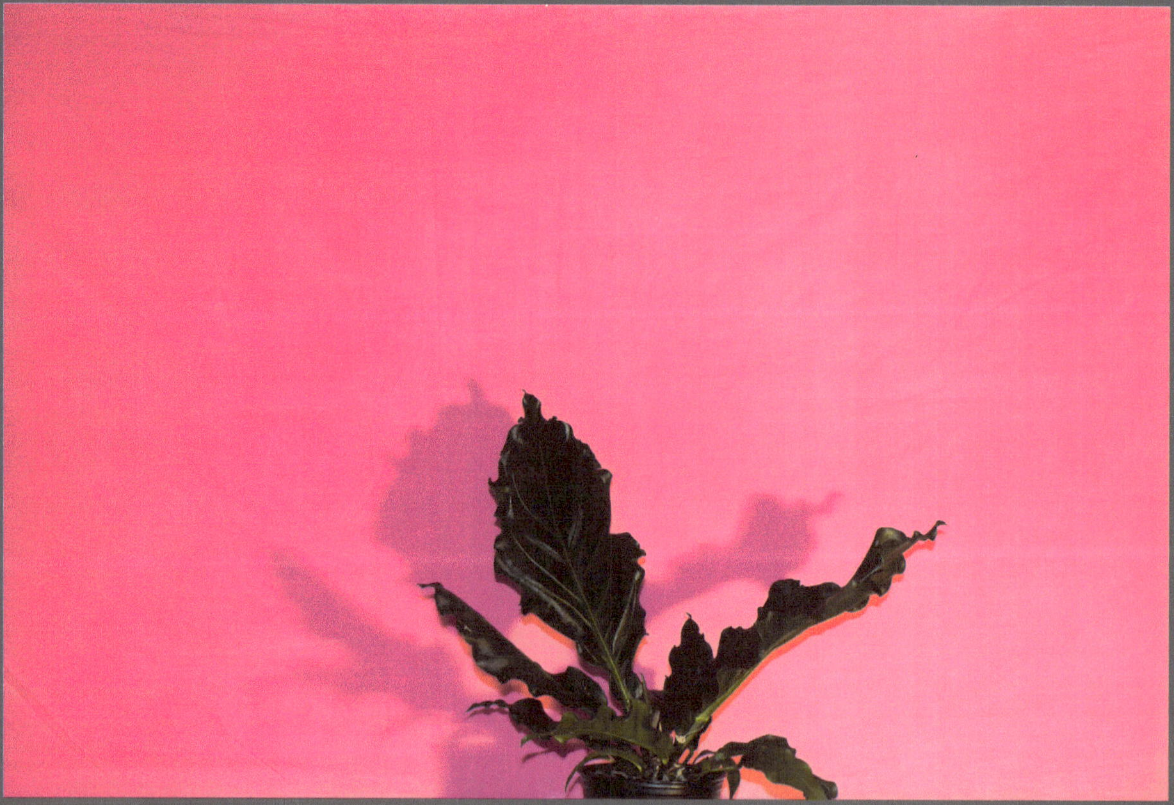

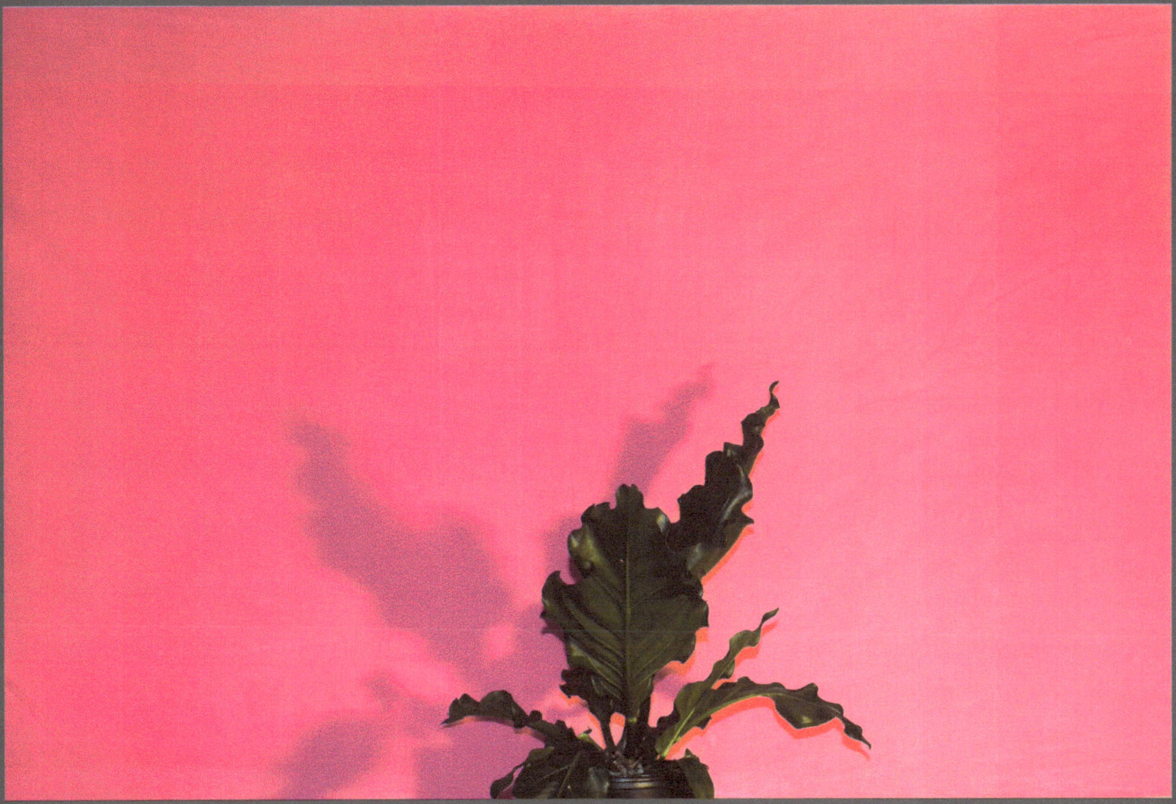

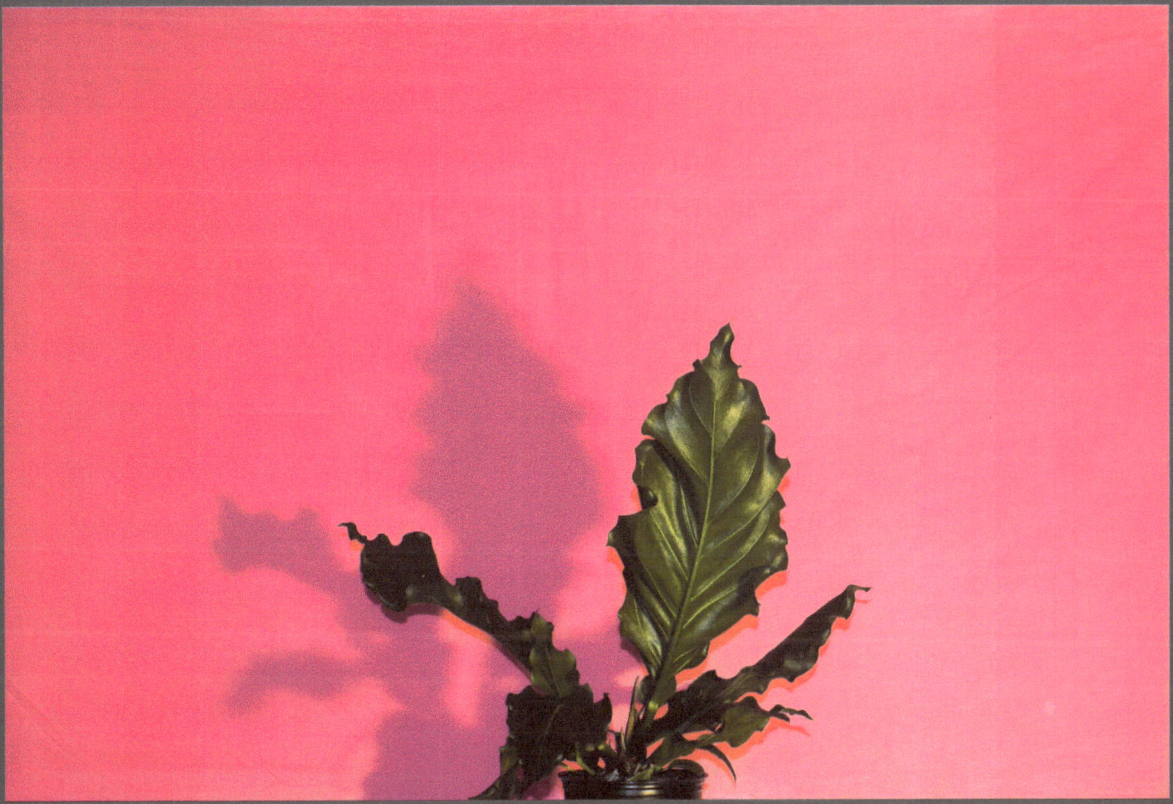

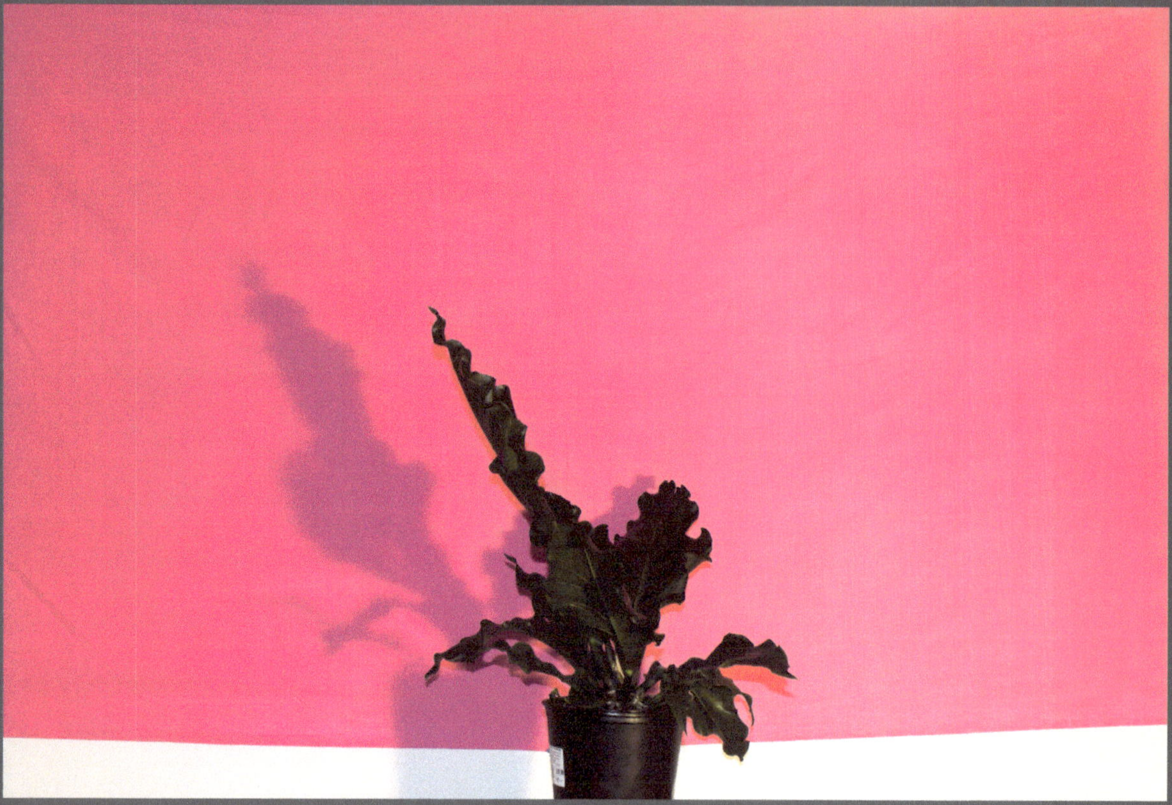

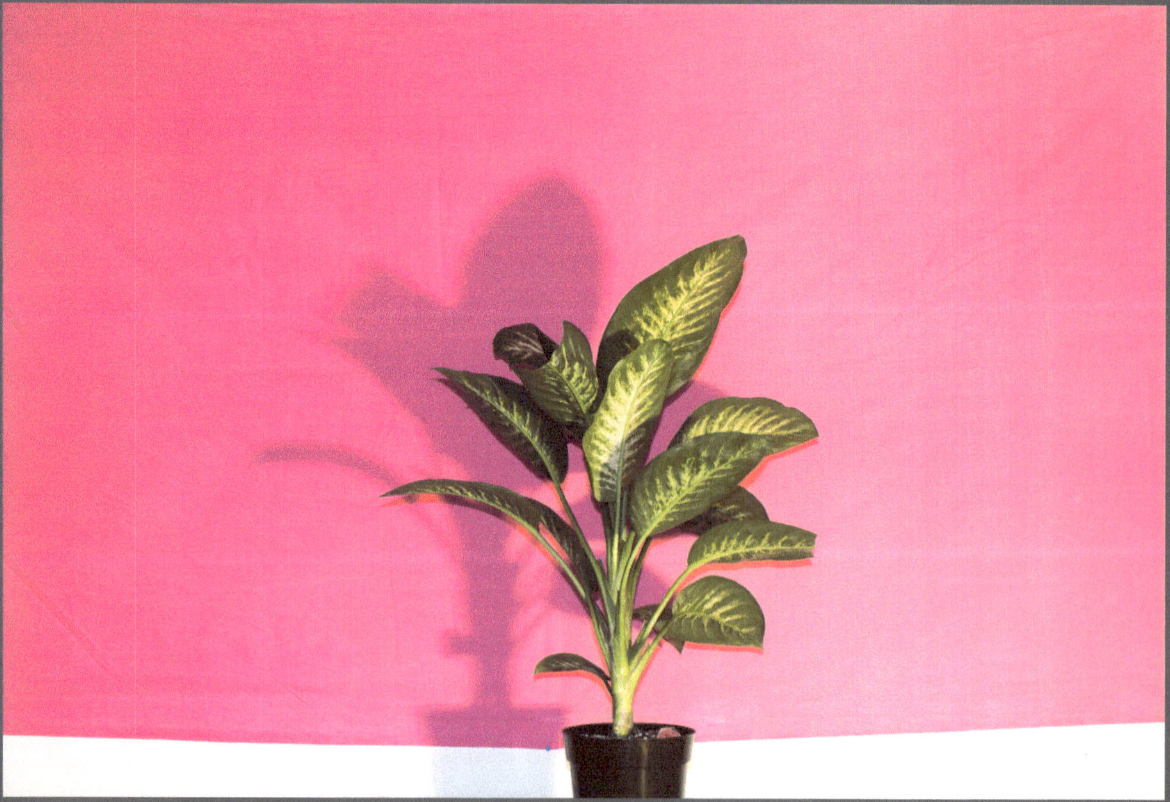

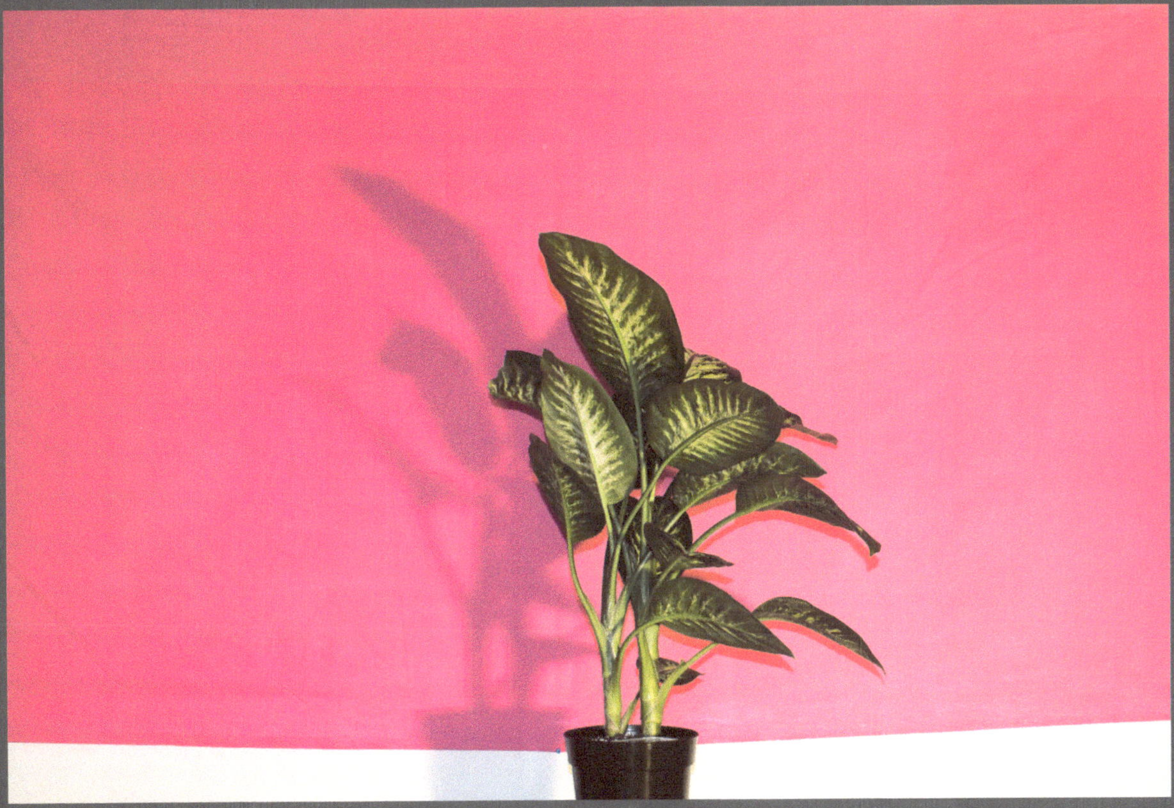

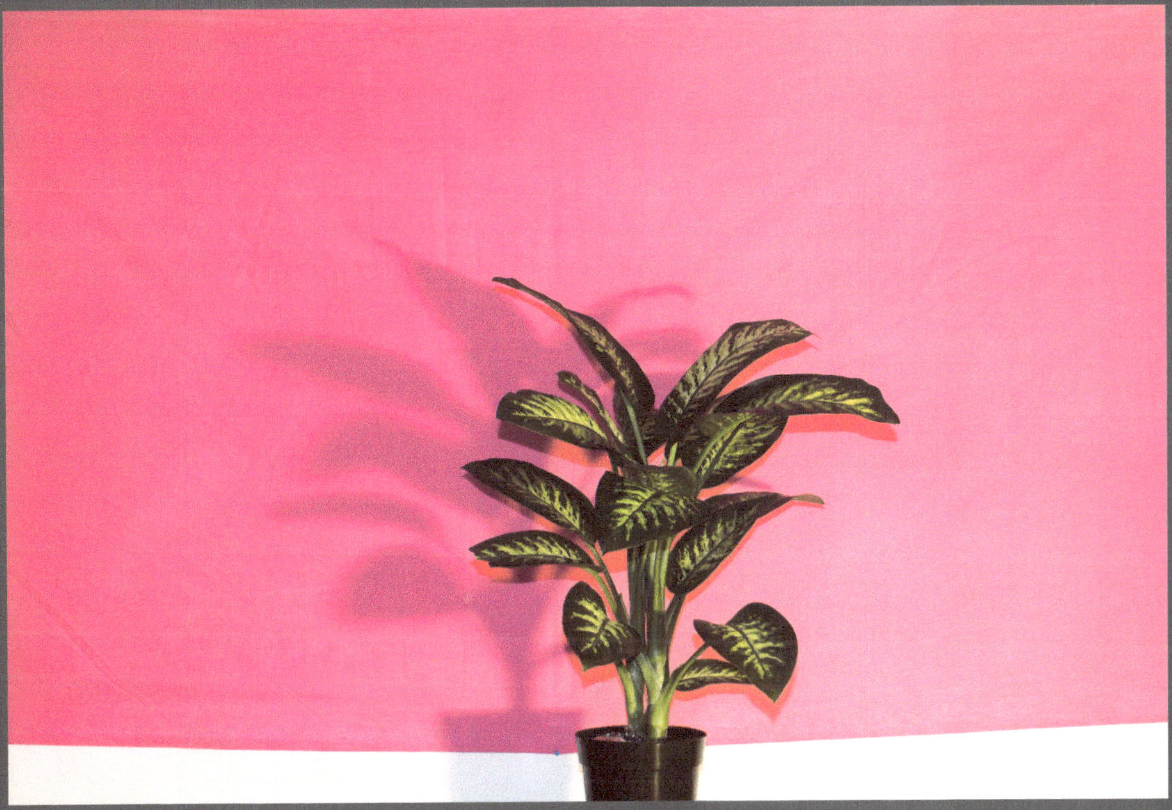

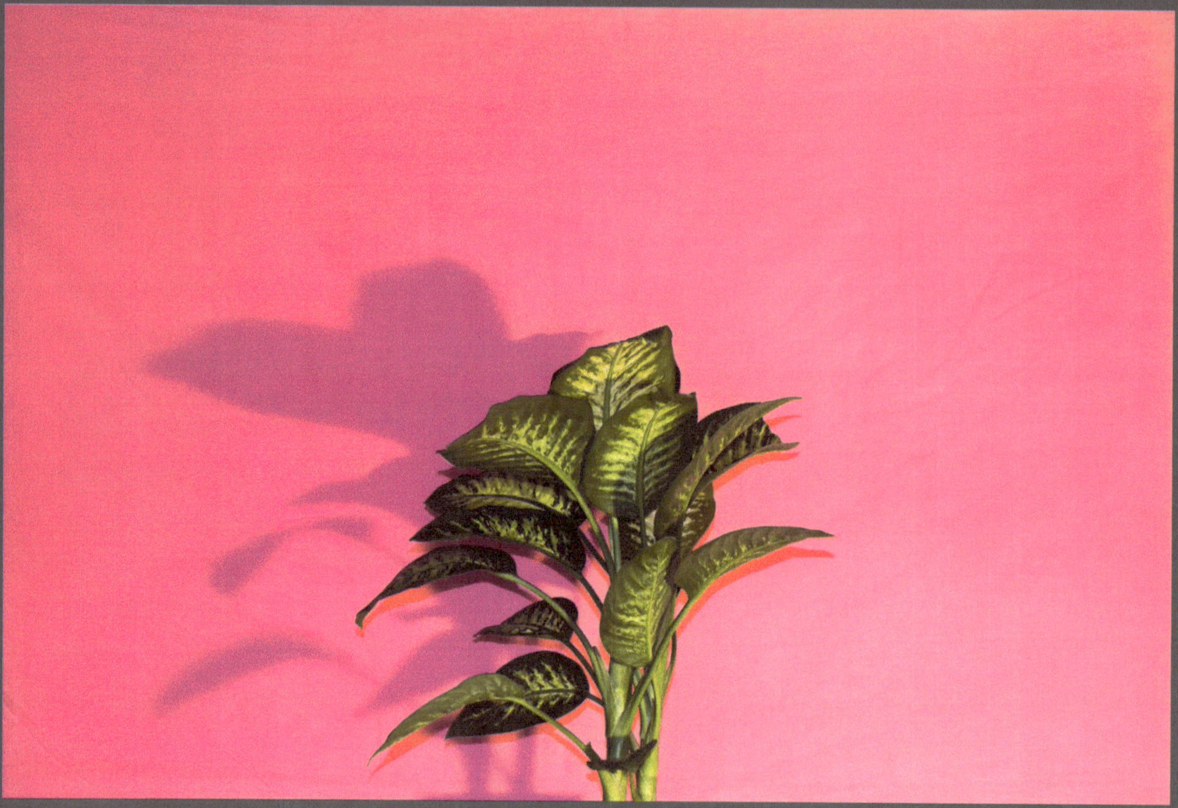

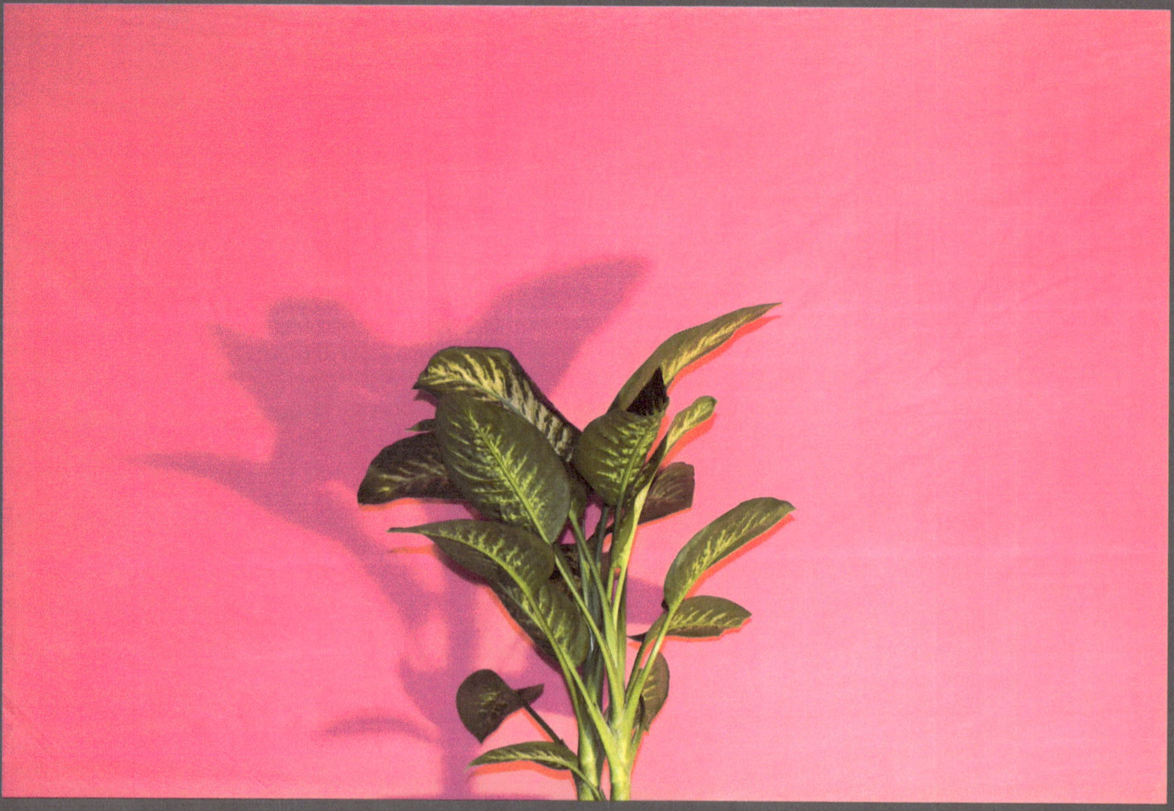

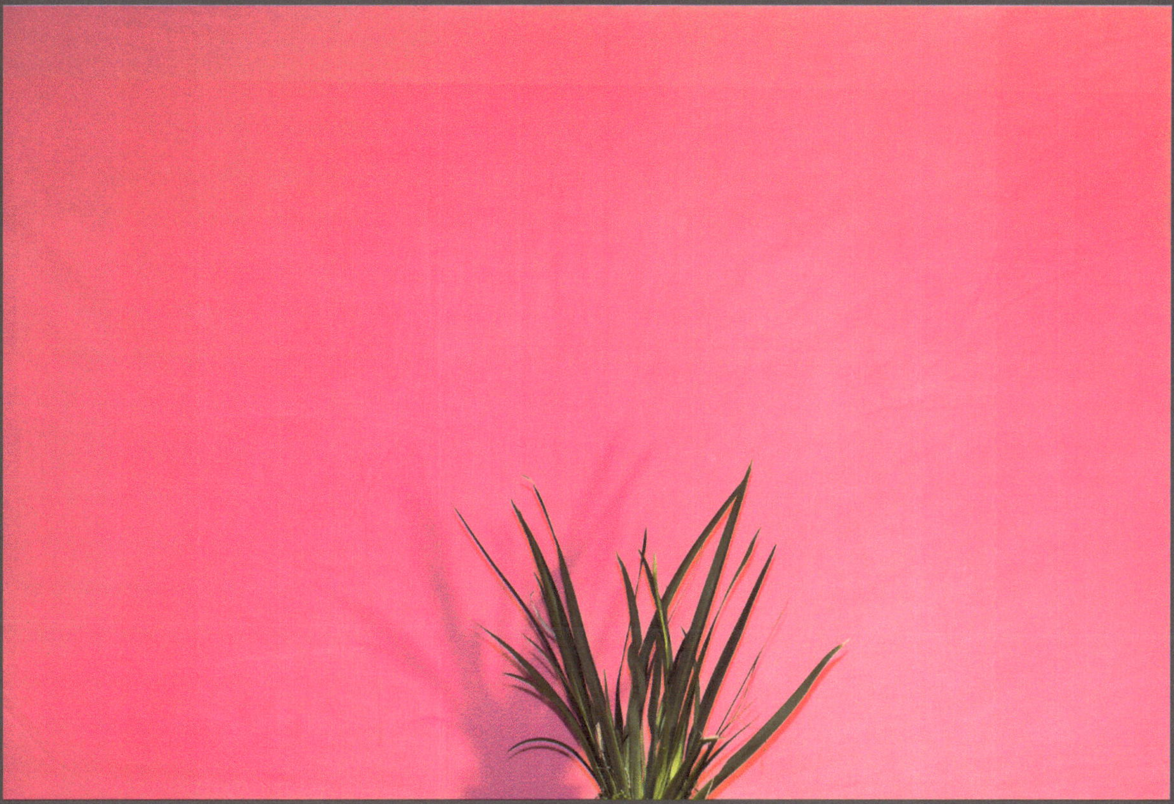

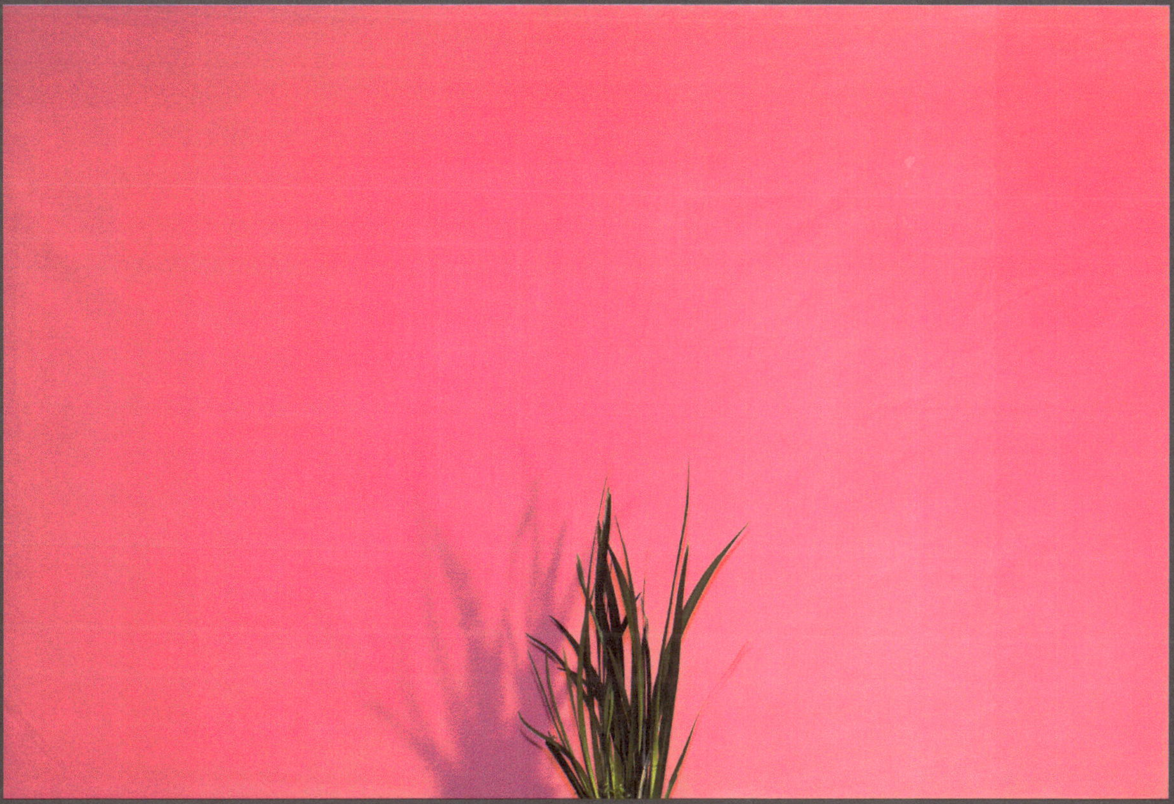

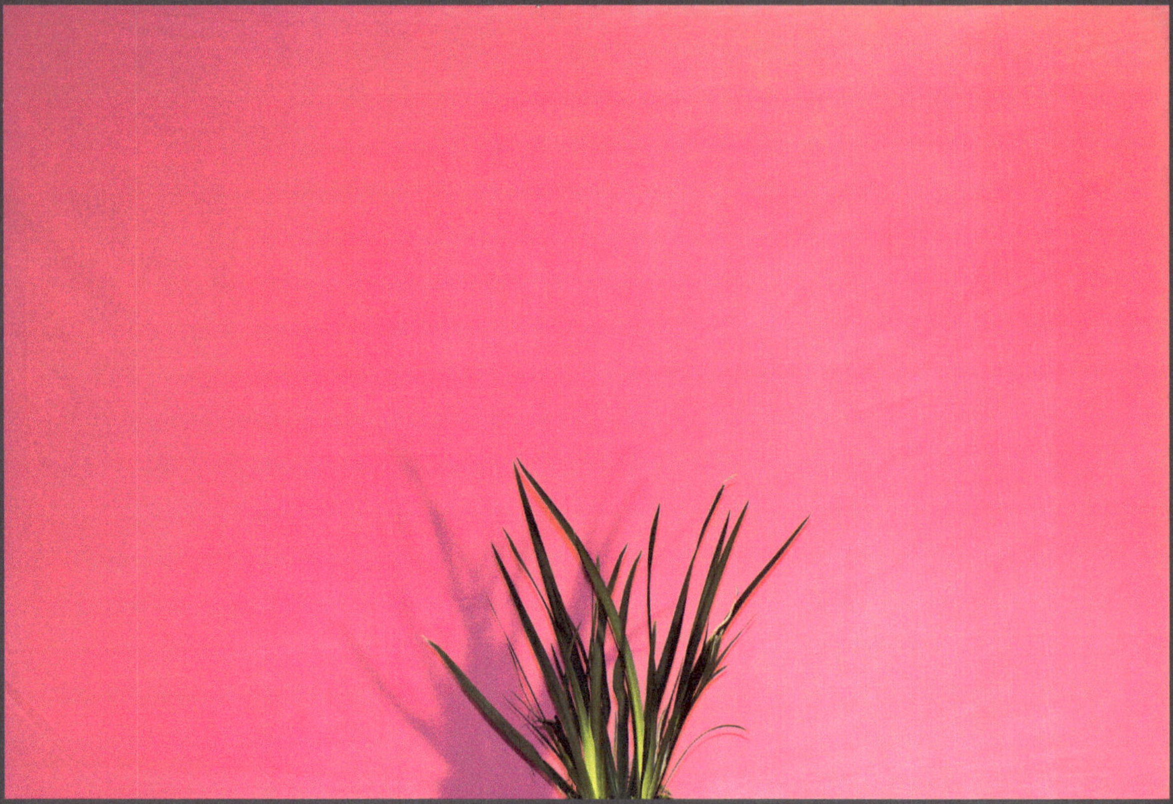

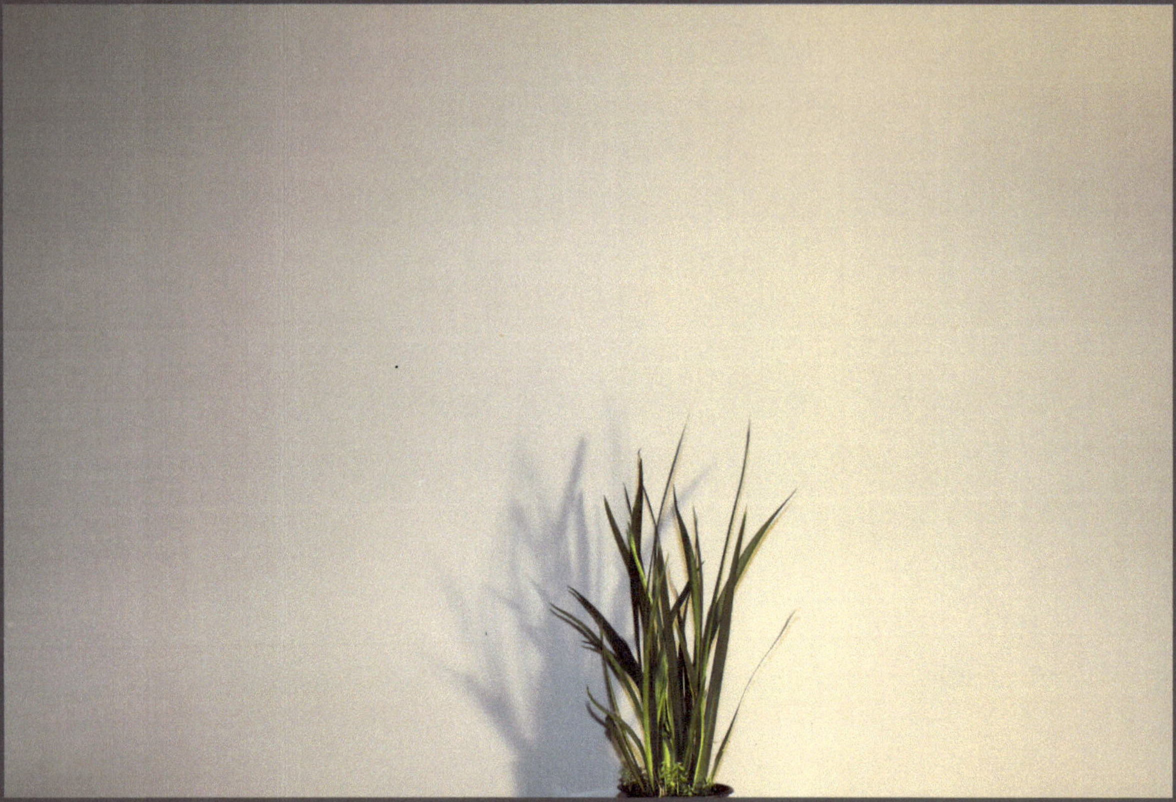

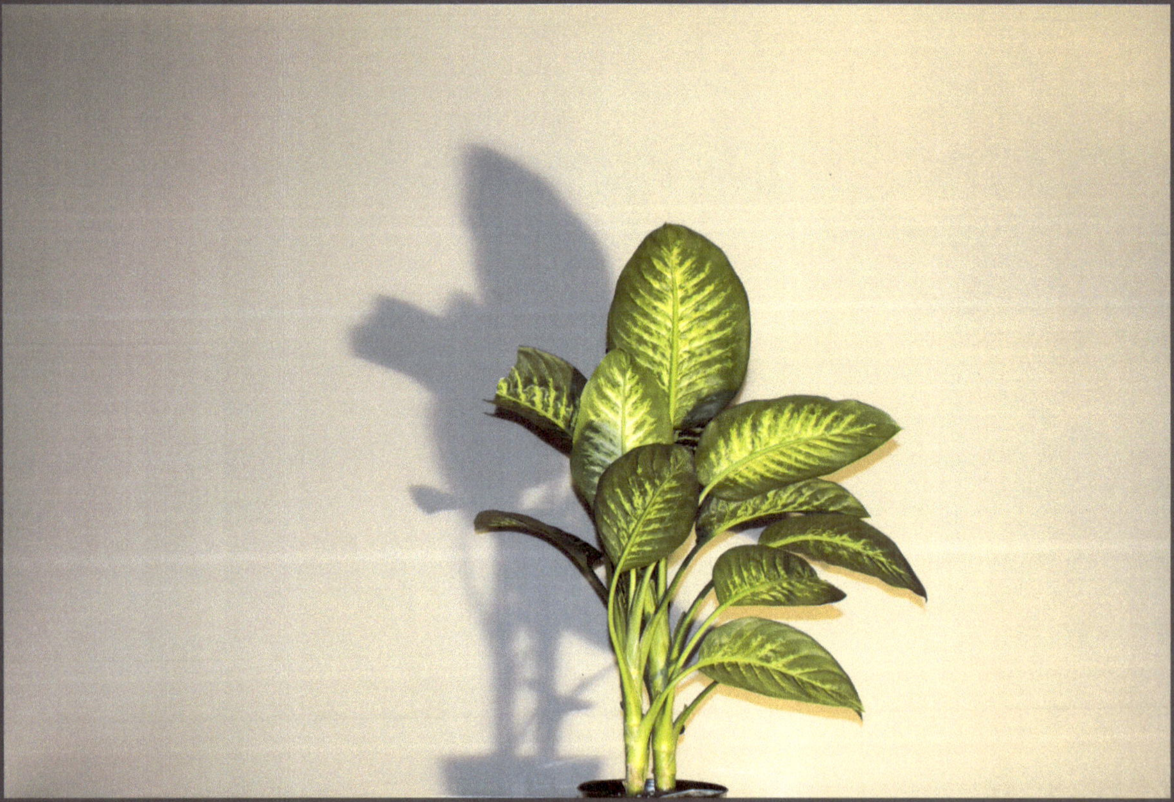

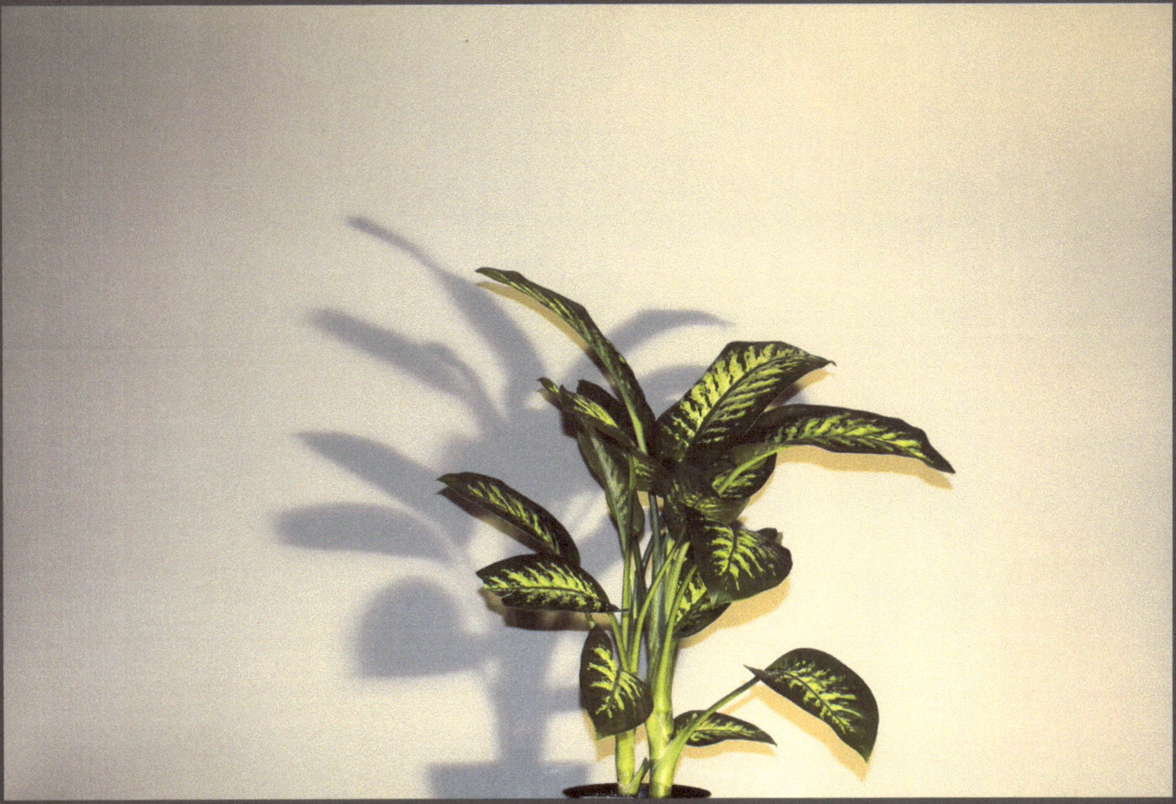

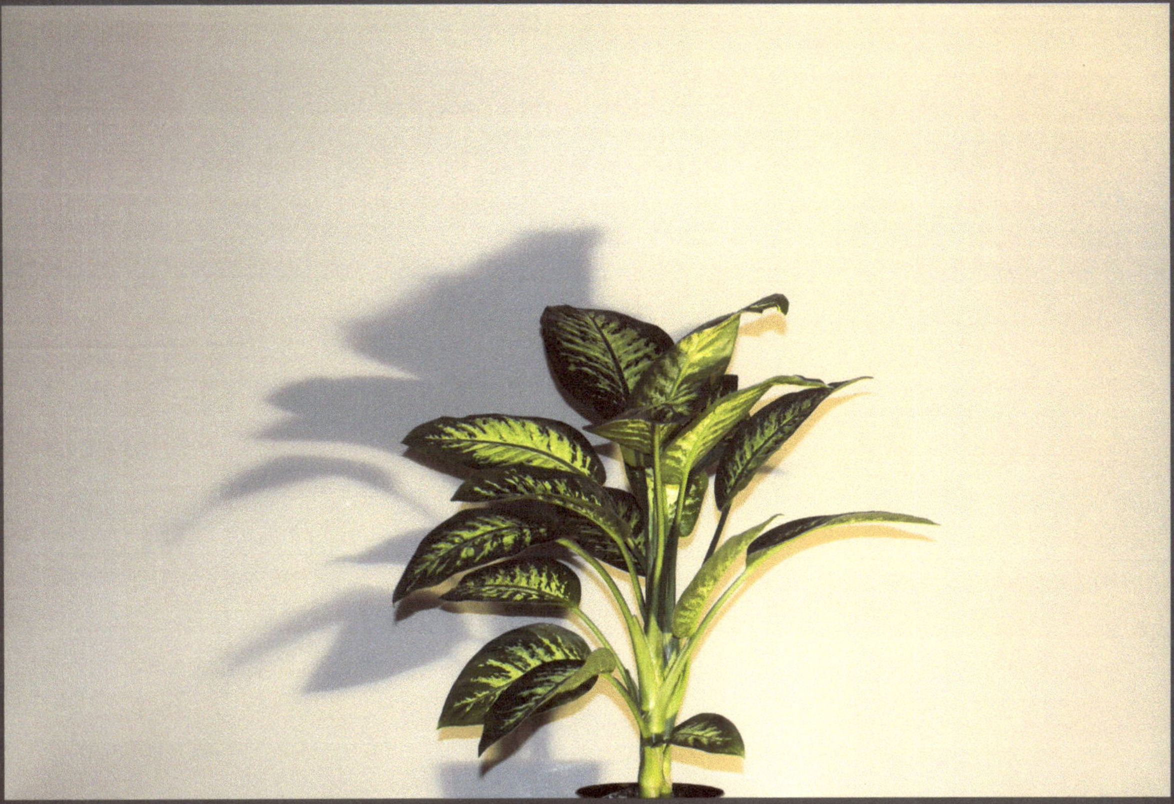

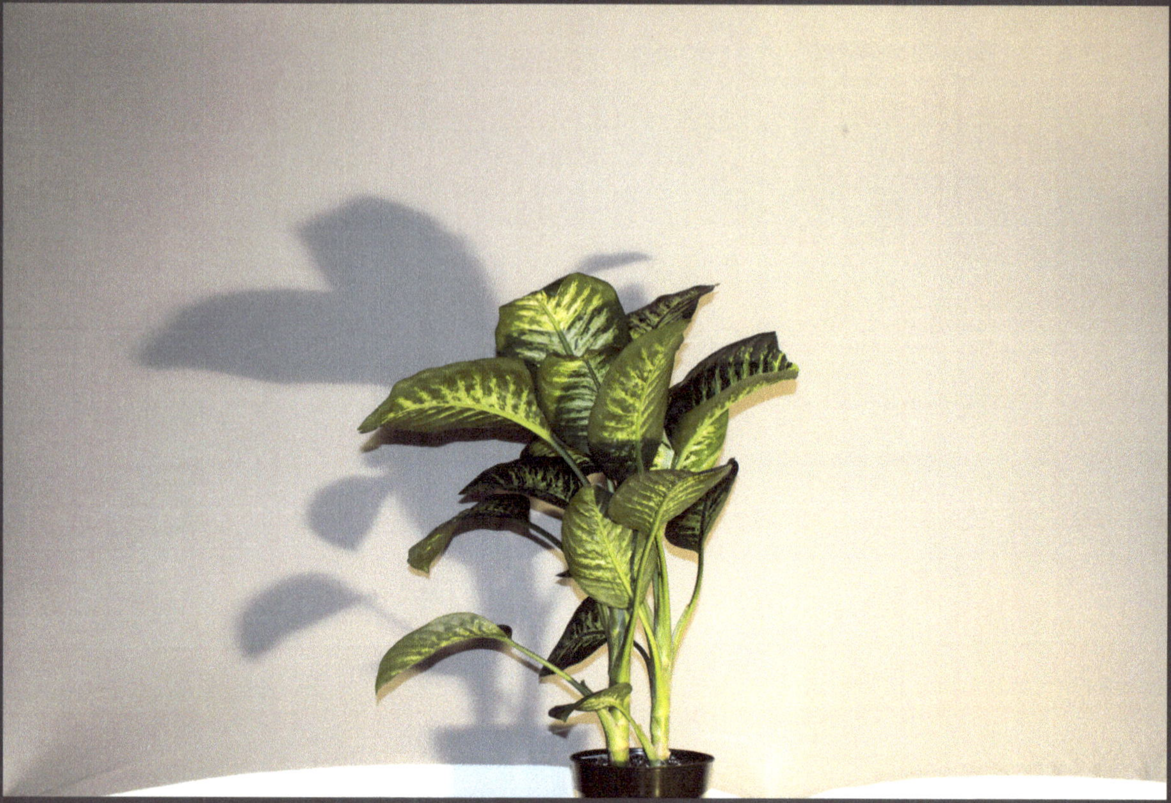
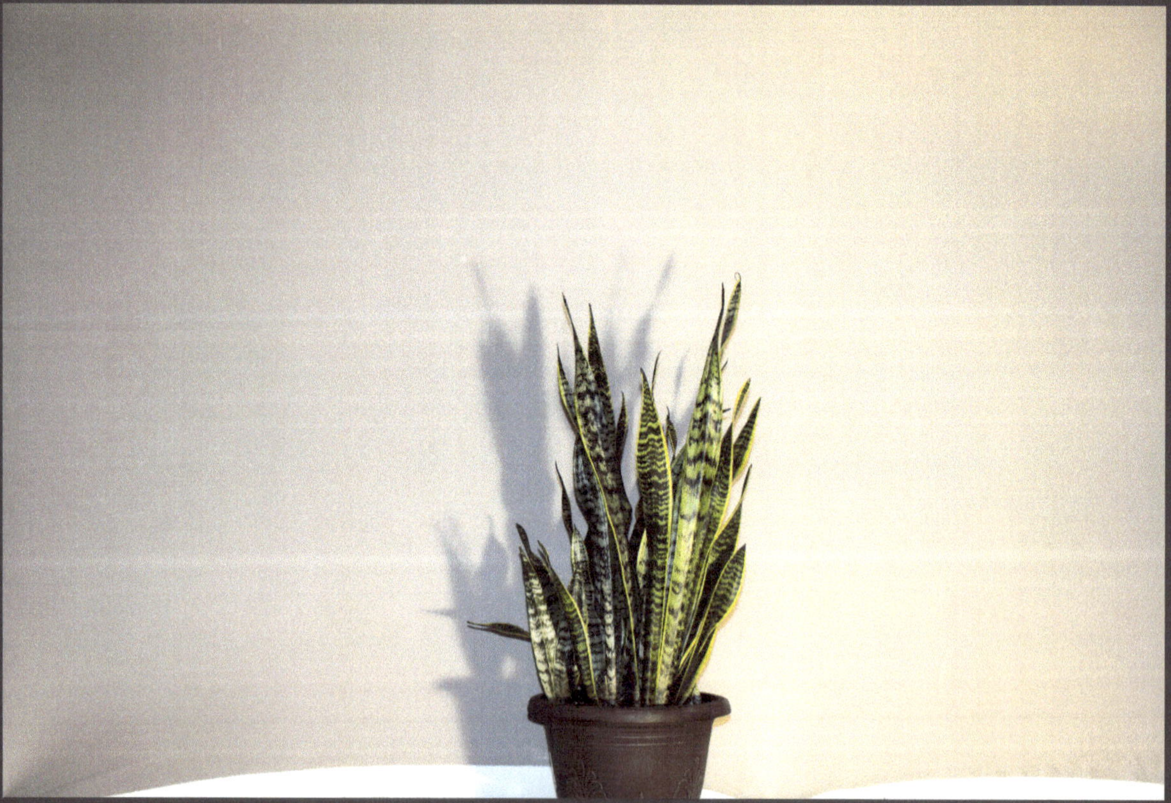

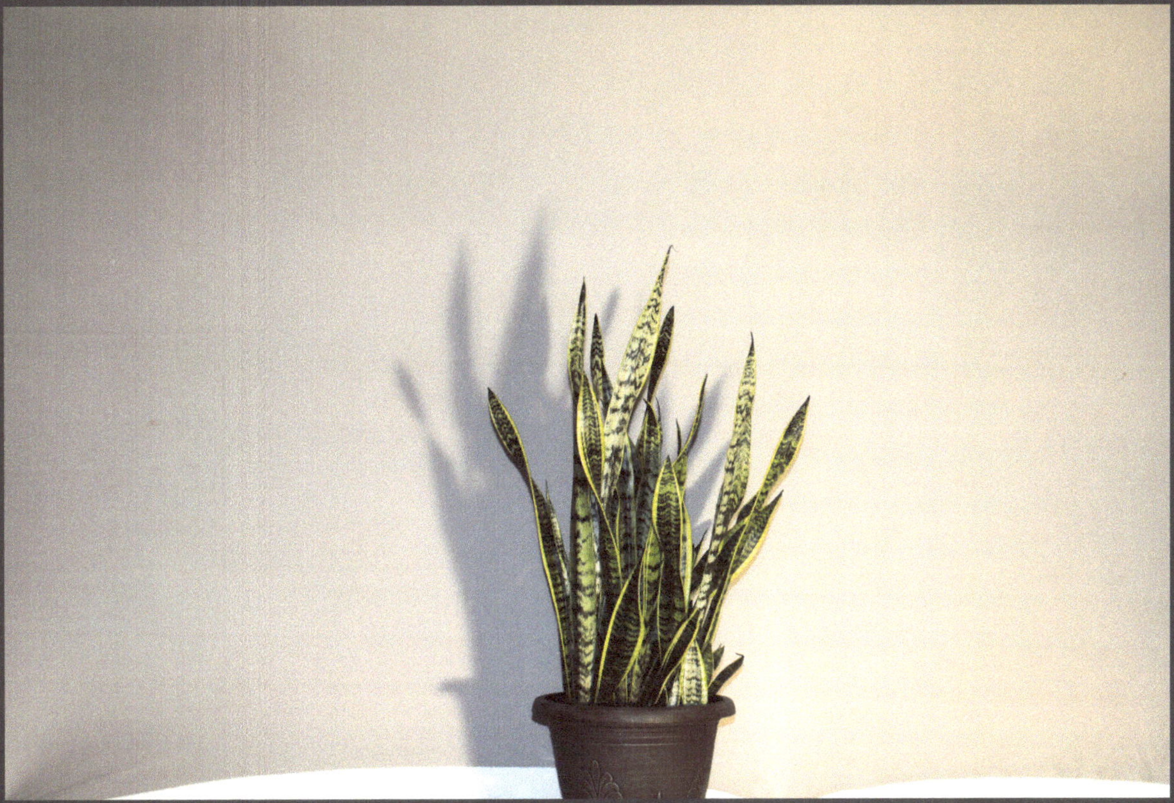

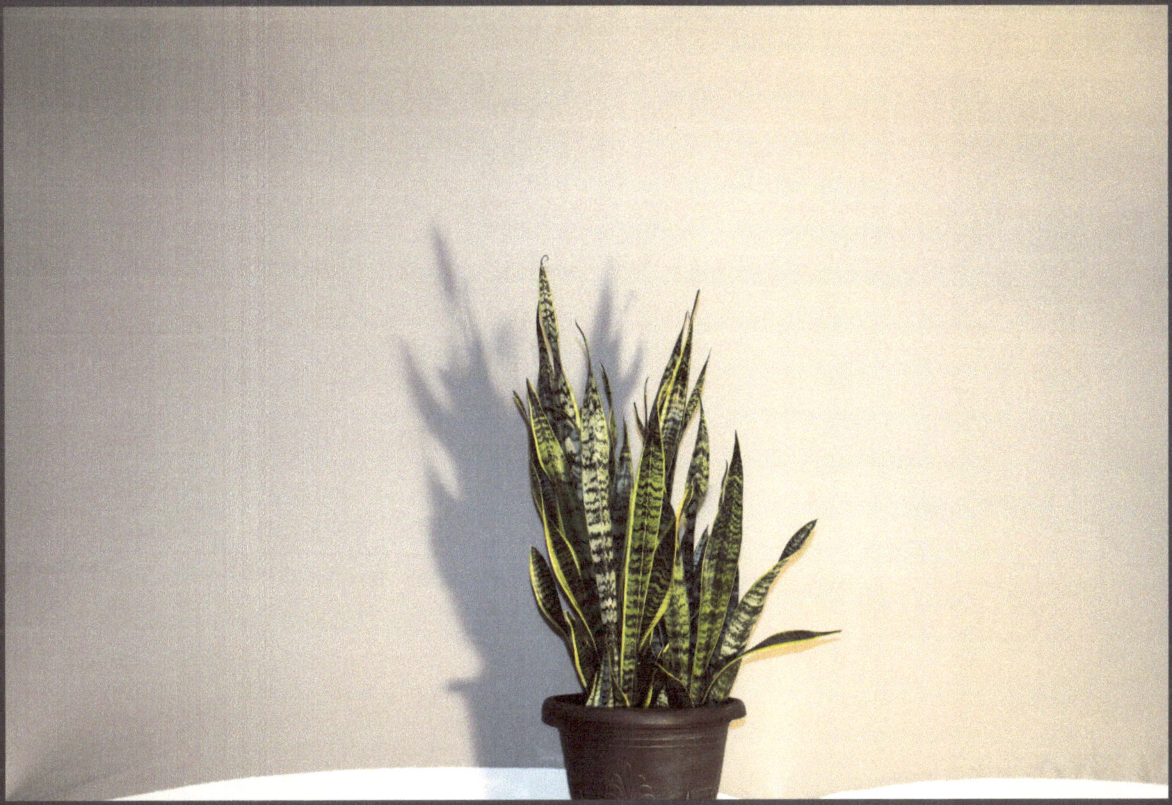

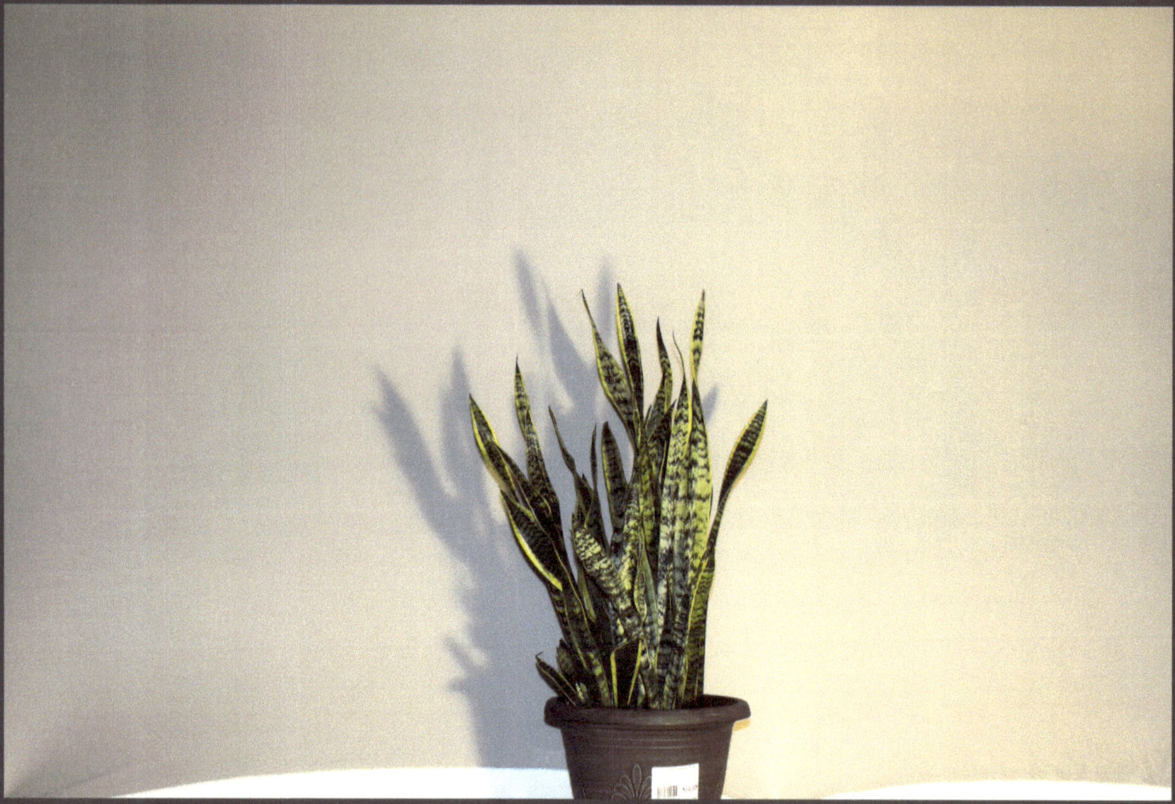

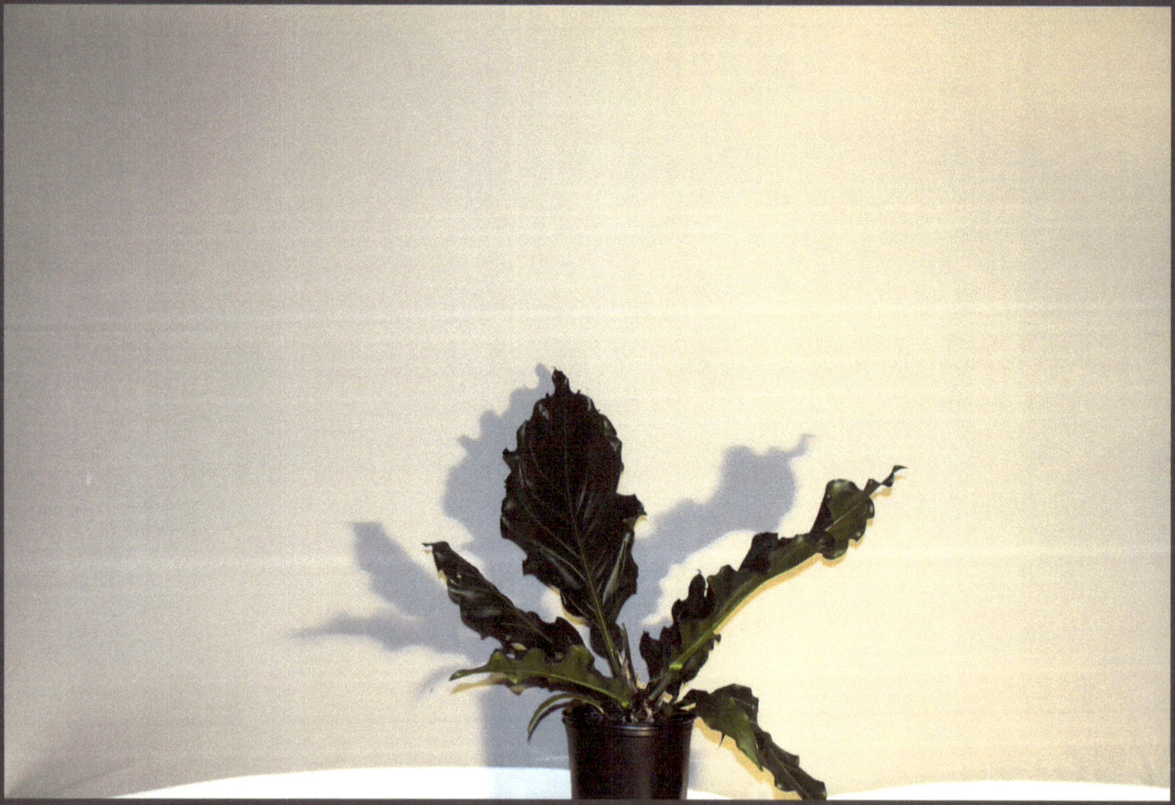

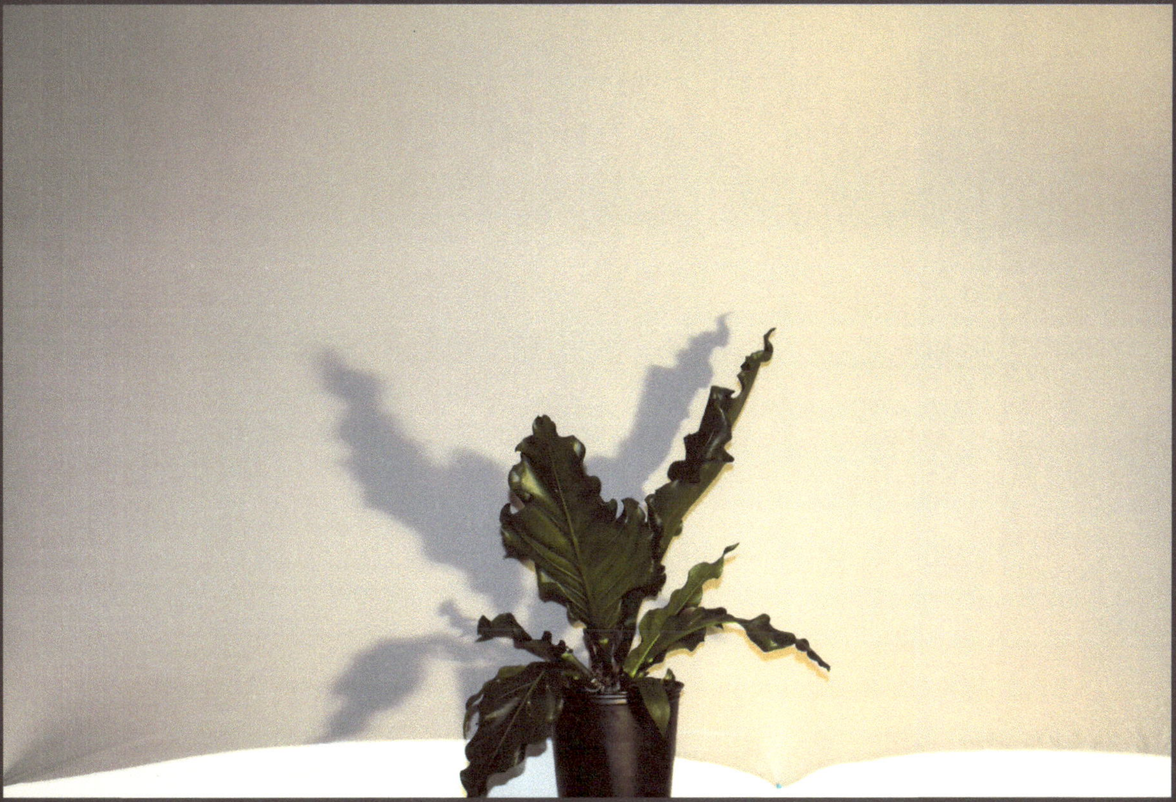
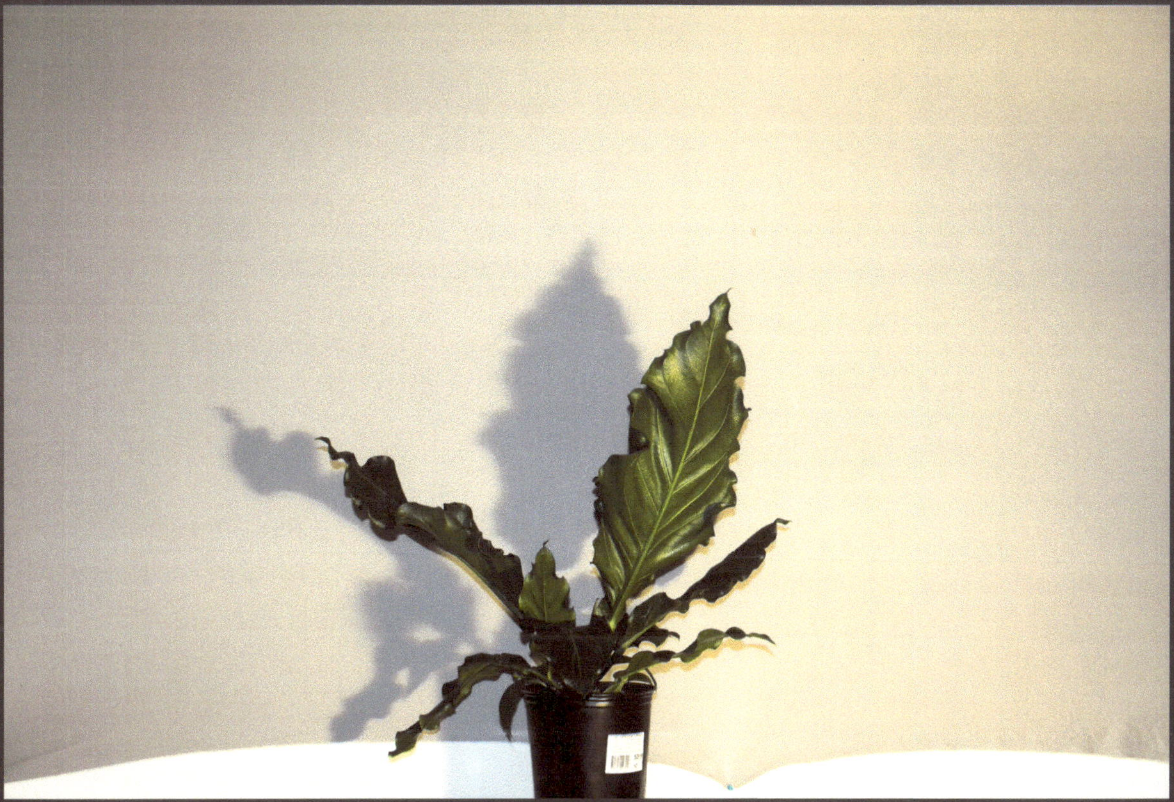

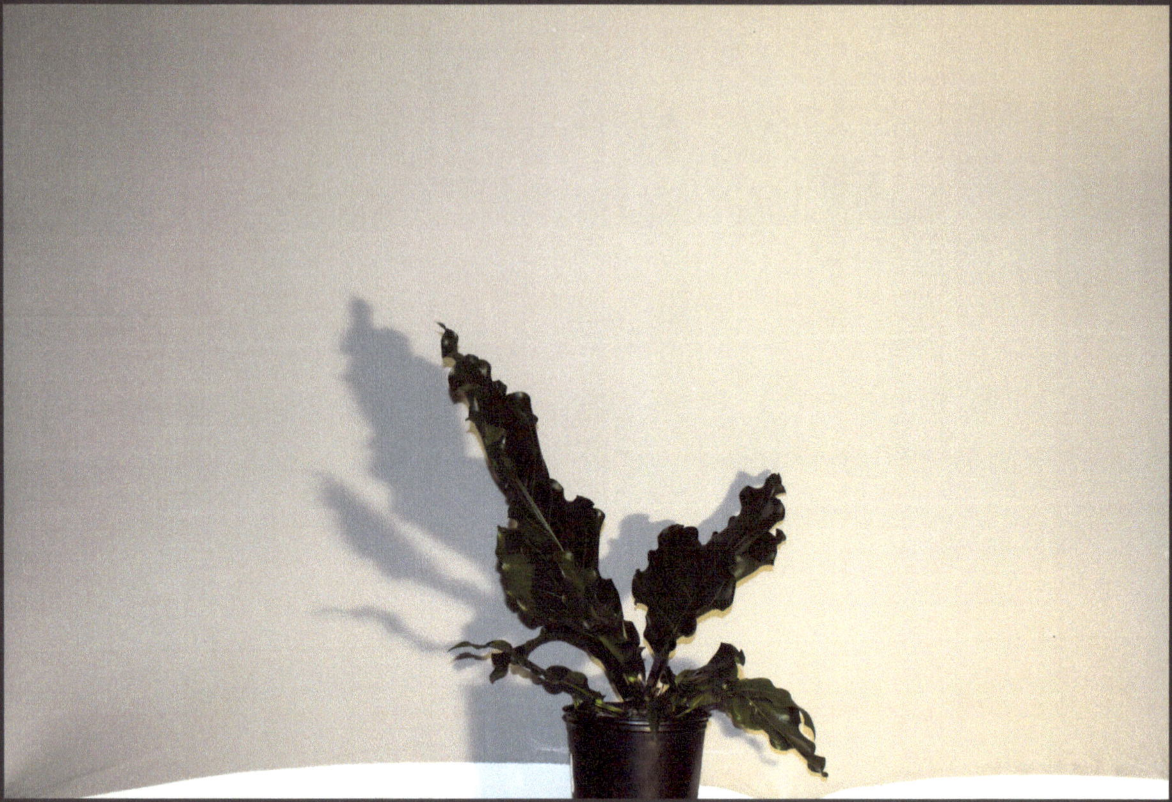

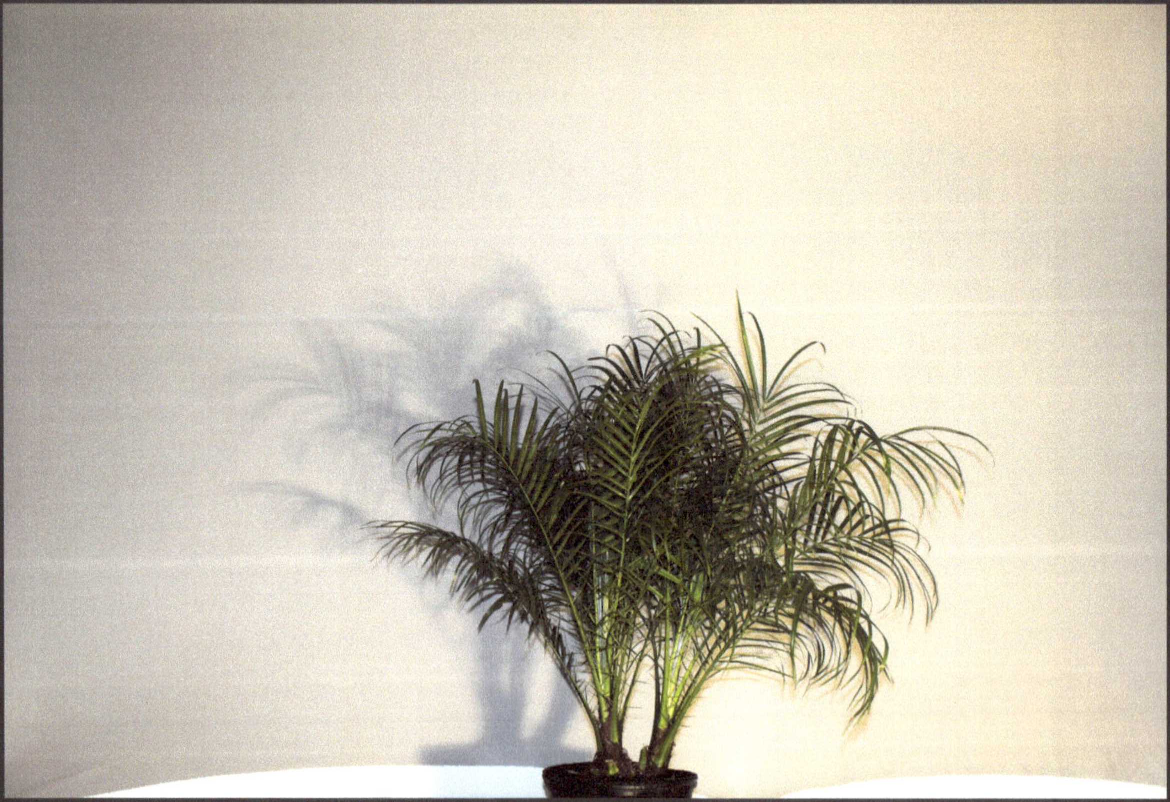

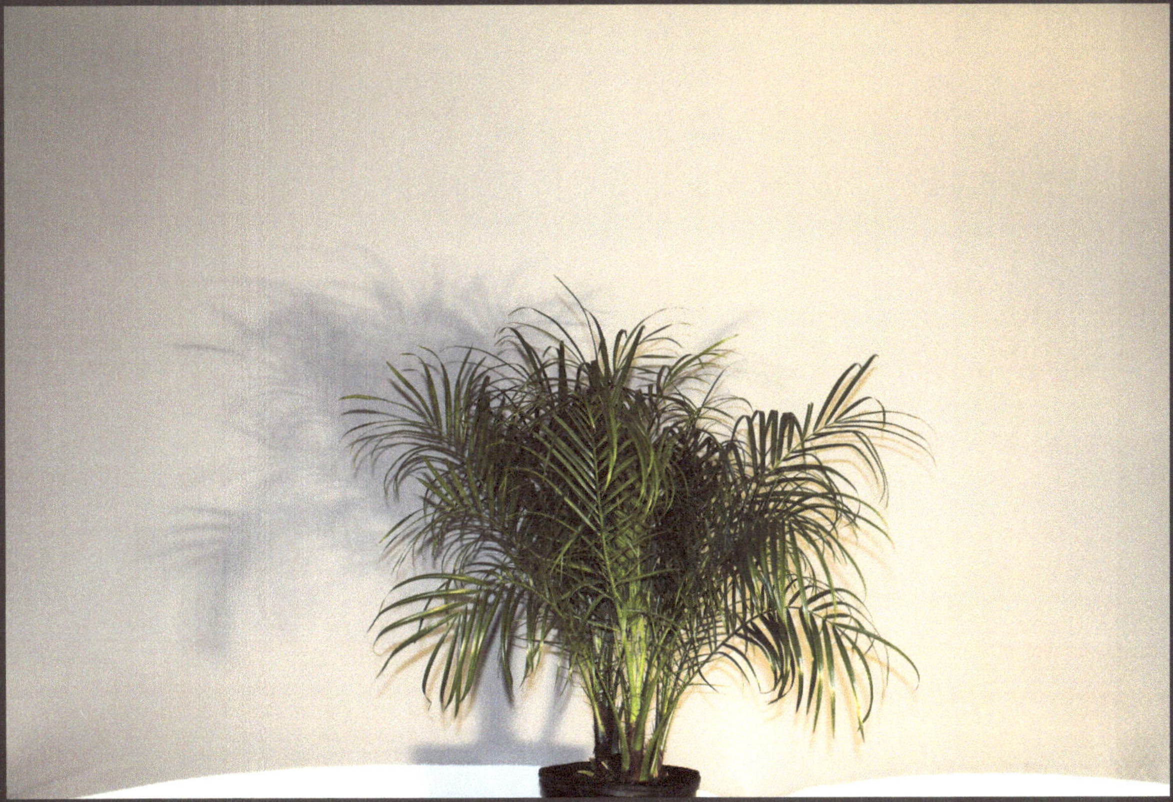

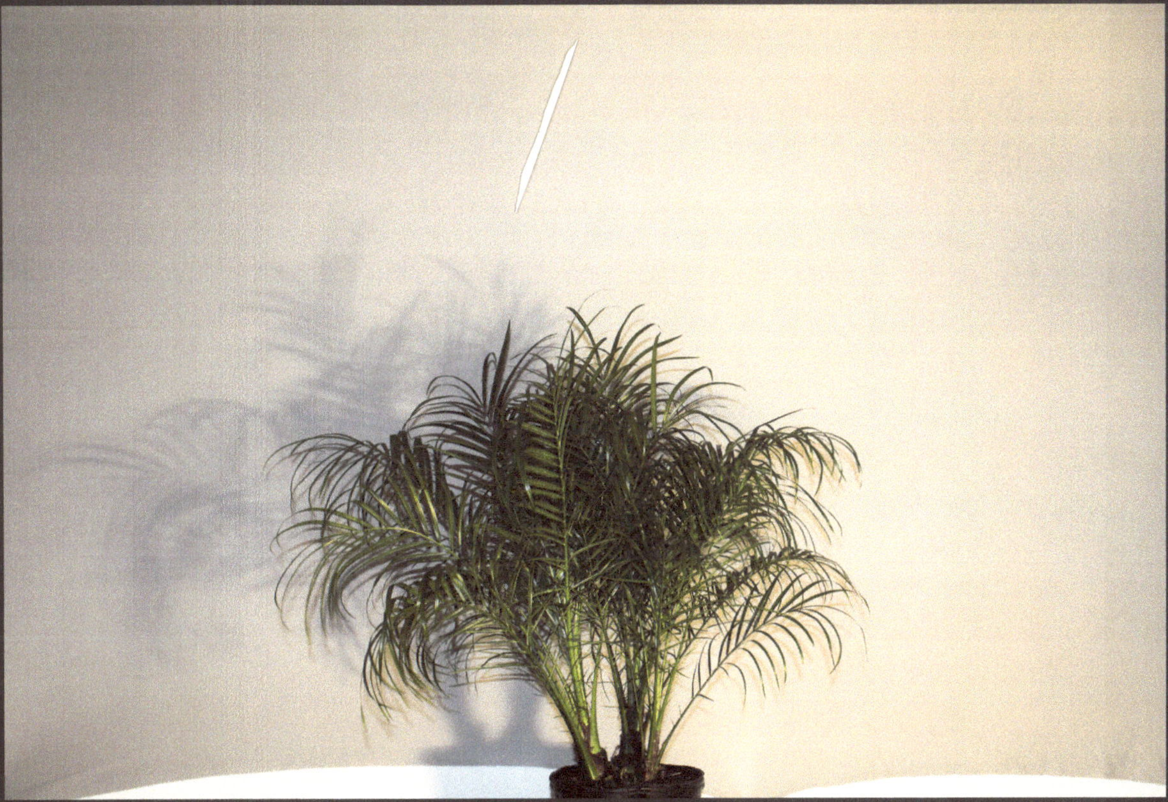

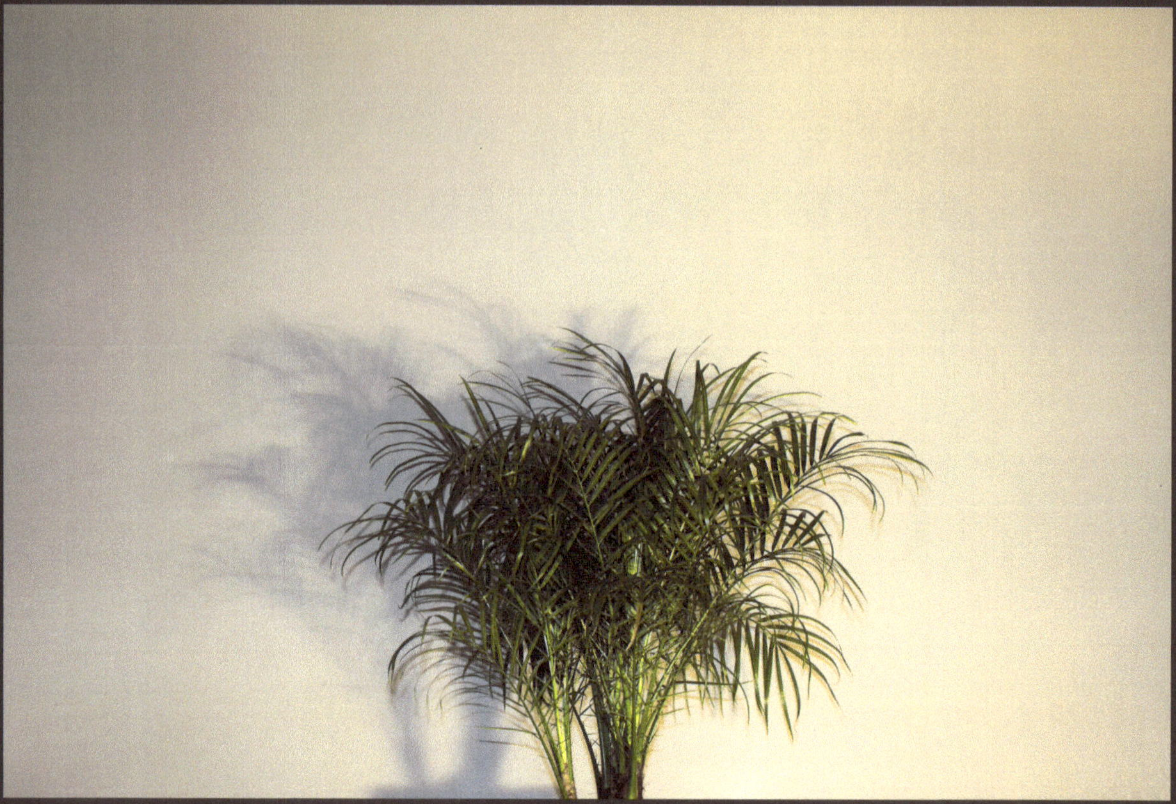

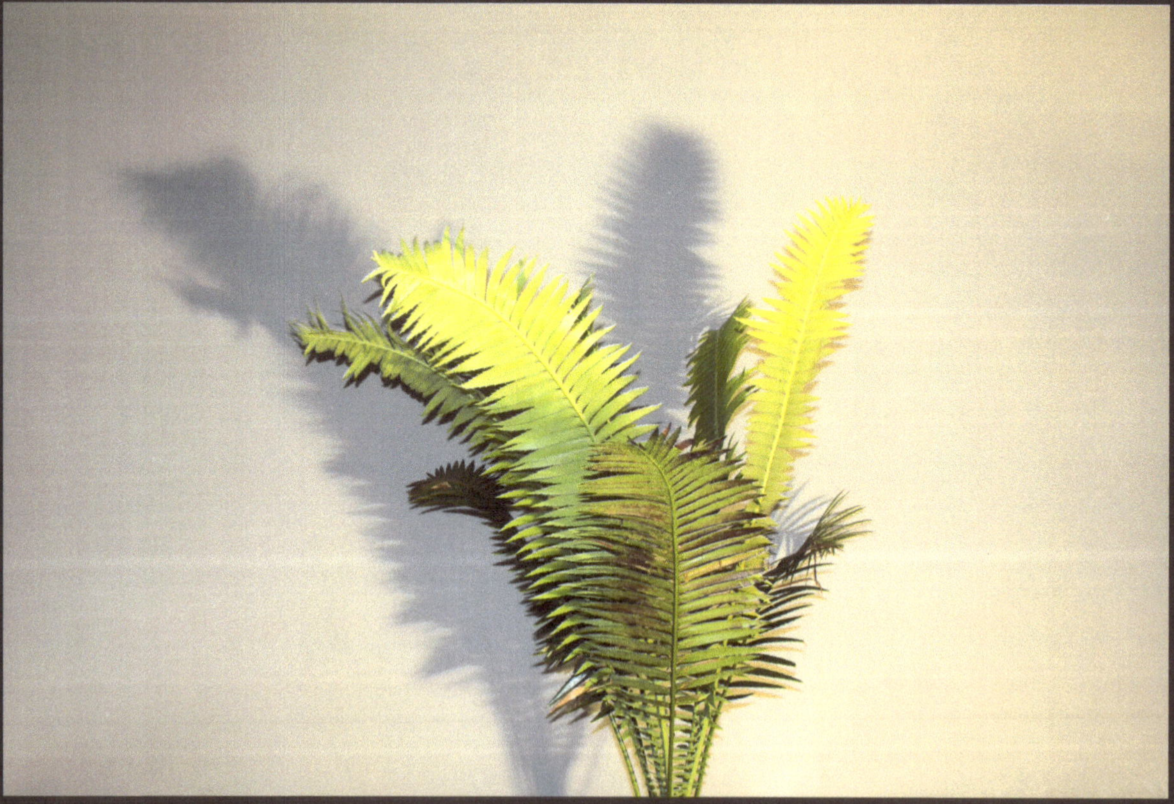

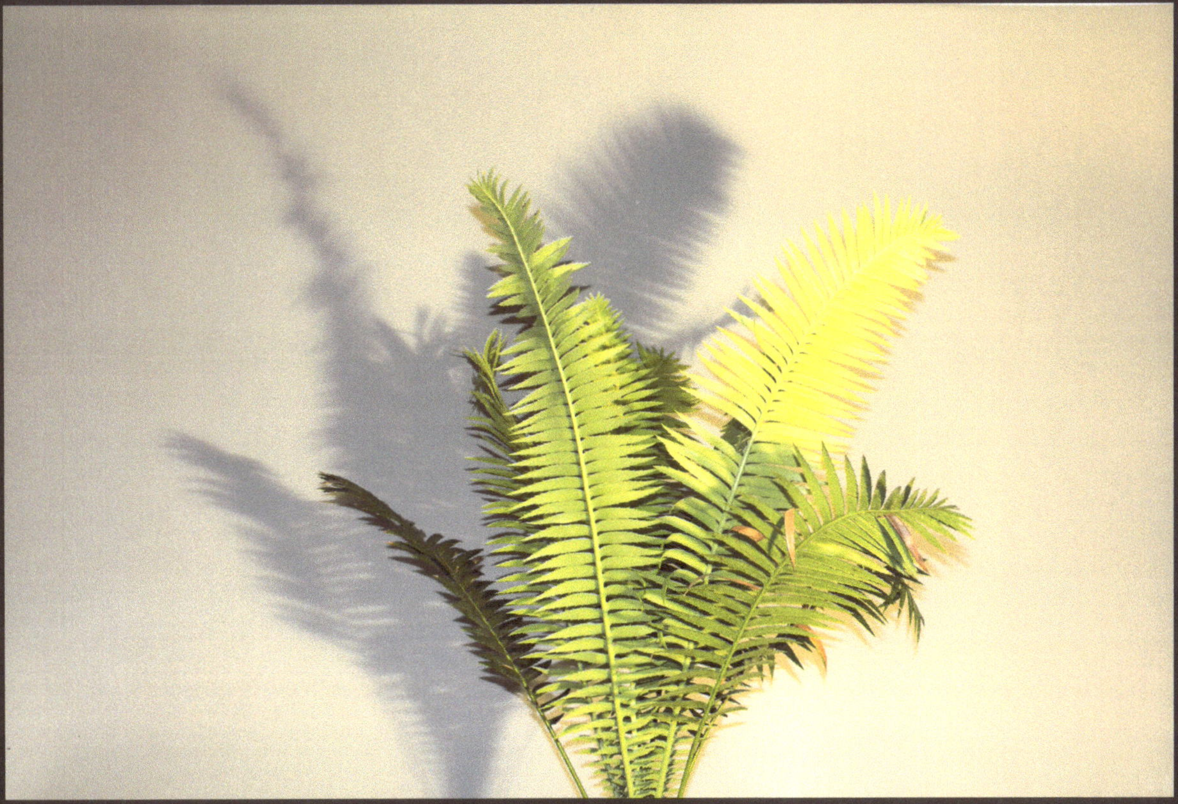

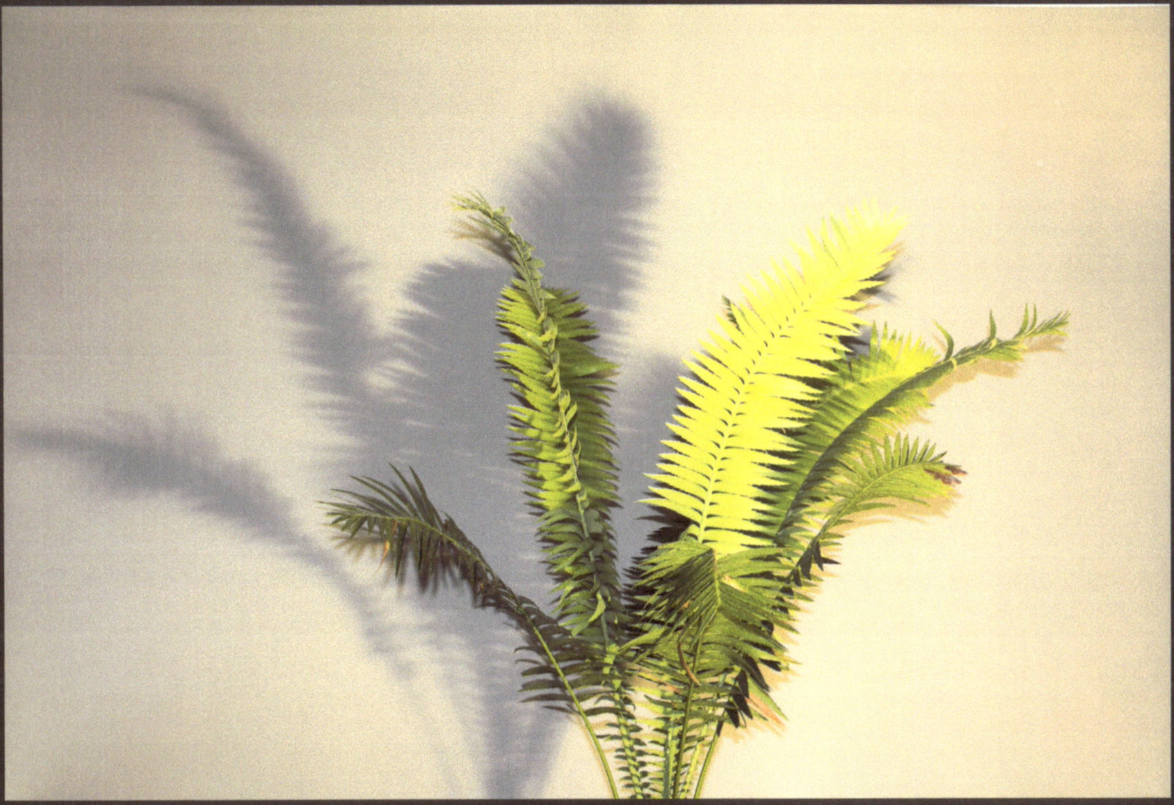

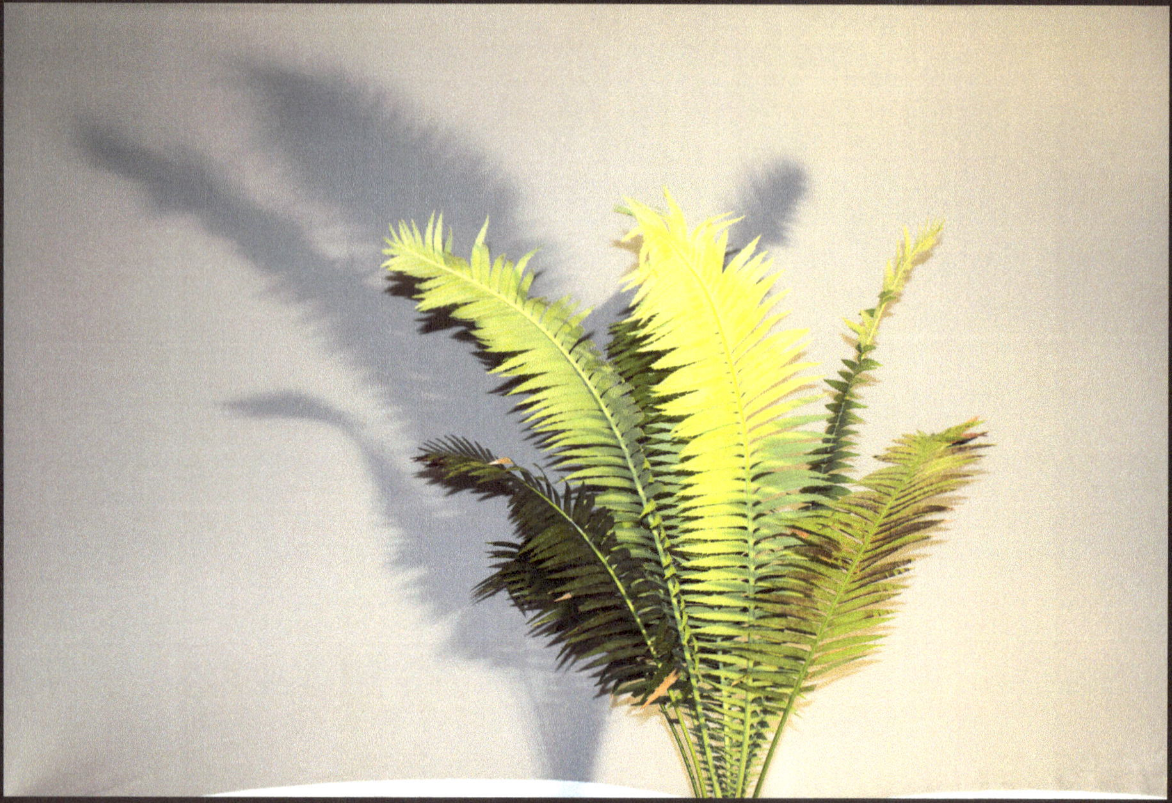

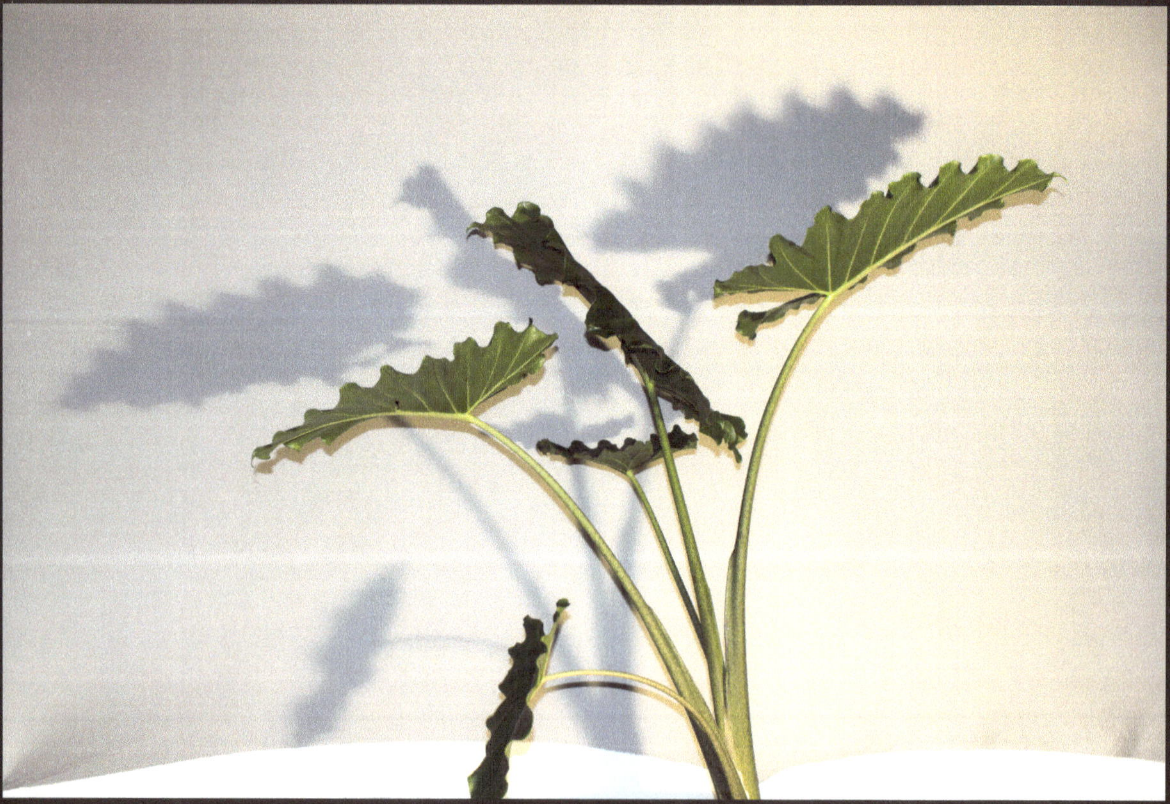

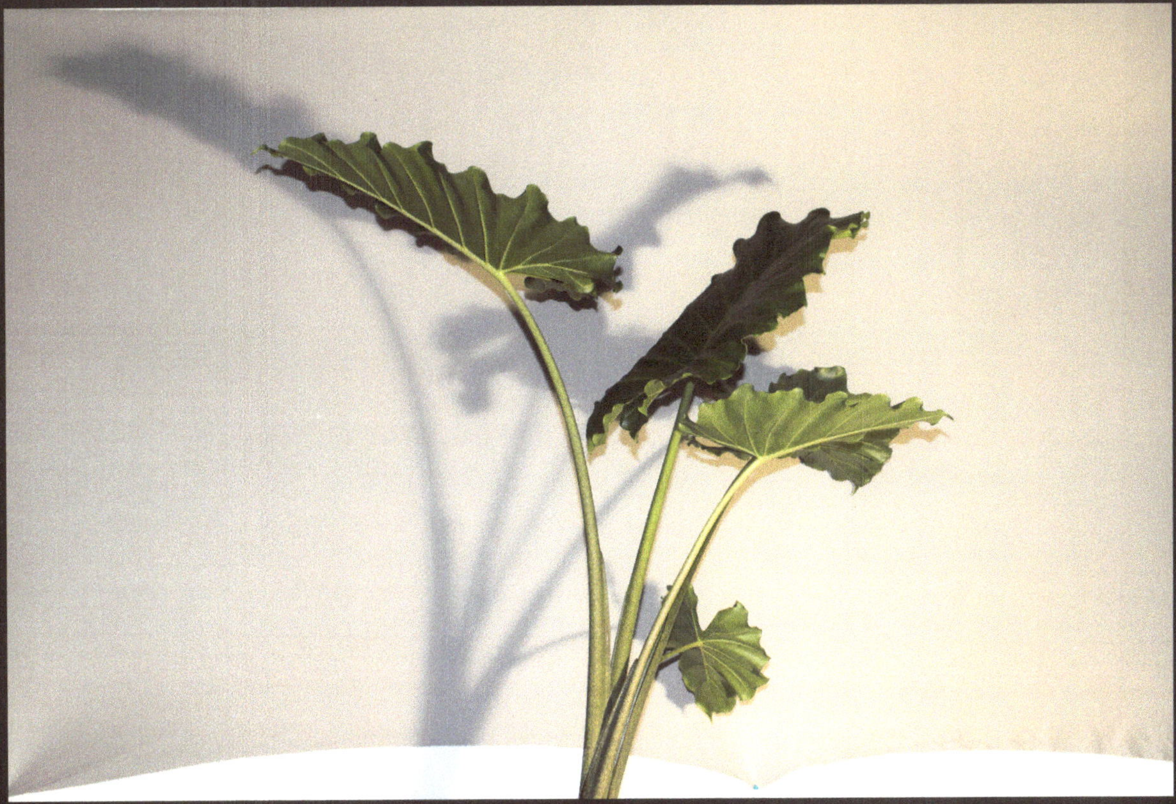

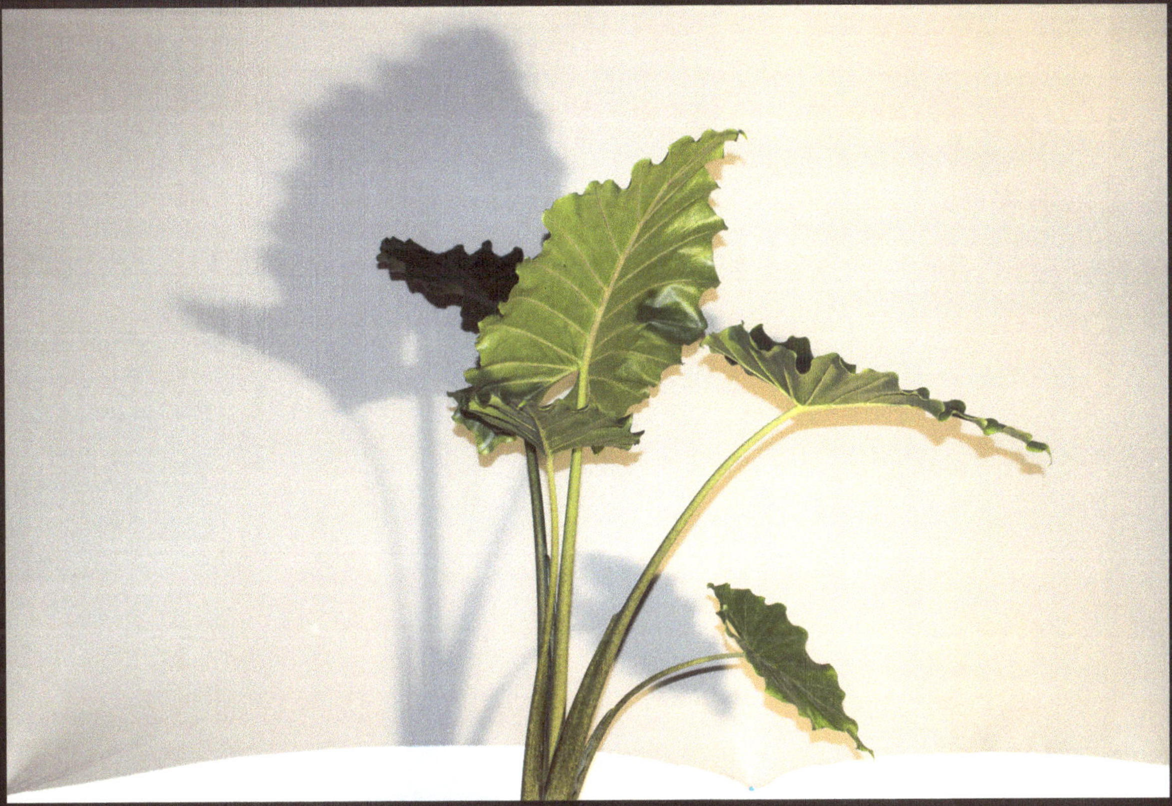

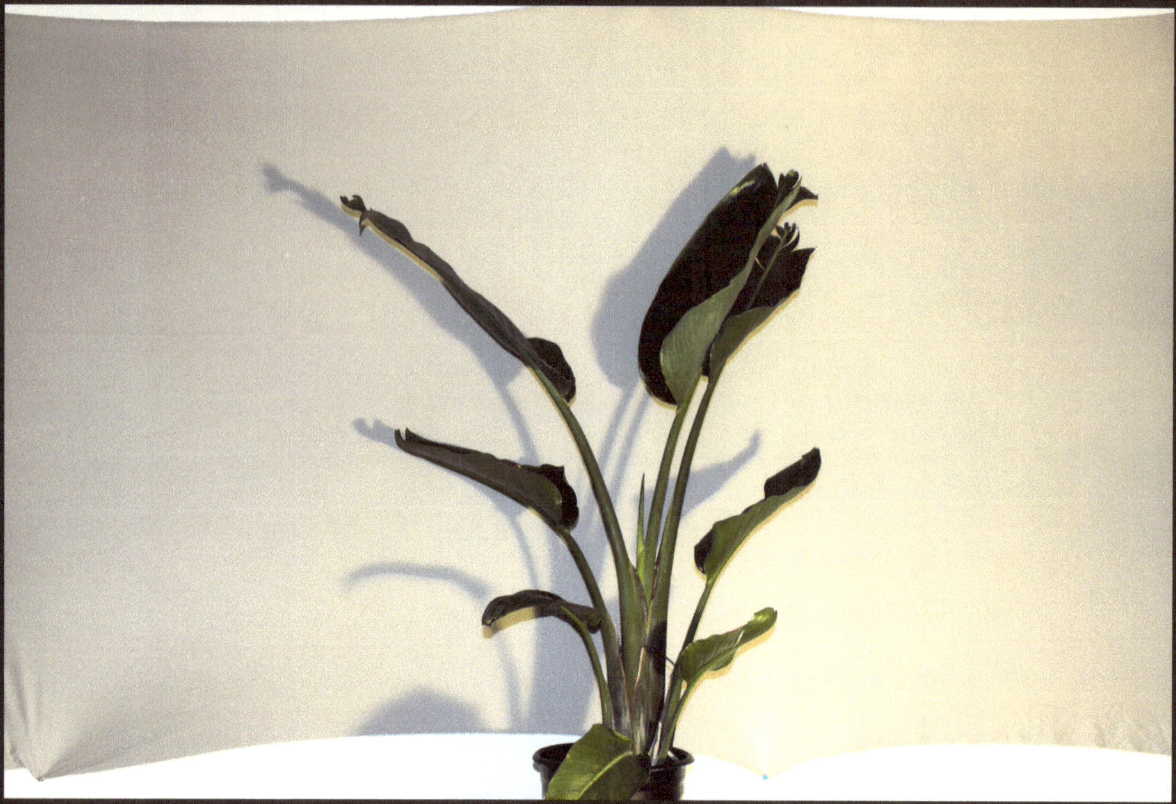

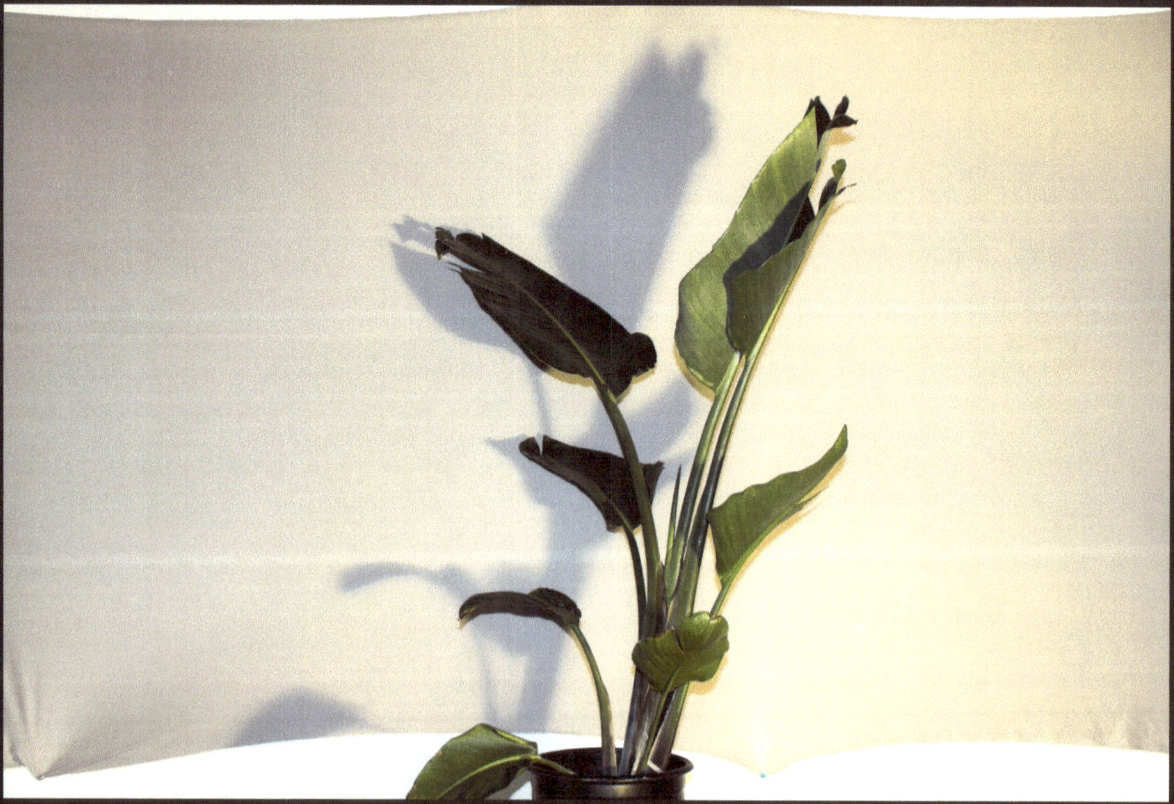

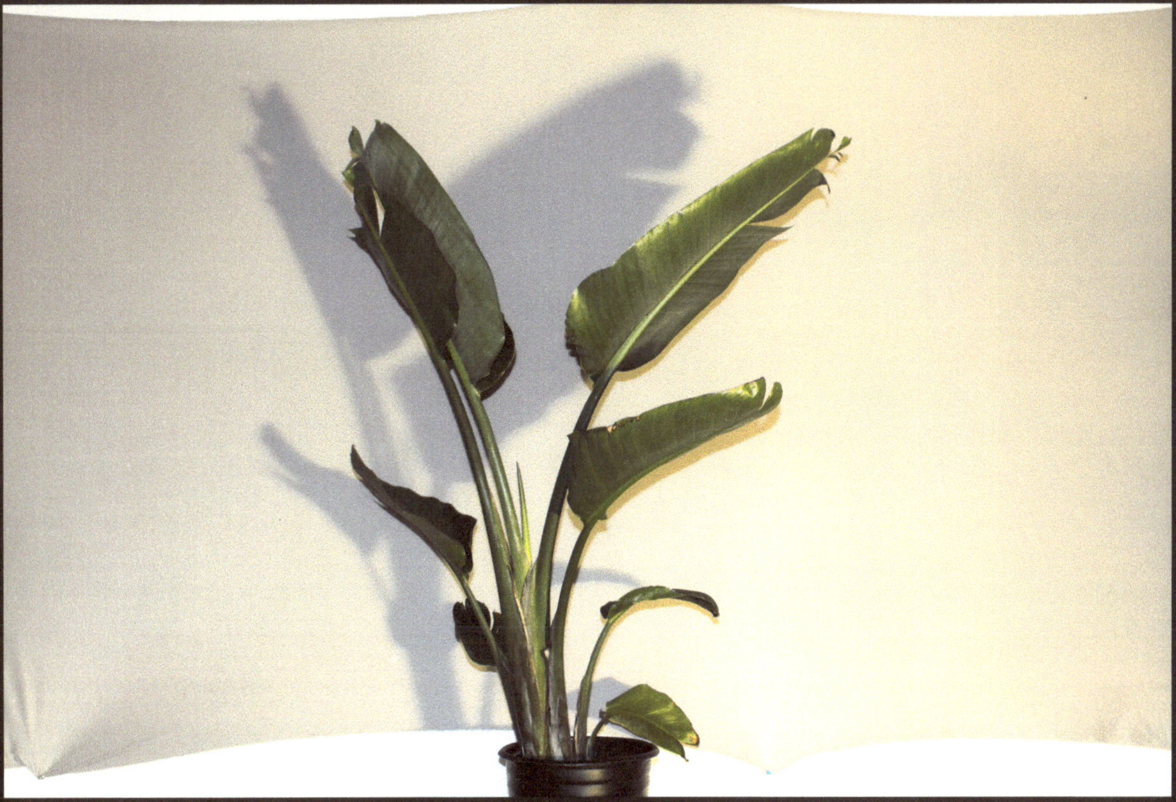

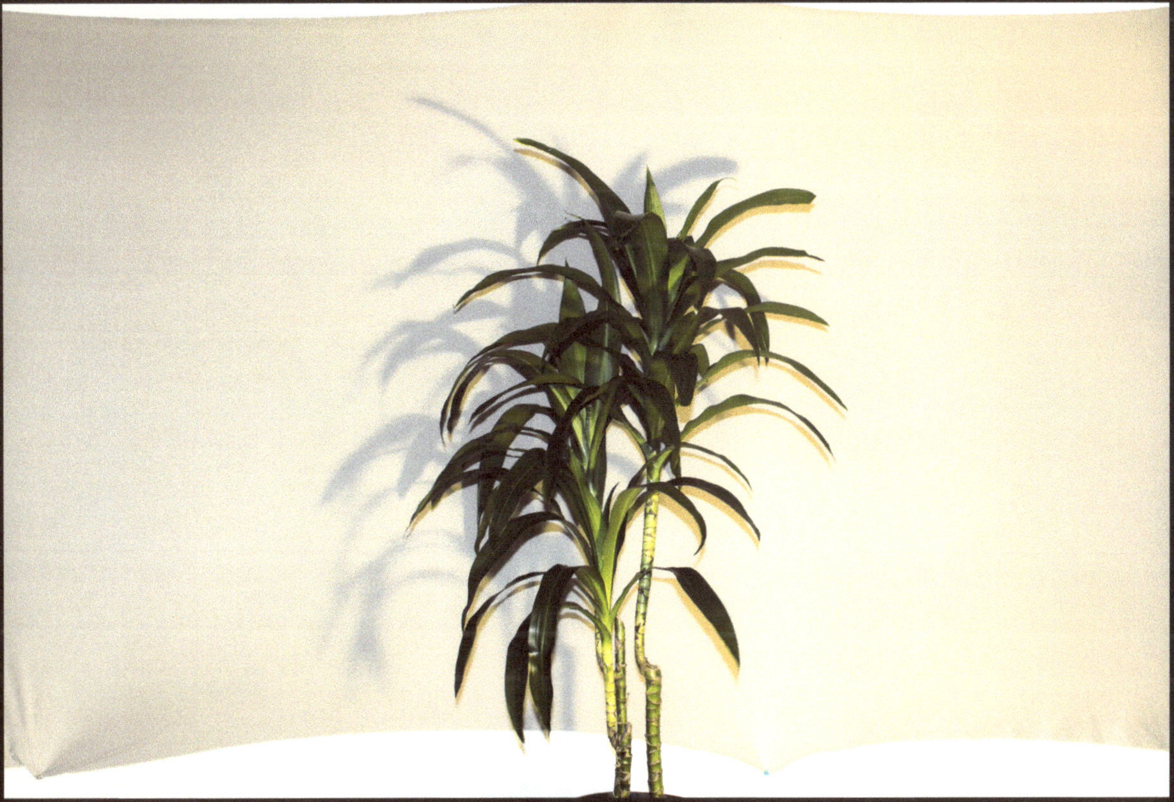

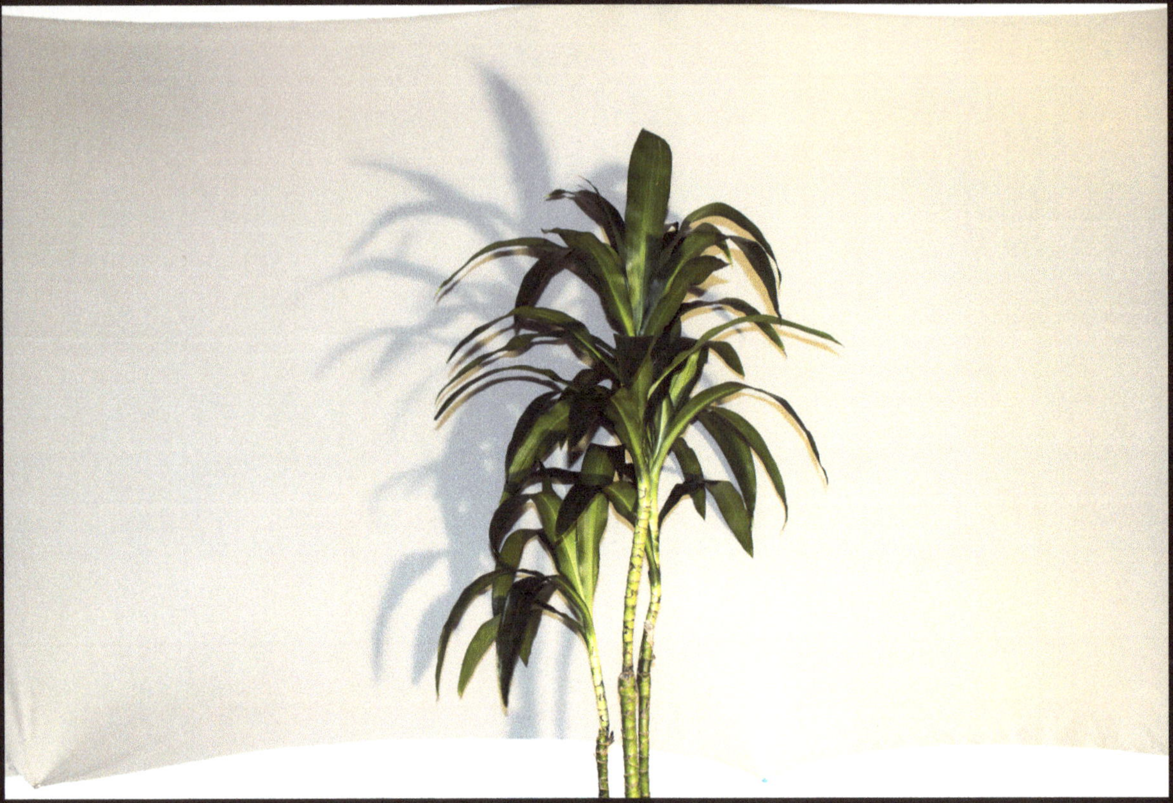

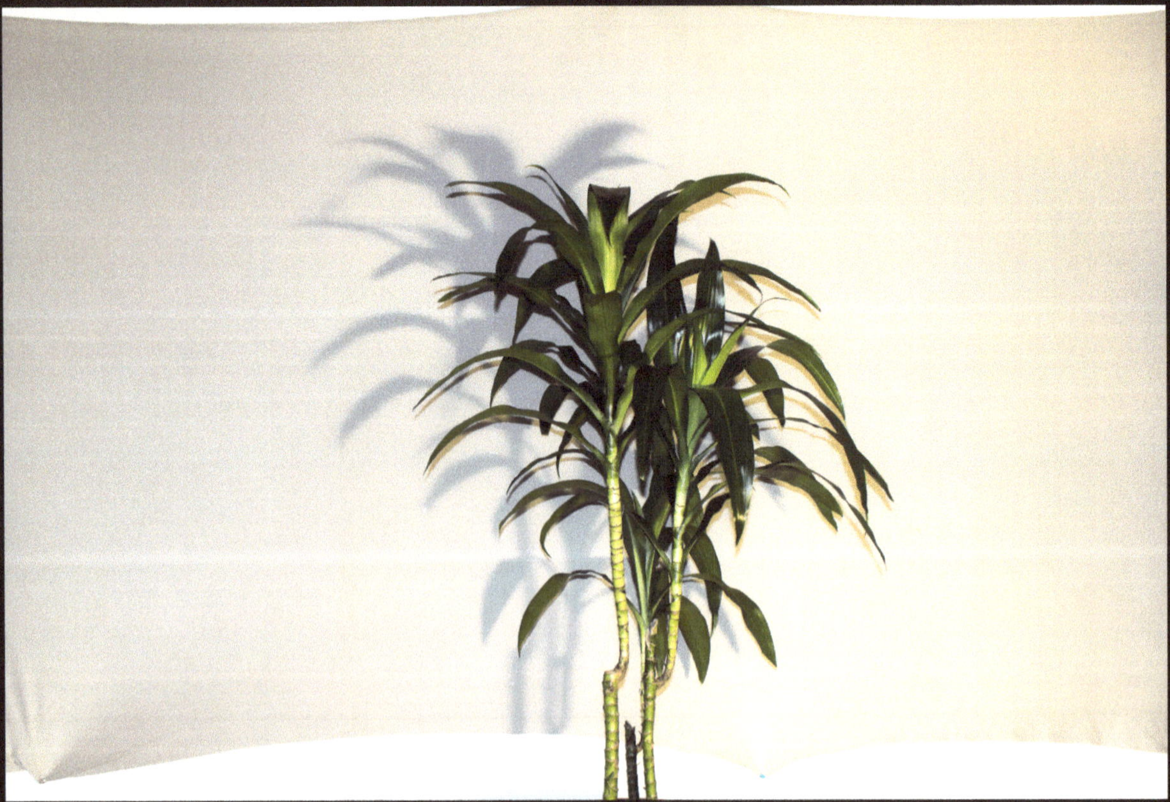

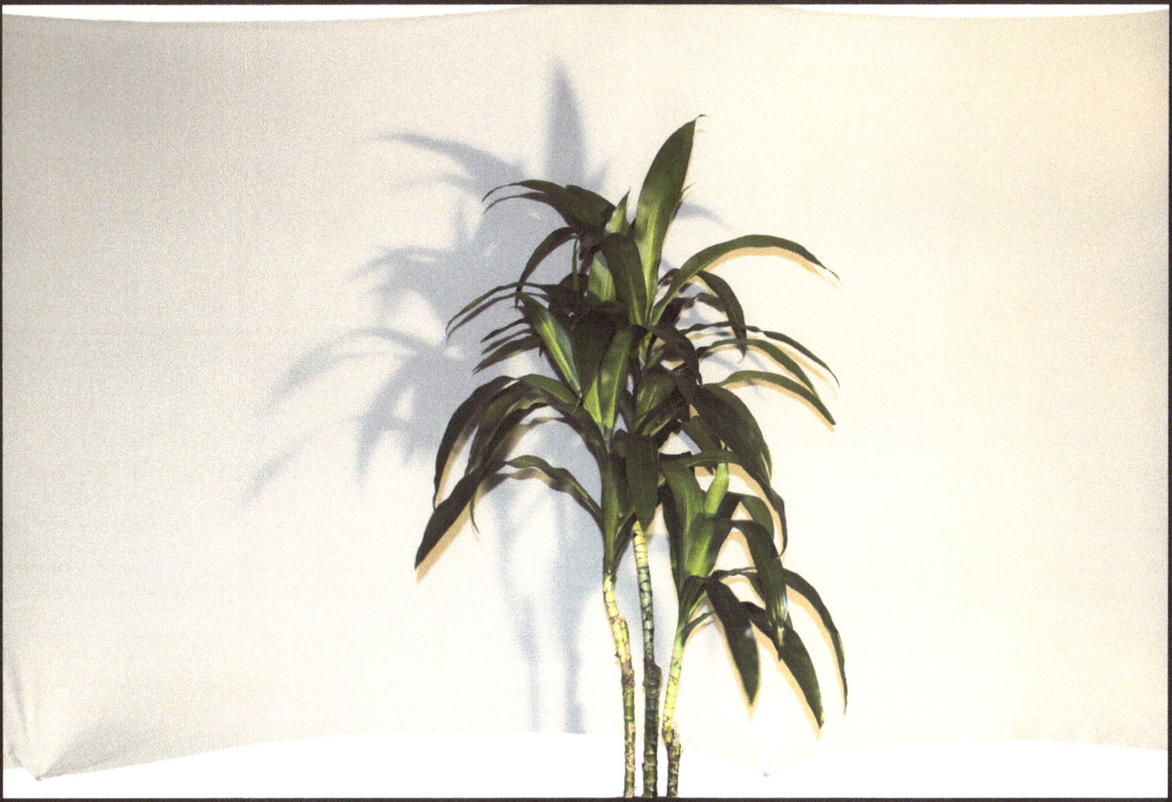

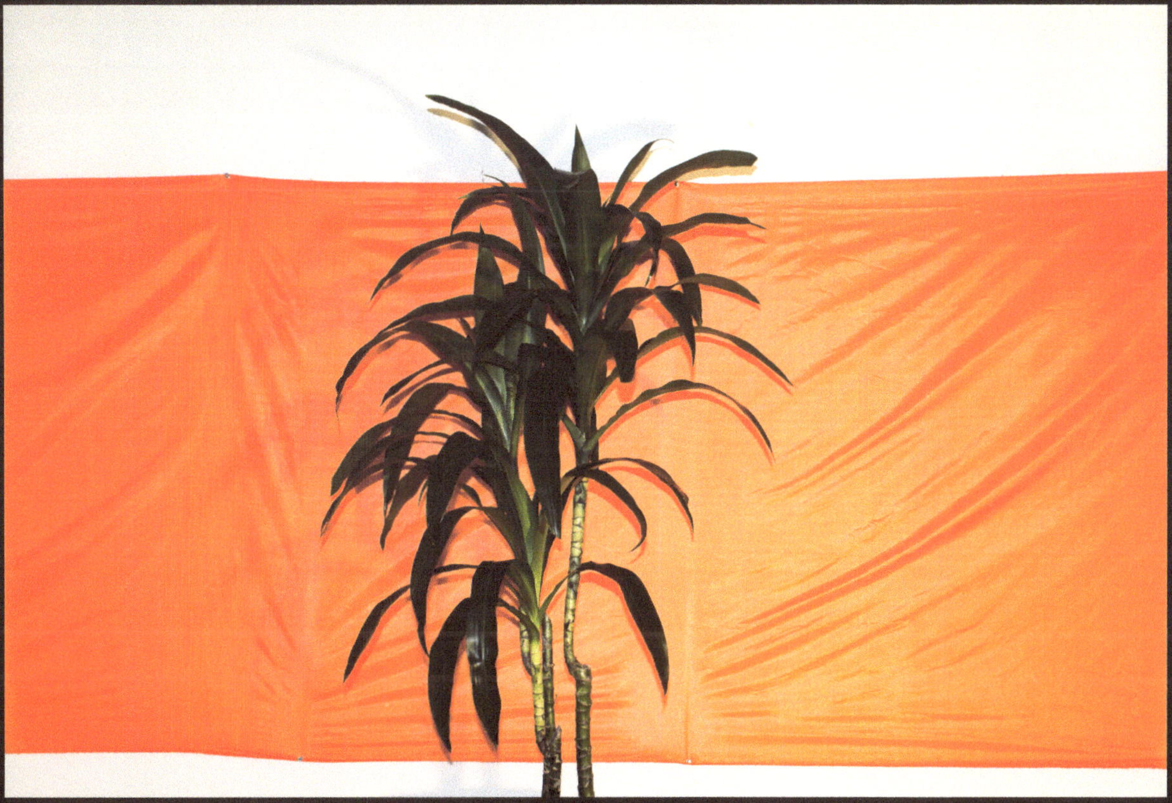

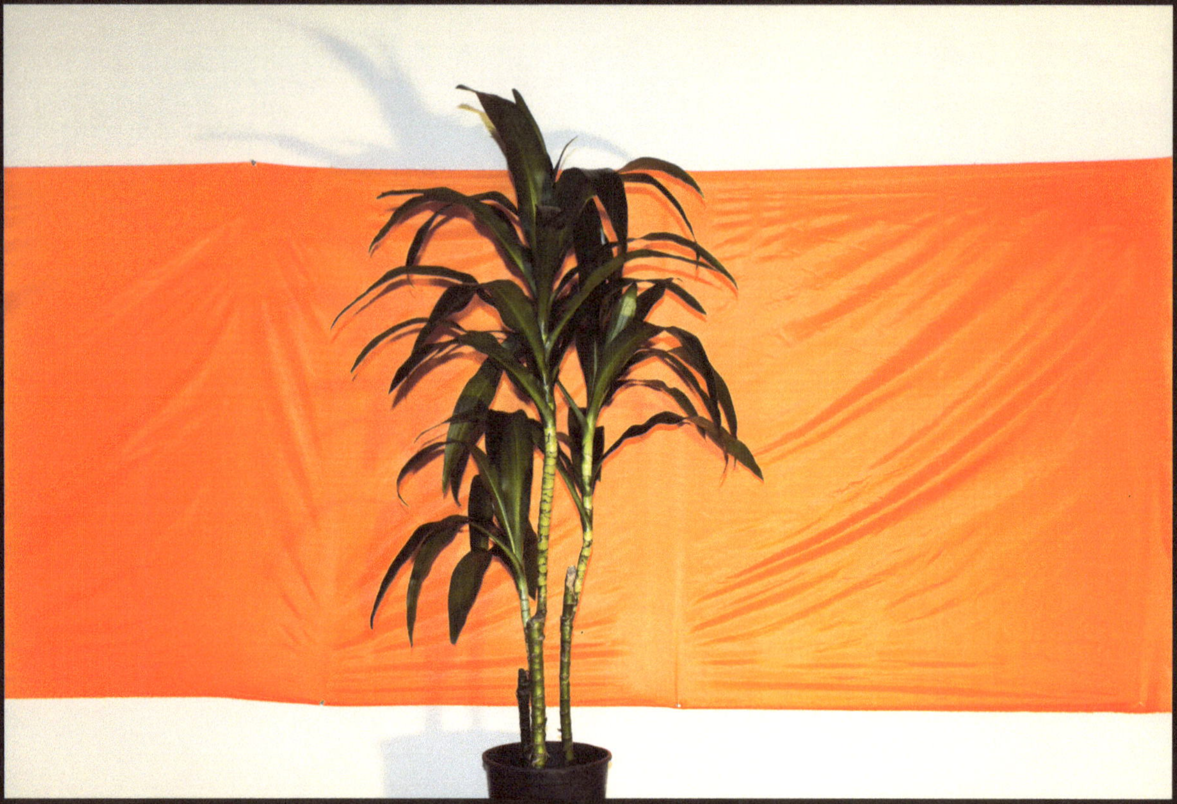

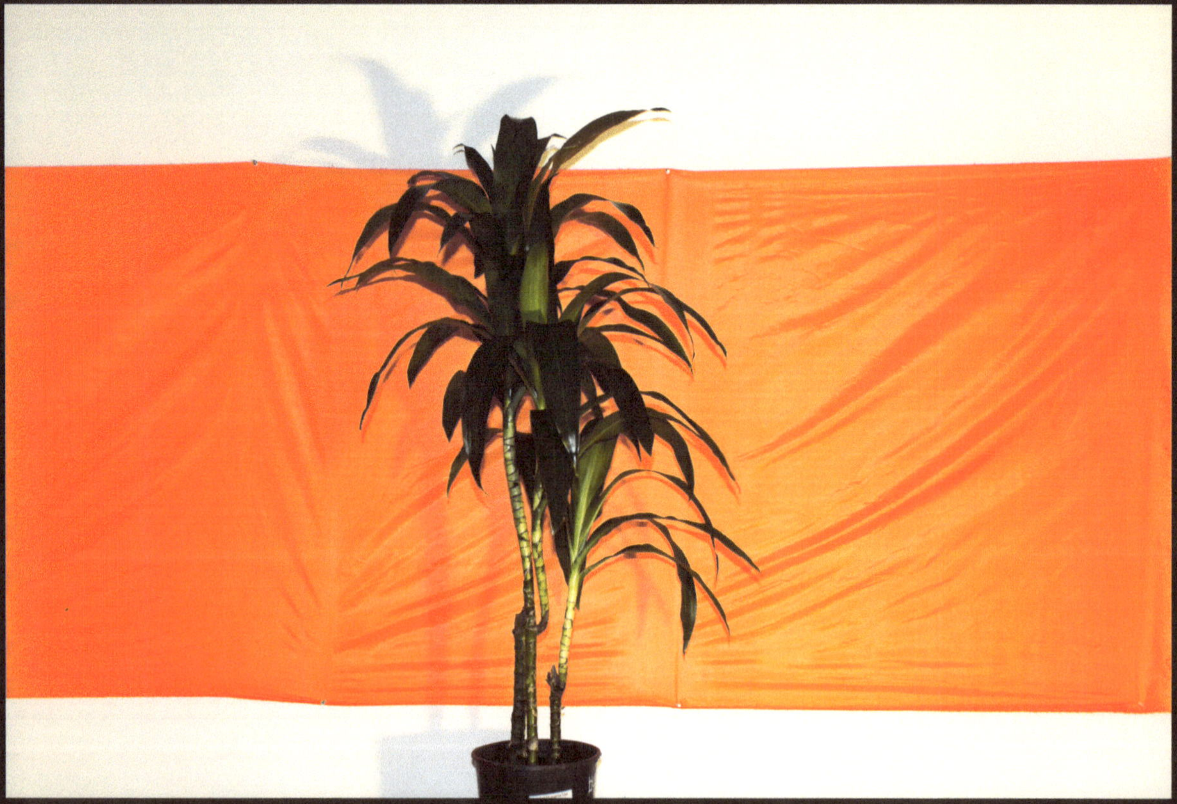

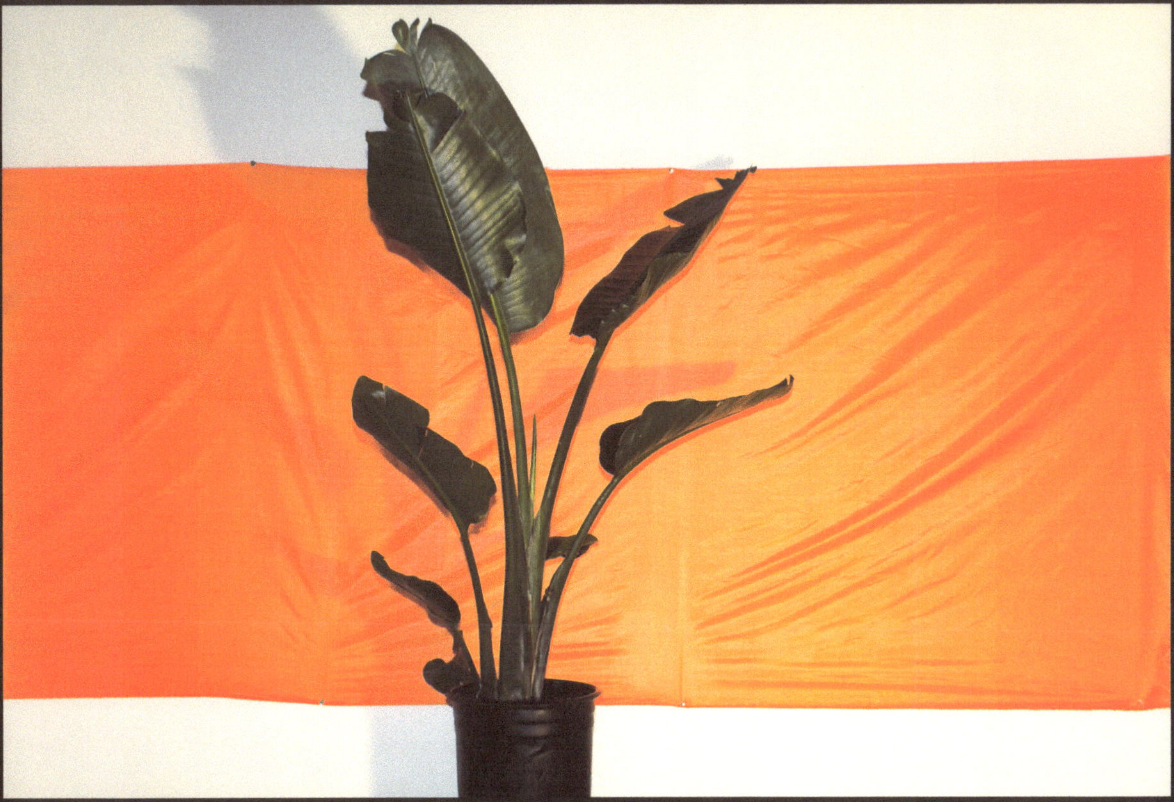

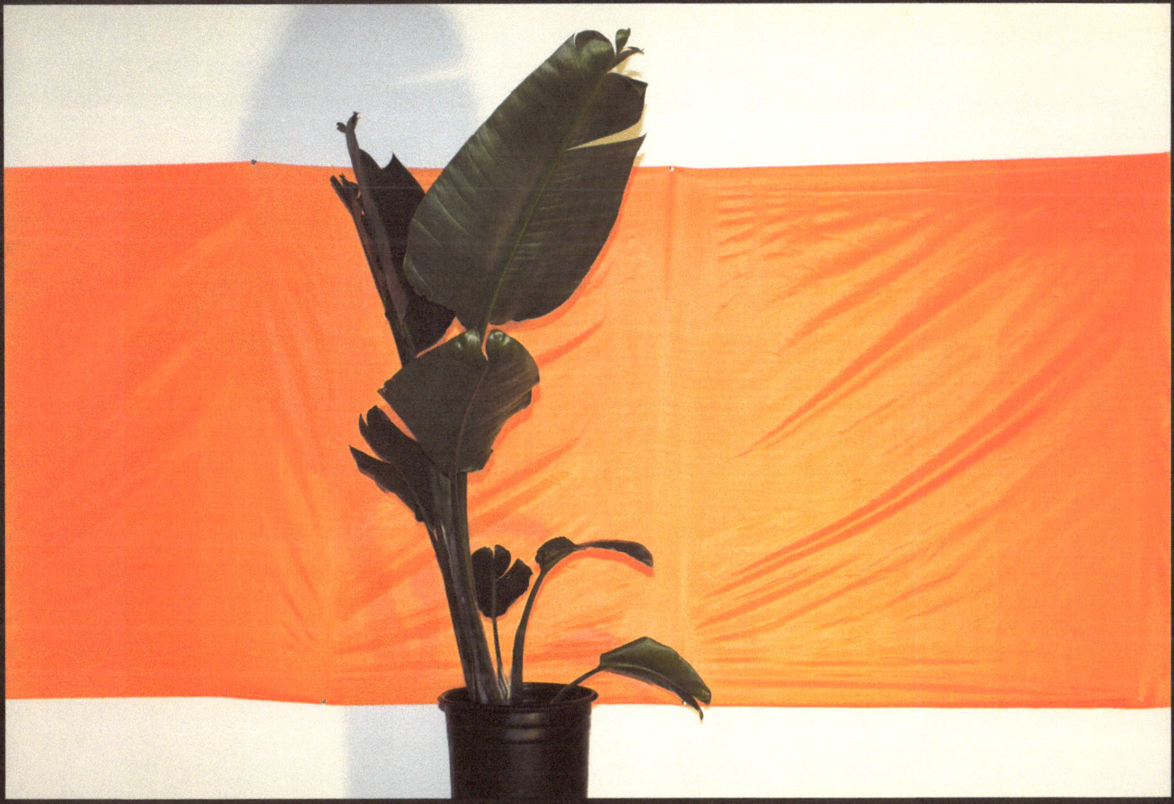

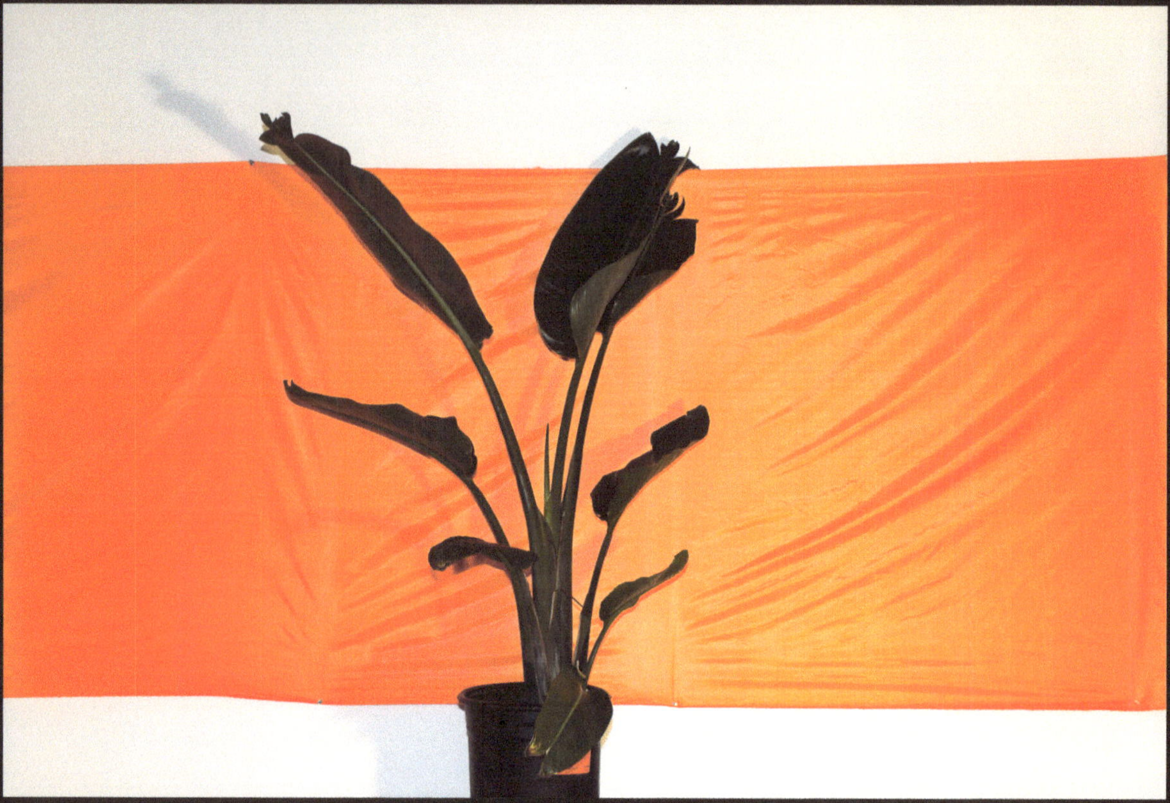

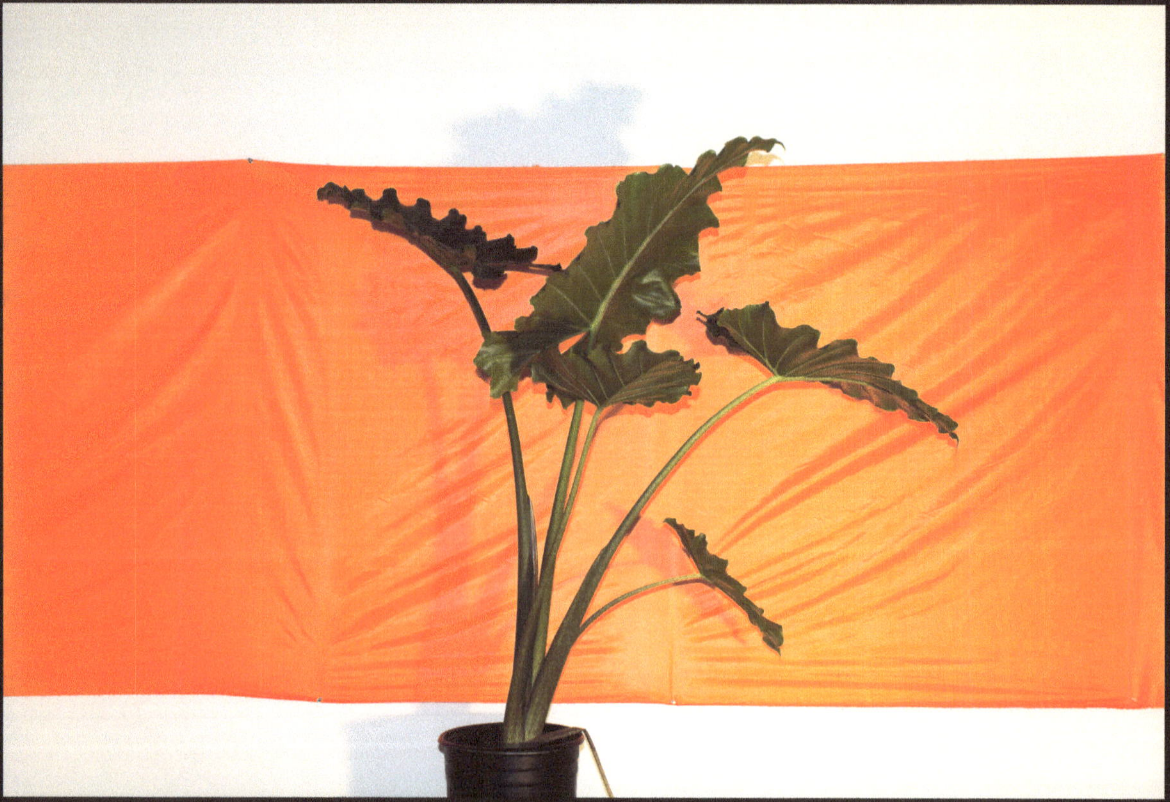

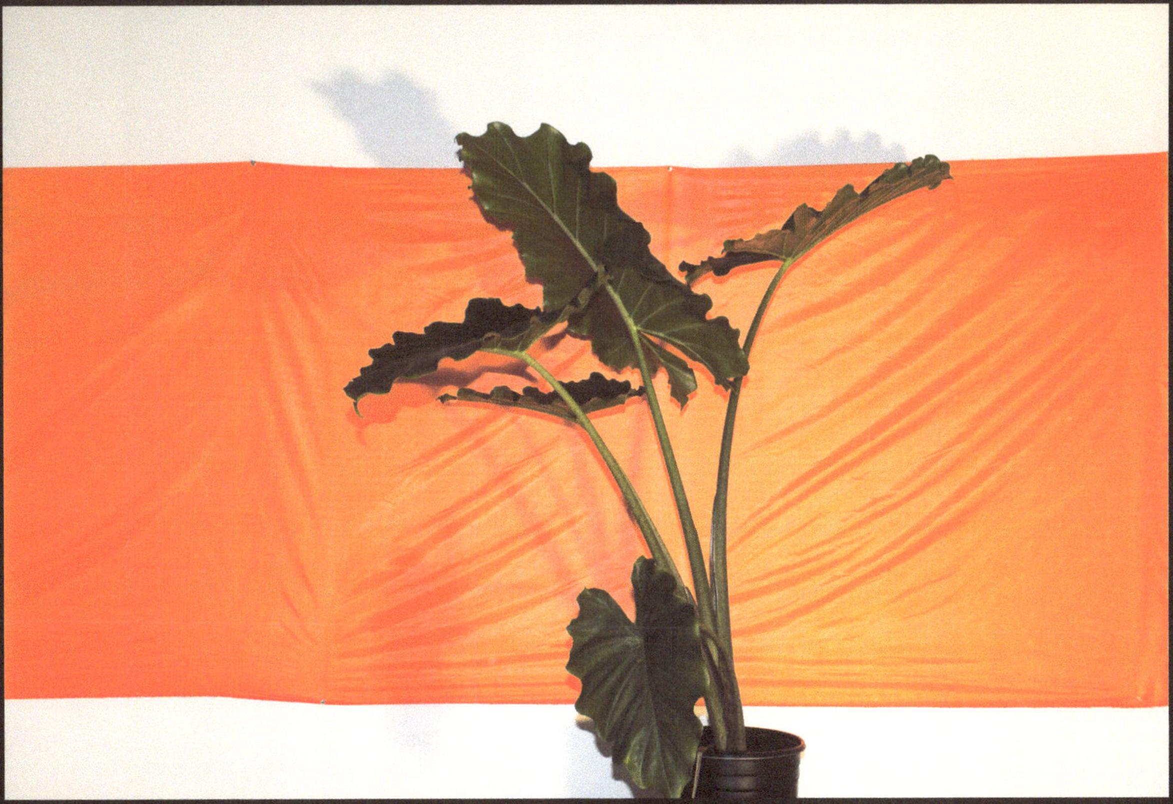
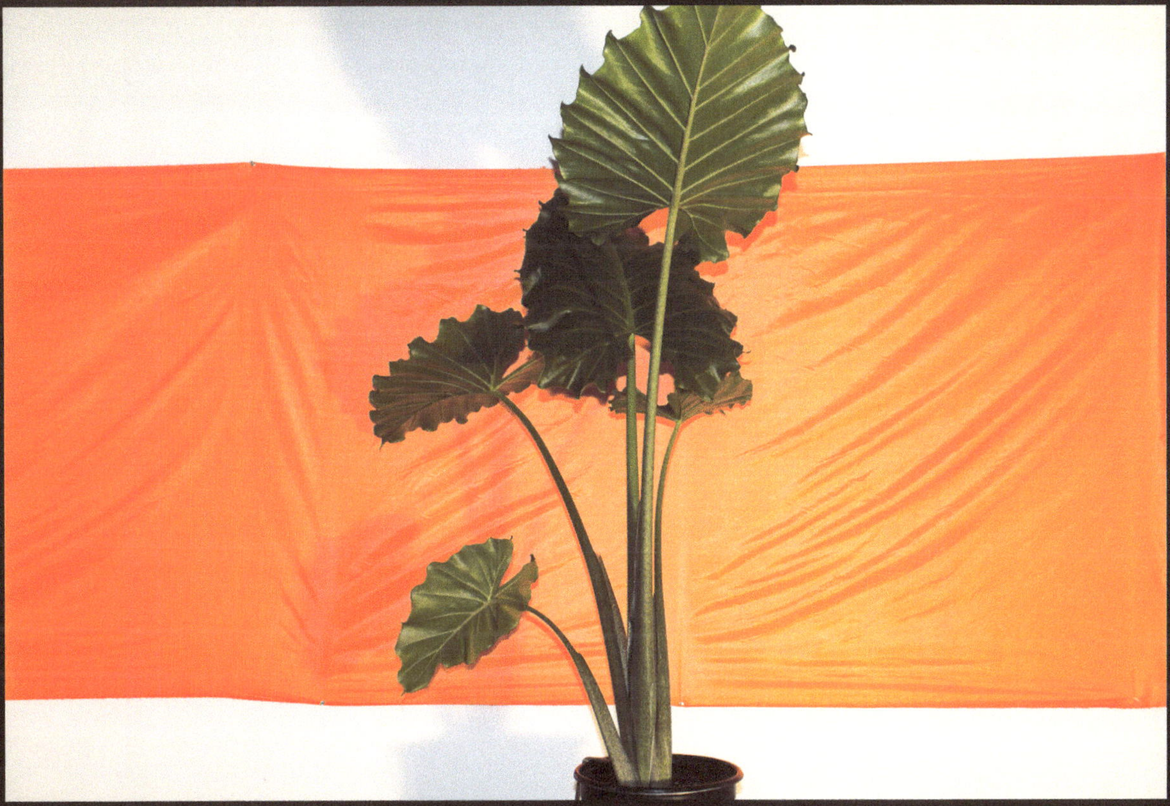

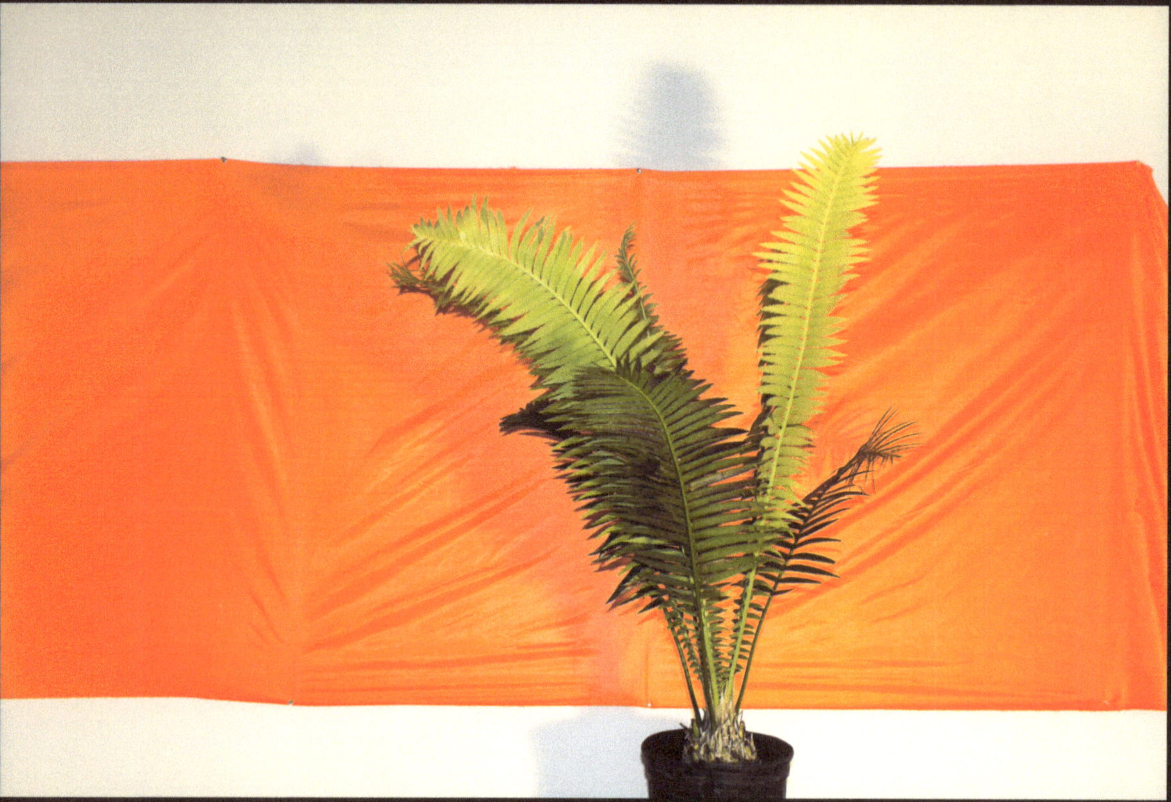

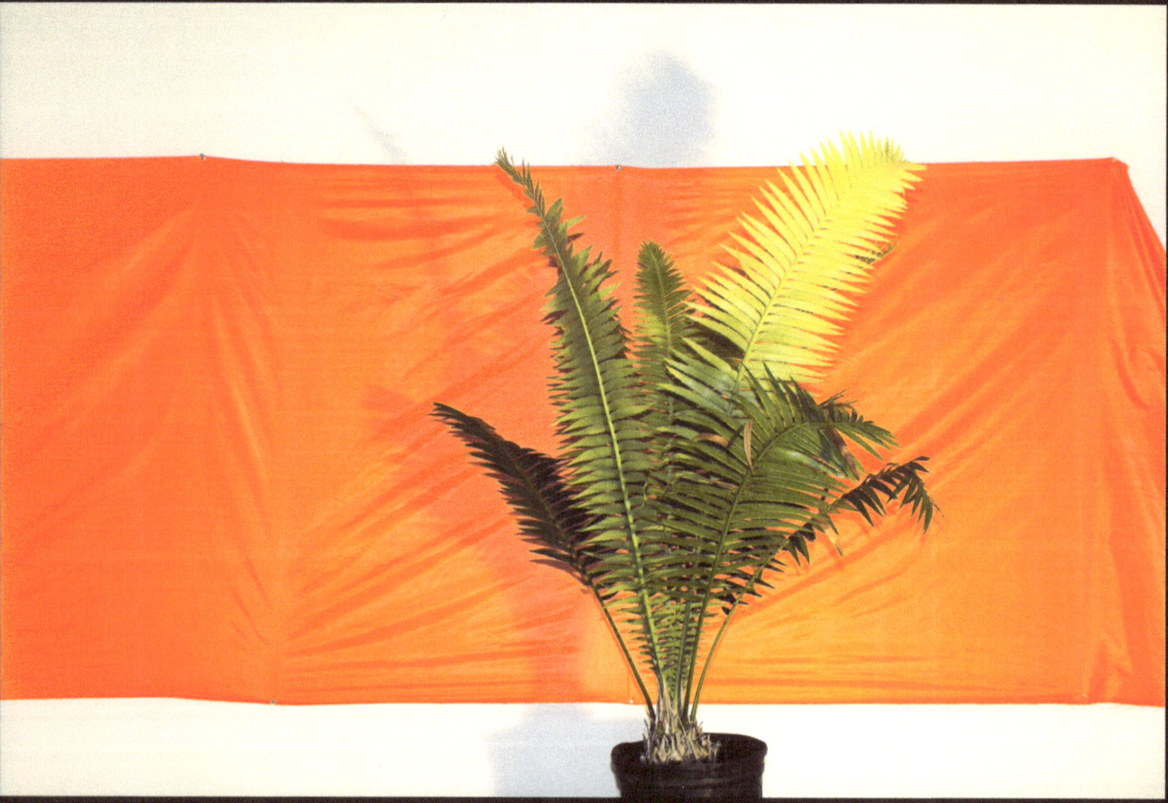

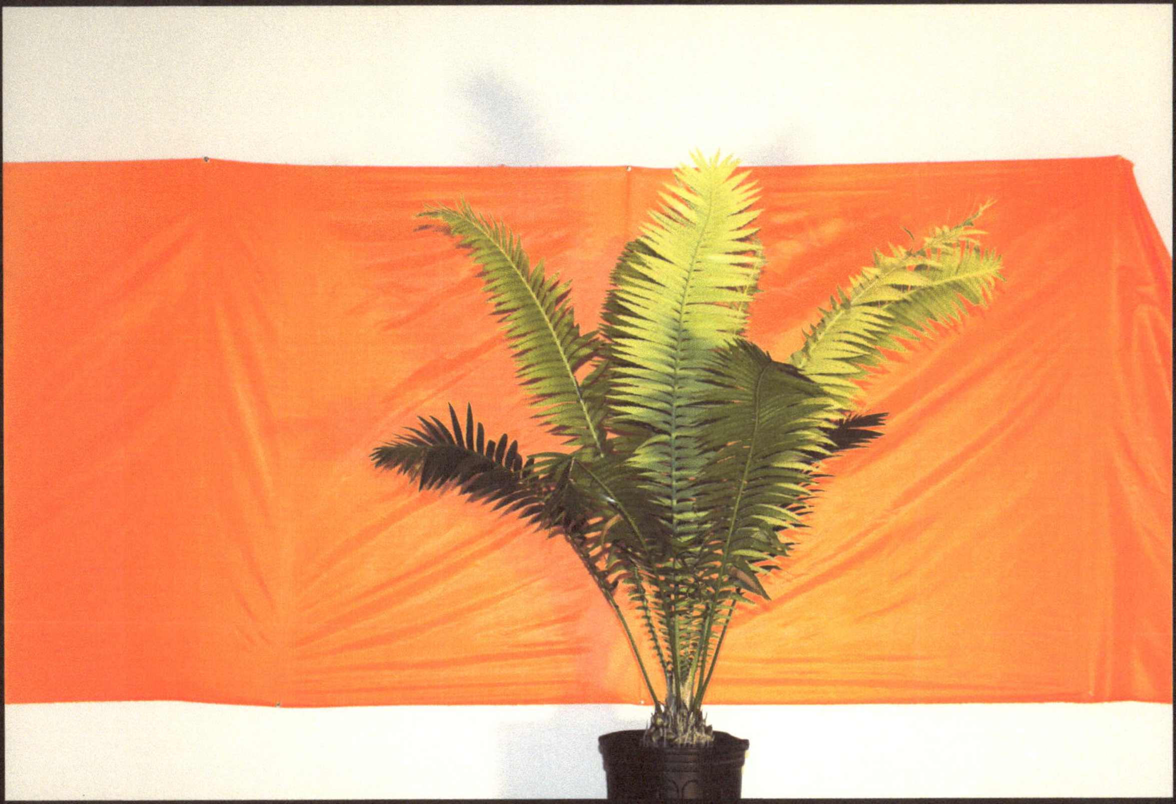

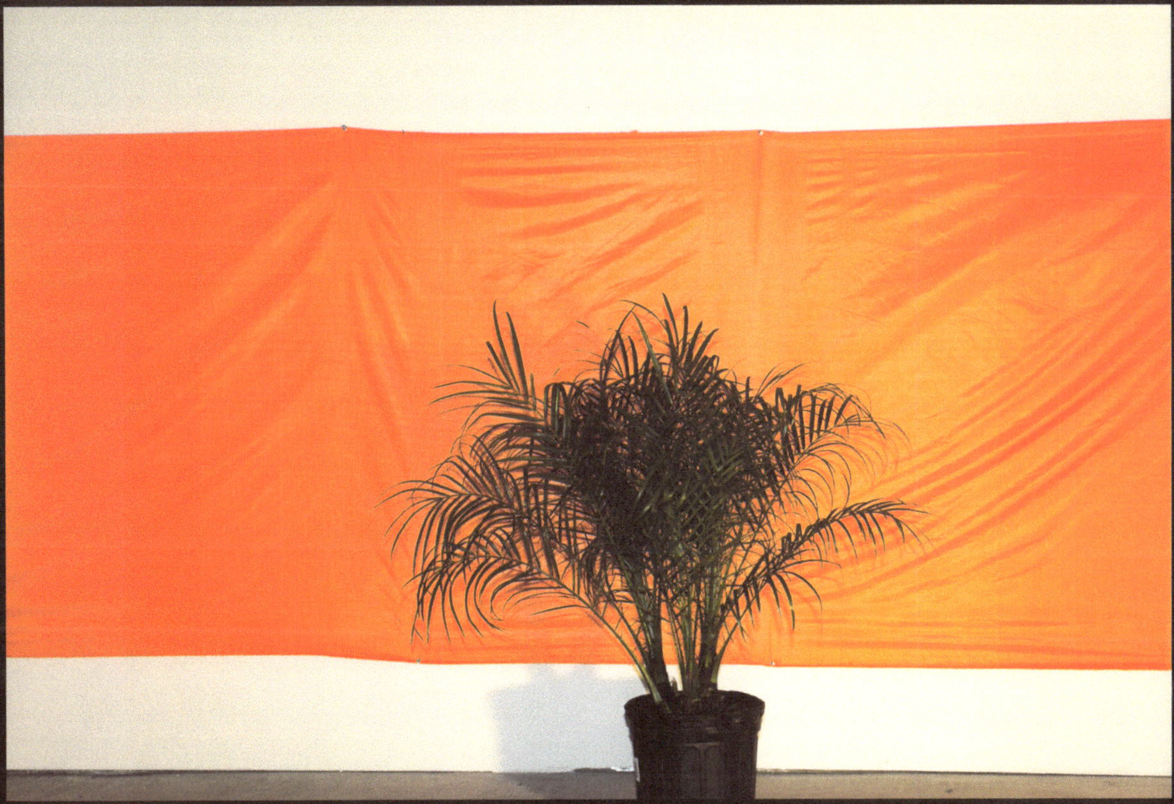

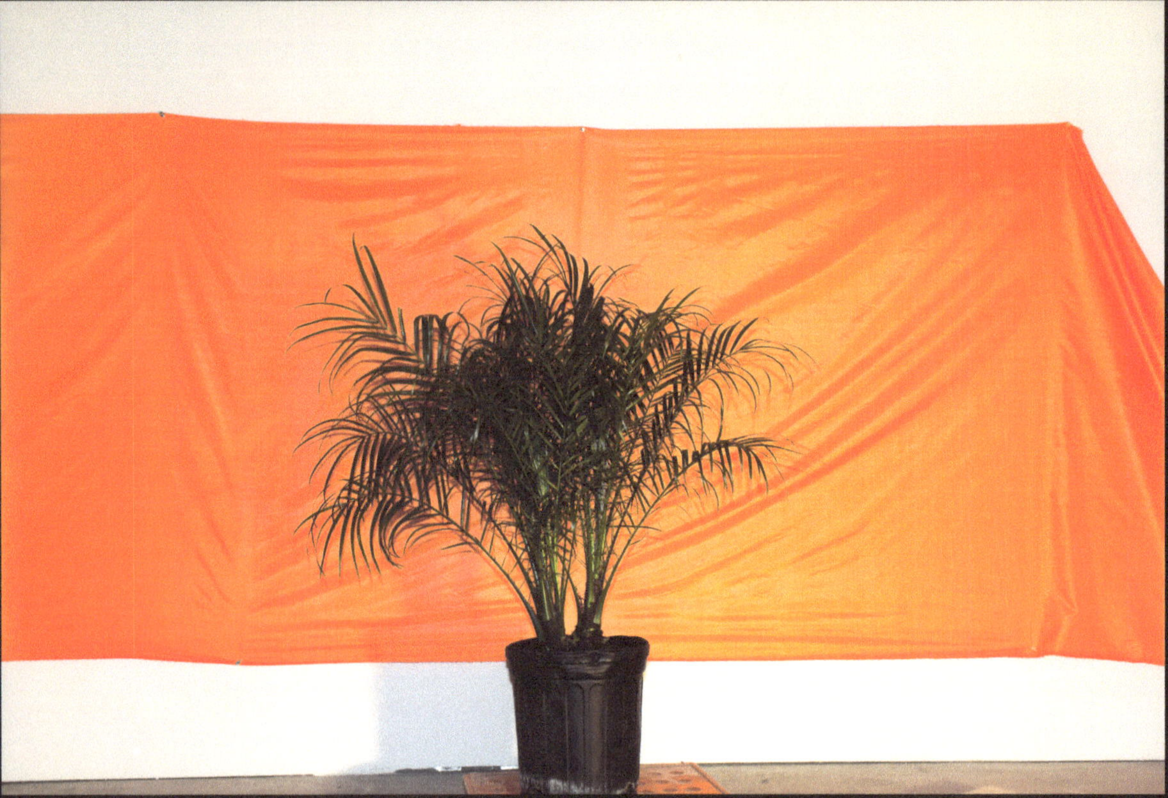

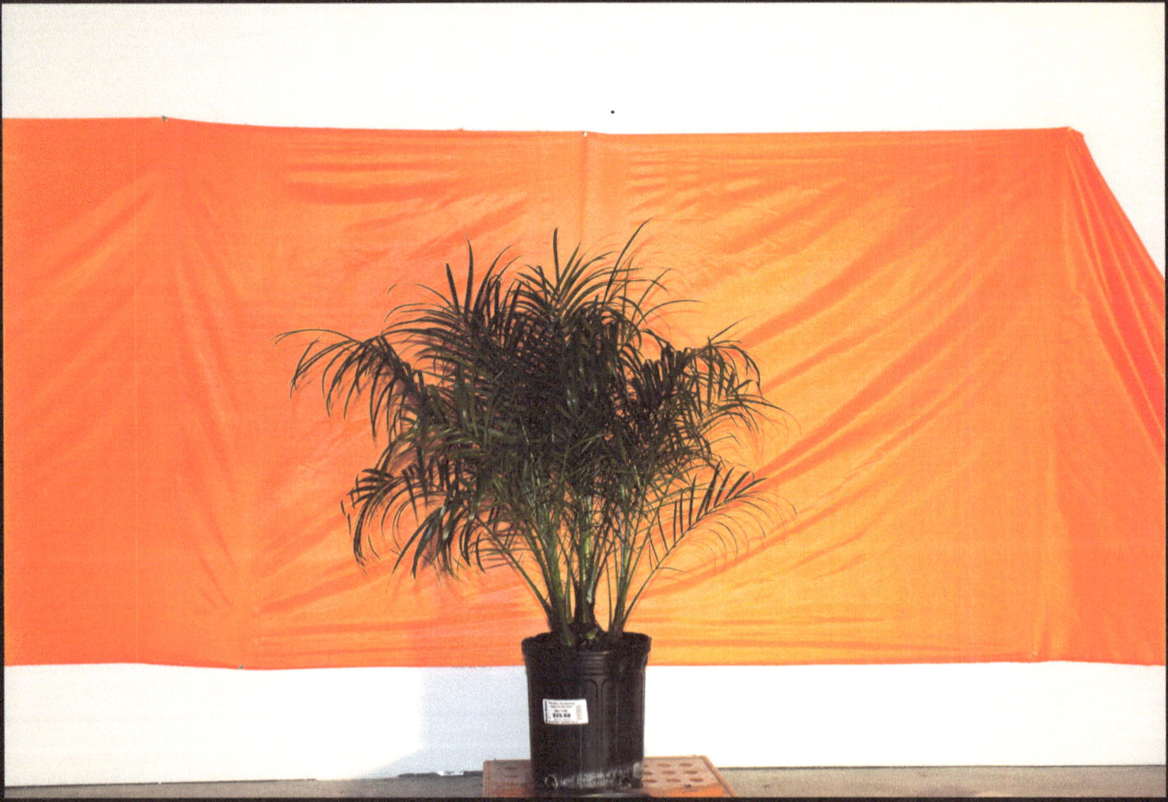

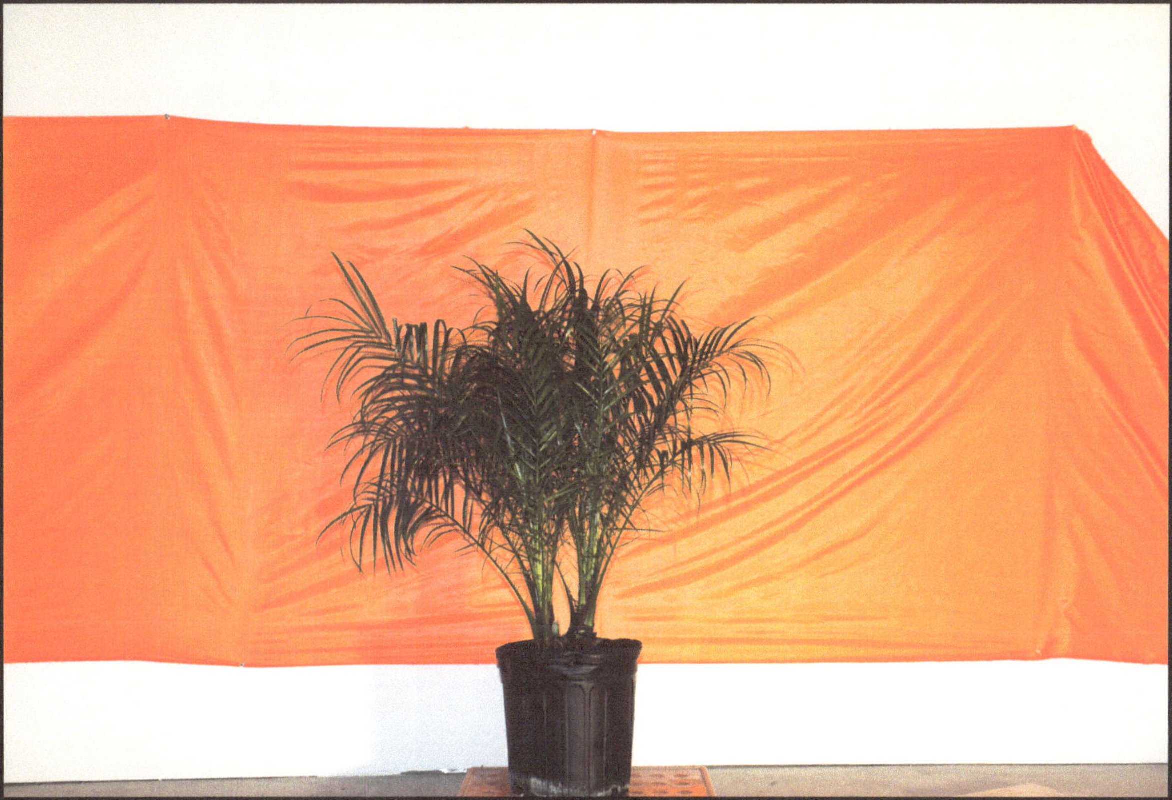

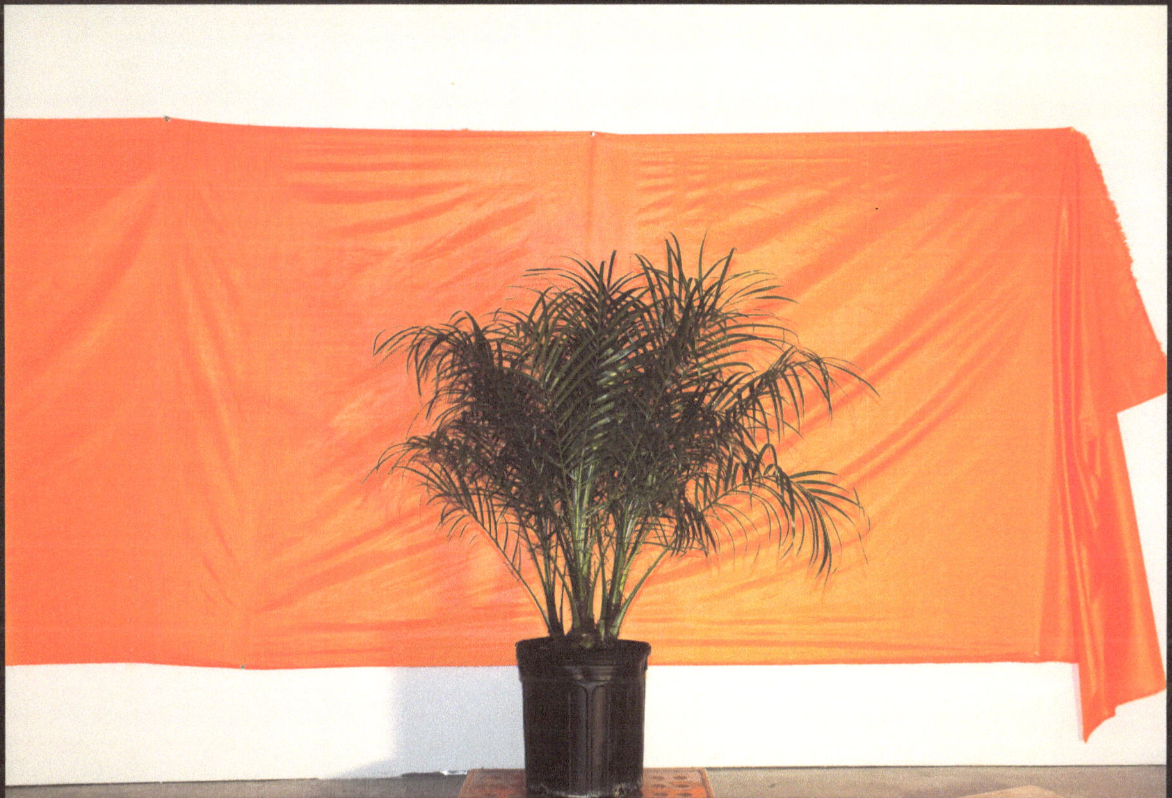

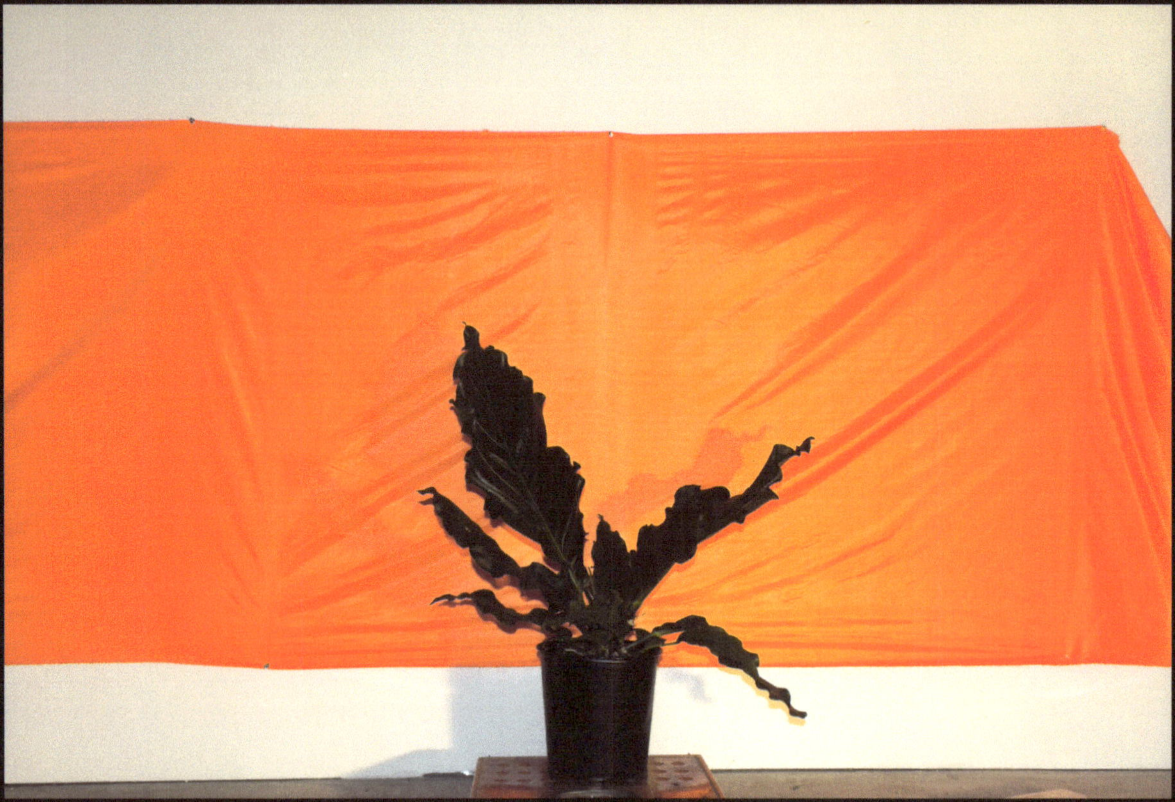

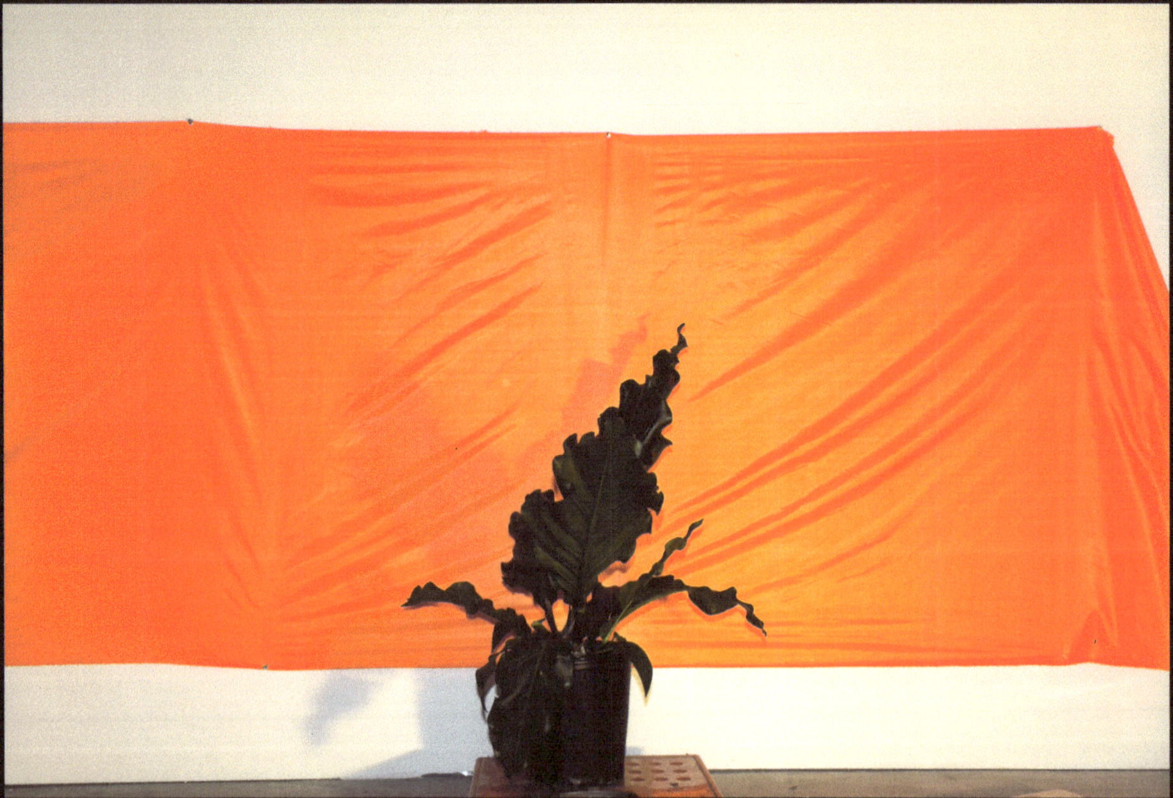

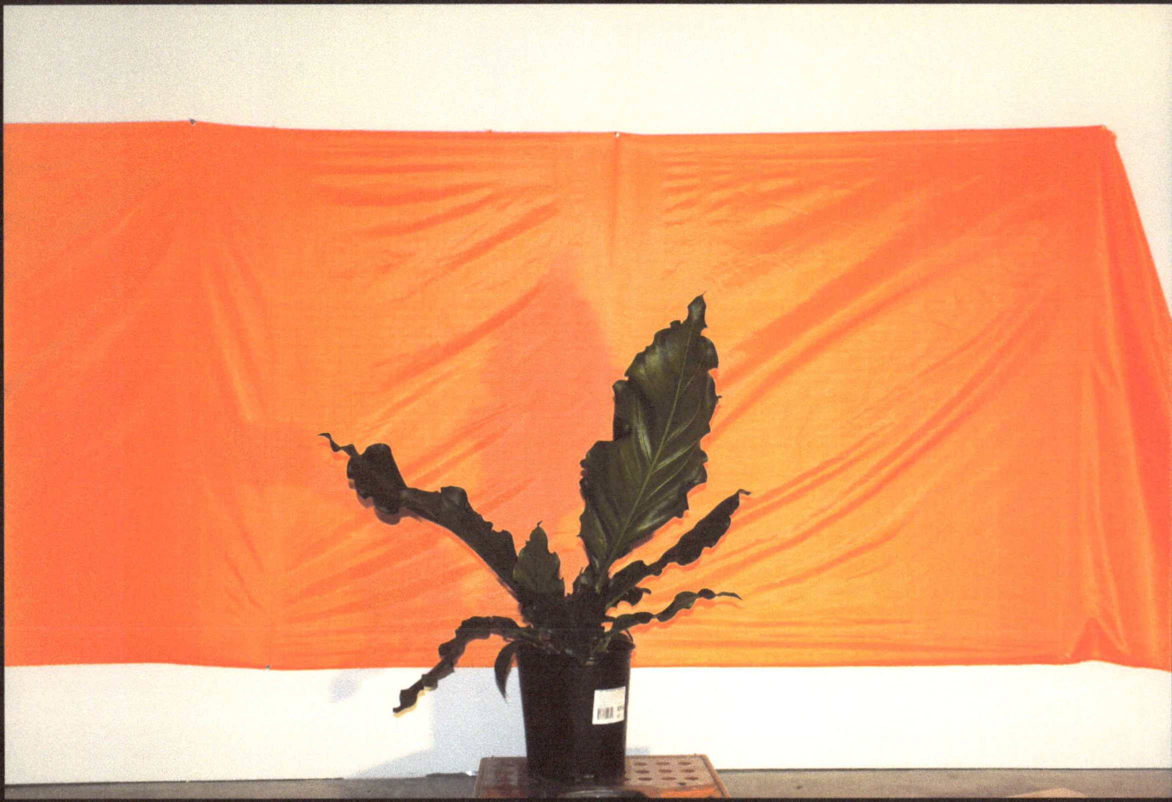

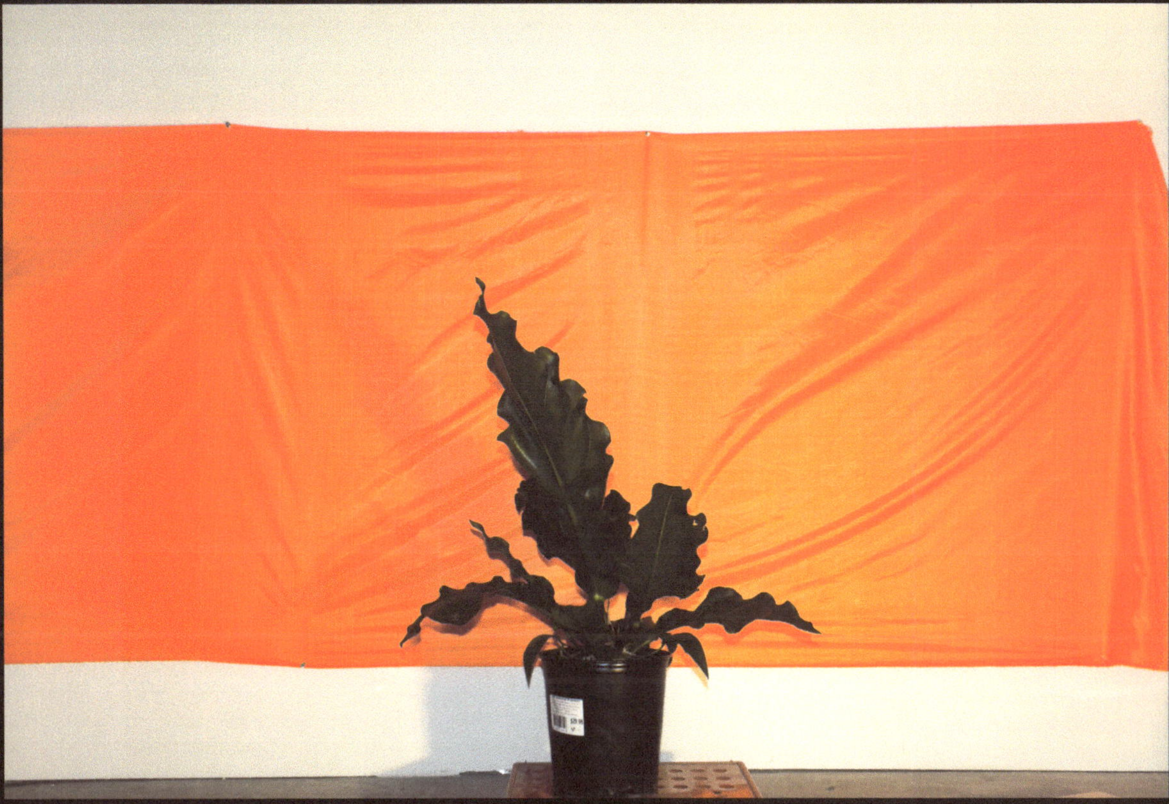

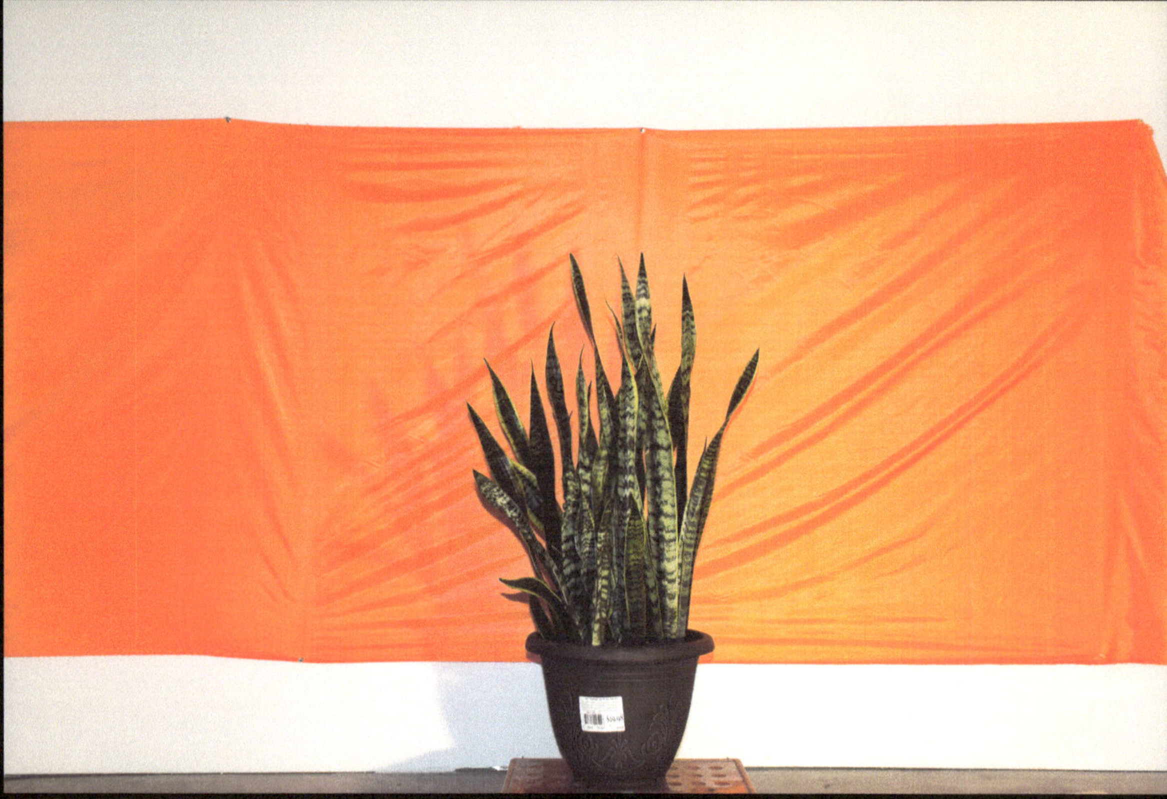

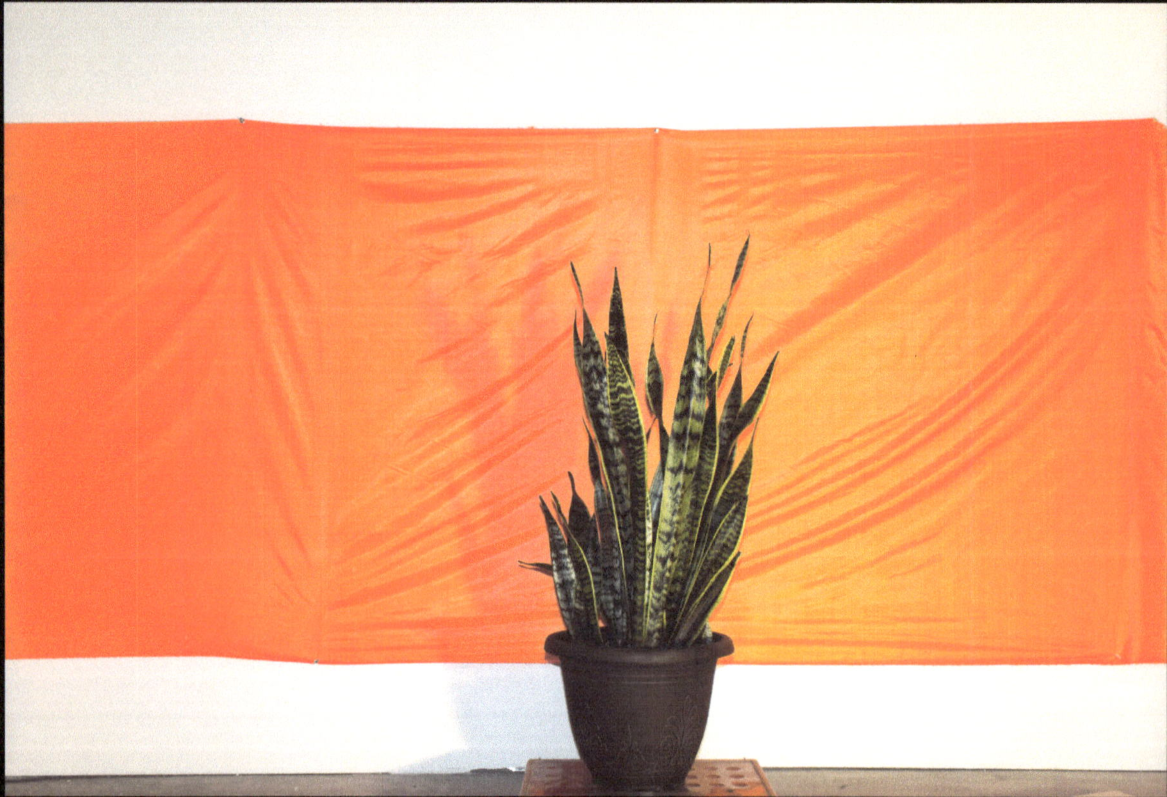

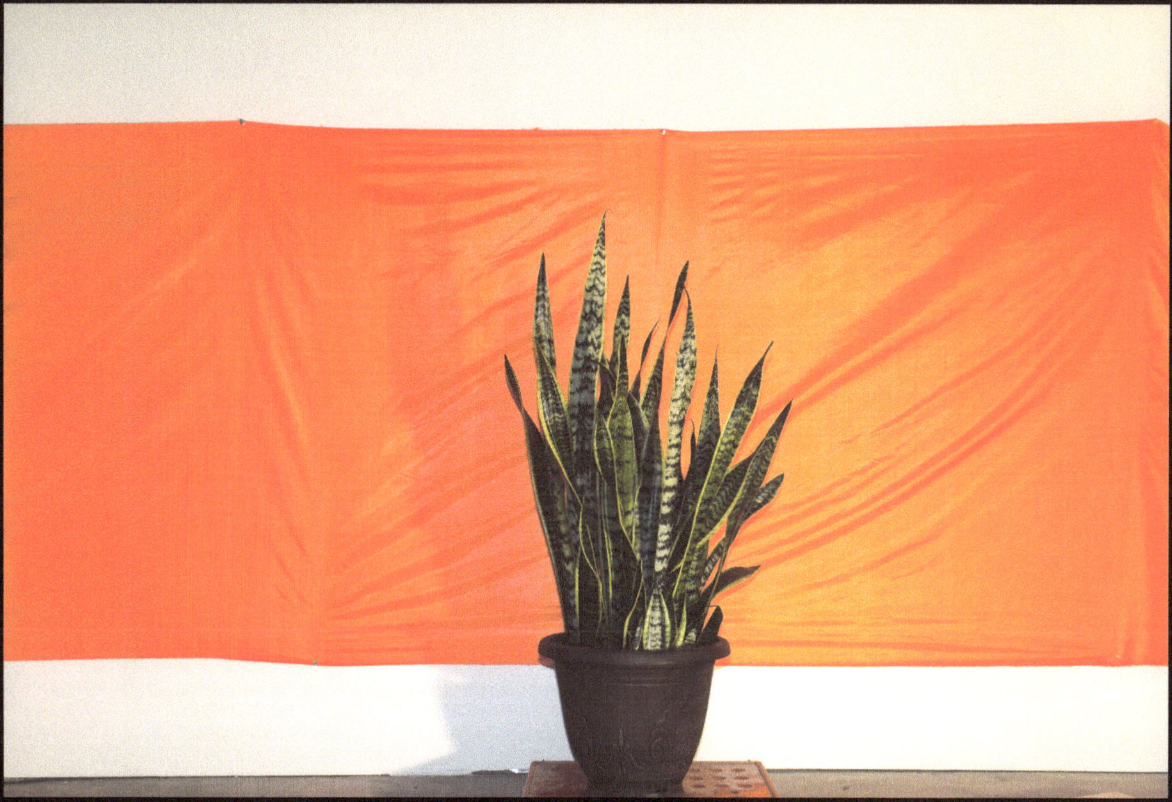

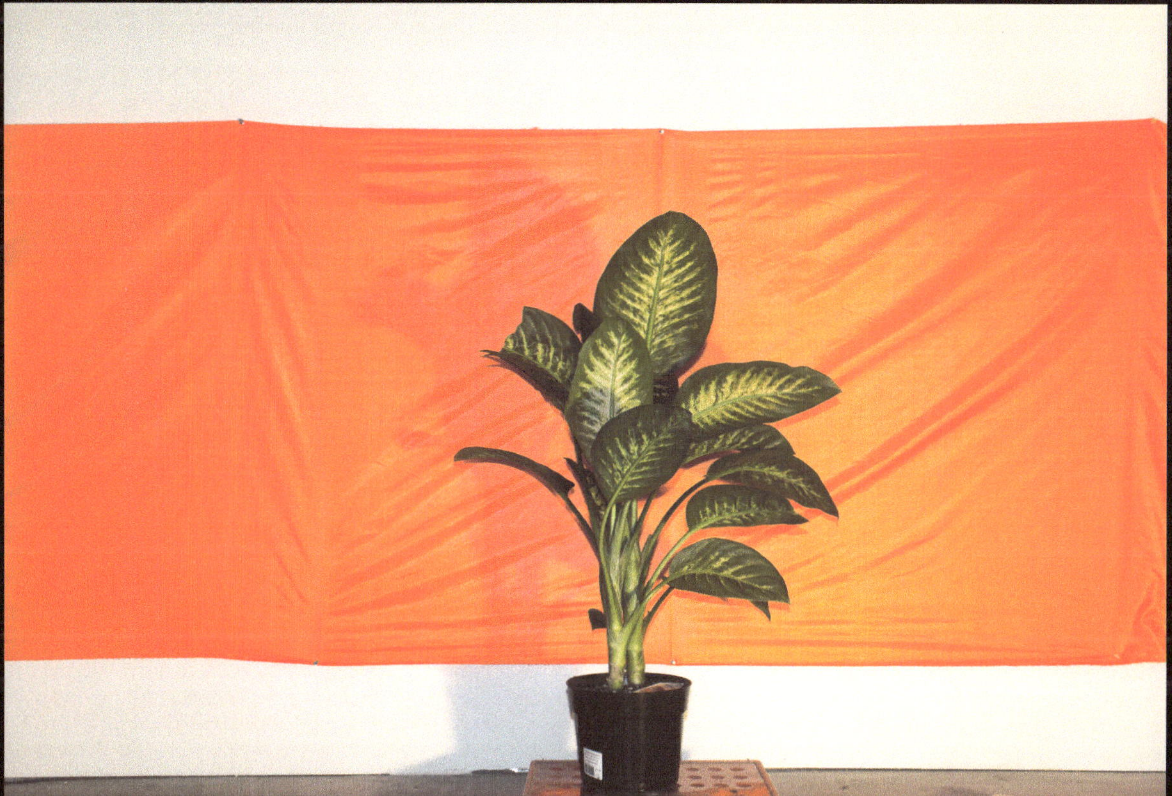

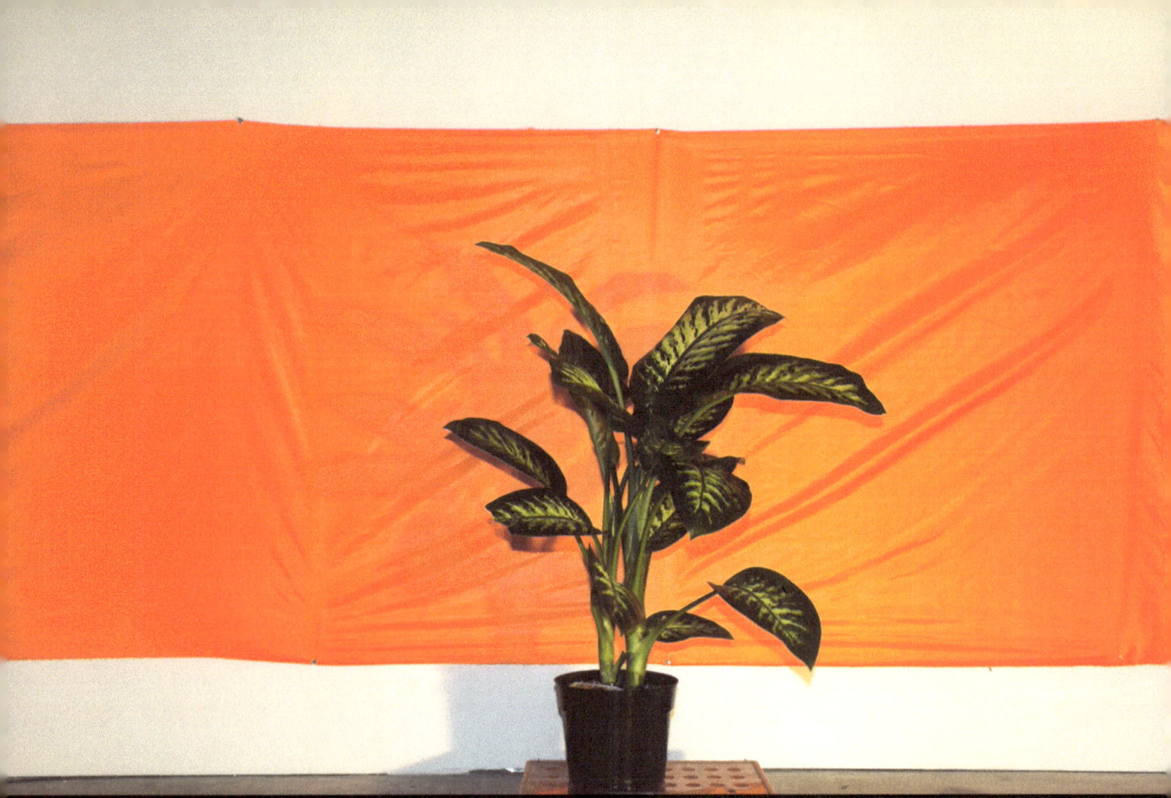

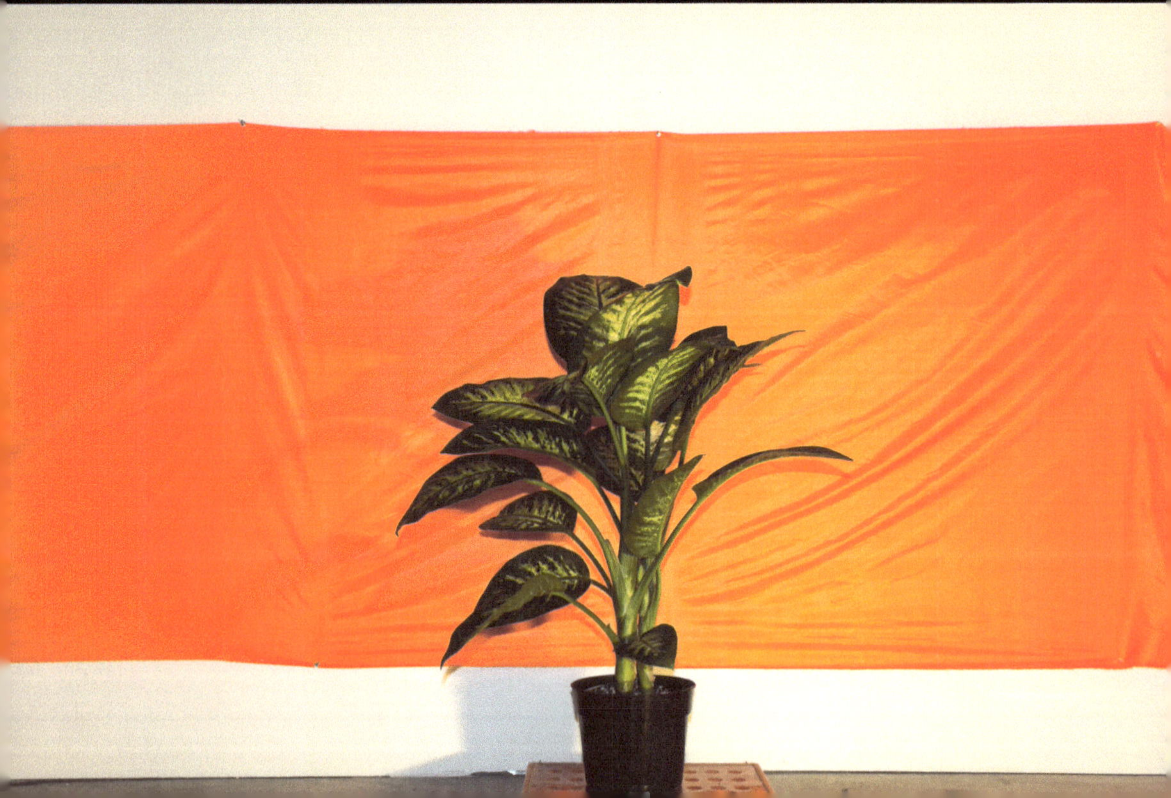

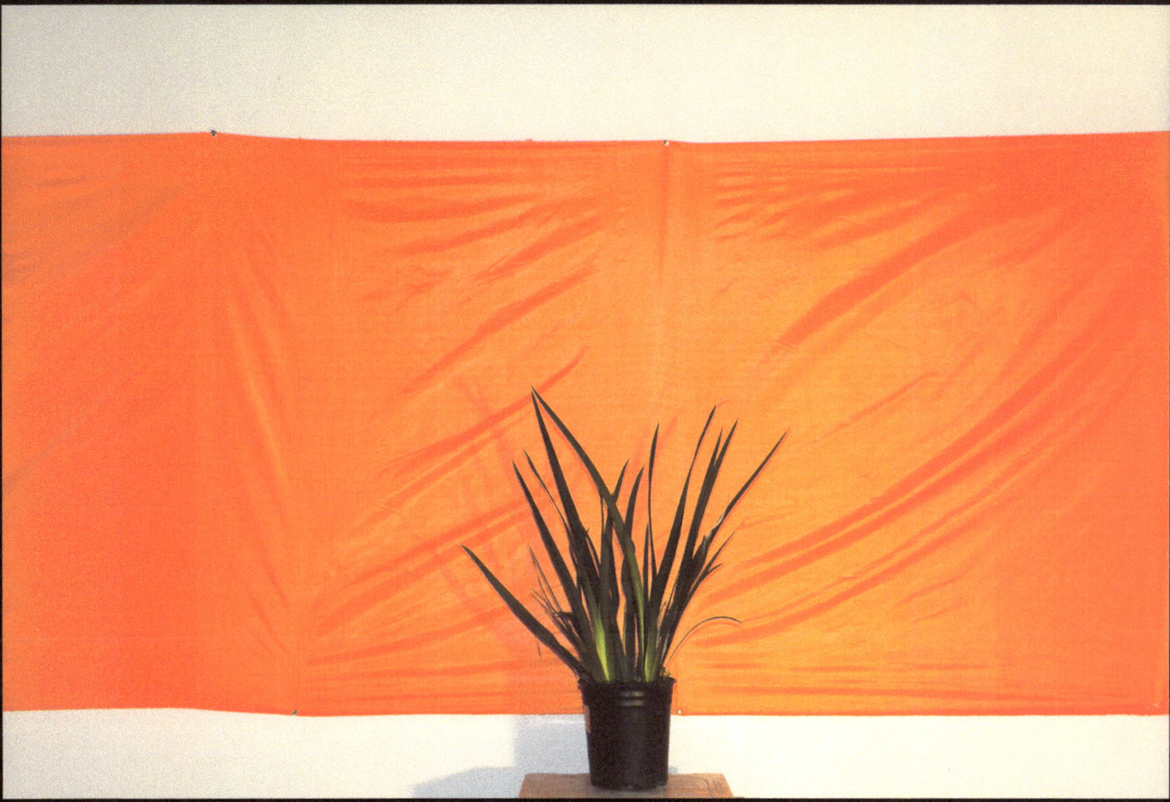

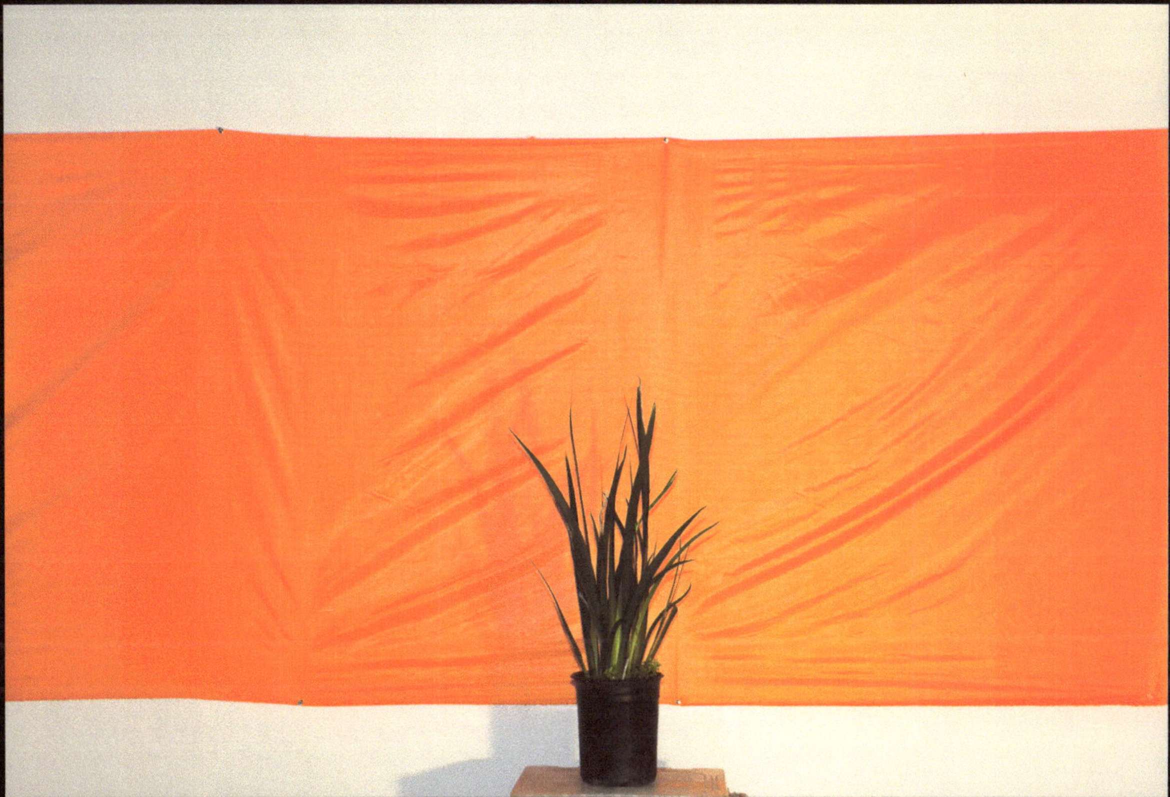

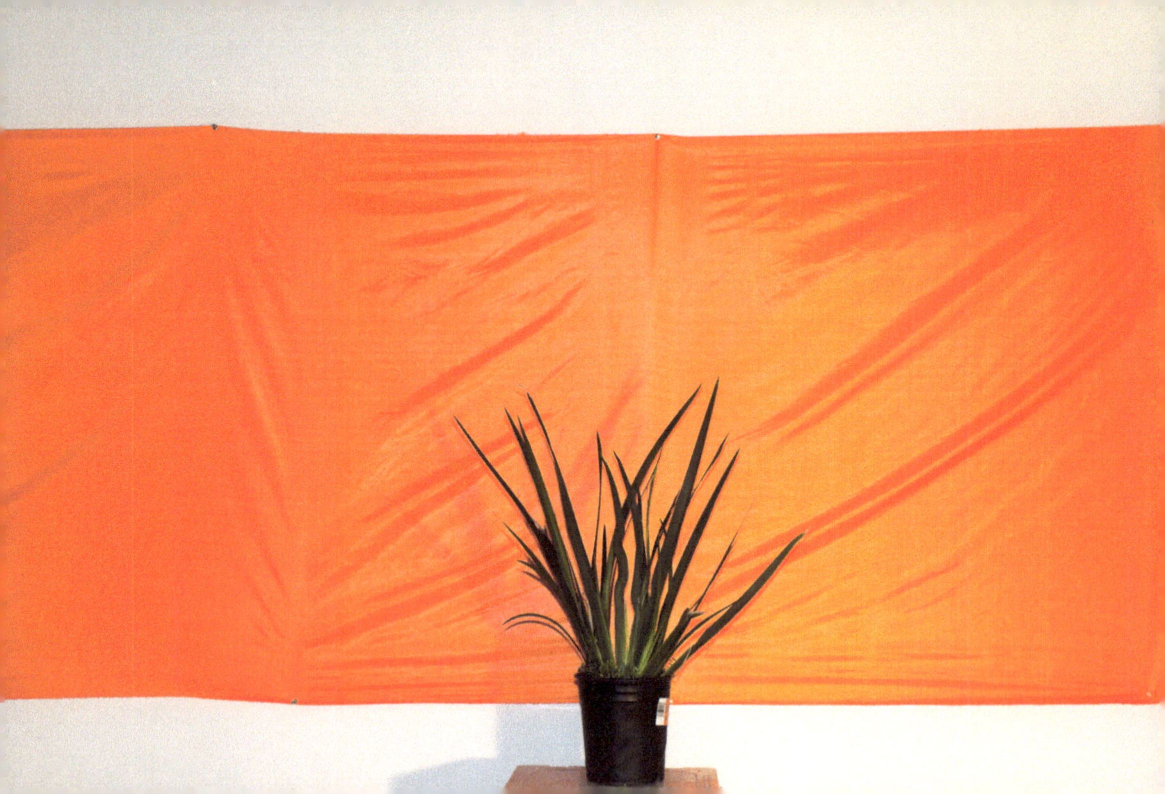

www.ingramcontent.com/pod-product-compliance
Lightning Source LLC
Chambersburg PA
CBHW050913180526
45159CB00007B/2904
9780996169660